Managing People as Assets

C. Kenneth Meyer, Lance J. Noe, Jeffrey A. Geerts, Garry L. Frank

Managing People as Assets

Copyright © 2012 by Millennium HRM Press, LLC. All rights reserved. No part of this publication may be reproduced, stored in a retrieval system or transmitted in any form or by any means, electronic, mechanical, photocopying, recording, or otherwise, except as may be expressly permitted by the United States Copyright Act of 1976 or in writing by the publisher.

For more information, write:

Millennium HRM Press, LLC
P.O. Box 41278
Des Moines, IA 50311

ISBN-10
0-9770881-2-X

ISBN-13
9780977088126

Printed in the United States of America

Dedicated To:

Professor Alex J. Kondonassis, Ph.D., David Ross Boyd Professor of Economics Emeritus and Regents' Professor of Economics Emeritus, University of Oklahoma, who has inspired three generations of students and practitioners in the field of comparative management, politics, and economics not only throughout North America, but also in Asia, Africa, Central and South America, Europe and the Middle East. His dedication to disciplined empirical research and effective teaching has enabled those whose lives he touched to deal with others with a spirit of accomplished civility, comity and openness — emulating the idealized philosophy of his ancestral Greek democratic heritage. Although we now value the importance of comparative and global economic and political understandings, he labored in the academy long before most in our society realized how people and countries are interconnected and interdependent. For those of us whose lives he touched, we will always owe him our gratitude and enduring love, for he always put students first and did so with a charitable and joyful heart.

C. Kenneth Meyer

Lance J. Noe

Jeffrey A. Geerts

Garry L. Frank

Preface

Human Resource Management (HRM) is no longer primarily fixated on the "nuts and bolts" of traditional, transactional employment management, such as job and position descriptions, employee record maintenance, remuneration and benefits, and labor-management relations. Today the HR director is as essential to the management team as are executives and senior managers in operations, production, distribution or legal and planning. The HR department has become a key component of management and is increasingly being integrated into the strategic planning activities of the contemporary organization.

Some things we know for sure as HRM and strategic planning activities change and take on a life of their own, and these trends and issues are imbedded in the 57 cases that make up *Managing People as Assets:*

1. Workplace diversity will continue to grow, especially in the areas of race and ethnicity, gender, age, disability, veteran status, national origin, religion, language and sexual orientation.

2. The HR strategic planning process has become increasingly sensitive to the global dimensions of organizational behavior and understanding of the importance that diverse political, economic and cultural environments, laws and regulations, etc., play in managing people as assets.

3. Organizations increasingly find it beneficial to recruit and hire people who are representative of the categorical traits of their clientele or customer base, especially by gender, race/ethnicity, and sexual orientation.

4. A 21st century organization has characteristics that make it distinctively different from its 20th century counterparts, especial in terms of structure, organization design, reach (domestic versus global), resources, job expectations, and style (structured versus flexible). These changes, in addition to others too numerous to mention here, *demand* that our organizations move from being simply resource driven bureaucracies, to performance, mission, and result based enterprises. The scope of these changes is so transformative and fundamentally accepted that they require no further explanation or comment.

5. New technology and social media are transforming organizational management and service delivery in the areas of communication, information systems, record management, personnel accountability, and inventory systems.

6. Employee health insurance, professional and continuing education, training, wellness programs, Employee Assistance Programs (EAPS), telecommuting and workplace flexibility (time, location, tour, shift, and benefits) are viewed as important motivators and job satisfiers, while simultaneously undergoing scrutiny in terms of their effective Return-on-Investment (ROI) HR metrics.

7. HR management and line managers need to continually increase their understanding in crucial areas of non-discrimination, safety and health, energy and environment, ethics and privacy if they wish to be successful in implementing the voluminous number of federal and state laws, rules, regulations and judicial decisions.

8. The workplace of tomorrow will become more heterogeneous, especially in terms of its aging (graying at the temples) and immigration characteristics.

9. Increasingly, transactional HR activities will become a part of electronic Human Resource Management (eHRM) in areas such as pay and compensation, benefits (vacation time, personal time-off, health and insurance payments, pensions, 401(k) and retirement, direct payroll deposits, recruitment), and other administrative and record keeping areas. Also, more and more of these transactional activities are being outsourced to organizations that specialize in HR management and development — or Professional Employer Organizations (PEOs). Most modern organizations have moved toward Web based HR systems and employees are encouraged to self-inform and manage their employment portfolio on a system that is always accessible 24 hours a day, seven days per week.

10. Management is torn between the "bi-polar twins" involved in balancing work and family. Workplace flexibility (flex-time, flex-place, telecommuting, etc.) is now commonly found in organizations, although management continues to struggle with the increased employee autonomy, empowerment, and responsibility that these changes imply.

11. Last, there is a cache of HRM and eHRM issues that are of enduring importance, yet how HR and line managers deal with them remains problematic. A sample listing of these concerns includes these salient topics and how we deal with them: retention, pluralistic workforce, working mothers (nearly 70 percent of mothers with children under 18 are employed), paternity-maternity leave programs, dual career families, glass and bamboo ceilings, limited or low skilled educated employees, gender pay inequities, work/family issues, child and elder care, sequencing mothers (drop out and then reenter employment market), age and disability discrimination, and immigration and work policies. Also, team or group evaluation methods remain unresolved, along with individual performance evaluation, succession planning, bench-marking, broad banding, e-learning, team building and career planning, and the uses of technology. All of these issues, unresolved as they might be, are part of the staple diet of the HR manager; they also beg for solutions which blend the theory of our multidisciplinary field with known best practices.

It is the collective perspective of the authors of *Managing People as Assets* that contemporary HRM can be largely summarized by the following dozen or so important concepts that pertain to the world of work and how these notions are interconnected: *changing, dynamic, global, diverse, flexible, customer driven, legalistic, fair, entrepreneurial, de-bureaucratized, uncertain, performance based, quality driven, team work, constant innovation and improvement, and people as assets rather than costs or liabilities.*

Most HRM practitioners and academics provide the following sage advice to line managers, supervisors and those generally interested in the processes and stages associated with the management of human resources: "If you hire the right person, with the right set of knowledge, skills, abilities and values, at the right time, for the right job — EUREKA! If not, it is next to impossible to find a management system that will help you resolve your problem."

In the cases that make up *Managing People as Assets*, there are hundreds of concepts that directly pertain to the field of human resource management. For example, included are major pieces of federal legislation that are relevant to the discussions and analysis, such as the Americans with Disabilities Act (ADA), Family Medical Leave Act (FMLA), Civil Rights Act of 1964 and 1991, Health Insurance Portability and Accountability Act (HIPAA), and Worker Adjustment and Retraining Notification (WARN), to mention just a few. Also, many of the concepts that make up the "stock and trade" of *Managing People as Assets* are imbedded in the cases: Affirmative Action, telecommuting, cutback management, defined contribution or benefit plans, employee counseling, outsourcing, contracting-out, ergonomics, offshoring, childcare and eldercare discipline, flexibility (benefits, time, place, tour, etc.), sexual harassment, women in management, grooming standards and dress codes, immigration, ethics, employee rights, Employee Assistance Programs (EAPs), globalization, pay equity, career planning, pay equity, career planning, performance management, leadership and management style, diversity, nonprofit 501(c)(3) organizations, interviewing, employee recruitment, selection, evaluation and retention, and retrenchment, team building, motivation and workplace violence and security. The combinations of these many concepts are presented in the **Index of Topics**.

Nine of the cases included in this book are suitable for group or teamwork analysis: *Patronage or Cronyism at DHS; Interns: An Underutilized Assets; A Hiring Dilemma: Recruitment from In-House or Outside; New Direction for the Department of Personnel; The "Pink Slip" Support System; Competition from Behind Bars; What Questions are Lawful or Unlawful; Jimmy's 53 Questions: Team Interviewing; and Keep Your Stick on the Ice or Your Views to Yourself.* These cases may be assigned to different groups or teams and then presented to the "community of learners" at the end of the course. This is an excellent way to build team membership and encourage the inculcation of positive team attitudes and behavior. This is especially important in contemporary organizations that use teams for nearly all work related tasks and projects.

In addition, *Managing People as Assets* provides a chapter dealing with the *Analysis and Interpretation of Case Studies*—a comprehensive treatment of the uses and salient arguments supportive of problem centered learning and several recommended methodological approaches to case dissection, analysis and decision making. Further, given the fact that the workforce, workplace, and technology are being changed at warp speeds in today's society, a chapter entitled *The World of Work in the 21st Century: Security to Ubiquitous Risk* is presented to further our understanding of the changing nature of work, the new psychological contract, and trend from left to right brain work activity. In the discussion, the reader will not only be introduced to the impact that the changing nature of work and organizational behavior and living has upon the workplace, but how these changes will affect how we value work, human dignity, and how we deal with the most elementary emotions of personal shame, guilt, and risk.

Managing People as Assets is distinct from other casebooks due to these six unique features: 1) It has a comprehensive listing in the Index of Topics of the human resource management and administrative concepts that are keyed to the case(s) in which they are of major importance. In those cases in which the concept(s) pertain, the case numbers associated with the relevant concept or topics is designated by an asterisk (*) symbol. 2) Each case study is presented in a table that lists all of the major and important concepts that pertain to its analysis, dissection, and presentation and is presented in **Appendix A, Case Histories Keyed to Topics**. 3) A table of names of key actors and organizations found in the cases studies is listed in **Appendix B, Index of Names, Positions and Organization Types**, for a quick reference to a specific case study in this volume or a name or organization recalled from class discussion. 4) In **Appendix C, Summary Guide to Application Pre-Employment Questions** is presented. This appendix is particularly valuable since it provides an up-to-date listing of inquiries that most frequently are raised during the interview process that may violate federal and state laws. 5) **Appendix D, Avoiding Discrimination During the Hiring Process**, provides an enlarged discussion of the rationale for each unlawful question dealing with topics as varied as drug or alcohol use and testing, age, religion, race, gender, sexual orientation, national origin discrimination, marital status, veteran status, etc., and provides a quick and essential study and overview of questionable pre-employment inquiries.

Finally, this book presents in **Appendix E, Selected Online Resources for Human Resource Management Topics and Issues**, literally several hundred websites pertaining to HR and eHRM that are useful in the everyday research activities associated with the world of management. The websites are delineated into 21 useful HRM categories such as jobs and internships, gender issues, federal personnel systems, unions and collective bargaining, pay, compensation and benefits, and recruitment and selection. It is the collective experience of the authors that as we use these sites and become familiar with their strengths and weaknesses, we save valuable time in our daily HR management and planning activities. Also, crucial information that once was laboriously obtained through traditional means is now a "click" away on these easily accessed websites, electronic libraries and data systems.

The authors wish to thank our editor, Jennifer Hart, for her continued support, advice, and efforts to make this book of cases applicable to the real-world of daily HR practice, and she did so with grace, gentle encouragement and competency. We appreciate and value the assiduous attention to detail and style that she provided to this volume of cases. She made them more readable and interesting by her careful choice of words and her insistence that the major case concepts not be camouflaged by complicated sentence structure and obtuse language, and for these suggestions we are thankful.

Also, we are thankful to those professors who provided a peer review of the book and offered suggestions too many to chronicle here, but nevertheless important to the overall integrity of this book. We gratefully thank Professors Richard C. Kearney, School of Public and International Affairs, North Carolina State University and Laura Wilson Gentry, School of Public and International Affairs, University of Baltimore, and a host of HRM practitioners who reviewed the manuscript and whose comments, corrections, and additions were heeded and addressed in this book.

Last, the authors acknowledge that any errors of omission or commission that may have entered these pages are inadvertent ones and that any names of organizations or of actors involved in the incidents, scenarios, and cases are fictitious in style and substance. Every attempt has been made to make these real case studies come to life and provide a learning experience that will truly integrate theory and practice. Now, fasten your intellectual seatbelts and prepare to take a "practical" educational journey in which you are encouraged to experience first-hand the concepts, issues, and dynamics involved in HRM management; you are further invited to appreciate and *savor* the value and importance of *Managing People as Assets*.

Table of Contents

Dedications v

Preface vi

Index of Topics ix

Introduction: The Understanding and Analysis of Case Studies 1

The World of Work in the 21st Century: Security to Ubiquitous Risk 10

1. Keep Your Stick on the Ice or Your Views to Yourself 23
2. Patronage or Cronyism at DHS 29
3. Jimmy's 53 Questions: Team Interviewing 35
4. What Questions are Lawful or Unlawful? 45
5. Making Meetings Work 55
6. Time and Time Again 63
7. The Dress Dress Code 69
8. Supervising God 73
9. Ergonomics in the Workplace 79
10. Severe Acute Respiratory Syndrome (SARS) 85
11. Pictures are Worth a Million Words 89
12. Interns: An Underutilized Asset 97
13. Lingering 9/11 Concerns 113
14. A Hiring Dilemma: Recruitment from In-House Versus from Outside 119
15. Other Duties as Assigned 137
16. City Bargaining 145
17. Doing the Zoo 151
18. Printing, Politics and Personal Preference 157
19. Employee Health Benefits 167
20. Was Her Privacy Violated? 177
21. New Direction for the Department of Personnel 181
22. Betting on Family Life 189

23. AIDS in the Public Workforce 193
24. The Sweet Smell of a Good Appearance Policy 199
25. Leave it to Bereavement 203
26. Madison County's Zero Tolerance of Harassment and Discrimination Directive 209
27. A Proud Tradition of Affirmative Action 213
28. Competition from Behind Bars 219
29. Life at Quality Care House (QCH) 229
30. The Expectant Mother 235
31. Managerial Succession 239
32. Crossing the Ethical Divide 245
33. The Downward Spiral of Founder's Hospital 251
34. Daughter Dearest: Nonprofit Nepotism 259
35. Entrepreneurialism or Exploitation 267
36. An Instance of Racial Bias 273
37. What Should it Be? CEO or Executive Director 277
38. The "Pink Slip" Support System 283
39. Language Has Meaning 293
40. A $5,000 Anonymous Phone Call? 299
41. A Campaigner for Equal Rights 305
42. Sick Leave or AWOL 315
43. What Color is Your Coded Message? 321
44. Problems with Volunteer Workers 327
45. Pressing a Harassment Suit 333
46. Many Faces of Discrimination 341
47. Many Sides of Downsizing 347
48. To Quit or Not to Quit 355
49. Freda is Sick Again 361
50. Regional or Racial Bias in Diversity Training 367
51. American vs. Immigrant Labor 377
52. The Good/Bad Administrator 383

53. The Far Side of Fifty 389

54. A Problem of Motivation... 395

55. Special Privileges for Officials? 401

56. Balancing Work and Life Activity 405

57. Management Helpful or a Hindrance?... 413

Appendix A: Case Histories Keyed to Topics... 419

Appendix B: Index of Names, Positions, and Organization Types 427

Appendix C: Summary Guide to Application Pre-Employment Questions 433

Appendix D: Avoiding Discrimination During the Hiring Process................................. 437

Appendix E: Selected Online Resources for Human Resource Management Topics & Issues 451

xiii

Index of Topics

The test gives major emphasis to topics in cases marked by asterisks.

1. Absenteeism
    Case *6, *13, 25, 31, *42
2. Accountability
    Case *2, 34
3. Acquired Immunodeficiency Syndrome (AIDS)
    Case *23
4. Administrative Advocacy
    Case 14
5. Administrative Discretion
    Case 14, 40
6. Affirmative Action, See Equal Employment
7. Affirmative Action Goals
    Case 27
8. Age Discrimination
    Case *53
9. American Federation of State County Municipal Employees (AFSCME)
    Case *22
10. Americans with Disability Act (ADA)
    Case *10, *22, *49
11. Anger Management
    Case 6
12. Annual Leave
    Case *6, *42
13. Application for Employment
    Case *4
14. Arbitration, See Union-Management Relations
15. Assisted Living Center
    Case 29
16. Attendance Management
    Case *6, *42, 49
17. Authority, See Power and Authority
18. Benefits, Employee
    Case 6, *19, 25, 55
19. Benefits, Health Care
    Case 19
20. Bereavement Policy
    Case *25

xv

Index of Topics

21. Board Membership
    Case *33
22. Board of Directors
    Case *17, 833, 34, 40
23. Brainstorming Technique
    Case *5
24. Bullying, *See* Workplace Violence
25. Bureaucratic Abuse
    Case 34, 40
26. Bureaupathology
    Case *57
27. Case Workload/Overload
    Case *57
28. Censorship
    Case 8
29. Centralization-Decentralization
    Case *21, 40
30. Change
    Case 19, *21, 28
31. Change, Resistance to
    Case 1
32. Child Care
    Case 6, 22
33. Civil Rights Act, 1964 (CRA, 1964)
    Case *4, 8, *45
34. Civil Rights Act, 1991 (CRA, 1991)
    Case 8
35. Clientele Relations
    Case *11, *29, *32, 43, 44, 48, *49, *57
36. Client Relationship Management System (CRMS)
    Case 32
37. Cocaine, *See* Drug Abuse
38. Collective Bargaining, *See* Union-Management Relations
39. Communication
    Case 2, 8, 10, 11, 18, 25, *29, 33, *39, *43, 52, 54
40. Community Relations, *See* Public and Community Relations
41. Community Services Block Grant (CSBG)
    Case *38
42. Compensation and Benefits
    Case *16, *19, *21, *33
43. Complaints of Public
    Case 2, *31, 33, 40, 51
44. Computer Hacking
    Case *32

Index of Topics

45. Conduct Codes
    Case *7, 17, *34, 40, *42, 50
46. Confidentiality, *See* Secrecy and Confidentiality
47. Conflict of Interest
    Case *17, *18, 32, *34
48. Conflict Resolution
    Case 5, 8, 13, 25, 29, 31, 33
49. Consultants
    Case *2, *33
50. Contingent Employee
    Case *30
51. Contract Administration
    Case *18
52. Contract Negotiation
    Case 16
53. Contracting for Service
    Case 17, 18, *51
54. Contracting Out
    Case *2, 18, 19, 28, 33, 35, *38
55. Cost of Living Allowance
    Case *16
56. Cronyism
    Case *2, 33
57. Cultural Values
    Case 25
58. Cut-Back Management, *See* Downsizing
59. Delegation of Authority
    Case 15, 21, *44
60. Discipline
    Case *1, 24, 25, 29, 40, *42, 46, 49, *52, 56
61. Discrimination, *See* Equal Employment
62. Dishonesty and Corruption
    Case *32
63. Diversity
    Case 3, 13, 25, 26, 27
64. Diversity Training
    Case 46
65. Downsizing
    Case *15, 16, 38, *47, 48, *57
66. Dress Code/Grooming Standard
    Case *7, *24, *40, *50
67. Echolalia
    Case *29

xvii

Index of Topics

68. Economic and Planning District
    Case *38
69. E-mail
    Case 43
70. Elder Care
    Case 6
71. Emergency Leave
    Case *6, 25
72. Emergency Management
    Case *10, *43
73. Employee Counseling
    Case 11, *13, *24, *29, *39, 49, 52, *56
74. Employee Evaluation
    Case 11, 31
75. Employee Orientation
    Case 55
76. Employee Placement
    Case 31
77. Employee Retention
    Case 21, *57
78. Employee Rights
    Case 3, *8, 10, 13, 28, 29, 40, 45, *46, 48, 51, 52
79. Employee Separation
    Case *48
80. Entrepreneurialism
    Case 17, *21, 28, *35
81. Equal Employment
    Case 3, 4, *13, 26, *27, 28, 30, *36, *37, 39, *41, *45, 46, *50, 53
82. Equity
    Case 36, 39, 46, 55, 55
83. Ergonomics
    Case *9
84. Ethical Questions
    Case *4, *17, *32, 34, 42, 49, *50, 55
85. Ethnocentrism
    Case 25
86. Executive Search Company
    Case *37
87. Fair Labor Standards Act (FLSA)
    Case 3
88. Family Friendly
    Case 22
89. Family Medical Leave Act (FMLA)
    Case 30, 49

Index of Topics

90. Fiduciary Responsibility
    Case 17, 19, *34, 47, 48
91. Field-Central Office Relations
    Case *14, *40
92. Firing Policies, *See* Termination Policies
93. Fiscal-Budgetary Matters
    Case 16, 19, 35, 38, 47, 57
94. Flex-time
    Case 21, *55
95. Flexible Benefits
    Case 21
96. Fraternal Order of Police (FOP)
    Case 16
97. Freedom of Religion
    Case 8
98. Freedom of Speech
    Case *1, *50
99. Fundraising
    Case 17
100. Gambling
    Case 22
101. Gender Discrimination
    Case 37, *41, *46, 53
102. Green Job Growth
    Case *38
103. Grievances
    Case 41
104. Health and Safety, *See* Quality of Work Life
105. Health Care
    Case *19, 20, 30, 49
106. Health Care Policy
    Case 6, *10, 19, 23
107. Health Insurance
    Case 19
108. Health Law and Regulation
    Case 10, 19
109. Health Insurance Portability and Accountability Act (HIPAA)
    Case 20, *30
110. Hepatitis
    Case 23
111. Hiring, *See* Recruitment and Selection
112. Hiring Quota
    Case 4, 27

Index of Topics

113. Homeless Persons
     Case *35
114. Homophobia
     Case *26
115. Homosexuality/Lesbianism
     Case *26
116. Hostile Work Environment
     Case *15, *26, *29, 45
117. Human Immunodeficiency Virus (HIV)
     Case *23
118. Human Resource Management Issues
     Case 3, 10, 13, 19, 30, 43
119. Human Resource Planning
     Case *14, 19, 43
120. Image Management
     Case 11
121. Immigrant Employees
     Case *51
122. Immigration Issues
     Case *13, *57
123. Incentives and Awards, *See* Motivation
124. Incompetency and Inefficiency
     Case *31, 57
125. Infectious Diseases
     Case 23
126. Insubordination
     Case *42
127. Interagency and Intra-agency Relations
     Case 16
128. Interagency Issues
     Case
129. Intergenerational Issues
     Case 46, 53
130. Intergovernmental Relations
     Case 31
131. Intern Evaluation Form (sample)
     Case *12
132. Intern Selection and Placement
     Case 12
133. Intern Supervision
     Case *12
134. International Association of Fire Fighters (IAFF)
     Case 16

Index of Topics

135. International Brotherhood of Teamsters (IBT)
     Case 16
136. Internet
     Case 21, 32
137. Internship Memorandum of Understanding (sample)
     Case *12
138. Internship Program (sample)
     Case *12
139. Internship Program Management
     Case *12
140. Interpersonal Conflict
     Case *50
141. Interpersonal Relations
     Case 5, 8, 10, 13, 15, *17, *20, 36, 41, 42, 44, 46, 48, 49, 50, 51, *52, *56
142. Interview Questions
     Case *4, 14
143. Interviewing
     Case 14, 24
144. Interviewing Panel
     Case *3, 14
145. Interviewing Privacy and Confidentiality Issues
     Case *4
146. Intranet
     Case *32
147. Invitation-to-Bid (ITB)
     Case *18
148. Job Classification and Placement
     Case 3, 21, 36, 49
149. Job Description
     Case 3, 14, *15
150. Job Satisfaction
     Case 6, 33, 48, 52, 53, 54, 57
151. Jurisdictional Conflicts, *See* Interagency and Intra-agency Relations
152. Kaizen
     Case 9
153. Leadership
     Case 8, 15, 21, 29, 33, *34, 39, 57
154. Legal Requirements
     Case 33, 46
155. Legislative - Executive Relations
     Case 2
156. Legislative Oversight
     Case 2

157. Liability
    Case 9
158. Lifestyle
    Case 50
159. Management or Leadership Title
    Case *37
160. Management Style
    Case 17, *34, 41, *52, 55, *56, 57
161. Marijuana, *See* Drug Abuse
162. Marketing
    Case *11, *18, 24, *39
163. Meeting Planning and Management
    Case *5
164. Methamphetamine, *See* Drug Abuse
165. Military Administration
    Case *42
166. Minority Employment, *See* Equal Employment
167. Minority Relations
    Case 26
168. Moonlighting, *See* Outside Employment
169. Morale
    Case 6, 33, 48, 52, 57
170. Motivation
    Case 11, *19, 52, *54, 57
171. Multiculturalism, *See* Diversity
172. Munchausen's Syndrome
    Case *49
173. National – Origin Discrimination
    Case *50
174. Native American Tribes
    Case
175. Natural Resources Management
    Case 14
176. Negligent Hiring
    Case 3
177. Negligent Retention
    Case *49
178. Nepotism
    Case *34
179. News-Media Relations
    Case 2, 18, 51
180. Nonprofit Organization
    Case 2, 3, *17, 29, 33, 34, *37, 49

Index of Topics

181. Non-Verbal Behavior
    Case *5
182. Offshoring
    Case 38
183. Ombudsman
    Case 44
184. One-Stop Shop
    Case 38
185. Opium, *See* Drug Abuse
186. Organization Behavior and Change
    Case 5, 8, 11, 15, 19, 21, *29, 50, 52, 57
187. Organization Culture
    Case 11
188. Organizational Structure and Design
    Case 14, *21
189. Outside Employment
    Case 18
190. Outsourcing, *See* Contracting Out
191. Pandemic Disease
    Case *10
192. Participatory Management
    Case 16, 56
193. Partisan Politics
    Case 2
194. Patronage
    Case *2, 14
195. Perception
    Case *11
196. Performance Evaluation
    Case 14, 52, 53, *54, *56
197. Personal Hygiene
    Case 24
198. Personality Conflict, *See* Interpersonal Relations
199. Philanthropic Organization
    Case 17
200. Planning and Goal Setting
    Case 17, 19, *21, *34, 37
201. Plant Closure
    Case *38
202. Pluralism, *See* Diversity
203. Policy Formulation and Implementation
    Case 19, *21, 46, 47, 51
204. Political Favoritism
    Case *2

xxiii

Index of Topics

205. Political Violence
    Case 1
206. Pollution Prevention Intern Program
    Case 12
207. Polycentrism
    Case *25
208. Power and Authority
    Case *15, 17, 31
209. Preferential Treatment
    Case *31, *34, 55
210. Pregnancy Discrimination Act (1978)
    Case *30
211. Press Relations, *See* News-Media Relations
212. Prison and Business Relations
    Case *28
213. Prison Labor
    Case *28, *35
214. Prisoner Rights
    Case *28
215. Privacy and Confidentiality Issues
    Case *15, *20, 29, 30
216. Problem Employee
    Case 6, *13, 42, *49, 50, 56
217. Productivity
    Case 6, 31, 54
218. Professional Air Traffic Controllers Organization (PATCO)
    Case 16
219. Professionalism
    Case *6, 7, *15, *17, 29, 32, 34, 40, 45, 55
220. Program Evaluation
    Case *21, *33
221. Promotion Policies
    Case *37, *53
222. Protest Organized by Employees
    Case *52
223. Public and Community Relations
    Case 28, *33, 35, *39, 40, 43, *49, 51, 57
224. Public Employee Rights
    Case *1
225. Purchasing/Procurement
    Case *18
226. Quality Management
    Case *21

Index of Topics

227. Quality of Work Life (QWL)
     Case *9, 21, 22, 29, 43, 45, 56
228. Racism
     Case *13, 50
229. Rank and Privilege
     Case *55
230. Recruitment
     Case 24, 28, 44
231. Recruitment and Selection
     Case 3, *4, *14, *17, 18, 19, 21, 27, 31, *34, 36, 37, 51, *53
232. Recruitment Application Form
     Case *4
233. Recruitment Discrimination
     Case *4
234. Reduction-in-Force, *See* Downsizing
235. Re-Engineering
     Case 19, *21
236. Reinvention
     Case *21, *35
237. Relevancy Challenges
     Case *5
238. Religious Discrimination
     Case *8, *13
239. Religious Practices
     Case 8
240. Reorganization
     Case *2, 16, *21, *37, 57
241. Resignation
     Case 40
242. Responsibility
     Case 52
243. Retention
     Case 6
244. Retrenchment, *See* Downsizing
245. Right to Work
     Case 16
246. Rules and Regulations
     Case 13, 21, 29, *34, 35, 37, *46, *55, 57
247. Secrecy and Confidentiality
     Case 32, 42
248. Severe Acute Respiratory Syndrome (SARS)
     Case *10
249. Sexual Harassment, Title VII, CRA
     Case 15, 26, 29, 45

xxv

250. Sexual Orientation
    Case *26
251. Sick Leave
    Case 42
252. Small Group Behavior
    Case 5, *52
253. Speech Writing
    Case *39
254. Staff – Client Relations
    Case *29
255. Stereotyping
    Case *28
256. Strategic Management
    Case *33
257. Strategic Planning
    Case 26, 37
258. Stress Management
    Case 31, *54, 56
259. Succession Planning
    Case *14, *33, *37, *53
260. Supervisor - Staff Relations
    Case *8, *11, 14, *15, 19, 25, *29, *31, 37, 41, 43, 49
261. Tax Increment Financing
    Case 38
262. Teamwork and Cooperation
    Case 2, 34, 44, *52, 56
263. Telecommunication
    Case 34
264. Termination
    Case 29
265. Termination Policy
    Case *15, 29, 34, 38, 47, *48, 49
266. Terrorism
    Case *13
267. Theft
    Case *32
268. Time Management
    Case *6, 31, *56
269. Total Quality Management (TQM)
    Case 21
270. Training
    Case *11, *26, 43, 44, *50
271. Tuberculosis
    Case 23

Index of Topics

272. Turnaround Management
    Case *31
273. Turnover
    Case 18
274. Underutilization
    Case *27
275. Unemployment
    Case 38
276. Unfair Labor Practices
    Case 16
277. Union-Management Relations
    Case *16, 25, *28, 38, 41, 48, *50
278. Value Clarification
    Case 39
279. Volunteer Management
    Case 44
280. Volunteer Workers
    Case *44
281. Volunteerism
    Case *44
282. Vulnerable Person
    Case *29
283. Wagner-Peyser Act
    Case *38
284. Wellness
    Case 6
285. Whistle-Blowing
    Case 55
286. Women in Management
    Case *21, *39, 41, *56
287. Work-Life Balance
    Case 6, 22, 42, *56
288. Work Schedules
    Case 42, 55
289. Worker Adjustment and Retraining Notification (WARN)
    Case *38
290. Worker Investment Act (WIA, 1998)
    Case *38
291. Workfare/Work Program
    Case *35, *54
292. Workforce Development Programs
    Case *38
293. Workplace Security
    Case 13, 28, 32, 35, *43, 49

Index of Topics

294. Workplace Stress
   Case 45
295. Workplace Violence
   Case 1, *43
296. Wrongful Discharge
   Case 15, 29
297. Zero-Tolerance Policy
   Case *2

Introduction

The Analysis and Understanding of Case Studies*
by
C. Kenneth Meyer, William S. Brown, Lance J. Noe, Jeffrey A. Geerts, and Garry L. Frank

It is a "truism" that learning takes place in a variety of ways, some traditional and others non-traditional and experimental. Over the years, curriculums have developed in schools of education and in psychology departments that focus on the many different theories of learning and the methods that are most congruent with acquiring and retaining factual knowledge, knowledge synthesis, knowledge integration, knowledge comprehension, knowledge application, and the actual communication of knowledge. Historically, classroom learners, regardless of age or level of experience, were taught as if they had little or nothing to contribute to the discussion at hand or had limited insights that might be applied to the problem solving process itself. This pedagogical or youthful learning model was considered *sacrosanct* and the teacher/professor/authority figure was assumed to have the answers — the right answers, of course — to the many challenges and problems inherent to a specific discipline or area of study. Although this construct was endorsed by many, it was only partially believed by the teacher — at least by those learned teachers who truly understood the amazing breadth of their parent discipline (management, political science, sociology, engineering, medicine, law, public administration, and so on), and knew from their attempt to solve problems that most issues they faced were essentially multi-disciplinary (involving theories, facts, notions, techniques, and methods, etc.), associated with several or many disciplines or that problems were best addressed when the trans-disciplinary approach was fully exploited.

The authors of these cases collectively have nearly 150 years of experience in staff and front-line organizations and have been directly connected as well in the extensive teaching, analysis and research of management and policy issues. With this considerable experience, however, we have learned beginning nearly five decades ago, that "...doing constitutes a good basis for learning." In the regular courses that we have "taught" during our collective college, university and professional training experiences, whether in the facilitation and coaching of learning in organizational behavior, leadership, policy analysis, human resources management, program planning and evaluation, and quantitative and qualitative methodology and statistics, we *discovered* the useful and imperative need to get learners involved actively, and hopefully passionately, in their own learning. This essentially mandates that the *learning process* must be *"owned"* by the learner! As such, we have experienced and have received considerable feedback from those with whom we have mutually learned within a variety of formal classroom and training milieus, that *not* every word set out in our lectures, handouts, illustrative models, and multi-media presentations — no matter how thoughtfully and carefully prepared, "scripted," and presented — has been cognitively absorbed (the transmission or absorption theory of learning). To think otherwise would be quite delusional at worst and naive at best. Therefore, we feel that the case studies presented in this book are written in such a manner as to present the factual evidence of the situation, but also to provide enough about the dynamics and environment surrounding the scenario as to inspire learning (noun) versus its verb counterpart. This is one reason that case-centered-problem-learning is effective, especially when the twin goals of teaching and learning methodology (medium) are married to the substantive material (content) that is to be learned (noun). To more fully attain these desired goals, care was given to the **Questions and Instructions** component tied to each case in this book. They provoke the intensive learning that can be accomplished through the challenging activity of identifying the major issues, concepts, and dynamics in the case, coupled to the experiential background of the learner — no matter how limited or substantial the learner's record is in the "field" of real life involvement and "practice." This theoretical model of teaching and learning as described above, requires learners to employ critical thinking and search-out and explore new ways to be active in the learning process. Effective, long lasting, relevant learning is not a passive "sport." In far too many of the learning mediums and teaching methods used in higher education, learning has become little more than a passive, nearly "spectator" activity, with some of the properties often attributed to "edu-tainment."

Strengths of Experiential Learning

In learning new management and policy analysis ideas, theories, techniques, methods, and notions, what we strive to learn and integrate into our experiential framework and bundle of knowledge, skills, abilities and values, is temporary, transitory and perhaps even "fleeting," in the sense of retention. Although most experienced teachers, facilitators, coaches, and mentors would subscribe to the idea that active learning pays real retention dividends, just like in a traditional financial investment sense, the empirical evidence for this assumption has not been as widely presented as one might suspect. However, one model that is often cited in case study and problem-centered and other active learning approaches, especially in the fields of public administration, economics, and management, is the "data and empirical findings" attributed to the research on the "Learning Pyramid"; although, unfortunately, the original research that gave credibility to the model has been lost, nevertheless it is attributed to the National Training Laboratory (NTL). In terms of learner-participant retention learning levels, the average amount of learning retained varies considerably by teaching method. **Table 1** shows the following distributions for learning by teaching method. Accordingly, as one descends the rows in which the various teaching method types are presented, we observe that the average retention rate increases. It is the lowest, only five percent, with the lecture method — a method that tends to hold a dominant position in the academy; and is the highest, 90 percent, when learners teach others and can use what is learned immediately. In the final analysis, it might be further argued that the team approach that is often used today as a learning medium in many academic and professional curriculums is also supported by the NTL findings.

Having stated some of the strengths and deficiencies associated with experiential learning, a *caveat* is in order. There will be times when the lecture and other methods of learning are most appropriate in enabling the learning of knowledge, and thinking differently would be certainly arrogant, "elitist," and foolhardy. For the tasks that the authors have set out here to meet, however, we suggest that new information and knowledge in management and policy analysis is best learned, integrated, evaluated, discussed, debated, communicated, and most of all, *"discovered,"* when learners are exposed to the case-study and problem centered method as "learning enablers," and when they are asked to use their critical reflection abilities and experiences in the process. In the final analysis, self-discovery of knowledge might result and the true genius of our individual and collective "brainware" or "intellect" might be fully unleashed as we take on and apply our minds to solving some of the key problems confronting day-to-day contemporary managers.

Table 1. Average Retention Rate for Learners by Type of Teaching Methodology Used (in percentages)

Teaching Method	Average Retention Rate (%)
Lecture	5
Reading	10
Audio-visual	20
Demonstration	30
Discussion group	50
Practice what has been learned	75
Teaching others/immediate use	90

Source: Permission granted by: NTL Institute for Applied Behavioral Science, 300 N. Lee Street, Suite 300, Alexandria, VA 22314. 1-800-777-2227.

Now, the case-study and problem-solving approach to learning has once again been placed in its rightful and valued position among the several approaches to learning: as a method in which learners are not *asked* to recount, analyze, and synthesize their experiential knowledge base, but are actually required to do so in a systematic, careful, and thoughtful manner from an empirical perspective. This approach requires that we use our human senses to observe the world around us, whether that be the magnificent world of nature on a grandiose scale or, from a less imposing perspective, the organizational milieu in which we spend a good share of our adult lives directly involved in the activity we call "work." On a moment by moment basis, we observe, we sense, we conceptualize — in short, we apply our minds to the many stimuli we have encountered — and we try to make sense out of a world that literally fills our "perceptual pail" full of data that then becomes part of our own life experience.

This reservoir or experience, then, is what we attempt to "drill into," tap, and bring to the problem-solving platform and the decision-making process. As we intuitively know, especially if we are concerned with reflecting on our view of the world in which we live, work, play, and love, that as we mature, at least for most of us, we begin to see things quite differently (change), and we develop added skills in transferring what we have learned from past experiences to present situations. In this example, our world of sensed perceptions has been screened and filtered through the bundle of assumptions we hold about people, places, things, events, occurrences, institutions, relationships, etc., and these forms, albeit in the most simplistic of terms, are our mental picture or view of the world. Of course, as we again know experientially, we observe pretty much what we want to observe, see what we want to see, look for clues that tend to reinforce what we hold dear, valued, and precious, and avoid those "stimuli" that tend to produce discomfort, pain, uncertainty and the like. In other words, we selectively observe. Also, we are aware that our assumptions about nature, people, organizations, groups, and institutions can influence what we observe. We hopefully become sensitized that our casual observances of our surroundings may be filled with errors — errors of selective observation, over-generalization, and even "group-think." This concept is easily demonstrated by the fact that we generally have beliefs about people of different backgrounds or characteristics, such as race, ethnicity, gender, socio-economic status, lifestyle, ways of thinking, and sexual orientation, although we may have little or no "direct" contact or experience with these many and varied "real-life" conditions. In some instances our perspectives are right on target and at other times they could not be further from the truth. It is difficult to be sure, to sort out "fact-from-fiction" — what we factually and accurately observe (sense) from stereotypical beliefs. Of course, we understand that when reality is correctly observed, that this forms a basis for factual knowledge, and eventually, effective problem-solving. When reality is "clouded" or emotionally colored by the assumptions we hold, it is called prejudice, bias, or intentional or unintentional loading, and distorts what is real.

With this set of informed insights in mind, we begin to appreciate the experiences that have been acquired through life's journey. As learners, our collective backgrounds and experiences are quite varied. Some learners have received many years of formal education to the point of having obtained undergraduate or even graduate degrees; others may not have had a systematic exposure to "chunks of knowledge" presented didactically through a college or university curriculum. Alternatively, some have more limited formal educational experiences, yet have attended and learned through the College of Hard Knocks (CHK). Those who are alumni of CHK, however, have a *repertoire* of experiences that may be equally prized or valued in comparison with those who are more fully credentialed by specialized institutions (universities, colleges, technical schools, etc.). This recognition is now more completely acknowledged and rewarded through credit-for-life experiences that some institutions of high learning assess and validate. So, whatever the basis for our knowledge or experience might be, there is value in what we have seen, observed, felt, or simply experienced. It is this experience that we must recognize as valuable and release in the classroom or laboratory setting where real examples of organizational living (cases) are examined. Then, and only then, many of the issues, dilemmas, and problems embedded within the content and context of case studies might be more adequately addressed and, perhaps, even resolved.

Interaction Among Learners

In addition, groups of learners are typically comprised of those who have actually worked in a number of different "fields" over their lifetime. Some may have broad experiences acquired in positions in the private sector, and others may have gained their experiences by working in the public sector at the local, state, regional, national or even international level. Still others have worked in the nonprofit sector or third sector. This vast richness of experience acquired from working in different environments, if properly mined, can bring new insights to the world of understanding how organizations actually work and behave, and the multiplicity of factors associated with problem identification and resolution. Thus, it is important that we know one another's background, range of experiences, type of positions held, level of formal and informal education in a specific discipline, etc., and that we encourage this richness of experience to be mutually shared, listened to, and reflected upon, during our group discussions and deliberations.

As learners we can help facilitate this "unlocking" of experiences and talent, thereby enabling it to "bubble-up" to the surface and be shared by all group members. Further, the experienced learner-facilitator (teacher) may have some added insights into how to most effectively unleash the talents of the group. When the knowledge and special insights of the group are primed, pumped, and "spilled-out," miracles happen in the learning process. Insights that would have remained hidden are revealed; facts in a case that may be obfuscated are brought to life; problems that were unanticipated become anticipated; and relationships among people, agencies, departments, etc., that were once deemed inconsequential, may be shown to have consequences of great magnitude and importance. The list of other valuable insights could

Introduction: The Analysis and Understanding of Case Studies

be expanded here, but the point is adequately made that if we collectively probe, analyze, synthesize, evaluate, and communicate, the learning process will be vastly improved and our experiential resource base further enriched!

Learning is enriched by the diversity of the group's background and experience, which is associated with the different occupational positions that group members may have had during their work lives. On the average, the typical worker will have seven or more careers— not just different jobs, but actual careers. Also, the notion that a person has a single job within one organization for life has become the exception rather than the rule during the latter part of the 20th century. In the past, it was assumed that if you worked hard, did what was required to earn the knowledge needed for a job (permit, license, registration, certificate, or degree), came to work on time dependably, and conscientiously contributed value to the organization, that you would have a job-for-life. In this relationship, employees and employers shared a mutuality of loyalty and trust that went from cradle to grave. Today, although this "old psychological contract" still exists in some organizational cultures, it is quickly dissipating. It is now more commonly assumed that an employer will provide for job mobility and learning, but it is the responsibility of the employee to search out the opportunities for skill and knowledge enhancement and continually be prepared to invent and re-invent oneself during an entire lifetime. This means that a "new psychological contract" has been struck and that management and labor largely agree that job retention and tenure are largely a 20th century phenomenon. People must be ready and able to move, provided they have the requisite set of knowledge, skills, abilities and values to move from one organization to the next. In other words, jobs have become short-term at best and throw-away at worst. Indeed, the new college graduates essentially apply for and accept their very first job with an eye to how the first job will lead to a second, the second to a third, and so on, with multiple organizations.

To complicate this work-life dilemma even further, the lines that once separated the three economic sectors from one another are no longer precise and clear. Indeed, during the last several decades there has been a blurring of distinction between what genuinely and uniquely constitutes the private, public, and the nonprofit sectors. This trend has been further augmented by the "privatization of the public sector," e.g. contracting out, outsourcing, and providing public grants and contracts to faith-based organizations. With these changes taking place at nearly warp speed, it leaves little stability to the once relied upon definitions that drew lines of demarcation and distinguished the different economic sectors in a unique, comprehensive, and even meaningful manner. It is this mixture of sectors that increasingly provide the experiential base for members of a learning group. As the old saying goes, "They have been there and done that." Their experiences are no longer mono-bureaucratic. Indeed, they have become poly-bureaucrats with deepened understanding of how all the economic sectors interact with one another and how they have become increasingly interdependent. Under proper encouragement and facilitation, understandings of these peculiarities can be drawn from those class participants and applied to the resolution of the problems presented in the case studies.

In analyzing and critiquing the case studies associated with *Managing People as Assets,* a variety of your colleagues' occupational titles and roles that they have held or continue to play will become evident. Similar to the background characteristics of those who may be learning in this course, you may find health care workers, police officers, emergency medical personnel, sheriff deputies, and risk managers. One might also encounter a fund manager for a charitable organization, a transportation employee, a counselor for dealing with persons with disabilities, a city planner, bus driver, grader operator, a teacher, a paralegal, and a park and recreation employee. Or, perhaps, you will have someone who once worked in public housing, inspections and compliance, municipal or state libraries, a weatherization program for lower-income property owners, or a volunteer in an elementary school, prison, museum or homeless shelter. The range of backgrounds and experiences associated with the sampling of occupations that may be present again shows the richness and diversity of the collective experience present among learners. Of course, our mutual task is to bring to the discussion platform that which is relevant and transferable from this experiential base. It is also important to keep in mind that just because one has held a job for years, that does not mean that over the years an increasingly complex set of learning experiences have been acquired. As is often found, some individuals have been involved in performing the same programmed, mundane and routine tasks, over and over, year after year. In those instances, the pool of relevant and substantial experience may be indeed a shallow one!

In the processes associated with critical thought and reflection on the issues associated with the case studies, participants will be encouraged to share their personal experiences and perspectives with each other. When experiential learning is utilized in an open, honest and safe environment, the learning is usually more effective and the experiences encountered become more memorable and meaningful. As the cases get discussed, the richness of the collective background of the course participants will become apparent. The variety and magnitude of your colleagues collective leadership experiences will reveal — whether they have occurred in the more traditional public, nonprofit, or private organizations or in diverse "hybrid" community-based organizations, the general workplace, the family or other organizations — an impressive array of observations and examples. For instance, in dealing with valuing differences or diversity (pluralism), specific discussions might take place on how the scenarios presented in the cases affect African-Americans, Asians, Latinos, gay/lesbian, bisexual, transgendered, questioning, and persons with disabilities. But diversity goes well beyond these traditional areas of interest and includes veteran status, socioeconomic status, age, ways of thinking, appearance, national origin, gender, and lifestyle.

When the critical components of the cases are analyzed and discussed, many divergent perspectives will emerge and personal beliefs, values, and ideologies will reveal their sometimes "passionate" and not so easily compromised or resolved perspectives or choices. During this hopefully vigorous exchange between members of the group, new interpersonal relationships will be formed. How the class participants deal with these newly formed relationships will affect the overall course effectiveness and be associated with the zeal, enthusiasm, or reluctance in which the learners take on the various challenges presented in the case studies.

Further Case Insights

In the analysis and understanding of things managerial or those that fit into the general area of public policy analysis, there is a cautionary tale. Although the picture has been painted with the clean brush strokes of using, understanding and valuing the talents and rich, diverse backgrounds of our colleagues, and what they bring to the "table," we as academicians and practitioners must be aware that often common sense explanations are not always what they are thought to be in terms of their validity and reliability. As such, our story is narrated cautiously and punctuated with less than optimistic endorsements. It should be noted that in dealing with some situations, the common sense explanations that may be freely given and are conveniently converted to less than thirty-second sound bites may be detrimental. In the field of management we have come to understand, from decades ago, that solutions to complex systems, such as corporations, municipalities, state agencies, nonprofit organizations, or even the U.S. economy, more than likely, do not submit to simple "one-line" solutions. Indeed, more frequently than we like to admit, our common sense solutions will not remedy a difficult problem. Rather, our intuitive approach will often produce the wrong answer, the wrong remedy, etc., and make the problem worse, rather than producing an ameliorating result. Simply stated, complex systems often behave in a counter-intuitive way.

This fact has been amply demonstrated in many areas that you might have knowledge or even direct experience. For instance, California's Proposition 13 was overwhelmingly approved by Californians at the poll (direct democracy), with the anticipation that the resulting property tax reduction of 50 percent would satisfy their "angry thirst" for a modern day "Boston Tea Party." Of course, the data is now in, the analysis has been conducted and the findings reveal that as *ad valorem* taxes went down, more service and user charges, fees and taxes were imposed — revenue receipts that are both restrictive and regressive. Or, contemporaneously, imagine the suggestion that some politicians made, that the cost of ethanol as a substitute for gasoline, for instance, would remain stable, even though the price of a barrel of crude literally "skyrocketed" from the mid-$20 range to over $70. Unfortunately, intuition does not reveal what scientists and technological specialists patently know: that ethanol is made with the use of calories (heat) produced with the burning of petroleum. Many other examples can be explicated here that reinforce the notion of using common sense explanations cautiously when dealing with complex systems. The counter-intuitive nature of these organizations juxtaposed with the "spillover," "unintended" or "secondary consequences" associated with problem resolution must be also understood and appreciated for their own worth.

The attempt is made here to neither "sanctify or vilify" the respective strengths and deficiencies that stem from our individual, *ad hoc* experiential backgrounds, nor to suggest that we need an elite corps of highly experienced Ph.D.'s to deal with the major problems and issues that confront us in our day-to-day decision making regime. However, it would be erroneous for us to proceed with unrestrained enthusiasm for practical, feasible, commonsensical decision making, without also placing the analysis spotlight on its associated or attendant problems.

Changing gears for a moment, let us assume that those who work in organizations, regardless of the sector, are conversant with the notion that decisions are nearly always made with incomplete information. As the adage is so frequently stated, "The information we need is not what we get; and the information we get, is not what we want." In that sense, managers and policy analysts constantly search for evidence that is simultaneously valid and reliable and can be used in problem resolution. But, this search for the "legitimate grail" of truth is often obscured and elusive due to the "politics of organization." From a bureaucratic perspective, albeit a cynical perspective, the twin imperatives of organizational living are associated with organizational survival and personal survival. If these imperatives are held, then analysis may be performed on the basis of conducting "pseudo evaluations" rather than ones conducted on the basis of scientific rigor and critical thinking. All too often, organization behavior is replete with examples where "appearance replaces reality," "politics substitutes for science," and "obfuscation and pedantry replaces effective communication." And, how often can it be shown that an agency goes through the gestures and rituals of being objective, professional, and "scientific," in its administrative reports and studies, but it is commonly known to "insiders" that the "analysis and study" are little more than a charade, a tightly scripted and ritualistic play on the "flanks of legitimate research." These observations just noted may be appropriately tempered due to the exigencies often associated with administration and management activities — the multiple pressures of time, talent and finances that help shape the environment in which we make choices. These forces often help propel us into waters that if we are not careful, can produce dangerous, perilous, unintended results. This wave of unanticipated consequences must be carefully weighed when we make choices. Simply stated, all choices, decisions, judgments, etc., we make have their own *repertoire* of consequences: some immediate and temporary and others delayed and long-lasting, but consequential nonetheless!

Comparing Organizational Types

Last, it should be also explained that the case studies included in *Managing People as Assets* take place in many different organizations. **Appendix B** lists the agency names with the associated cases for speedy reference. Although this information is useful, it is essential that as we begin our readings, assessments, and deliberations, that we understand those organizational features that help distinguish, at least partially, the three sectors from each other: public, nonprofit and private. As one scholar so aptly put it decades ago, "All three sectors are alike, except in areas where they differ." This simplistic assertion is unbelievably factual and helpful for the uninitiated manager. Of course, the areas in which they vary are the critically important ones and are briefly discussed below, and must be understood if error in judgment is to be avoided. Keep in mind that the business of public service organizations is the business of the people! Public organizations are designed for and required to serve the public interest and, thereby, treat citizens equitably and fairly. In contrast, business firms exist to serve the private and capital interests of their owners. They segment their customers based on the customers' ability and willingness to pay for products and services offered by the firm and, therefore, are not required to treat all customers alike. In addition to public organizations and business firms, about one and one-half million nonprofit entities populate our society. These nonprofits fit between public organizations and business firms. Like public organizations, nonprofits are required to serve a public purpose (e.g., feed and shelter the homeless, conduct medical research, provide for private education) in society in exchange for their tax exempt status. Yet, similar to business firms, nonprofits must be managed with an eye toward the bottom line to remain in business, and their mission statements determine what clientele they will or will not serve in society.

Despite the fact that there are managerial differences among public organizations serving the public interest, nonprofits serving a public purpose, and businesses serving private interests, there are two things that do create similarities among these three types of organizations. First, across all three sectors, there is an increasing emphasis on the importance of governance, accountability, and the "sunshine twins" of openness and transparency. Second, all three types of organizations must become "learning communities" to effectively and efficiently adapt to their dynamic and changing environments so that they can produce and deliver quality products and services to their citizens, clients, and customers.

Enough has already been presented on the case study method as a useful problem-solving approach. It is now our desire that these cases of real-life experiences be put to the test. It our hope that your active involvement in the analysis and resolution of the myriad problems and dilemmas incorporated into these cases will enable you to see and value the depth and breadth of the concepts associated with effectively and fairly managing people as assets in the 3rd millennium, and engender a spirit of acknowledgement that managing public sector organizations is indeed a high calling and worthy profession.

*Adapted and reprinted with permission from *Managing Public Service Organizations,* by C.K. Meyer, G.L. Frank, J.A. Geerts & L.J. Noe, 2006, Millennium HRM Press, Inc.

Introduction: The Analysis and Understanding of Case Studies

The World of Work in the 21st Century: Security to Ubiquitous Risk

by

C. Kenneth Meyer, William S. Brown, Benjamin Bingle, Lance J. Noe, Jeffrey A. Geerts, Garry L. Frank

The nature and experience of work has undergone changes over the course of history. In the earliest times of colonial America, work was predominantly agrarian. Work which we might now term "industrial" was confined to the small cities springing up on the East Coast. This type of work was not large in scale, and often done by guilds or craftsmen. As the United States grew in the early 19th century, a debate was waged among our leaders: what should be the economic base of our country. By the latter half of that century it was clear, the industrialization of the U.S. economy had won out. This development brought with it very important changes in the experience of work for the worker. No longer did the worker toil out of doors on his or her own land — in charge of their own work and responsible only to themselves and their families for their work product. Now the worker worked indoors in factories, where they labored for an employer, either an owner of the business or as a manager representing the owner. Control of many aspects of their lives passed out of their hands as a result of entering what has been termed the Modern Age (for more on this, see: Beniger, 1986).

As the nature of work changed, so too did the American landscape. Mass industrial cities such as Pittsburgh grew in and around massive industrial complexes. The resulting urbanization permanently changed the lives of the workers. Workers had to adopt new values to be successful in the new system. The workplace values of this new Modern Age developed with the growth of the United States' economy. After World War II, the U.S. was in a position of unparalleled world economic hegemony.

The Evolving Organizational Environment

William Whyte, in the classic book *The Organization Man* (1956), studied the values operant in the work world of the 1950s where large blue-chip industrial organizations ruled the day. These corporations were, perhaps, the greatest manifestation of the post-agrarian industrial movement of the Modern Age. What Whyte found were values of mutual loyalty between the worker and the organization. The "cradle to grave" implicit social or psychological contract between worker and employer consisted of an exchange of lifetime employment and protection for loyal hard work, and compliant, conforming workplace behaviors.

Whyte saw this mutual loyalty between employer and employee as fundamental to the psychological well-being of the individual worker, "…greater fealty to The Organization can be viewed as a psychological necessity for the individual. In a world changing so fast, in a world in which he must forever be on the move, the individual desperately needs roots, and The Organization is a logical place to develop them" (1956, 161).

However the advent of the 1980s saw the beginning of a change in the nature of work and the experience of work for the employee. Writers such as Best and Kellner (1997) see this change in recent decades as part of a larger social change in our global culture. They see recent decades as a pivotal point

Introduction: The World of Work in the 21st Century

in human history, a transition from the Modern Age to the Postmodern Age. We are in what Best and Kellner term the "Post-Modern turn" — a period in which the values of both periods exist simultaneously. The new Postmodern Age, they represent, is characterized by complexity, chaos, spontaneity and contingency.

The nature and experience of work as described by Whyte has changed during the period from the 1980s to the present. In a study of how the values of the workplace have changed, Leinberger and Tucker (1991) interviewed the children of the organization men in Whyte's study. They concluded that the new generations of workers no longer were imbued with the same level of organizational loyalty that their parents had displayed. The 1980s ushered in a period of mass layoffs and downsizings that broke the implicit social contract of the Modern Age. Organizations no longer concerned themselves with the long-term employment of their workers; they let workers go when this action was perceived to be in the short-term interests of the organization. As Leinberger and Tucker note "In the past corporate giants kept longtime salaried employees on the payroll through good times and bad. That is no longer the case. Nor are staff reductions any longer confined to ailing companies, since restructuring has made massive cuts routine even at the healthiest concerns. During the 1980s, more than a million managers were fired or pushed out by companies that were fighting off hostile takeovers" (1991, 210). It is estimated during the 1980s that a staggering 3.1 million jobs were cut from the Fortune 500 corporations alone. This does not include small-to medium-sized businesses or the public sector.

The "Old Deal" vs. the "New Deal"

As a result of this turbulence in the workplace, employees during this period began to develop a new set of workplace values, predicated on career mobility, often changing organizations and industries, including shifts between the private and public sectors over the course of a career. Pfeffer (1998) sees these changes in the work relationship as constituting a new social contract between worker and employer, "In the relatively recent past, employers both valued and rewarded employee loyalty. Today, downsizing, outsourcing, and the externalization of employment, the use of contingent work arrangements, reign supreme…the implication emerges that since the organization won't look out for your interests anymore, you should look after them yourself, taking individual responsibility for your career" (Pfeffer 1998, 162). The result is that organizations now imbue workers with values such as the need to be "career self-reliant" and "career resilient" thus always maintaining a high "employability" career stance in case one is suddenly found to be out of work.

The upshot of this is that traditional careers of the past have been replaced with a more "Protean" concept of careers that do not root themselves in a particular industry, organization, or sector (for more on Protean careers, see Hall, 1996). This approach appears to be an adaptive response to the turbulent dynamics and uncertainty of the postmodern labor market. Pfeffer concurs, "Today, mobility across employers and even across industries is expected and reflected in most individuals' career histories" (1998, 161).

Introduction: The World of Work in the 21st Century

The New World of Work

The uncertainty that accompanies the career dynamics described above has generated some additional values prevalent in Postmodern society generally, and Postmodern work particularly. German sociologist Ulrich Beck (2000) describes these values in what he terms the brave new world of work. The new world of work Beck perceives is saturated with risk. He notes that there is a worldwide reshaping of work relationships predicated on the concept of risk. "Paid employment is becoming precarious…'labor market flexibility' has become a political mantra…Flexibility also means a redistribution of risks away from the state and the economy towards the individual. The jobs offered become short-term and easily terminable… work society changes into a risk society…For a majority of people, even in the apparently prosperous middle layers, their basic existence and life world will be marked by endemic insecurity" (Beck 2000, 3). This is largely due to the fact that while labor power is local (at best), the power of large trans-national corporations is global, and often beyond control of most national and local governments and unions.

This reshaped work relationship between employer and employee, combined with increasingly flexible organizations now viewing workers at all levels as completely dispensable, has had a tremendous impact in the way individuals view the organizational entity, virtually eroding any thought of forming a long-term relationship with their employer. Richard Sennett (1998), of New York University and the London School of Economics, believes there have been limited, if any, true advancements in the workplace since the assembly line days of Fordism. He argues in his book, *The Corrosion of Character*, that the modern employer's focus on flexibility, short-term projects, and episodic labor hinders the workers ability to build a consistent narrative of their lives. Moreover, since character development depends upon loyalty, trust, commitment, and mutual respect – traits that are lacking in the modern workplace – the very essence of personal development is at risk.

Furthermore, due to the ever-changing nature of work, Beck sees adaptive forms of employment on the rise throughout the world. One such form is what he terms the "Brazilianization" of work. As he describes it, "in Brazil those who depend upon a wage or salary in full-time work represent only a minority of the active population…people are traveling vendors, small retailers or craft workers, offer all kinds of personal service, or shuttle back and forth between different fields of activity…" this creates a dynamic wherein "a rapidly spreading variant in the late work societies, where attractive, highly skilled and well-paid full-time employment is on its way out" (Beck 2000, 1-2). Thus Beck believes that in the very near future only one-half of all those employed will hold full-time employment for any significant period in their careers. The other half will work "*a la brasilienne.*" The harvest of this type of dynamic is a political economy shot through with risk and insecurity.

From Working Poor to the Globalized Workforce

Several authors (Shipler 2004; Shulman 2003; and Ehrenreich 2001) have demonstrated how over 30 million United States citizens can be classified as the "working poor." These are individuals who, despite full-time employment, find themselves on the edge of poverty. This situation is prompted by low wage jobs with few to no benefits. As a result, large numbers of the working poor qualify for social assistance programs such as Medicaid, rental assistance, and food stamps. Ehrenreich (2001, 219) reports

Introduction: The World of Work in the 21st Century

that "…according to a survey conducted by the U.S. Conference of Mayors, 67 percent of the adults requesting emergency food aid are people with jobs." Shipler describes the situation of the working poor in the most fearful of psychological terms, "Poverty is like a bleeding wound. It weakens the defenses. It lowers resistance. It attracts predators" (2004, 18). Shulman (2003, 12) sees an equally fearful result at the national level, "…if work does not work for millions of Americans it undermines our country's most fundamental ideals. We are permitting a caste system to grow up around us, consigning millions of Americans to a social dead-end." At the same time as this new social dynamic in the nature and experience of work unfolds, globalization of industry has reduced the power of unions in the United States to adequately represent the needs and interests of the working poor. The impact of this is to exacerbate the insecurity of feeling "at risk" in the workplace, causing workers to choose the temporary security of the new work relationship over the need for autonomy and an authentic and independent self.

Simon Head in his book *The Ruthless Economy: Work and Power in the Digital Age* (2003), describes how not only the working poor, but also white collar jobs are being subjugated to unparalleled management control. He details how traditional industrial management techniques such as standardization, measurement, monitoring, and control have become fused with the electronic power of new technological advances to create the platform for the most powerful managerial hegemony in the history of management. He terms this phenomena "techno-Taylorism" in homage to Frederick W. Taylor, one of the early thinkers in the field of industrial/scientific management. Technology exists today to give management the ability to know and see any aspect of an employees work or personal life.

Privacy in the Workplace

Data gathering devices currently used by management include pre-employment checks such as motor vehicle history reports, criminal history reports, credit reports, telephone usage pattern reports (indicating 800 and 900 numbers called), magazine subscription reports, worker's compensation claim reports, and potential clandestine surveillance by private investigators, which may include interviewing a potential employee's neighbors. Most major corporations require a post-offer, pre-employment physical examination including EKG, chest x-ray, blood pressure data, as well as urine and blood samples.

While in the past employers could engage in pre-employment genetic testing of job candidate blood samples, a recent legal development has now prohibited this practice. The passage of the Genetic Information and Nondiscrimination Act in 2008 (GINA, 2008) outlawed this practice. The EEOC issued final regulations on this Act on November 9, 2010. The regulations stated in part that GINA "…prohibits employers and other entities covered by GINA...from requesting or requiring genetic information of employees or their family members" (Smith, 2010).

Once hired, the employee may be issued a "smart" ID card that can provide management with real-time information on the location of the badge wearer, how long they have been in a specific location, and the identities of other badge wearers in the same location. Smart card technology or "Hygiene Guard" is also utilized in some hospitals, hotels, and restaurants to monitor the bathroom activities of badge wearers. Workers who do not wash their hands, use an inadequate amount of soap in hand washing, or who spend time in excess of the system allotted bathroom time will have their behavior brought to management's attention by the system. Furthermore, once in the workplace a worker's computer use will be monitored to include email and voicemail monitoring, computer files scans, and continuous work performance monitoring. Some organizations use clandestine closed-circuit television monitoring (CCTV) to observe workers' performance. Additionally, off-duty conduct may be regulated to include prohibition of certain hobbies deemed dangerous, like skydiving and motorcycle driving, off-duty smoking and alcohol consumption, diet and exercise regulation via mandatory cholesterol screening, and prohibition of dating and marriage with employees of their own organization or that of their competitors (for more on workplace privacy issues see: Brown 2000).

Some technologies, however, have supported the advent of a more mobile workforce. Cellular telephones, Global Positioning Systems (GPS), fixed-mobile convergence, and wireless connectivity are standard fare among private and public organizations in the 21st century. These technological capabilities and devices afford efficiencies that were previously unheard of and allow employees to work from home, airport terminal, hotel room, construction site, or public space. The emergence of technology has made the workforce more dynamic and responsive, while also satisfying the demands of today's worker, namely, a more proportionate work-life balance. Studies conducted by IDC, a global provider of market intelligence, predict that nearly 75% of the United States workforce will be mobile by 2011 and worldwide, one billion workers will be mobile within the same timeframe (Reuters, 2008).

Incorporating these technologies carry risks; for organizations, a primary risk is loss of sensitive data that can easily be misplaced, deleted, or mishandled by small technical devices and their users. As well, organizations must trust employees to use these devices as workplace tools and not for entertainment, amusement, or personal gain. It seems, by all practical measures, that organizations do not have this sense of trust and workers pay for this distrust in the form of surveillance and monitoring.

While mobile workers enjoy more autonomy and freedom of flexibility, employers utilize surveillance to maintain control and monitor work activity. The extent of employee monitoring has grown to unprecedented levels that border on the rights of privacy. In court cases such as Bourke v. Nissan (1993), Smyth v. Pillsbury (1996), and Shoars v. Epson (1994) (Privacy Rights Clearinghouse, 2008), however, the legality is upheld. This surveillance is not always disclosed to workers, which creates a sense of distrust among traditional and mobile workers alike. A constant watchful eye saddles the employee with feelings of contempt, a loss of independence, and unnecessary anxiety.

Technological advancements have emerged as a double-edged sword in the workplace. On the one hand, their capabilities offer increased productivity and efficiency while providing for a more mobile workforce. On the other hand, technology has allowed for a marked increase in employer surveillance, and, since the monitoring is easily hidden inside a shiny new device or is carried out behind the closed doors of IT departments, employer surveillance has been incorporated into the workplace under a veil. Current practices now in place take on Orwellian proportions and the invasion of individual privacy by employers is furthered fueled as this technology becomes ever more sophisticated and intrusive. Writers call this ability to see all regarding their employees' private and public lives "panoptic power." The result is that workers never know when management is monitoring or surveying their behavior, but are constantly aware that they could be monitored or watched at any moment.

Introduction: The World of Work in the 21st Century

Responding to the Nature of Work

Employees who feel the constant insecurity of being at risk in the world of work, who are "infanticized" by ubiquitous technological supervision and control, who are precariously perched on the brink of poverty due to low wages and low or no benefits, and often who are unable to care adequately for their families as a result, must deeply feel shamed by the experience. In the book *Shame, Exposure, and Privacy* by Carl Schneider (1977) the argument is advanced that people who have a perception of themselves as inferior, small, weak, or helpless, feel shamed by the experience. Schneider argues that loss of privacy and control also creates feelings of vulnerability, violation and shame. Clearly, the workplace dynamics we have articulated above have the potential to meet the criteria outlined by Schneider.

Christopher Lasch (1984) describes the psychological reaction individuals may have to prolonged feelings of victimization and powerlessness in the experience of their lives. He terms this adaptive response, "narcissistic survivalism" and compares it to the adaptive behaviors manifested by individuals in total institutions or extreme situations.

Narcissistic survivalism is characterized by the creation of what Lasch calls the minimal self by drawing in the boundaries of self to less vulnerable and more defensible parameters. The rest of the frontiers of self are surrendered to conformity, compliance, and docility in the face of overwhelming authority. Thus, the self-presented in everyday life is not an authentic one, but rather the self that the individual believes the powers in authority wish to see. This presentation of an inauthentic self leads to feelings of unworthiness, shame, and alienation. The alienation felt is multi-layered: from the authentic self, from others (by the presentation of an inauthentic self in everyday life), and from a feeling that they can "be" in the world (alienation on a grand scale).

The corrosive nature of work in new capitalism may be the human reaction to the changing nature and experience of work as described here (Sennett, 1998). Sennett states that "in order to be reliable, we must feel needed" however the contemporary experience of work "radiates indifference" and "absence of trust" (1998, 146). It seems clear that an experience of work that is imbued with indifference and distrust, and is predicated on ubiquitous risk and insecurity will have a corrosive and destructive result on perceptions of self and perceptions of one's ability to be in the world. Sennett, perhaps, states it best "a regime which provides human beings no deep reasons to care about one another cannot long preserve its legitimacy" (1998, 148).

Depth of Change

Also of note is the depth of change occurring in the workplace. The change is ongoing and transformational in nature; organizations have experienced, or are in the midst of experiencing, a shift from the heavy-lifting, programmable, analytical, "left-brain" approach of the past to an entrepreneurial, creative, conceptualizing, "right-brain" composition. The new psychological contract between employees and organizations is not rooted in the loyal, work-a-day mantra of the past, but rather has evolved to reflect an erosion of trust in the relationship between employee and employer.

Introduction: The World of Work in the 21st Century

The emerging workforce is contingent, with employees working part-time, contractually, seasonally, and, in many cases, having multiple careers. This shift impacts the nature of the workplace and the physical makeup of the organization. No longer do all workers report with briefcase in hand each morning; instead, technological capabilities, combined with the contingent nature of work, has resulted in employees telecommuting and working non-traditional hours.

This transformation extends to the very structure of the workplace as organizations transition from a hierarchical makeup. David Osborne and Ted Gaebler analyzed this shift in their book, *Reinventing Government*, which describes organizations that once featured a clear, albeit, at times irrational, chain of command shifting from hierarchy to a network-based structure in an attempt to de-bureaucratize their operations. This transformation is made possible by decentralizing the workforce, technological advancement, and a transition toward self-management. Flattening the organization creates a more anticipatory, proactive, and nimble workforce that is better suited for today's challenges. According to Osborne and Gaebler, "hierarchical centralized bureaucracies designed in the 1930s or 1940s simply do not function well in the rapidly changing, information-rich, knowledge intensive society and economy" (1992, 12) of today.

Beyond these changes, lies a dramatically diversified cross-generational workforce with different viewpoints, management styles, approaches, preferences, and lifestyles. The current workplace features multiple generational cohorts; veterans amidst the upper organizational stratums, baby boomers at the senior executive level, Generation X constituents populating middle management, and members of Generation Y are now working and rising to leadership positions. This powerful mix contributes to the depth of change occurring in today's workplace and results in serious organizational implications that demand thoughtful consideration from leaders and human resource managers alike.

Future Occupations

With these changes, and the fundamental shifts in the global economy, come increased demand for certain occupations in the future. Increasingly, due largely to an aging population and the influx of immigrants, healthcare professions will be in high demand throughout the United States. Niche direct healthcare positions are expected to rise as the anticipated number of home health aides needed by 2016 exceeds one million (Altman, 2009). Recent findings indicate that health informatics specialists, who develop systems to assist doctors and nurses in making fact-based diagnoses, and patient advocates that are hired by insurance companies, hospitals, and individuals to guide patients through the increasingly confusing healthcare system, will both be more common in the future. Demand for computational biologists and behavioral geneticists is also predicted to increase steadily as the cost to fully sequence a person's genome declines. Those working in these occupations will play a leading role in new medical discoveries related to cancer, diabetes, heart conditions, and countless other diseases (Nemko, 2008).

As the digital world continues to play an ever-expanding role in daily life, more and more technology careers will be generated. The number of information technology jobs is projected to increase 24 percent by 2016, more than twice the overall job growth rate (Altman, 2009). Data miners, for example, will play a larger role as they sort through digital information related to preferences, buying habits, brand-loyalty, and demographics that users submit online, and then, based on their analysis, provide businesses with valuable information about what products and services to offer and how to individualize marketing efforts. Simulation developers, on the other hand, create video simulations for entertainment, education, and training purposes so that thrill-seekers can have the excitement of piloting a jet aircraft without the safety hazards or a medical student can gain experience conducting advanced surgery without threatening a real patient's life (Nemko, 2008).

Asia's rise to global prominence may also have an impact on future vocations. Business development specialists will be needed to help American firms establish partnerships and collaborations with foreign companies while offshore managers will also be in demand to oversee these new joint ventures (Nemko, 2008). These highly specialized vocations will likely be contingent in nature and rely heavily upon digital systems for efficiency and cost savings.

Green jobs focused on environmentalism and sustainability are also projected to be more abundant in the future. The United States government has taken steps to prompt this growth by designating more than $60 billion to clean energy projects in an effort to stimulate economic activity and $600 million towards green job training programs (Walsh, 2009). These "green collar" jobs may range from solar panel installation specialist to sustainable building auditors (Nemko, 2008) and some experts predict that green employment could make up 10% of all job growth through 2040 (Walsh, 2009).

A sample of selected occupations that now contain a "critical mass" of employees and a listing of some of the newest, emerging occupations are presented in **Table 2**. Based on the preceding discussion, many of these occupations reflect the changing global, economic, technological, and scientific nature associated with the "dynamic" world of work that is presenting itself.

Table 2. Newest Emerging Occupations

Acute Care Nurses	Adaptive Physical Education Specialists
Advanced Practice Psychiatric Nurses	Anesthesiologist Assistants
Biochemical Engineers	Biochemical Engineers
Biofuels Processing Technicians	Biofuels Production Managers
Bioinformatics Scientists	Bioinformatics Technicians
Biomass Plant Technicians	Biomass Production Managers
Biostatisticians	Brownfield Redevelopment Specialists & Site Managers
Business Continuity Planners	Business Intelligence Analysts
Chief Sustainability Officers	Climate Change Analysts
Clinical Data Managers	Clinical Nurse Specialists
Compliance Managers	Critical Care Nurses
Customs Brokers	Cytogenetic Technologists
Cytotechnologists	Data Warehousing Specialists
Database Architects	Document Management Specialists
Electroneurodiagnostic Technologists	Electronic Commerce Specialists
Endoscopy Technicians	Energy Auditors

Introduction: The World of Work in the 21st Century

Table 2. Newest Emerging Occupations, continued

Energy Brokers	Energy Engineers
Environmental Economists	Fuel Cell Technicians
Genetic Counselors	Geneticists
Geodetic Surveyors	Geographic Information Systems Technicians
Geospatial Information Scientists and Technologists	Geothermal Production Managers
Geothermal Technicians	Green Marketers
Histologic Technicians	Histotechnologists
Hospitalists	Human Factors Engineers and Ergonomists
Hydroelectric Plant Technicians	Industrial Ecologists
Informatics Nurse Specialists	Instructional Designers and Technologists
Intelligence Analysts	Logistics Engineers
Mechatronics Engineers	Midwives
Molecular and Cellular Biologists	Nanosystems Engineers
Nanotechnology Engineering Technologists	Network Designers
Neurologists	Neuropsychologists
Non-Destructive Testing Specialists	Online Merchants
Ophthalmic Medical Technologists and Technicians	Photonics Engineers
Photonics Technicians	Physical Medicine and Rehabilitation Physicians
Precision Agriculture Technicians	Preventive Medicine Physicians
Quality Control Analysts	Radio Frequency Identification Device Specialists
Recycling and Reclamation Workers	Recycling Coordinators
Regulatory Affairs Managers	Remote Sensing Technicians
Robotics Engineers	Securities and Commodities Traders
Security Management Specialists	Solar Photovoltaic Installers
Solar Thermal Installers and Technicians	Spa Managers
Speech-Language Pathology Assistants	Supply Chain Managers
Sustainability Specialists	Transportation Planners
Transportation Security Officers	Validation Engineers
Video Game Designers	Water Resource Specialists
Water/Wastewater Engineers	Weatherization Installers and Technicians
Web Administrators	Wind Energy Engineers
Wind Energy Project Managers	Wind Turbine Service Technicians

Another dynamic that must be considered when dealing with future occupations and the changing nature of work is that more people are compelled to find a variety of ways to make their living. People out of fear and risk aversion go back and forth between several jobs as they perhaps attempt to start a cottage business on the side (one that they can operate out of their homes or apartments). Simultaneously, there is the palpable rise of "techno-Taylorism" — workers are tethered to their machines, but the processes are technical rather than merely repetitive and purely mechanical. As we have known for decades, most people derive personal value and worth directly from their organizational attachments. To lose this "true connection" leaves a devastating imprint on the personhood of the individual that is downsized, terminated, or as the British might say, "has become redundant."

Further, it is particularly relevant to the post 2007-2009 recession in the United States, that those who suffer job loss are prone to blame themselves, although in all likelihood their individual behaviors had nothing to do with the reduction-in-force (RIF). Still, all words of blame aside, in losing their jobs they have lost their organizational affiliation, which in turn attacks their basic self — who they think and believe they are. All too frequently, job loss is associated with feelings of low self-esteem, powerlessness, personal weakness, and inferiority. These opinions that further and directly undermine the credibility of self may also exist after a layoff. Eventually, as Karl Marx observed nearly a century ago, alienation is manifested and feelings of shame and unworthiness raise their mutually devastating heads; in turn, the worker then begins to present a portrait, as shown earlier, of himself/herself as inauthentic, shameful, and alienated.

William Brown, in summarizing important recent material on the nature of work makes the keen observation that the new trend is explained with mental abstractions such as "career self-reliance," "career resiliency," and in the final analysis, "maintaining employability." He also notes with interest that we are entering a new era in the world of work — one in which *risk* is the most *ubiquitous* factor connected with the work experience. Citing the work of Beck (2000) he makes the compelling argument that the power of labor is local, whereas corporate power is global and this global hegemony shapes the world of work not only nationally, but worldwide.

An understanding of the changing world of work in the third millennium will help in the analysis of the cases that follow. Knowing the salient characteristics of the Postmodern – an era that is pervasive in its implications for managing and understanding human behavior – will help us grapple with these uncertain, turbulent, and "changing times."

References

Altman, Alex. (2009, May 25) High Tech, High Touch, High Growth. *Time.*

Beck, Ulrich. (2000). *The Brave New World of Work.* Cambridge, UK: Polity Press.

Beniger, James R. (1986). *The Control Revolution: Technological and Economic Origins of the Information Society.* Cambridge, MA: Harvard University Press.

Best, Steven and Kellner, Douglas. (1997). *The Postmodern Turn.* New York: Guildford Press.

Brown, William S. (2000). "Ontological Security, Existential Anxiety, and Workplace Privacy," *Journal of Business Ethics,* 23: 61-65.

Ehrenreich, Barbara. (2001). *Nickel and Dimed: On (Not) Getting By in America.* New York: Henry Holt and Company.

Hall, Douglas T. (1996). "Protean Careers of the 21st Century," *Academy of Management Executive,* 10(4): 8-16.

Head, Simon. (2003). *The New Ruthless Economy: Work and Power in the Digital Age,* Oxford, UK: Oxford University Press.

Lasch, Christopher. (1984). *The Minimal Self: Psychic Survival in Troubled Times.* New York: W.W. Norton & Company.

Leinberger, Paul and Tucker, Bruce. (1991). *The New Individualists: The Generation After The Organization Man.* New York: HarperCollins.

Nemko, Marty. (2008, December 4). Ahead of the Curve Careers. *U.S. News & World Report.* Retrieved from http://www.usnews.com/money/careers/articles/2008/12/04/ahead-of-the-curve-careers-2008.html

Osborne, David, and Gaebler, Ted. (1992). *Reinventing Government: How the Entrepreneurial Spirit is Transforming the Public Sector.* Reading, MA: Addison-Wesley Publishing Company, Inc.

Pfeffer, Jeffrey. (1998). *The Human Equation: Building Profits by Putting People First.* Boston, MA: Harvard Business School Press.

Privacy Rights Clearinghouse. (2008, July 1). Employee Monitoring: Is There Privacy in the Workplace? Retrieved from http://www.privacyrights.org/fs/fs7-work.htm#1

Reuters. (2008, January 15). IDC Predicts the Number of Worldwide Mobile Workers to Reach 1 Billion by 2011. Retrieved from http://www.reuters.com/article/pressRelease/idUS122779+15-Jan-2008+BW20080115

Schneider, Carl D. (1977). *Shame, Exposure, and Privacy.* New York: W.W. Norton & Company.

Sennett, Richard. (1998). *The Corrosion of Character: The Personal Consequences of Work in the New Capitalism.* New York: W.W. Norton & Company.

Shipler, David K. (2004). *The Working Poor: Invisible in America.* New York: Alfred A. Knopf.

Shulman, Beth. (2003). *The Betrayal of Work: How Low-Wage Jobs Fail 30 Million Americans and Their Families.* New York: The New Press.

Smith, A. (2010, November 9). Legal Issues/Federal Resources, *EEOC Issues Final GINA Regulations.* Retrieved from: http://www.shrm.org/LegalIssues/FederalResources/Pages/EEOCFinalGINARegulations.aspx

Walsh, Bryan. (2009, May 25). It Will Pay to Save the Planet. *Time.*

Whyte, William. (1956). *The Organization Man.* New York: Simon and Schuster.

1

Keep Your Stick on the Ice or Your Views to Yourself

by
C. Kenneth Meyer and Lance Noe

John Snow was saddened about the way his childhood sport of hockey had changed since he was a young boy growing up in Duluth, Minnesota. Sure, the coaches demanded as much then as now and there was the physical contact involved in checking other players, but the skills of skating fast and precisely always had to be finely honed. Some banter on the ice was permitted, but it was not mean spirited and filled with obscenities, profanities, and statements about one's "mother."

Today John Snow became quite agitated as he read and reread the front page story that appeared in his metropolitan newspaper, and he presumed that it had also received top billing in other newspapers across the country. For sure, it was the lead sensational story on all national and cable television news. The newspaper article featured two fathers who had argued and then fought over the extent to which violence was being played out by adolescents in an ice arena in New England, until one father ended up killing the other father, who was the game's umpire, while their children watched. "How can this be?" he wondered. Why can't the senseless level of violence end in America? What is happening, he thought, to our children who are fed a high caloric diet of violent encounters on a daily basis?

"Enough is enough," he said to himself. He opened a new document on his computer and wrote a letter to the editor of the local newspaper, *The Publics' Messenger*. His thoughts came quickly about a topic over which he had become outraged. It was during normal working hours to be sure and he knew that what he was writing was his own personal opinion, but someone had to say something, if only to decry the magnitude and viciousness of violence in society. He wrote:

> **Dear Editor:**
>
> **Today, there is a low level of confidence and trust and a high level of cynicism and verbal abuse for those in positions of authority: police, government employees, teachers, social workers, librarians, members of Congress and the judiciary. Indeed, over the last thirty years, this trend is augmented by the declining confidence in the basic institutions of society, such as medicine,**

colleges/universities, journalism, and large companies. Correspondingly, is there any wonder why people don't trust/respect referees, umpires, coaches, and other players or fans? The legitimacy of coaches, umpires, referees, etc., as authority figures is challenged when they are spit upon, cursed, punched, shoved, and in a myriad of other ways, have pain, injury or suffering intentionally inflicted upon them by players and managers--and these acts take place in the non-combative sports. On the extreme side of the sports industry exist the totally obscene, decadent, and sought after forms of behavior and "entertainment" displayed in boxing," an ear or so for an alleged bunt," or in basketball, "a threat and choke for a reduction in pay and a short suspension," "professional" wrestling or "psycho-sexual sadism," twisted around the themes of female objectification and the crudest forms of barbarism and human debasement, and the other combative "sports" of "Ultimate fighting," "kick boxing," and the totally cruel and vicious "tough man" contests. These later "sports" go well beyond the concern of this letter.

Violence in sports should be categorized as a type of workplace violence (similar to violence that occurs in offices, factories, lumber mills, farms, taxicabs, warehouses, schools, and in "stop and robs," convenience stores. If the safety and health of workers (players, umpires, coaches and agents) and spectators is of concern, then the level of violence taking place on the court, field, floor, track, or in the arena might appropriately be addressed by the U.S. Centers for Disease Control and Prevention (CDC), the Occupational Safety and Health Administration (OSHA), by professional labor unions, management, and team owners. The rationale underpinning a governmental policy that deals with sports violence is easily justified.

It is common to see players fighting one on one or as a "gang" on the field. Coaches routinely curse, rant and rave, and scream at players; they even throw clipboards, chairs, or other objects that are within immediate reach, onto the playing floor, and get "close and physical" with their charges. The players scrawl and act viciously at the umpires and other players, fight with, trip, hit, kick and physically and verbally lash-out at the spectators, and throw their bats, sticks, racquets, hats, etc., to the ground as if they are millionaire spoiled kids having a tantrum, which they largely are. Mothers of cheerleaders fight with one another and one went so far as to put a contract for murder on another girl's mother. Predictably, parents act violently toward their own kids who are involved in little league play. Most recently, the player agents have entered into the fray and some even attempt to show that the spectators desire to see players snarl, scratch, claw, and be physically and mentally brutal and purposively violent in the arena. In fact, members of The Associated Press recently voted three out of the top twelve national sports stories as ones dealing with violence: Tyson bites Holyfield (ranked 2), Marv Albert sex (biting) scandal (ranked 10), and Sprewell attack on Coach Carlesimo (Ranked 12). Perhaps, violence and winning, in a perverted way, have become the "brass ring."

Violence does not end on the field or in the arena. Too often, violence continues after the game and some players get involved in acts of domestic spousal abuse against wives, girlfriends, and paid or unpaid sexual partners, and engage in other types of violent behavior, drug pushing, physical assault, and even rape. Even some of the "all-stars" on the U.S. Olympic Hockey Team "trashed" their hotel room in Nagano, Japan, when they found out that their crude, violent and bullying behavior was not successful against their opponents. One might reasonably conclude that we spend more time reading the indictments by grand juries of those engaged in sports, than we spend reading about "play of the day" and the ultimate "slam dunk."

Management, union officials and player agents all too frequently portray these attacks and outbursts as lapses in character or that the player "was driven over the edge," by some unidentifiable cause, as if to justify a temporary aberration. They then do everything possible to keep them on the team so that a "win" can be marked-up, because winning is everything. The character and discipline formation of athletics gets lost in this "win-at-any-cost" mentality. To add to the problem, some club owners and sports announcers deride other owners, players, associations, and even engage in a unique type of violence, racism. The latest foray into the culture of spectator approved violence were the simulated violent attacks by the San Diego Chicken against a purple dinosaur figure who resembles Barney, a television favorite of young children. As the chicken attacks, pounces upon, and strikes the dinosaur, the cheers and applause are nearly palpable from the stands. These, of course, are all acts of violence.

Sports are not the sole proprietor of violent behavior in society. Generally, it is easy to uncover varying levels or intensities of violence in politics (injury by infringement, profanity, outrage, distortion, and need to control electoral politics and the actions of special prosecutors come to mind); in musical lyrics from country to rap; in the media; in public policy (laws directed against women, minorities, children, elderly, lower income, and the underclass); in video games, and in such areas as police-citizen interaction. More years of life are lost to violence each year than the total losses associated with cancer, strokes, and heart disease, according to the American Medical Association. Indeed, violence is of pandemic levels and is a major medical and public health problem. Each year, nearly one-half million visits to trauma and ER care centers involve violence. A recently conducted national survey of doctors, reported in the *Annals of Internal Medicine*, revealed that 87 and 94 percent of surgeons and internists, respectively, thought that gunshot wounds *should* be treated as a public health epidemic. The published report projected that death by gunshot will eclipse death by auto accidents by 2003. Further, some aspects of our society have become so violent that we can't seem to have the two sexes trained together, as is suggested as a means of dealing with the recent allegation of rape, sexual abuse and harassment in several of the military branch services.

Perhaps there is still some particle of hope among most of us that violence can be addressed in our systems of entertainment, economics, and politics. The public outrage concerning the "slap on the wrist" given to a NBA player who choked his coach provides some solace. If an employee in your workplace choked the CEO, CFO, or supervisor, would this result in employee suspension, termination or the filing of a civil or criminal charge? Perhaps it is painfully evident for most to see how far we have permitted our society to depart from those idealized standards that ought to govern basic relationships among us: trust, caring, civility, compassion, and understanding.

He read and re-read the letter. It included all the issues he wanted to put on the table at this time and the tone had to be dramatic, he reasoned, if readers were to pay any attention to what he had to say.

Case 1: Keep Your Stick on the Ice or Your Views to Yourself

No topic was more important to society than that of violence and he had spoken his mind and now he would let the chips fall where they might. Believing he had engaged in an act of citizenship, he proudly signed the letter: John Snow, Human Resources Counselor, city of Plainview. Now all he had to do was wait for the reactions of his friends and co-workers. He expected that other "Letters to the Editor" would follow, and he knew he would be ridiculed by some and praised by others. What he did not anticipate was his director's reaction. The email was crisply written:

> "John, you have done it again! Your job is to counsel employees of the city of Plainview and their family members. It is not in your job description to take on every liberal, bleeding-heart cause that is presented on TV. To add insult to injury, your recent letter to the editor was signed using your official position title, which, as you know, is forbidden in the "City of Plainview Employee Manual." I wish to discuss this irresponsible act with you and determine what steps need to be taken to ensure that you are appropriately disciplined. As you may already know, several members of the city council are fed up with your public tirades."

Questions and Instructions:

1. As the director of the Human Resources Department, what do you find objectionable, if anything, in what John Snow has penned to the editor? Is the content of the letter relevant to your meeting with Snow? Be specific.

2. Does public employee John Snow give up any rights that he otherwise enjoys as *Citizen Snow*? If no, what is your reasoning or rationale? If yes, can you specifically identify any employee rights that are limited for public employees and why they are curtailed?

3. Should John Snow have signed his name and given his official organization affiliation? Was it acceptable, in your opinion, for John to write the letter he sent to the newspaper while at work and on the city time clock? Please elaborate. Would you see his expressed "opinion" as a concern for the HR director if he had signed it and given only his home address? Please explain.

Case 1: Keep Your Stick on the Ice or Your Views to Yourself

Name:

Case Log and Administrative Journal Entry

This case analysis and learning assessment is printed on perforated pages and may be removed from the book for evaluation purposes.

Case Analysis:
Major case concepts and theories identified:

What is the relevance of the concepts, theories, ideas and techniques presented in the case to that of public management?

Facts — what do we know *for sure* about the case? Please list.

Who is involved in the case (people, departments, agencies, units, etc.)? Were the problems of an "intra/interagency" nature? Be specific.

Are there any rules, laws, regulations or standard operating procedures identified in the case study that might limit decision-making? If so, what are they?

Are there any clues presented in the case as to the major actor's interests, needs, motivations and personalities? If so, please list them.

Case 1: Keep Your Stick on the Ice or Your Views to Yourself

Learning Assessment:
What do the administrative theories presented in this case mean to you as an administrator?

How can this learning be put to use outside the classroom? Are there any problems you envision during the implementation phase?

Several possible courses of action were identified during the class discussion. Which action was considered to be most practical by the group? Which was deemed most feasible? Based on your personal experience, did the group reach a conclusion that was desirable, feasible, and practical? Please explain why or why not.

Did the group reach a decision that would solve the problem on a short-term or long-term basis? Please explain.

What could you have done to receive more learning value from this case?

2

Patronage or Cronyism at DHS

by
Mary Beth Mellick and C. Kenneth Meyer

On January 4th, two-year-old Kaitlin Dalby died after being beaten to death while in the care of her mother and mother's boyfriend. It appeared she had suffered weeks of abuse before her death. Area residents claimed they had made numerous calls to the Department of Human Services (DHS) to report the abuse before Kaitlin died. One call was made on December 12th, less than a month before Kaitlin's death. Another call was made just four days later. The department's internal review had no record of the December 12th call, nor had DHS employees mentioned such a call. Under closer inspection, however, the department records revealed that a call had been received and had been checked out.

DHS Director Debra Foster felt department workers followed all procedures in the Dalby case, but also stated that she had "grave concerns" about whether her employees responded properly to allegations that Kaitlin Dalby was being abused in the weeks before she died. The governor's office was notified about the incident and began an investigation. The investigation was barely underway when another development unfolded that again questioned the credibility of the Department of Human Services and its director, and overshadowed the Dalby case almost entirely.

As Foster apprehensively tried to cover for her department and its handling of the Dalby case, state officials were examining the budget, in particular the executive branch's growing reliance on contractors to perform various services. The state spent $430 million on service contracts in the last budget year, compared to $161 million it had budgeting for contracts ten years earlier. Indeed, last year, one-third of the state's total budget went to private contractors. Governor Jack Bartlett said previous leaders might have created the reliance on outside help by reducing the number of state workers. "The workload remained the same, and the state hired consultants to fill in for full-time employees," he said.

Upon examining the increase in contractors, a special state audit was conducted on two consultants in DHS: Matt Schilling and Kathy Kramer. Foster, the human service director, hired Kramer. She was a professional acquaintance of Foster when she worked as director of the human services department in a neighboring state. State auditors discovered Kramer was paid nearly $22,000 for a month's worth of work in the previous year. Three days after her consulting contract ended, Kramer was hired full time as the department's chief deputy director of policy. Her salary was fixed at $89,544 per year. As a state employee, her pay was set at $1,700 per week, compared with the $5,500 per week she made as a consultant. The auditor's office found little evidence of what Kramer did during her month of consulting. In response to the auditor's request for evidence of Kramer's work, the department turned

Case 2: Patronage or Cronyism at DHS

over four typewritten pages, including an informal and fragmented summary. The following excerpts are illustrative of the material presented in Kramer's "Summary of Responses" after she had worked in the DHS for a month as a consultant. Taken from Kramer's report were the following representative statements:

"Most would say that communication has come a long way in the last few years, but will also say there is still a ways to go."

"Teamwork has another theme throughout the responses. Teamwork including line staff, field staff, central office, between divisions, at every level. 'Lead by example' and 'walk the talk' were expressions noted."

"Contracting out was mentioned in several papers. Feeling is this should be discontinued and the funding be used for additional staff to do the work."

The following are additional excerpts from a one-page report by Kramer titled "Specific Areas of Focus":

"Establish partnerships based on shared decision making, shared responsibilities, and shared accountability…"

"Establish a human service system founded in quality, i.e., best/promising practice, customer satisfaction, continuous improvement…"

By nearly any standard, some of the state politicians judged these statements to be little more than trite phrases or simple statements and many members of the department were upset that the consultant was paid in one month what they would receive in an entire year. Representative Dennis Newman (R), Speaker of the House of Representatives, said, "The arrangement with Kramer smacks of cronyism and appeared to be a misappropriation of state money."

The second case involved Texas consultant Matt Schilling who was hired by the state to explore a new payment system for service providers that would link pay to performance for companies, counselors, child-welfare workers, and others who did business with the DHS. Like Kramer, Schilling had a previous relationship with Foster stemming from the consulting he previously provided for an agency that she directed in another state. Upon close examination, state auditors were surprised to learn that under Schilling's contract with the state, he was paid $380,000 over 22 months.

Under Schilling's new payment system, social-service providers would be made more accountable. For example, under the old system, the DHS would pay providers for work produced, not results. A counselor under the existing system would receive payments based on the number of sessions with a troubled teen. Under Schilling's system, pay would hinge, at least in part, on changes in the teen's life such as getting a job, staying in school, avoiding drug use. Providers disagreed with Schilling's system, stating that they didn't think their payments should depend on progress. However, Lutheran

Social Services, the state's largest non-profit social service agency was "... supportive of the direction of Schilling's recommendations," said Ron Green, the agency's president and chief executive officer. He said, "The public demands that payments be linked to results!"

Whether Schilling's payment system would be successful, in the final analysis, was a contentious issue. Some lawmakers wondered publicly in the interviews they gave and the letters they wrote to the editor of the state's major newspaper, whether he was worth the astronomical salary he received for his work. They stated that Schilling's idea of holding providers accountable sounded great, but for $380,000, he had failed to answer the question, "How?"

State senator Marcia Bergman said, "Schilling's proposals are heavy on jargon and light on ordinary common sense solutions." In his defense, Foster said Schilling was not expected to provide details on how to make his concepts work. "The answers for 'how to' are going to come from our front lines, not from in here," she retorted.

The auditors' findings of private contractors' salaries were met with intense public scrutiny. Senator Diane Reynolds, a Legislative Oversight Committee member, said, "It was difficult for average citizens to understand why a department does not have enough people to do their job, but has some $400,000 to have an outsider come in and tell us what we're doing wrong."

"There's hardly anybody worth that much money. The way these consultants were taken care of was ridiculous," said Woodward Mayor George Meyer, referring to Schilling's frequent stays at Embassy Heights, an exclusive hotel located close to the capitol building complex, and the costs associated with round trip airfare from Texas. In addition to Schilling's $380,000 salary over 22 months, he also incurred $54,000 in travel expenses that were paid without proper authorization, State Auditor Doug Davidson revealed. He further stated, "Schilling should repay the money to the state."

Democrats suggested Republicans were trying to stir up trouble for Governor Bartlett, a Democrat, as the two parties geared up for the fall legislative elections. Representative Phil Abbott, a Democrat from Cedar Valley, charged that committee co-chairman Richard Stone, a Republican from Connelly, was playing gotcha politics with the governor. Abbott also questioned the timing of the Schilling audit report by Davidson, a Republican, late last month.

DHS director Debra Foster was finally confronted by her critics at a hearing at the state Capitol. She surprised lawmakers by accepting full responsibility for the contractual flaws identified by auditor Doug Davidson in Schilling and Kramer's lucrative consulting contracts. She stated that she might seek help from the Attorney General in recovering the $54,000 for Schilling's travel expenses. Foster also stated she intended to heed the advice of Davidson and other state officials in improving the department's handling of contracts. She defended the work, however, of both Schilling and Kramer, by characterizing their improved service. Lawmakers treated their meeting with Foster as a fact-finding session, not an interrogation.

Case 2: Patronage or Cronyism at DHS

Schilling even admitted that the recommendations of consultants aren't always accepted and implemented, based on his experience as an official during the 1990s in his home state's mental health department. When a local reporter asked him in 1997 if the agency had become overly reliant on consultants, he replied, "State agencies don't really listen to consultants."

Questions and Instructions:

1. What political and management issues are you able to identify in the case? Please list them.

2. Is there a difference between patronage and cronyism? If yes, please make the distinction. What forms does patronage take in government at its various levels today? Please elaborate.

3. Is patronage, cronyism, and favoritism only found in government operations or is it also present in other areas of the economy — the private and nonprofit sectors? Please explain.

4. If you were in Debra Foster's position, would you have made the political concessions that are presented in the case?

5. Would you have defended the quality of the work provided by Kathy Kramer? If so, why? If not, why not?

Case 2: Patronage or Cronyism at DHS

Name:

Case Log and Administrative Journal Entry

This case analysis and learning assessment is printed on perforated pages and may be removed from the book for evaluation purposes.

Case Analysis:
Major case concepts and theories identified:

What is the relevance of the concepts, theories, ideas and techniques presented in the case to that of public management?

Facts — what do we know *for sure* about the case? Please list.

Who is involved in the case (people, departments, agencies, units, etc.)? Were the problems of an "intra/interagency" nature? Be specific.

Are there any rules, laws, regulations or standard operating procedures identified in the case study that might limit decision-making? If so, what are they?

Are there any clues presented in the case as to the major actor's interests, needs, motivations and personalities? If so, please list them.

Case 2: Patronage or Cronyism at DHS

Learning Assessment:
What do the administrative theories presented in this case mean to you as an administrator?

How can this learning be put to use outside the classroom? Are there any problems you envision during the implementation phase?

Several possible courses of action were identified during the class discussion. Which action was considered to be most practical by the group? Which was deemed most feasible? Based on your personal experience, did the group reach a conclusion that was desirable, feasible, and practical? Please explain why or why not.

Did the group reach a decision that would solve the problem on a short-term or long-term basis? Please explain.

What could you have done to receive more learning value from this case?

3

Jimmy's 53 Questions: Team Interviewing

by
C. Kenneth Meyer and Lance Noe

Jason Klineworth was anxious about being placed on the Team Selection Committee for the Northup Community Center. He understood that hiring was about the most important activity performed by the Human Resources (HR) Department. In his 15-year tenure as a line manager, he frequently heard his peers reiterate, as if it were a mantra, these words, "If you select the right person, for the right job, at the right time — congratulations on a job well done! If you do not make the right personnel choice, there isn't a management system known that will fix your problem!"

Klineworth was conscientious about his newly assigned duty and wished to become a full participant in the process. He looked at this task as one that would build added competency as well as contribute to his overall body of accumulated experience. In preparation for serving on the selection committee, he prepared a detailed list of the information he sought: job description; essential tasks to be performed; major qualifications; copy of the application form; advertising venues used to build the applicant pool; guidelines to be followed during the interview process; recommended criteria for applicant screening and selection; and any data that the HR Department had from their position-audit and exit-interview that might help inform his decision.

Most of the information that Klineworth requested was quickly identified and sent to his office, as some of the information had already been asked for by other members of the selection team. As the application deadline approached, he was taken by surprise to receive an email from James Lightfoot, director of the Human Resources Department, which solicited questions that should be asked of the interviewees. Although he had some ideas of his own, he went on-line and searched for suggested tips. The literature identified was voluminous, and from it he deduced the following suggested questions, which he itemized and then forwarded to Director Lightfoot:

1. Please describe your work experience to date.
2. What would you say are your strongest personal strengths?
3. Do you have any personal weaknesses? If so, what are they?
4. How do you plan to strengthen your positive attributes and overcome your deficiencies?
5. How would you classify the quality of your past performance? Below average, average, above average, or excellent?
6. What do you know about Northup Community Center ~~and where did you get your information~~?

Good b/c shows interest in center

Case 3: Jimmy's 53 Questions: Team Interviewing

7. If selected for this position, what position do you expect to hold at Northup Community Center five years from now?
8. What skills or attributes do you believe are needed to successfully meet the requirements of this position? How would your management strengths contribute to the mission of Northup Community Center? Please explain.
9. Do you bring any added personal traits or experience that other applicants might not possess?
10. In what ways have you maintained your professional currency after graduation from college?
11. In looking at the job description and listed duties, which one would you pursue most ardently and why?
12. In your last job, what would your immediate supervisor say was your strongest attribute?
13. What would your co-workers suggest as constituting your two most serious weaknesses?
14. Over the past five years, what were your most important management achievements? *Goes to expertise*
15. What are the characteristics that you value in a successful manager? *Management Style*
16. What is your favorite book of all time? *Priorities*
17. Are you looking for a job or a career with Northup Community Center?
18. In the past year, what movie did you see that you really enjoyed? *Visionary*
19. When clients think of the center, what image would you like them to hold? *Mission*
20. What concerns, if any, should a manager have about the role of safety in the workplace?
21. Have you ever applied for Worker's Compensation? If so, for what reason and for how long?
22. Do you have a religious belief that would prevent you from working on certain days or on weekends?
23. Is there a difference between leadership and management? If so, how do they differ?
24. Have you ever been arrested for a crime? What crime?
25. How long do you plan on staying with Northup?
26. Do undocumented immigrants have the "right" to work in the U.S. even if it violates U.S. law?
27. List three characteristics of your last supervisor that you found distasteful.
28. Do you believe that women should be in positions that supervise men?
29. Why do you want to work for Northup?
30. How much compensation in either wages or salary did you receive last year? What is your expectation for remuneration for this position?
31. List three benefits that would be most important to you if you were hired at Northup.
32. On the following personal attitudes, indicate on a scale of 1-10 your strength: (1 is weak, 5 is neither weak nor strong, and 10 is strong).

Character

Integrity

Courage

Masculinity

Need for Achievement

Case 3: Jimmy's 53 Questions: Team Interviewing

Need for Dominance

Vision

Trustfulness

Humor

33. Please identify two nationally recognized leaders that you presently admire. What attributes do they have that you deem laudatory? —
34. Do you take any drugs or illegal substances? If so, what are they? — AD
35. Do you have any disabilities that the selection committee needs to know about before you are hired? Explain. — ADA
36. Can you provide the committee with at least five personal references, with one from a pastor or member of the clergy? — Title VII Religion
37. Do you plan to have children? — Title VII
38. Do you favor a short or long commute to work?
39. What criteria do you use in sizing up the organization for which you want to work?
40. What achievement or accomplishment in the past best prepares you for this position?
41. What job related factors do you rank high on your list of requirements?
42. What qualities in your opinion, does a successful manager need to have?
43. How would your best friend describe you as a person?
44. Overall, what specific factors serve as a basis for your personal motivation?
45. Identify a troublesome situation you had with a problem employee. How did you resolve the personal dilemma? In retrospect, how would you solve the problem today?
46. Do you have any children? If so, what are the ages? — Illegal   Narrative ?'s
47. Do you have any children or dependents that have a disability?   Did you learn from experience
48. What is your credit score? —
49. On average, how often do you take a day or so off for sickness? — ADA
50. Do you own your own car? —
51. Have you ever belonged to a labor union? If so, which one? — Not Illegal. Doesn't Pertain.
52. Where were you born? — National
53. In what year did you receive your high school diploma? — Age Descrimination

Klineworth realized his list had become an ambitious one, but these were the questions he wanted to have posed to the job applicants. He understood that many of these were "standard-fare" but others were reflections of trouble spots he had encountered with the outgoing incumbent. Now, he would sit back and wait for the director of HR to respond about the appropriateness of his 53 questions.

The first document he received from Lightfoot provided the following position description as presented in **Exhibit 1**. As such, it included the essential elements and scope of the position, the working conditions, and the physical effort required for satisfactory performance.

Case 3: Jimmy's 53 Questions: Team Interviewing

He reviewed the list of questions he had formulated and sent to the director and wondered if all of them were really relevant — especially given the way the HR department had defined the position.

Questions and Instructions:

1. Do you think that the qualifications listed in the position description are "objectively" related to the successful performance of the task, duties, and responsibilities connected to the position? If so, why? If not, why not?

   Degree is non-specific
   No Supervisor requirement. 5yr

2. If you were James Lightfoot, which of the questions suggested by Jason Klineworth would you strike from the list? Why?

3. Out of the 53 questions raised, identify the five most relevant ones that pertain to the position description? Why do they meet your standard of appropriateness?

   1, 6, 14, ~~17~~, 19, ~~40~~, 45. Work experience is a green light

4. Of the many questions suggested, which ones are the most blatantly unlawful inquiries given the position described? List and indicate why they are illegal ones.

5. List any other questions you would ask and explain why.

Case 3: Jimmy's 53 Questions: Team Interviewing

Exhibit 1. Position Description

Name:

Department: **Title:**   DIRECTOR-CAREER SERVICES

Reports To: **SPVR Title:**   BOARD OF DIRECTORS

Northrup Community Center

JOB DESCRIPTION

Essential Job Functions

Conduct individual/group sessions with clients and stakeholders regarding career-related issues.	25%
Manage positions and personnel to make best use of employees; select employees and develop their capabilities; counsel employees effectively; administer discipline; handle human resource matters in accordance with Northrup's policy and procedures.	20%
Develop and facilitate workshops/programs on career-related topics.	10%
Develop departmental budget, monitor such budget and supervise department's staff.	10%
Liaison among departments, functions, or groups within the center. Communicate information to appropriate personnel.	10%
Measure outcomes for client placement and report the information to Board of Directors.	5%
Assist in client testing programs that assist in assessing goals and progress in personality and career development. Maintain test records. Interpret test results to clients and parents.	5%
Meet with staff to work on assessments of needs and the development of an action plan to meet requirements which surface.	5%
Direct the development of the center's strategic plan consistent with the established overall strategic plan and ensure their proper execution.	5%
Performs other duties as assigned.	5%

Comments:

FOR HR USE

Exempt   X   Non-Exempt

Approval Date   Position Control #

The above assignments are intended to describe the general nature and level of work being performed by people assigned to this job. They are not intended to be an exhaustive list of all responsibilities, duties and skills required.

Essential Elements

Education: Baccalaureate Degree - Knowledge of specialized principles or techniques normally obtained through a four-year college/university academic program or an equivalent in-depth specialized training program directly related to the type of work being performed.

Experience: Considerable: 3-7 years.

Other Essential Training and Skills:

Computer Experience (Macintosh and/or PC): Spreadsheet/Database Applications (i.e. Microsoft Excel, Access, FileMaker), Word Processing Applications (i.e. Microsoft Word, WordPerfect), Publishing Applications (i.e. PageMaker), Presentation Software (i.e. PowerPoint), Web Development Applications (i.e. Visual Page, FrontPage), Other **Scope of Management:** Number of Direct Reports - 3.

Scope

Complexity:	Work is basically non-standardized and widely varied, involving many complex and significant variables. Analytic ability and inductive thinking are required to devise new methods to situations where previously accepted methods have proven inadequate.
Consequence of Error:	Errors are usually discovered in succeeding operations where most of the work is verified or checked and is normally confined to a single department or phase of organization activities.
Decision Making:	Greater latitude and discretion is warranted in making decisions, which affect principal areas of the organization as well as customers/constituents. Reviews and approves decisions and/or recommendations that could affect the entire organization.
Impact:	Considerable Impact - Causing risks or improvements to relationships, significant efficiencies or delays in operations, and/or significant financial gains or expenses.

Case 3: Jimmy's 53 Questions: Team Interviewing

WORKING CONDITIONS & PHYSICAL EFFORT

	Seldom Or Never	Monthly	Weekly	Daily	Hourly
1. Lift objects weighing up to 20 pounds.	X				
2. Lift objects weighing 21 to 50 pounds.	X				
3. Lift objects weighing 51 to 100 pounds.	X				
4. Lift objects weighing more than 100 pounds.	X				
5. Carry objects weighing up to 20 pounds.	X				
6. Carry objects weighing 21 to 50 pounds.	X				
7. Carry objects weighing 51 to 100 pounds.	X				
8. Carry objects weighing 100 pounds or more.	X				
9. Standing up to two hours at a time.			X		
10. Standing for more than two hours at a time.		X			
11. Twisting or turning head or back.		X			
12. Stooping, bending, kneeling, or crawling.	X				
13. Ability to reach and grasp objects.		X			
14. Manual dexterity or fine motor skills.		X			
15. Color vision - the ability to identify and distinguish colors.	X				
16. Ability to communicate orally.					X
17. Ability to hear.					X
18. Pushing or pulling carts or other such objects.	X				
19. Proofreading and checking documents for accuracy.		X			
20. Using a keyboard to enter and transform words or data.				X	
21. Using a video display terminal.				X	
22. Working in a normal office environment with few physical discomforts.					X
23. Working in an area that is somewhat uncomfortable due to drafts, noise, temperature variation or the like.	X				
24. Working in an area that is very uncomfortable due to extreme temperature, noise levels, or other conditions.	X				
25. Working with equipment or performing procedures where carelessness would probably result in minor cuts, bruises or muscle pulls.	X				
26. Operating automobile or van.	X				
27. Operating heavy equipment.	X				
28. Extreme temperatures, such as cold or heat.	X				
29. Hazards such as mechanical, electrical, burns/explosives, unprotected heights, or moving objects	X				

Case 3: Jimmy's 53 Questions: Team Interviewing

Case 3: Jimmy's 53 Questions: Team Interviewing

Name:

Case Log and Administrative Journal Entry

This case analysis and learning assessment is printed on perforated pages and may be removed from the book for evaluation purposes.

Case Analysis:
Major case concepts and theories identified:

What is the relevance of the concepts, theories, ideas and techniques presented in the case to that of public management?

Facts — what do we know *for sure* about the case? Please list.

Who is involved in the case (people, departments, agencies, units, etc.)? Were the problems of an "intra/interagency" nature? Be specific.

Are there any rules, laws, regulations or standard operating procedures identified in the case study that might limit decision-making? If so, what are they?

Are there any clues presented in the case as to the major actor's interests, needs, motivations and personalities? If so, please list them.

Case 3: Jimmy's 53 Questions: Team Interviewing

Learning Assessment:
What do the administrative theories presented in this case mean to you as an administrator?

How can this learning be put to use outside the classroom? Are there any problems you envision during the implementation phase?

Several possible courses of action were identified during the class discussion. Which action was considered to be most practical by the group? Which was deemed most feasible? Based on your personal experience, did the group reach a conclusion that was desirable, feasible, and practical? Please explain why or why not.

Did the group reach a decision that would solve the problem on a short-term or long-term basis? Please explain.

What could you have done to receive more learning value from this case?

4

What Questions are Lawful or Unlawful?

by
C. Kenneth Meyer, Susan Brady and Stephan Clapham

Larry Shapiro had a penchant for detail and precision. Around the state department of human resources he was known as being pedantic and somewhat erudite. Of course, no one ever told him as much to his face. Rather these remarks were the fodder of lunch room "chit-chat" and "spontaneous staff meetings" that coalesced around the hallway water cooler. Shapiro, however, would not have been personally offended by being labeled erudite and his flair for the use of the English language, spiced with Latin phrases and romantic French words was well known.

Larry Shapiro had worked diligently on building a "powerful vocabulary" and he felt it symbolized the mark of a truly educated person. Of course, he also was quick to add, that pedantry can impede effective communication, especially when polysyllabic words are used inadvisably or inappropriately. For instance, as it was affectionately retold by a friend, a colleague told him he was being too meticulous! Not to be offended when his colleagues would raise or roll their eyes in disbelief that he had reached for and found a word or phrase that they may never have heard of before — especially a word that was rightfully placed into a complex, compound sentence — he would politely respond, "Do you mean to say that was I was being assiduously meticulous?" He knew that his personal, idiosyncratic demeanor projected an ambiance of sophistication, but deep into the marrow of his bones his colleagues trusted him and valued him as a capable leader and team player.

Shapiro had a different agenda today. He had been given the task of preparing the members of his team for the peer interviews they would be conducting later on in the afternoon. The human resource department had scheduled three interviews to be conducted with prospective employees for the position of Information Systems Analyst, State Office of Education. As such, Shapiro had fully prepared himself for the task that he had been assigned, and went online and researched the kind of questions that would be within the permissible legal parameters surrounding the interviews. He knew he had been given a daunting task. In the past, he had listened to his co-workers inquire about the personal and familial attributes of the potential incumbents. He wanted to make certain this scenario was not replicated.

In the midst of researching the various nuances and legalisms that surrounded or accompanied the interview process, he thought that this might be best accomplished if he prepared a illustrative Application Form and ask the team to determine, utilizing the job description for the Information Systems Analyst position, as a point of reference (see **Exhibit 1**), which were appropriate and inappropriate, lawful and unlawful questions that might be fielded.

Case 4: What Questions are Lawful or Unlawful?

Upon meeting with his group, he passed out the job description, explained why he had been asked to facilitate a pre-interview training program, and then passed out the application form (See **Exhibit 2**). He asked his co-workers to seriously reflect on the type of questions that would be within bounds and identify a minimum of five questions that they thought would be inappropriate and another five questions that they considered off-limits. He also asked them to think about the type of additional questions that might be asked that would improve the Application Form. Due to time constraints and the fact that he wanted to have time for questions and discussion, he limited the individual assessment to ten minutes.

When the ten minutes were up, he went to the large "Post-It" papers that he had attached to the walls of the training room, and asked for their feedback. He had previously labeled the sheets with the following categories: Essential Attributes of the System Analyst Position; System Analyst Desired Qualification; Most Relevant Questions; Least Relevant Questions; Unlawful Inquires; and, Additional Appropriate Questions.

Questions and Instructions:

Exercise: Please use an assessment technique similar to the one devised by Larry Shapiro for his team members, or one that you feel would "more" appropriately enable you to satisfy the training objective. Provide the class with a similar set of instructions, not unlike those that Larry provided. Limit the assessment to ten minutes and then have your class members report what they have discerned. In preparation for this exercise, it is important that you have personally researched the many questions found in **Exhibit 2** (The Application Form) and be prepared to indicate their lawfulness. In the final analysis, identify those questions that were most relevant to the position; those that were least important; those that were unlawful; and those that "should have" been asked.

Solution Verification: Upon the completion of the assessment exercise as detailed above, ask your colleagues to refer to **Appendix C**, **Summary Guide to Application Pre-Employment Questions** and **Appendix D, Avoiding Discrimination During the Hiring Process**.

In these appendices, a compilation of the numerous laws of the United States as interpreted by the U.S. Equal Employment Opportunity Commission (EEOC), and the State of Iowa Constitution and statutory laws as viewed by the Iowa Civil Rights Commission (ICRC), are presented. In both instances, a brief description of the enabling legislation that prohibits discrimination is presented, whether it is Title VII of the Civil Rights Act of 1964 (gender, race, color, religion, or national origin), the Age Discrimination in Employment Act of 1967 (ADEA), Americans with Disabilities Act of 1990 (ADA), and so on, or the Iowa Civil Rights Act (ICRA) that prohibits discrimination on the basis of age, race, creed (religion), national origin, disability, or sexual orientation and gender identity. As such, clarity is given to those questions that often appear on application forms and are raised during the interview process. It should be noted that unlawful inquiries can largely be avoided if questions deal with the applicant's education, experience level, knowledge, skills, and abilities that relate to the actual job. Generally, if the employer cannot objectively demonstrate that the question is related to successful job performance, it should be avoided!

Case 4: What Questions are Lawful or Unlawful?

The appendices are informative on inquiries related to age, arrests and convictions, reference and background checks, polygraph examinations, childbirth and pregnancy, citizenship and immigration, disability and health, and a myriad of other topics. *Note:* These documents only pertain to the state of Iowa and you may, if you think it is more appropriate, use the specific laws of your own state in completing this exercise.

Verification:

[Handwritten notes: Marital Status (only if can meet Req of Job) — Title VII]

1. What questions did your colleagues identify as problematic as shown in Appendix C and D?

   [Handwritten: Family Info — Title VII; Race — Title VII; Workers Comp?; US Citizen — Title VII; Age; Photo; Gender — Title VII]

2. Which questions were correctly identified by the group as discriminatory? Please make a list.

   [Handwritten: Age Discrimination Act of 1967; Title VII]

Exhibit 1. Job Description: Information Systems Analyst: State Office of Education

---

CLASSIFICATION TITLE: Information Systems Analyst

DEFINITION
Under general direction acts as a lead to develop, design, document, maintain, evaluate, support and provide problem resolution for computer systems applications; performs a variety of technical and analytical services for business, finance, payroll and personnel departments; analyzes, evaluates and trains users on mainframe computer system; performs other related duties as assigned.

DIRECTLY RESPONSIBLE TO
Appropriate Administrator

SUPERVISION OVER
None; however, may lead, train, and provide assistance to other staff.

DUTIES AND RESPONSIBILITIES (Any one position may not include all of the listed duties, nor do all of the listed examples include all tasks which may be found in positions within this classification.)

Information Systems Management
Develops and produces physical design of databases based upon logical data models by employing program and business requirements and analysis; works closely with system users to ensure information system strategies are aligned with business, finance, payroll, and personnel needs; researches and develops database administration; coordinates and aligns information systems with user objectives;

develops and reviews standards and procedures regarding business, finance, payroll, and personnel systems; troubleshoots and resolves issues with software functionality; performs technical adjustments and installs technical updates to system; maintains, analyzes, evaluates and updates database integrity and security settings; maintains detailed accounting of users and security access to system software; audits, modifies, and amends data in systems; monitors and reports on system usage.

Training and Technical Assistance
Provides technical direction to users; formulates, assists and supports users with application training and technical support; sets up and maintains users on mainframe computer system including creating and maintaining all facets of software functions for users; creates, assembles, and distributes procedure/training manuals and materials to users; sets up processes and procedures, and assists users in implementing new system modules; reviews, evaluates and implements recommendations for improved methods or procedures; plans and implements departmental processes and projects.

Office Operations/Data Reporting
Monitors and reports to management any deviation from procedures or policy; oversees and manages multiple concurrent projects; supports internal operations, budget management, and project planning; supports existing products and services by acting as an agent for problem and operational issue resolution; establishes and maintains a variety of file systems; reviews user requests and requirements; organizes and analyzes material for efficient reporting and retrieval; assists users to retrieve data from system; develops procedures, forms, and other organizational tools to implement and manage office automation used in the department; plans and prepares correspondence related to all facets of the position.

MINIMUM QUALIFICATIONS
Education, Training and Experience
Any combination of education, training and experience equivalent to possession of a Bachelor's degree that demonstrates the ability to perform the duties and responsibilities as described. Experience in school district, county and/or state office business, finance, and payroll and personnel information systems; experience using various computer software and networks.

Knowledge of:
Utilization and purposes of management information systems; personal computer hardware and software; principles of office automation systems, basic principles of computer system analysis, principles of organization; common office procedures and practices; advanced knowledge of school district/county or state Office of Education business applications and office procedures and practices.

Skill and Ability to:
Communicate effectively in both oral and written forms; explain technical concepts in non-technical terms; research and problem solve inquiries; demonstrate initiative and work independently with a minimum of supervision; work under time constraints to meet deadlines; set priorities, and make decisions on a variety of complex matters; organize, schedule, and coordinate a variety of activities and projects; establish and maintain cooperative working relationships with those contacted during the course of work; research and evaluate office computer applications and information systems software; learn new

Case 4: What Questions are Lawful or Unlawful?

software and hardware packages and adapt to changes in technology; retrieve data to prepare documents, and produce a variety of reports from the database.

Other Characteristics
Possession of a valid state driver's license, and willingness to travel using own transportation with mileage reimbursed.

Revised and approved by the Personnel Commission on 1/13/2009.
Department of Education
An Equal Opportunity Employer/Program
Employment Application: Information Systems Analyst

Exhibit 2: Application Form

Applicant Personal Information				
Last Name	First		M.I.	Date
Street Address		Apartment/Unit #		
City	State		ZIP	
Phone	Email Address			
Date Available	Social Security No.		Desired Salary	
Position Applied for				
Time available to: Day ☐ Evening ☐ Night ☐	Combination of shifts ☐	Application is for: Full-time ☐	Part-time ☐	Labor – no benefits
Gender Male ☐ Female ☐	Race (optional):		Age:	
Are you a United States citizen? YES ☐ NO ☐	If no, are you authorized to work in the		YES ☐ NO ☐	
Have you ever worked for this state? YES ☐		NO ☐	If so, when?	
Have you ever been convicted of a felony? YES ☐		NO ☐	If yes, explain	
Marital Status: Married ☐ Single ☐ Divorced ☐ Separated ☐			Domestic Partner ☐	Widowed ☐

Case 4: What Questions are Lawful or Unlawful?

If single, do you plan to have a family in the future?	YES ☐	NO ☐

If you have children, what child care arrangement will you make? Please be specific.
If you are married, where is your spouse employed?
What names if any have you worked under (AKA;

Are you legally able to work in the United States?	YES ☐	NO ☐

Are you available for work?	Full-Time ☐	Part-Time ☐	Shift Work ☐	Seasonal Work ☐

May we contact your former employers to verify this information?	YES ☐	NO ☐
May we contact your present employers?	YES ☐	NO ☐

Please complete this personal data section by including a 1½" by 2" recent photograph.

Note: Federal and state law prohibit discrimination in hiring due to race, color, creed, age, gender, national origin, religion, disability or veteran's status

Please provide any additional information about your abilities or interests that makes you a good candidate for this position:

_____

_____

_____

Education and training

What is the highest grade you completed?	1 ☐	2 ☐	3 ☐	4 ☐	5 ☐	6 ☐	7 ☐	8 ☐	9 ☐	10 ☐	11 ☐	12 ☐	GED ☐

Have you earned any certificate or academic degrees?	No ☐	Yes ☐	If yes, please provide the information solicited below.

College			Address		
From	To	Did you graduate? YES ☐ NO ☐			Degree
College			Address		
From	To	Did you graduate? YES ☐ NO ☐			Degree
College/Other			Address		
From	To	Did you graduate? YES ☐ NO ☐			Degree

Case 4: What Questions are Lawful or Unlawful?

Have you earned any professional licenses or certificates?		No ☐	Yes ☐	If yes, please provide the information solicited below.
Profession:	Issued by:		License or certificate name:	
If multiple licenses or certificates, provide added information on appendix page.				
Have you ever had your professional license or certificate revoked, suspended, or limited in any way?			No ☐	Yes ☐
If yes, give the reason for the disciplinary action:				

Previous Employment

Begin with your most recent employer or present employer; then account for all the time during the last ten (10) years. Be sure to include, if applicable, any period of unemployment and all unpaid work done. Additional pages may be appended to this application as needed. Reason for leaving may include voluntarily quit, termination, health or disability reasons, among many others.

Company			Phone ( )	
Address			Supervisor	
Job Title		Starting Salary $	Ending Salary	$
Responsibilities				
From	To	Reason for Leaving		
May we contact your previous supervisor for a reference?		YES ☐	NO ☐	
Company			Phone ( )	
Address			Supervisor	
Job Title		Starting Salary $	Ending Salary	$
Responsibilities				
From	To	Reason for Leaving		
May we contact your previous supervisor for a reference?		YES ☐	NO ☐	
Company			Phone ( )	
Address			Supervisor	
Job Title		Starting Salary $	Ending Salary	$
Responsibilities				
From	To	Reason for Leaving		
May we contact your previous supervisor for a reference?		YES ☐	NO ☐	
Did you ever collect unemployment insurance while working at any of these organizations?			YES ☐	NO ☐
Did you ever utilize worker's compensation benefits for injury(ies) sustained while working for any of these employers?			YES ☐	NO ☐
If yes, how much and over what time were you paid?				
Was this the first time you collected unemployment or worker's compensation?			YES ☐	NO ☐

Case 4: What Questions are Lawful or Unlawful?

What is the lowest salary you would be willing to accept?	
Military Service	
Branch	From To
Rank at Discharge	Type of Discharge
If other than honorable, explain	

Specialized Skills, Training, Abilities and Knowledge
List the special areas in which you have highly developed skills, abilities, training, and knowledge. This may include knowledge of languages, computers, specialized equipment and laboratory techniques, etc. and technical machinery.

Organization membership or affiliate
Name: **Membership Date:**

Address:

Name: **Membership Date:**
Address:

Family Information
Names of children:
Ages:
Maiden Name if applicable:

Employment Agreement and Understanding Disclaimer and Signature
The information provided here for employment purposes is true and any misrepresentation or omission of facts may be grounds for denial or termination of employment (if hired) at the time it is discovered. This is an at-will employer and you or the employer may terminate the employment at any time for good or bad reason and with or without cause. Upon completion of this application, submission to drug and alcohol screening is required. I authorize the organization to check my work references, personal references and obtain any and all information requested and waive my rights and release these individuals from liability. The same standard applies to checking my background for any and all arrests and convictions.

Signature _____   Date _____

Case 4: What Questions are Lawful or Unlawful
Name:

Case Log and Administrative Journal Entry

This case analysis and learning assessment is printed on perforated pages and may be removed from the book for evaluation purposes.

Case Analysis:
Major case concepts and theories identified:

What is the relevance of the concepts, theories, ideas and techniques presented in the case to that of public management?

Facts — what do we know *for sure* about the case? Please list.

Who is involved in the case (people, departments, agencies, units, etc.)? Were the problems of an "intra/interagency" nature? Be specific.

Are there any rules, laws, regulations or standard operating procedures identified in the case study that might limit decision-making? If so, what are they?

Are there any clues presented in the case as to the major actor's interests, needs, motivations and personalities? If so, please list them.

Case 4: What Questions are Lawful or Unlawful?

Learning Assessment:
What do the administrative theories presented in this case mean to you as an administrator?

How can this learning be put to use outside the classroom? Are there any problems you envision during the implementation phase?

Several possible courses of action were identified during the class discussion. Which action was considered to be most practical by the group? Which was deemed most feasible? Based on your personal experience, did the group reach a conclusion that was desirable, feasible, and practical? Please explain why or why not.

Did the group reach a decision that would solve the problem on a short-term or long-term basis? Please explain.

What could you have done to receive more learning value from this case?

5

Making Meetings Work

by
Jack Fellers and C. Kenneth Meyer

Jim Jorgeson angrily walked down the hall, into his office, and slammed his door shut. That's it! He thought. I have had it with these lousy weekly department meetings! We get nothing down, waste a lot of time, and end up mad at each other. I would love to stop going to these meetings, he thought, but I can't stop going. I am the department manager!

Jim had a richly experienced childhood compared with others in his department. His youthful experiences in the national parks (Yosemite, Grand Canyon, Zion, Big Bend, and Glacier), and in the sand dunes of the high deserts in southern Idaho were often mentioned when he talked about his travels and adventures. His parents made sure that he was well grounded in travel and geography and they gave "short-shrift" to any feelings or talk which degraded or diminished the humanity of others. Jim's parents made sure he attended his studies while in school with diligence and their stern attitude gave way to "uncommonly" good praise when Jim participated in drama, the choir, orchestra, and debate. He, too, felt good when he was able to please his parents and he "…knew they had his best interests at heart."

He was close to his mother, and she often admonished him with statements such as, "James, you'll appreciate what your father and I are doing for you someday"; or, "If you work and study hard, the barriers that stand in the way of success will vanish!" And, "Be careful what you wish for — your wishes may be granted." Playfully, she would tease him when he wanted something beyond the financial means of the family and in a smiling manner paraphrase the lyrics of a popular country song that "God's greatest gifts are unanswered prayers."

Jim understood that parents, generally, use a variety of statements to motivate and direct their offspring and sometimes the admonitions they utter were those that were passed down from their parents as the matured into adulthood. "Oh yes," he mused, "…it is interesting the way we learn from tradition and authority." Yet he learned early on in life that he had to chart the course in life he would navigate and was keenly aware that not all of his decisions would be congruent with the deeply held Christian values which his parents espoused and cherished, and, for the most art, practiced. In brief, his training and education led to a listing of personal and organizational behaviors he detested and would not countenance as a manager, such as domestic spousal and child abuse, racism, child or adult pornography, or discrimination on any basis including appearance and sexual orientation. He was also sensitive of the twin problems of ageism and nativism.

Case 5: Making Meetings Work

In conversation with his closest friends, he would proclaim that public servants behavior off-duty had to be beyond reproach in terms of respect, dignity and honor and never bring discredit to the individual, agency or department. He said, "I learned the meaning of honor as a young man at my father's knee and I intend to instill this value, especially in my son." Organizational loyalty was one of the major pillars of strength in his moral house and whistleblowers were, in his view, little more than disloyal snitches. He said, "You can call me old fashioned, but if we have dirty laundry that needs cleaning, such as poor performance, abuse of authority, doubtful legal behavior, or wasteful activities, we'll clean it in private and not hang it out to air on the public clothes line." Although he had a penchant for fairness as a manager, he was not above using his power as a manager indirectly and subtly, even if that meant getting even with those he considered disloyal or untrustworthy. In his view, not everyone should be able to become a public servant, for it was a truly noble profession and high calling.

As Jim walked out of the Center for Justice building into the bright sunlight he thought about his problems with meetings. He wondered why meetings often became contentious, and why his colleagues talked in gossiping terms about other departments and people not in attendance. Why did his colleagues not put the interest of the department before their own personal, selfish concerns? He asked himself about the fading concept of workplace trust and organizational loyalty. He reflected on his upbringing and wondered where his colleagues got their belief and value systems from, for they were quite different from his own.

It was a rare day when Jim didn't have several meetings on his agenda. While he clearly understood the need for and value of meetings, he was often fed up with the participative process. He knew he was not alone in his disdain for meetings and some of his staff expressed similar frustrations with the time spent, or wasted as they put it, in meetings.

Anyway, he thought, while he was headed to another meeting, at least this one should be fun! He was having lunch with an old college friend who happened to be in town to lead a workshop. He didn't really know what Bill Mortenson did for living, he just knew it would be fun to get away from the office and catch up with an old friend he hadn't seen in several years.

Lunch turned out to be a fun diversion. Jim and Bill spent the first half of the meal catching up on wives, kids and friends, as well as reliving past college glories. When they moved on to current events and careers, Bill could clearly see that Jim was troubled. The frustration with the morning meeting was still foremost on his mind. Bill asked him to describe the meeting. Jim hesitated at first, but Bill reminded him that sometimes it helps "…to just talk things through to help think about and learn from them." As it turned out, the workshop Bill was in town to facilitate was entitled: "How to Effectively Manage Meetings!"

Jim talked about some of the problems he had encountered, not only with this morning's meeting, but with others as well. Some of the things that constantly eroded the effectiveness of the meetings included getting off track, people dominating the discussion while others said little or nothing; people posturing, while others were quick to judge the ideas of others, which in turn cut-off the generation of new ideas and shut off participation. Also, it seemed that the same things were repeatedly placed on the agenda with little or no resolution, and that there was little follow-through on what had been decided.

Case 5: Making Meetings Work

Bill listened intently, focused on what Jim had to say, and then he asked, "Jim, how many people do you have at these weekly department meetings?" "Probably between 15 and 20, depending on work-related travel and vacations," Jim answered. Bill went on to explain that having such a large group in a meeting can lead to a host of problems. He suggested that some of the people who do not say much are quiet because they don't have anything to contribute to the discussion, or in other cases are too shy to speak up in front of a group that is so large. "A good metric to use for meetings is that unless a person can be actively engaged in at least two-thirds of the items on the agenda, they shouldn't be at the meeting. Sometimes you need more than one meeting, depending on your agenda and outcomes," Bill opined.

"How many agenda items do you have at a typical meeting?" Bill asked. It turned out agendas and outcomes were another problem. Jim had recently inherited the weekly department meetings from his previous boss. Jane Worthy was one of those rare individuals who could walk into a meeting with no agenda and masterfully lead the group through a series of issues until they were all resolved. Jim did not have those skills and talents and, to make matters worse, never much thought went into meeting preparation.

Bill walked Jim through some meeting planning steps, including determining the goal(s) for the meeting. "Goals drive agenda; agenda determines who needs to be invited. If it turns out that only some of the people are needed for each agenda item, then you probably need multiple smaller meetings, not one big meeting," Bill stated. Jim realized that this was an area in which he needed to improve. While he had some ideas in his mind, and occasionally emailed out some things "to think about" as he put it for the next meeting, he really did not prepare an agenda or have specific desired outcomes for each meeting.

"Having an agenda, sent out in advance, will help in a number of ways," Bill added. He went on to explain that an agenda needs to be sent out at least 24-48 hours in advance, if not even earlier, if possible. This will allow people time to prepare for the meeting. "Better prepared people tend to participate more. Some people are quiet because they haven't been given the opportunity to prepare; they don't want to speak up at a meeting because they haven't had time to either think through an issue or to do some pre-meeting research."

There are two other major advantages to having set outcomes and a published agenda, Bill noted and then outlined them in detail. One of the major time wasters in meetings is getting off track. Bill talked about the need for people in a group to get to know one another, to catch up with what may be going on, or to even blow off some steam during a meeting from time to time. However, he went on to state, "When up to 50 percent of the time spent in organizational meetings is wasted each year, there is a time to get off task and a time to get back on track."

Bill then taught Jim the use of Relevancy Challenges, a simple communications technique designed to help groups stay on task. "If someone says something that could potentially take the group off task, it is the leader's responsibility to keep the group moving forward. Let's say I start talking about the game from over the weekend. Interestingly enough, but not particularly germane to what the group needs to do. A weak leader may just watch in frustration as the group takes off on the game. What the leader needs to do is to acknowledge the comment, ask how it relates to the outcome at hand, then if the person can tie it to the outcome, great, then continue to lead the discussion. If they can't, thank them, make a note of the topic, indicating that you will come back to the topic later if there is time, and move back to the outcome at hand. But, to use this technique requires that you have specific outcomes that must be addressed. Without having the outcome in mind, it is difficult to determine what is relevant to the discussion and what is not."

Jim thought about that for a moment and commented, "You know, I tried that kind of thing once, and it blew up in my face. I challenged Joseph about a comment he made and he thought I was picking on him. He wouldn't look at me the rest of the meeting and it took an apology from me and a week or two for him to cool off. But I can see now, looking back, that we didn't have a clearly defined outcome we were discussing at that point."

"That's the key," Bill responded. "Without a clear outcome it is hard to determine relevance, so your challenge came across as a *personal* one, perceived to be directed at the person, not as a *process*-oriented one. Joseph probably felt picked on, even if you did not have that in mind."

Bill talked about other advantages of having set outcomes. He explained that if a specific outcome has been put forth, then evidence can be established to determine if that outcome is met at a later date. If there is no outcome, no evidence, how do we know whether or not we accomplished what we set out to do? Wow, Jim thought, "I never really thought about it that way! That would sure make the year-end appraisals of both department and individual performance a lot easier to carry out."

Jim wanted some suggestions for getting some of those who are quiet more involved and keeping others from dominating the discussion. Bill reminded him that having fewer people attending a meeting, who can be better prepared, will help with that issue. However, this is likely to still be a problem due to the patterns that have already been established within this group. Bill provided a couple of suggestions. First, he told Jim he could ask those who are quiet for their opinion. Sometimes people have great ideas; they just aren't comfortable bringing them up. By asking them to share you are giving them permission to put forth their ideas. Jim thought about that for a minute and Steve came to mind. Steve tends to be very quiet, rarely says much in meetings, but often would come up afterwards with just the right suggestion. When Jim asks Steve why he didn't say it during the meeting, he would look down, and stammer something about "I just came up with it now." Bill just smiled and then gave Jim another suggestion saying, "Another approach is simply to go around the table and ask each person to state his or her opinion. That gives each one person an opportunity to speak, which can let the shy folks speak and gives the talkative ones a turn to share, but then they have to wait until everyone else has spoken before they can speak again."

Jim asked, "Around the table? Is that a figure of speech? I mean, we tend to use a long narrow table?" Bill asked, "Do you sit at the head of the table?" Jim thought about that for a while, "I usually sit in the same place, in the middle on the north side. Does that matter?" Bill smiled, "Everything matters when it comes to planning and running effective meetings." They then discussed work place design issues that ranged from the use of round tables that provide for greater equality and collaboration among participants, while rectangular tables can demonstrate a more hierarchal relationship and make it difficult for the participants to see each other. Jim then smiled and said: "Are you telling me that the arrangement of the chairs is related to the successful outcome of the meeting?" "Exactly," Bill exclaimed. Then, Jim asked what should be done with two people who do not get along — that is, whatever Joyce suggests, her nemesis Henry opposes. Bill thought for a moment, then said, "Unfortunately, that is a common problem; the larger the group the more likely you will have personality clashes and lingering conflict, especially if you have been having problems during past meetings. One thing you can do, if you have two people who don't get along well, is to not allow them to sit across from one another, that is more of a confrontational setting and they are more likely to want to fight. Try and arrange it so that they sit side-by-side. It is a lot harder to fight with someone you are next to as opposed to someone who is directly across from you!"

Bill looked at his watch and said he had only a couple of minutes until he needed to go. "One last thing," he said, "How you end the meeting is also important, just like planning and running the meeting." Bill spoke of backtracking the meeting at the end to summarize all that had been covered during the meeting. Look for the subconscious nods of agreement from the participants, the body language, to make sure that the group members are in agreement. If you get the nods you are set; if you get puzzled looks, you need to go back and talk it through until you reach agreement on what was covered in the meeting. Although it was now time to leave, Bill indicated that they had not touched on the management or facilitation of the meeting or on the importance of reading the group, especially the non-verbal signals! Also, he quickly suggested, at the end of the session, make sure that everyone knows what their responsibilities are moving forward, what they will do and when they will have it done. Accountability is crucial. "And, by the way," Bill noted, "Indicate when the group will meet again and begin to talk about the potential meeting outcomes. When you return to your office, it is important to get minutes of the meeting out as soon as possible. Ask for corrections or clarifications and set a specific time limit for their submission. This is another tool for ensuring agreement."

Jim knew he needed to get back to work and let his old friend go. He thanked him and they talked about doing a better job of staying in touch. He gathered up the dozen or so napkins he had been taking notes on. Good thing we weren't at a restaurant with cloth napkins he thought! As angry and down as he had been in the morning, he was really excited to take all the things he had learned from Bill over lunch and put them into practice. So many good ideas he thought, I know that I can't make all of the changes at one time, but, I want to give it a try."

Questions and Instructions:

1. Based on your experience, why are meetings an important organizational tool?

2. What problems have you encountered that make meetings unproductive? Please explain.

Case 5: Making Meetings Work

3. Bill Mortenson has provided Jim with a lot of ideas on how to effectively manage meetings. Since Jim cannot try all the recommendations at once, which of the suggestions would you recommend he do first? Please prioritize the suggestions in order of importance.

4. What items, if any, would you delete from Bill's list of suggestions and why? Do have supporting evidence for your choices? Please be specific. Are their suggestions that you would add to Bill's list of recommendation? What are they and why do you feel they would contribute to meeting effectiveness? Please explain.

5. What does the Law of Diminishing Marginal Utility or the rule of inverse proportionality — that is, the least important issues take up the most time have to do with the conduct of meetings? Please explain.

6. The sage muses sardonically that meetings are generally a waste of time. If true, are the kept and published minutes a tangible confirmation that time was actually wasted? Your reaction please.

7. The case presents a detailed background on Jim's background. In your opinion, does it have any bearing on how Jim might manage a departmental meeting? Please explain.

Case 5: Making Meetings Work
Name:

Case Log and Administrative Journal Entry

This case analysis and learning assessment is printed on perforated pages and may be removed from the book for evaluation purposes.

Case Analysis:
Major case concepts and theories identified:

What is the relevance of the concepts, theories, ideas and techniques presented in the case to that of public management?

Facts — what do we know *for sure* about the case? Please list.

Who is involved in the case (people, departments, agencies, units, etc.)? Were the problems of an "intra/interagency" nature? Be specific.

Are there any rules, laws, regulations or standard operating procedures identified in the case study that might limit decision-making? If so, what are they?

Are there any clues presented in the case as to the major actor's interests, needs, motivations and personalities? If so, please list them.

Case 5: Making Meetings Work

Learning Assessment:
What do the administrative theories presented in this case mean to you as an administrator?

How can this learning be put to use outside the classroom? Are there any problems you envision during the implementation phase?

Several possible courses of action were identified during the class discussion. Which action was considered to be most practical by the group? Which was deemed most feasible? Based on your personal experience, did the group reach a conclusion that was desirable, feasible, and practical? Please explain why or why not.

Did the group reach a decision that would solve the problem on a short-term or long-term basis? Please explain.

What could you have done to receive more learning value from this case?

6

Time and Time Again

by
Mary Beth Mellick and C. Kenneth Meyer

The Springfield Cancer Research Center (SCRC) is a small public health-research clinic located in the Northeast. It is a satellite site to the main clinic located 100 miles away in Greenfield. The Greenfield clinic had been in operation for seven years when the Springfield clinic opened this past summer. The clinics represent two of fifty sites located across the country that are tasked with conducting a study on the prevention and treatment of breast cancer in women. The goal of each clinic is to recruit as many women as possible who have been diagnosed with breast cancer, and to follow them throughout their treatment. Kay Smith, RN, was hired as the clinic manager for the new clinic in Springfield, and recently hired a nurse practitioner, a data coordinator, and a project manager. The new project manager, Tammy Wells, previously worked at the central clinic in Greenfield clinic before she was transferred to SCRC.

The working hours for both Greenfield and Springfield cancer centers were identical: 8:00 a.m. to 4:30 p.m. with a half-hour for lunch. Tammy, the project manager, said that the Greenfield "...supervisors were *very* strict about hours, " and if anyone came to work even late--even just a few minutes late--they were required to take vacation time for the minutes lost. Tammy also said that Jan Benton, another project manager in Greenfield, would stand at the copy machine every morning and monitor the time of arrival for all employees. "Flexibility was not an option," she noted and "...no one was allowed to take an extra half-hour lunch and stay at work an extra half-hour at the end of the day," flexibility that some wanted.

When Kay heard about the attendance rules in Greenfield, she proclaimed that "...there was no way her clinic would operate in such an autocratic manner." She further explained that on certain high patient load days, her co-workers may not get a half-hour for lunch, but when the patient load was low they could take long lunches, as long as no one took advantage of the flexible time. Kay told her staff, "I refuse to be as rigid as the Greenfield clinic with hours. The way they treat their employees is so unprofessional; they might as well work in a factory. After all, we are not a colony of ants." By this time, everyone had come to like and trust Kay and they had formed an opinion that SCRC would be a great place to work. As a group of only four, the staff became almost like family, and they treated each other with dignity, respect and a caring professional concern.

If there ever was to be an exception principle in Kay's management outlook, it was the requirement that all members of her staff be at work by 8:00 a.m. every morning, no excuses, and no exceptions. It was easy for Kay to be at work by 8:00 a.m. She woke up every morning at 4:30 without an alarm, made her family breakfast and also dinner for that evening, did laundry, and left for work sometimes as early as 6:30. She loved to get things done in the morning. Her employees, however, did not have Kay's energy in the morning. Tammy lived one hour away and was a single mom with two kids. She had to get them to school and daycare before leaving for the one-hour drive to work. Sarah Parker, the data coordinator, had trouble being on time – especially in the morning. Sarah and Tammy were usually late, but usually not more than 5 minutes. Since they did not see patients, their work was not affected if they were late. Kathy Jones, the nurse practitioner, on the other hand, was usually at least 15 minutes late and had patients waiting for her when she reached the office. Kay reminded everyone that 8:00 a.m. was the time to be at work.

Staff members at the Springfield clinic were told that the patient load would be high and the rumor mill communicated that additional staff would be hired. During the next few months the clinic staff did an exceptional job of getting the work done. Although there were only four of them, the SCRC staff maintained a 98 percent retention rate, the highest of all the clinics nationally, and much higher than those clinics that had 15 or 20 employees. However, Kathy, the nurse practitioner, only did average and sometimes below average work. She had many personal problems that interfered with her job, including separating from her husband, taking care of her mentally ill daughter, and occasionally providing assistance to her elderly mother. The staff sympathized with Kathy, and didn't think twice about picking up the slack for her.

The employees at the Springfield CRC were busy, but not busy enough. They only had one research study, where the other clinics had between five and ten going on at one time. But new studies were pending, and it wouldn't be long, they were told, before they would be swamped. Until then, Kay told her staff it was okay to take long lunches while work was slow.

In the beginning, everyone started with a one-hour lunch break, but over time, the norm became two hours. With business slow, Kay seemed unconcerned. However, Kathy sometimes stretched the lunch hour to three-hours and kept patients waiting until she returned. Kay told her that three-hour lunches were too long, and that she could not keep her patients waiting like she did.

As months passed, work remained extremely slow. The new research studies that were pending had fallen through. And as the Springfield staff became more familiar with their jobs, they were able to get their work done well before 4:30. Not only did Kay allow her staff to continue to take long lunches, she also told them that once their work was done, they could do whatever they wanted – as long as they stayed at work. So the staff brought magazines, books, and crossword puzzles to work to make the days go by faster. On exceptionally slow days, Kay would let her staff go home a half-hour or more early. However, she still demanded that everyone be at work by 8:00 a.m., even if there was no work to be done and no patients to see. No one argued with Kay about the 8:00 a.m. rule because they didn't want to cause friction. They really liked and respected her as a clinic manager.

Kay continued coming to work by 7:00 a.m. every morning, even if there were no appointments until later in the day. She read the newspaper or worked on crossword puzzles until the first appointment. But Kathy, Sarah, and Tammy did not change their habits, and still came to work late. They did not understand the rationale of "breaking their necks to get to work by 8:00," only to read magazines and do crossword puzzles as Kay did. Tammy wanted to use the extra time to spend with her kids, while Sarah wanted to sleep in longer in the morning. But Kay was adamant about being to work by 8:00 a.m., and became increasingly angry as the staff continued its late arrival. As Sarah and Tammy strolled in at 8:05 and 8:10, and Kathy between 8:15 and 8:30, Kay would be sitting at the front desk working on a crossword puzzle. She would not even say "hello," but would instead look up at the clock to see what time it was. She also would not talk to anyone for about the first half-hour of work, until she cooled off.

As tensions grew about the issue of time and hours, Kay decided to put her foot down. She said that if anyone on her staff were 10 minutes late or more, they would have to take vacation time for the lost time. Sarah and Tammy usually made it to work by 8:05, but sometimes it was 8:10. Kathy continued to be 15 minutes late or more. Kay had everyone filling out vacation slips for being late. Lunches remained flexible, although Kathy continued to take three-hour lunches, and Kay continued to confront her about it.

The vacation records that were filled out for lost time were sent to the main office in Greenfield where all staff benefits were handled. Of course, the Greenfield clinic was not happy with the numerous vacation records they had to process. All the five and 10-minute vacation slips going to Greenfield every week embarrassed Kay, so she decided to stop having Sarah and Tammy use vacation time when they were late, but continued having Kathy use it. Although tensions continued to be high, the staff, for the most part, remained a tight-knit group, and the clinic held on to its number one national ranking!

Sarah and Tammy knew Kay was at her wit's end and made a stronger effort to get to work by 8:00 a.m. They had hoped Kathy would do the same, but she did not. In fact, she only got worse. Kathy's work, although never more than satisfactory, started going further downhill. Her personal problems worsened, and she began to take between two and three weeks off each month for sick time, vacation time, or family leave. She continued to come to work late and take long lunches. Kay eventually started making Kathy fill out vacation slips for long lunches. As a rebuttal, Kathy began making up excuses to get out of work by saying she was going to the lab in another building, when really she was running errands or taking her mother to the doctor.

The staff's sympathy for Kathy grew to frustration. The more Kathy came to work late and took time off, the more Kay became angry and the more work everyone had to do to pick up the slack. Even when Kathy was at work, her mind seemed to be somewhere else. The clinic was becoming an unbearable place to work. But no matter how many rules Kathy broke, and no matter how angry Kay got with her, Kay would not reprimand her because she knew if she did, Kathy would retaliate. Kay felt that if she tried to fire her, Kathy would say that Kay allowed the staff to do crossword puzzles and read magazine at work. Kay – and everyone else at the clinic – could lose their jobs as a result. Kay felt the only thing left to do was to make Kathy's life hell so she would eventually quit. But it didn't work.

Months went by and Kathy showed no signs of leaving. Meanwhile, Sarah and Tammy started back in their routine of being five or ten minutes late for work. Kathy also continued to be late, keeping her patients waiting.

Case 6: Time and Time Again

Kay had finally had it. She told her staff that there would be no more long lunches, even if there was no work to do and no patients to see: "Half-hour lunches only. If you choose to run an errand for a half-hour and still want to eat lunch, you'll have to eat at your desk while you work." She continued to confront people when they were late, although no vacation time had to be used. Kay later pulled Sarah and Tammy aside and told them: "Since Kathy can't follow the rules, then everyone will have to be punished."

Over the next few months, morale and productivity at the clinic quickly dropped. The group of employees that was once like family slowly began distancing itself from one another. The tension between Kay and Kathy grew into shouting matches. Meanwhile, Tammy and Sarah began looking for new jobs.

Questions and Instructions:

1. Was Kay fair in how she handled "flex-time" with everyone? Why or why not?

2. What does flex-time really mean? Explain. What are the positive and negative implications associated with flexible scheduling of time? Elaborate.

3. Should Kay have fired Kathy? Why or why not?

4. Should Kay have reprimanded Tammy and Sarah for not getting to work on time? Why or why not?

5. If this case had transpired 20 years ago, do you think it would have been more acceptable to reprimand someone for being late? Is there a difference in management style when members of Generation X or Y are being disciplined? Please justify your response.

Case 6: Time and Time Again
Name:

Case Log and Administrative Journal Entry

This case analysis and learning assessment is printed on perforated pages and may be removed from the book for evaluation purposes.

Case Analysis:
Major case concepts and theories identified:

What is the relevance of the concepts, theories, ideas and techniques presented in the case to that of public management?

Facts — what do we know *for sure* about the case? Please list.

Who is involved in the case (people, departments, agencies, units, etc.)? Were the problems of an "intra/interagency" nature? Be specific.

Are there any rules, laws, regulations or standard operating procedures identified in the case study that might limit decision-making? If so, what are they?

Are there any clues presented in the case as to the major actor's interests, needs, motivations and personalities? If so, please list them.

Case 6: Time and Time Again

Learning Assessment:
What do the administrative theories presented in this case mean to you as an administrator?

How can this learning be put to use outside the classroom? Are there any problems you envision during the implementation phase?

Several possible courses of action were identified during the class discussion. Which action was considered to be most practical by the group? Which was deemed most feasible? Based on your personal experience, did the group reach a conclusion that was desirable, feasible, and practical? Please explain why or why not.

Did the group reach a decision that would solve the problem on a short-term or long-term basis? Please explain.

What could you have done to receive more learning value from this case?

7

The Dress Dress Code

by
C. Kenneth Meyer and Lance Noe

Comer, Welch, and Rassel Group is a prestigious policy research firm founded in 1970 by K. L. Comer. Mr. Comer set the tone at the research firm by setting a strict dress code policy in 1970 that was reluctantly updated as styles and public standards of grooming and dress changed. "The fact that we established a traditional dress code policy in 1970 gave our more liberal policy recommendations credibility. The same is true today," stated Comer, who was now chair of the Board of Directors. In spite of being in semi-retirement, Comer still took ownership of the dress code and worked one-on-one with the director of personnel in conducting the annual policy review and writing up the end of year report. Throughout the group's history, however, the basic code remained constant: Women are to wear skirts, nylons and dress shoes. Men must don suits and ties.

Leslie Sullivan was excited to begin work for Comer, Welch, and Rassel. She knew the history of the policy research firm and the reputation it had garnered as a cutting edge policy research firm, especially in the areas of revenue and taxation, corporate law, personnel policy, and environmental policy. A top graduate from a prestigious school of public policy, Leslie felt she was a good find for the firm and was proud to be hired.

On her first day of work, she was shocked to receive an email in the morning from the director of personnel. As she opened the email, she fully expected to find a congratulatory note expressing the group's pleasure that she had joined the organization and was now on-board. To her utter dismay, however, the email curtly informed her that she was not in compliance with the dress and grooming standard. Her wearing a suit with pants was considered a violation of the dress code. "I can't believe this. I just bought this designer outfit in order to express my commitment to presenting myself in a professional manner. Now they are telling me that I must wear a skirt? I don't wear dresses by choice and I didn't think that a firm that spent the last 35 years fighting for such things as women's rights should treat me this way," she sighed.

Sullivan was now upset. "What should I do now? I certainly feel humiliated," she mumbled. "I'll nip this issue in the bud immediately," she thought as she printed the "Will be back in 15 minutes" message to be posted on her office door. She walked down the hallway and spoke with a personnel assistant about the dress code and was quietly told that Mr. Comer had made the policy years ago and that he was adamant about it and insisted that employees dress to a traditional standard. "After all," he was quoted as saying, "That is a small price to pay to gain clients and access to the reins of power. And, everyone knows that appearance is everything."

Questions and Instructions:

1. Some surveys suggest that 75 percent of recent graduates consider an organization's dress code an important factor in making a decision to accept a position. How do you think Comer, Welch, and Rassel's dress code impacts hiring?

2. Discuss the issue of gender in creating a dress code? Can different standards be applied fairly to men and women? Explain.

3. What do you personally think about casual dress days in the office? Do you think that absenteeism, tardiness and productivity suffer because of a more casual work environment? Please be specific. What are the national trends in relation to dress and are they the same across the nation, or do they differ by geographical region, type of organizations, and sector in which people are employed? Identify the differences, if any.

4. To what extent should the factors of safety, health, comfort and type of position occupied influence the dress code policy of your organization? What about the issue of employees dressing in such a manner that there appearance creates a "disruptive" environment? How would you deal with issue? Explain.

Case 7: The Dress Dress Code

Name:

Case Log and Administrative Journal Entry

This case analysis and learning assessment is printed on perforated pages and may be removed from the book for evaluation purposes.

Case Analysis:
Major case concepts and theories identified:

What is the relevance of the concepts, theories, ideas and techniques presented in the case to that of public management?

Facts — what do we know *for sure* about the case? Please list.

Who is involved in the case (people, departments, agencies, units, etc.)? Were the problems of an "intra/interagency" nature? Be specific.

Are there any rules, laws, regulations or standard operating procedures identified in the case study that might limit decision-making? If so, what are they?

Are there any clues presented in the case as to the major actor's interests, needs, motivations and personalities? If so, please list them.

Case 7: The Dress Dress Code

Learning Assessment:
What do the administrative theories presented in this case mean to you as an administrator?

How can this learning be put to use outside the classroom? Are there any problems you envision during the implementation phase?

Several possible courses of action were identified during the class discussion. Which action was considered to be most practical by the group? Which was deemed most feasible? Based on your personal experience, did the group reach a conclusion that was desirable, feasible, and practical? Please explain why or why not.

Did the group reach a decision that would solve the problem on a short-term or long-term basis? Please explain.

What could you have done to receive more learning value from this case?

8

Supervising God

by
Lance Noe and C. Kenneth Meyer

Roscoe Jones was by all accounts a religious person who applied his beliefs to all aspects of his life. However, it was the expression of his religious views in the office that began the drama that resulted in his termination and subsequent lawsuit. When Jones was hired to direct the Department of Assessment for Regency County he made no secret of the fact that religion was the most essential element of his life. It was a core commitment and value! During the interview, Jones wore a small religious pin on his lapel and referred to his Christian religious beliefs when asked questions about how he would approach administrative problems. Jim Radick, Regency's county manager, thought it was slightly unusual if not peculiar that Jones' referred so often to his beliefs; in fact, it made him personally uncomfortable. However, since the previous director of assessment was fired for dishonest practices, he thought the change to a leader with strong religious principles would be refreshing for the department, and so a letter was sent to Jones offering him the position, which he immediately accepted.

Three months into the job, Radick began to receive complaints from some longtime members of the Department of Assessment. They complained that Jones allowed employees who shared his fundamental faith to read religious literature at their work stations during office hours. Other employees claimed he encouraged donations to various sectarian causes by supporting the distribution and routing of contribution envelopes for certain charitable programs in the office. It was noted that the envelope routing path always seem to end in the director's office and this caused some employees to become suspicious that he was "playing book" on who did and did not contribute. Still, others claimed that Jones would spend countless hours in his office talking with anyone willing to discuss their religious faith, provided, of course, it matched his own beliefs. No one claimed that he had purposively attempted to convert employees during working hours to his brand of religion or that he had harassed employees who didn't share his beliefs. Several employees complained, however, that they felt alienated and shunned by their director and that attitude was largely a result of religious disposition rather than performance or productivity.

When county manager Radick stopped by Jones' office to discuss the issues of potential religious discrimination, he was surprised to see a large framed picture of the "House of Faith and Works Center" dominating the space directly behind his chair. The center of the picture portrayed an enormous glass, stone, and steel architectural wonder that Jones was quick to point out had "recently won an international design award." Playing loudly on the speakers of his personal computer was live religious teachings and music from the House of Faith and Works Center. After the volume was turned down to allow conversation, Jim asked Roscoe, "Doesn't the picture and preaching create an inappropriate environment for a public department?" Roscoe replied, "I don't see how the picture is any different from photos of Rome, Paris, London, and Berlin that hang in your office. It tells me we both enjoy architectural wonders that happen to be religious buildings." Regarding the live teaching and music from the center, Roscoe noted that of course he turns it down when meeting with his co-workers, but emphasized that the teaching contributes to his good and honest job performance. "Many of my employees have told me that the teaching and music from the House of Faith and Works inspires them to do honest and quality work. It certainly is better that the shouting talk radio shows that I hear in other city departments," he opined.

When asked about the other complaints that had been registered by employees, Roscoe said he couldn't recall every conversation he has ever had with co-workers, nor does he remember every donation envelope that got passed around the office. And as for allowing employees to read religious publications or material while on the job, he said he assumed that the employees were reading the material during their personal and regular breaks. "Who am I to censor what people read? Maybe taking God out of the workplace is what got this department into trouble before you hired me!" Jones fired back. The meeting confirmed to Radick that Roscoe Jones was not going to modify his practices and would consider it a violation of his religious rights if either asked or pressed to do otherwise.

Manager Radick retreated to his office and began to consult with the county attorney. The county attorney warned Jim that he was exposing the county to considerable risk by allowing such a religiously charged atmosphere to continue in a department of county government. "There is the matter of separation of church and state you know," he said. Based on the legal advice, Roscoe Jones was next ordered to cease all religious activity at work or face disciplinary action that could include termination. As expected, he did not modify his practices and after consulting with the county commission, Roscoe Jones was given a notice of termination.

Ten months later a federal court brought back their decision in *Jones v. County of Regency*. Roscoe Jones was awarded $500,000 in damages for the "unwarranted and heavy handed order and subsequent action" which the court saw as excessively infringing on the right to free religious expression.

Questions and Instructions:

1. To what extent can a person's religious beliefs be expressed in public workplace? Does it matter if a person is in a supervisory position?

Case 8: Supervising God

2. Evaluate the perspective that the county manager brought to the first meeting with Roscoe Jones in his office.

3. Should a person be required to leave her/his religious beliefs at the door when seeking public sector employment?

4. What does this court decision tell the public sector regarding the role religion should play, if any, in the workplace?

Case 8: Supervising God

Case 8: Supervising God
Name:

Case Log and Administrative Journal Entry

This case analysis and learning assessment is printed on perforated pages and may be removed from the book for evaluation purposes.

Case Analysis:
Major case concepts and theories identified:

What is the relevance of the concepts, theories, ideas and techniques presented in the case to that of public management?

Facts — what do we know *for sure* about the case? Please list.

Who is involved in the case (people, departments, agencies, units, etc.)? Were the problems of an "intra/interagency" nature? Be specific.

Are there any rules, laws, regulations or standard operating procedures identified in the case study that might limit decision-making? If so, what are they?

Are there any clues presented in the case as to the major actor's interests, needs, motivations and personalities? If so, please list them.

Case 8: Supervising God

Learning Assessment:
What do the administrative theories presented in this case mean to you as an administrator?

How can this learning be put to use outside the classroom? Are there any problems you envision during the implementation phase?

Several possible courses of action were identified during the class discussion. Which action was considered to be most practical by the group? Which was deemed most feasible? Based on your personal experience, did the group reach a conclusion that was desirable, feasible, and practical? Please explain why or why not.

Did the group reach a decision that would solve the problem on a short-term or long-term basis? Please explain.

What could you have done to receive more learning value from this case?

9

Ergonomics in the Workplace

by
C. Kenneth Meyer and Steve Lewis

Niles Wabanaki was brought into World Parcel Service (WPS) procurement and delivery system in Houston, and as he told his friends, "I want to learn as much as possible about shipping and receiving. It is much more involved than just loading and unloading trucks."

Wabanaki was a recent college graduate and had majored in business and industrial engineering. While in college he played football and although alert, agile, quick, and with good hands, he did not have all of the physical traits required to become a National Football League linebacker. He had numerous job possibilities in the private sector, but his long-term goal was to work for the city that he loved and give something back to a community that gave him a good education and an excellent "start in life."

At WPS Niles received his work assignment from Elaina Lewis, the director of human resources, who was new to her job as well. Lewis told Watanabe that the Shipping and Receiving Department had a higher rate of workers' compensation claims than all of the other departments of the organization. The warehouse supervisor, Harry Coleman, attributed the excessive claims to the caliber of the people that were hired as material handlers. He believed that many of these workers were receptive to getting hurt and were looking to get a free ride or a free lunch — of course on the government's dime. "Niles you will come to see and appreciate what I have told you. It takes all kinds of people to make the world go around," Coleman said. Then, Coleman said something that appeared to Niles to be inconsistent with his earlier statement, "On a more serious note, the injury level has made it very difficult for me to field a consistent workforce and the claims are having an adverse financial impact on my department."

Niles Watanabe was now in a situation to take his zeal and enthusiasm for worker safety and health to his newly found position at WPS. He acknowledged in other milieus his passion to create a healthy work environment and was poised to get down to the job of better understanding the nature of the tasks performed in his department and the employees who performed them.

Being a careful observer of human behavior, Watanabe noticed that the men and women who handled the material worked diligently every day. He saw no shirking of responsibility or laggardness routinely unloading trucks, lifting and carrying packages weighing up to 70 pounds or more. The packages were then carried to the sorting area where they were placed into bulk container carts. Once filled, the carts were manually pushed to the docks where the cartons and packages would be positioned

Case 9: Ergonomics in the Workplace

in the awaiting trucks. When filled, the carts weighed one-half of a ton or more and had to be pushed up a slight incline and onto the delivery trucks. Often the trucks were of different sizes causing the material handlers to move ramps into place to provide smooth access to the delivery vehicles. Niles thought that this posed a potential risk for back and shoulder problems and an even more serious issue if workers lost control of the heavy bulk carts.

Niles also observed what was going on in the receiving and sorting areas. The material handlers were often reaching deep into the large bins and constantly bending over to reach, grasp and transport packages. When he first observed this physical activity, the writings of the Gilbreths and their "Therbligs" came to mind and for him the classical management theories took on an entirely new meaning. He also paid attention to the positioning of the computer terminals and noticed that the keyboards and the monitors could not be adjusted and that some of the workers actually had to twist the trunk of their bodies while on their stools in order to update the computer fields. Again, he thought, this provided another risk for back injury. Finally, Niles noticed that the stools did not provide adequate back or leg support and some of the people who had to sit on these stools for long periods of time complained that this led to decreased circulation, lower back pain, and poor posture.

Niles excitedly began to build a proposal to implement ergonomic improvements that he felt would reduce the risk that the workers in the Shipping and Receiving Department were regularly facing on a daily basis. His plan was to procure the following items and put them into place:

- New sit/stand or lean stools for the sorting and receiving areas. The stools would take two-thirds of the pressure off of the lower back and make it easier for the workers to get up and move around.
- Tilting package carts for sorting and receiving areas. The carts could be angled toward the worker and prevent awkward body twisting and lifting movements that might be injurious to the shoulders and lower back.
- Automated pull carts to replace the bulk container carts. An automated cart would require little to no effort and would provide better control of the transported material. Ultimately, the new carts would eliminate the back and shoulder strains that occurred so frequently in the department.
- Hydraulically controlled ramps. These ramps would be purchased and installed, eliminating the need to compensate for the differences in the dimensions of the delivery trucks that were loaded.

He had been on the job for only three months when he was invited to present his recommendations to the supervisory staff of the Shipping and Receiving Department. He told his wife before he left for work that he would be unveiling his plan to reduce the amount of loss time, reduce medical costs, and reduce workers' compensation. He felt his four recommendations were in line with what he knew about ergonomics.

Niles realized during his presentation that his ideas were not being well received by the others as they raised their eyebrows and some actually snickered. One department head stated, "This is a warehouse, not a playground," in response to the automated pull carts and hydraulic ramps. Still others felt there was no room in the budget for new equipment of the type proposed. Yet, in spite of the palpable antagonism, Niles was persistent in his explanation and justification and showed that the Bureau of Labor Statistics (BLS) reported that the average costs of a work-related musculoskeletal disorder (WMSD) was about $14,000. Niles patiently explained: "If the new equipment prevented only ten occupation injuries per year, WPS would save at least $138,100 a year and this yearly savings would produce a return on investment (ROI) in less than two years."

After the meeting was concluded, Harry Coleman, the Warehouse Supervisor, waited to speak alone with Elaina. Coleman stated, "We don't need to throw good money after bad. These college educated kids come in here and always want to spend money on new equipment. New equipment won't change a thing. If you ask me, we just need to pay higher wages and we'll get a better class of workers. You know yourself Elaina; you can't make a silk purse out of a sow's ear!"

Niles had tried desperately to make a difference at WPS. He felt that the suggestions he made to reduce worker injuries, worker compensation claims and improve the overall quality of work life were not taken seriously by management. He had objectively observed what people were doing and had compiled the empirical evidence that supported his recommendations for change. Now, frustrated with the lack of understanding and acceptance of basic ergonomic principles at WPS, he was ready to apply his talents and energies elsewhere.

Accordingly, he went online and searched for a new position. This time, he would tryout the public sector and he especially wanted to get a job with his hometown, the city of Holdenview. Holdenview was special to Watanabe and he loved the prospect of being able to live once again in a thriving metropolitan community. He knew that Holdenview had a questionable reputation for hiring Asians, and for that matter, most states, counties, and municipalities were not known for their progressiveness in this area, but he reasoned the fact that he had roots in his hometown would not hurt his chances.

Niles Watanabe was successful in his bid for a new career and although he had numerous job offers in the private sector, he told his friends that he wanted to give something back to a community that gave him a good education and excellent leg-up on life. Commenting further, he said, "Luckily, Holdenview had a position open in the Receiving and Distribution Department and I was selected to head the department."

Little did Niles realize at the time, but he was being tasked with doing the job of an ergonomist, even though he had little formal training and only a small amount of empirical knowledge of ergonomics or human factor engineering. He was innately drawn to examine the interaction between how ones anatomy, physiology and psychology related. He knew instinctively that if people were to exercise and realize their athletic abilities to the fullest extent, the whole anatomical structure needed to be understood. In short, he did not need to read any books to see how the physical dimensions fit with the cognitive domain — the way we process massive amounts of information daily and make decisions in an organizational setting. Niles realized the different kinds of work that his associates and others were asked to perform for the vast majority of their lives, varied from computer use to "heavy lifting," physically demanding tasks of moving boxes, standing stationery for long periods of time, completing routine,

Case 9: Ergonomics in the Workplace

repetitive and sometimes mundane tasks, to working in heavy industry or in service jobs that involved their own peculiarly distinct uses of equipment, processes, and systems.

Questions and Instructions:

1. After reading the scenario that involved Niles Watanabe, what would you have done differently to bring about the needed work-related changes at World Parcel Systems? Please elaborate.

2. Based on what you know about the field of ergonomics, were Watanabe's recommendations reasonably on target or were they misplaced? Please explain.

3. Putting on your own ergonomics hat, please examine your own work place and the tasks performed by your colleagues and yourself. In what areas would you be able to apply ergonomics in relation to these four factors: information design, equipment and systems, work arrangements, and working environment? Keep in mind that what you will identify as problematic will cross the boundaries of many disciplines, ranging from health and safety, engineering design, anatomy and physiology, biomechanics, psychology, design sciences and the total built environment.

4. Please conduct a Web crawl and summarize at least one finding that pertains to ergonomics and human size, shape and strength (anthropometry); human error; sound and vibration; and, vision. Please report these findings in a handout that is distributed to your colleagues.

Case 9: Ergonomics in the Workplace

Case 9: Ergonomics in the Workplace
Name:

Case Log and Administrative Journal Entry

This case analysis and learning assessment is printed on perforated pages and may be removed from the book for evaluation purposes.

Case Analysis:
Major case concepts and theories identified:

What is the relevance of the concepts, theories, ideas and techniques presented in the case to that of public management?

Facts — what do we know *for sure* about the case? Please list.

Who is involved in the case (people, departments, agencies, units, etc.)? Were the problems of an "intra/interagency" nature? Be specific.

Are there any rules, laws, regulations or standard operating procedures identified in the case study that might limit decision-making? If so, what are they?

Are there any clues presented in the case as to the major actor's interests, needs, motivations and personalities? If so, please list them.

Case 9: Ergonomics in the Workplace

Learning Assessment:
What do the administrative theories presented in this case mean to you as an administrator?

How can this learning be put to use outside the classroom? Are there any problems you envision during the implementation phase?

Several possible courses of action were identified during the class discussion. Which action was considered to be most practical by the group? Which was deemed most feasible? Based on your personal experience, did the group reach a conclusion that was desirable, feasible, and practical? Please explain why or why not.

Did the group reach a decision that would solve the problem on a short-term or long-term basis? Please explain.

What could you have done to receive more learning value from this case?

10

Severe Acute Respiratory Syndrome (SARS)

by
C. Kenneth Meyer and Gina DeVoogd

Donald and Jessica Forrester had saved as much as their middle-class lifestyle permitted. They skimped and cutback on Starbuck's latte and, instead, would have an iced coffee at the "Golden Arches." They cut their regular family vacation from nine to six days and stayed in economy versus more upscale motels. They had a single goal, to see and explore mysterious China. Finally, after twenty-five years of a silver marriage, a grown family, and an empty nest, their goal was in sight and they were not going to let anything get in the way of blocking their dream vacation — not even an outbreak of Severe Acute Respiratory Syndrome (SARS) in Guangdong, China.

The Forresters were savvy people, reasonably middle class by all standards, and professionally educated. They had the acumen to surf the internet with ease and they frequently visited the Centers for Disease Control and Prevention (CDC) website. They kept abreast on the outbreak of SARS and other communicable diseases in their destination cities and the several Chinese provinces they would be visiting. They were online and knew the U.S Department of State's (DOS) recommendation for travel in China and knew how seriously SARS was considered by the World Health Organization (WHO). Interestingly, they had read in the press how the People's Republic of China (PRC) had responded to SARS and their trusted travel consultant advised them to postpone their travel to China. But, in a single-minded act of determinism, they set off for a month long vacation in China. They did not get overly excited about SARS — after all, they reasoned, it was probably medical hype for the most part.

The trip went as planned and Don Forrester told his friends, "It went splendidly well and was uneventful. What else could you ask for? And, we didn't see anyone die from SARS. We didn't even need to wear those pale blue respiratory masks that our friendly pharmacist had recommended."

The Forrester's told their greeting family members who met them at the airport with hugs and affection, that tourism was down and they had few delays and experienced minimal hassles while they walked on the Great Wall and visited the Sacred City. In fact, they recounted with astonishment and delight how well their flight went from Beijing to Shanghai. Don explained to his oldest daughter how they regularly had their temperatures taken at the hotels they stayed in and that they were a constant 98.6 degrees Fahrenheit. The Forresters were happy to be home and glad they had discounted the SARS doom and gloom. Don chuckled, however, when he described the 18-hour delay in their return flight to the United States because only a small number of passengers were either eligible or willing to fly.

Case 10: Severe Acute Respiratory Syndrome (SARS)

What may have been normal for Don Forrester would not be considered standard fare for his employer. When he returned home, checked for any property damage or vandalism, and checked the basement for water leaks, etc., he dutifully emptied the dozens of messages that had been saved on his answering machine. One of the many messages he had received was urgent. It was from Maxie Davis, Director of Human Resources at Children's Hospital, where Don was the Chief Financial Officer (CFO). The message said, "Don. Please call me when you return home from your trip to China. Human Resources has discussed the ramifications of your trip to China in relation to your potential exposure to the SARS virus and has decided that it is in the best interest of your colleagues, hospital patients, and other hospital employees, that you not return to work for at least fourteen days. We just want to make sure that if you have the SARS virus, that it is not spread or transmitted throughout the hospital. We all hope that you and Jessica had a great time and cannot wait to hear about your travels and see the pictures you took with your new camera. Please call me immediately when you get this message. And, welcome home!"

Don hung up the phone and in disbelief and frustration told Jessica they had been effectively quarantined by the hospital and wondered if the Department of Human Resources had any resemblance of sanity left in its office.

Questions and Instructions:

1. Do you agree or disagree with the action taken by Maxie Davis to quarantine Donald for fourteen days? Please justify your answer.

2. Was the Department of Human Resources being overly cautious or merely prudent given the infectiousness nature of the SARS virus? Please elaborate.

3. If an individual (employee or not) is to be placed on quarantine, who should make this decision to avoid discriminatory complaints? Please explain.

4. Are there any other diseases that you know of such as Ebola or Avian flu, etc., that might justify an action as serious as that of requiring a quarantine to protect public health and welfare? Please elaborate.

Case 10: Severe Acute Respiratory Syndrome (SARS)

Case 10: Severe Acute Respiratory Syndrome (SARS)
Name:

Case Log and Administrative Journal Entry

This case analysis and learning assessment is printed on perforated pages and may be removed from the book for evaluation purposes.

Case Analysis:
Major case concepts and theories identified:

What is the relevance of the concepts, theories, ideas and techniques presented in the case to that of public management?

Facts — what do we know *for sure* about the case? Please list.

Who is involved in the case (people, departments, agencies, units, etc.)? Were the problems of an "intra/interagency" nature? Be specific.

Are there any rules, laws, regulations or standard operating procedures identified in the case study that might limit decision-making? If so, what are they?

Are there any clues presented in the case as to the major actor's interests, needs, motivations and personalities? If so, please list them.

Case 10: Severe Acute Respiratory Syndrome (SARS)

Learning Assessment:
What do the administrative theories presented in this case mean to you as an administrator?

How can this learning be put to use outside the classroom? Are there any problems you envision during the implementation phase?

Several possible courses of action were identified during the class discussion. Which action was considered to be most practical by the group? Which was deemed most feasible? Based on your personal experience, did the group reach a conclusion that was desirable, feasible, and practical? Please explain why or why not.

Did the group reach a decision that would solve the problem on a short-term or long-term basis? Please explain.

What could you have done to receive more learning value from this case?

11

Pictures are Worth a Million Words

by
C. Kenneth Meyer and Lance Noe

Maureen Ross had been a human relations trainer for as long as she could remember, and was presently a senior consultant for the Viva Consultant Group (VCG). She had facilitated training programs for a wide variety of organizations and was knowledgeable about many of the traditional topics connected with organization behavior, development and change. Her familiarity with the essentials of management theory put her at ease with her audiences regardless of their level of experience. She felt comfortable talking about the intricacies of job design and redesign, leadership traits, and the value of leadership inventories. She was conversant with the advantages and limitations of decision making techniques ranging from brainstorming, Nominal Group Technique (NGT), and the uses of the Delphi Method. She often stated that when supervisors speak derogatorily about group decision making and its accompanying low level of decision making adequacy, they are wrongly placing blame on the members of the team, rather than the technique or processes used to reach consensus.

Additionally, Maureen had a good understanding of Maslow's Hierarchy of Human Needs and could present Frederick Herzberg's Two-Factor Theory of Motivation with eloquence and "parsimony." Her colleagues often commented on the expertise she demonstrated with the notions of management gurus such as Fiedler, McGregor, Vroom, Argyris, Likert, McCleland, Waldo, Simon, and Juran. Her subject mastery was impressive and this roster of names and their contributions to the professional literature rolled off her tongue like "Life Savers." She could playfully interact with trainees, connecting their practical problems to the theoretical contributions of these historical giants and maintain an intellectual spirit of interest in the learning center. Of course, she was also informed and conversant with federal, state and local laws pertaining to discrimination and her knowledge of Supreme Court decisions and case law was extraordinarily impressive.

Maureen had been in the trenches and had earned her spurs the hard way as a training consultant. She understood the sundry training topics that her organization was called upon to teach. She often would quip, "I've been there and I've done it," when questioned about a specific presentation problem or training issue. She knew and understood things political and managerial and no one in her organization doubted her when it came to dealing with these sticky wickets. Although she was a seasoned veteran in sizing up organizations and that was a major reason why VCG's training know how was sought by other organizations, some of VCG's higher level executives had serious concerns about how well she was leading, managing, and motivating her own team. Maureen felt she was doing an outstanding job, of course, but there were rumblings in the hallways that not all was as well as it seemed.

Case 11: Pictures are Worth a Million Words

Maureen's team was asked to participate in an afternoon training session in which the climate of the unit would be talked about. As an advocate of continuing education she felt it was a good idea and that it was, in fact, long overdue. Her colleagues told her that initially they felt a bit threatened by the prospect, but now felt that their worst anxieties and fears would not be realized! Hearing this, Maureen, wholeheartedly embraced the training her team was about to receive.

The three-hour training period was duly scheduled and all member of Maureen's team were able to participate. Noteworthy, Maureen did not take part in the training exercise and could easily hear that the training and assessment was going well by the amount of laughing and periodic applause that she heard coming from the training room.

When the training was completed, the facilitator, Harold Glassner, an experienced organizational and leadership consultant in his own right, met with Maureen and revealed the results of a collage of pictures that her group had created and on which there was group consensus. The group was asked by Glassner to utilize the Web and select visuals (icons, symbols, words, etc.) from the thousands of pictures that were available, that accurately portrayed their own unit (see **Exhibit 1**), and contrast it with their idealized organizational model (see **Exhibit 2**).

The team was comfortable and pleased with what they had put together and Glassner learned what each panel on each row of the display symbolized. Glassner, who had a great deal of experience dealing with assessing organizational climate and culture, was not in the slightest surprised by what their idealized organization looked like. However, the pictures and symbols that the group selected as representative of their own unit portrayed some leadership and organizational problems that he had not anticipated.

Harold Glassner studied each frame, each picture of the two collages and tried to put down on paper what they symbolically represented. He was aided by the fact that Maureen's group interpreted each panel as part of the training assessment and debriefing they had just completed, but he wondered if there was more to the pictures and symbols than met the eye!

Questions and Instructions:

1. If you were Harold Glassner, what would you say the panels presented in Exhibit 1, The Organization in Disarray, represented? Please be specific.

   Confrentation   Ivory Tower
   Lack of Buy In   Is it Friday?

2. In five minutes or less, please explain to Maureen Ross what you have learned from her group and what she ought to do if some of the most obvious organizational problems were to be addressed. (Please select a partner to role-play or act-out your counseling.) Will you use directive or non-directive counseling techniques? Please explain and demonstrate.

   No Clue
   Direct to shake reality

Case 11: Pictures are Worth a Million Words

3. Similarly, in analyzing Exhibit 2, The Perfect Organization, what organization and leadership attributes and characteristics were desired by Maureen's team? Once more, please elaborate on the pictures and illustration and be specific as to their meaning.

Stop! Please complete Part 1 before proceeding to the next part of the case study.

Maureen Ross' team completed their pictorial assessment of how they perceived their training unit and provided the attributes that they wanted present in their idealized organization. Their collage was made up of pictures, words, symbols and icons that they felt would be representative of the traits that would be valued by VCG's customers. Accordingly, as revealed in **Exhibit 3**, The Idealized Customer View of VCG, the collage portrayed a number of images that one would suggest as common elements and thus were expected, yet others were clearly at the cutting edge of image marketing and management.

Questions and Instructions:

4. Please examine Exhibit 3 and indicate what attributes the team felt their customers /clients wanted Viva Consultant Group to exemplify? Please be specific.

5. From your own perspective and experience in dealing with organizations of different kinds and what you judge to be of worth or value, are there any attributes you found missing in Exhibit 3 that you would add to the collage? Please explain. Are there any attributions you would delete from the Exhibit 3? If so, please provide the rationale or justification for your decision.

6. If you were asked to make an assessment of the prevailing organizational climate and culture of your own organization, other than using a survey or questionnaire, what innovative approach would you suggest? Please prepare an example of what you would propose and what form your evaluative instrument might take.

Case 11: Pictures are Worth a Million Words

Exhibit 1: Organization of Disarray

Exhibit 2: The Perfect Organization

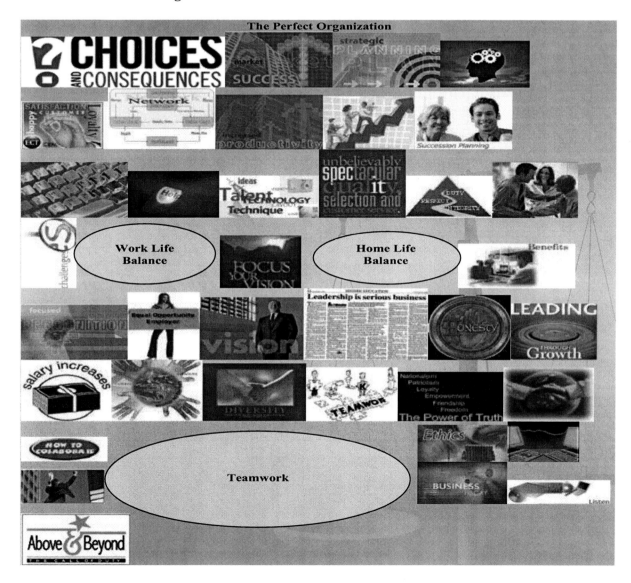

Exhibit 3. Organizational Attributes Desired by Customer

Ability to Answer Questions	Accessible
Accommodating	Accountable
Attentive	Caring
Commanding Presence	Common Sense
Considerate	Consistency
Courteous	Creativity
Easy to Understand	Educated
Effective Communication	Efficient
Empathetic	Even Handed
Experienced	Factual
Fair	Firm
Fiscally Conservative	Flexible
Friendly	Genuine
Genuine	Helpful
Helpful	Honest
Informed	Informed
Integrity	Kind
Knowledgeable	Objective
One-Stop Shop	Patient
Polite	Polite
Problem Solver	Prompt
Prudent	Respectful
Responsive	Skilled
Thorough	Timely
Unbiased	

> Case 11: Pictures are Worth a Million Words
>
> **Name:**

Case Log and Administrative Journal Entry

This case analysis and learning assessment is printed on perforated pages and may be removed from the book for evaluation purposes.

Case Analysis:
Major case concepts and theories identified:

What is the relevance of the concepts, theories, ideas and techniques presented in the case to that of public management?

Facts — what do we know *for sure* about the case? Please list.

Who is involved in the case (people, departments, agencies, units, etc.)? Were the problems of an "intra/interagency" nature? Be specific.

Are there any rules, laws, regulations or standard operating procedures identified in the case study that might limit decision-making? If so, what are they?

Are there any clues presented in the case as to the major actor's interests, needs, motivations and personalities? If so, please list them.

Case 11: Pictures are Worth a Million Words

Learning Assessment:
What do the administrative theories presented in this case mean to you as an administrator?

How can this learning be put to use outside the classroom? Are there any problems you envision during the implementation phase?

Several possible courses of action were identified during the class discussion. Which action was considered to be most practical by the group? Which was deemed most feasible? Based on your personal experience, did the group reach a conclusion that was desirable, feasible, and practical? Please explain why or why not.

Did the group reach a decision that would solve the problem on a short-term or long-term basis? Please explain.

What could you have done to receive more learning value from this case?

12

Interns: An Underutilized Asset

by
C. Kenneth Meyer and Sara Kurovski

It was Amy Greene's favorite day of the year, the day the summer interns started work at the Braxston Pubic Engineering and Consulting Group (BPECG) where she had worked for the past five years. This year, Amy was charged once more with overseeing the experiences that the interns would receive. BPECG was a respected engineering company in the area and received numerous applications from engineers from across the country who sought employment there. BPECG was an obvious draw for those engineering students who wish to launch their careers in a prestigious firm with a national reputation.

This year, Amy would supervise the interns selected to work at her company — interns who were by objective standards among the best and the brightest students at the neighboring major state universities. To be selected as a Braxston intern was a special honor since the company had a very competitive program and was able to choose from a stable of extremely qualified applicants.

The interns placed at BPECG worked during their summer vacations, were paid fifteen dollars an hour, and were expected to work at least 40 hours per week. In turn, the interns received college credit (three hours) for their experience and were required to write a paper that detailed what they did and how it contributed to their learning in their specific field of engineering-- mechanical, electrical, environmental, or chemical. In anticipation of her new "study" Amy had saved up a host of things to do and projects to be completed for her new charges.

Christina Kimball received one of the prized internships at BPECG. She was excited and nervous when she came to engineering office and knocked on Amy's office door. It seemed like minutes had gone by before Amy looked up from what she was doing and acknowledged her. She felt so awkward just standing in front of an open door and not being "properly" received. After five or so seconds had elapsed, Amy slowly turned toward the door, and looking up she said, "You must be my intern for the summer." Assertively, Christina stepped forward and courageously said: "My name is Christina and I'm so ex--" but before she could finish, Amy interrupted her.

"That's great," Amy somberly said, looking back down to what she had been reading. "Your cubicle is around the corner and there's a stack of files. You need to make two copies of each file, mail

Case 12: Interns: An Underutilized Asset

one to each of the clients that is listed on the letter and file the other one. It should take you about two days to do that. Take your half-hour lunch break whenever you would like."

Christina exited Amy's office quickly, determined to impress her "boss" and ready to get her task done in less than the expected two days. Christina had heard rumors from other interns that they did not get to do actual engineering work when interning at Braxston, but she was going to be different and she knew the value of having BPECG's name on her resume. Delighted by her selection, but not surprised since she was the top student in her class, she was anxious to get some "applied experience" and then move on to graduate. But now, she had to get through this summer internship. She figured that during the first week she would do some assistant type activities and then after that she would get to work on some small projects. After Christina got settled into her cubicle, she quickly began working on the large stacks of files that swamped her desk.

Four weeks later Amy was humming to herself as she entered her office; she spotted Christina at her cubicle, "Is my coffee on my desk?" "Yes ma'am," Christina responded.

It had been nearly a month and Christina was still doing pedestrian kinds organizing, filing, and "light house-keeping" activities such as getting coffee for Amy, faxing papers, making copies, pulling files, running to the post office to purchase supplies and mail items, and even putting all of the books and manuals in Amy's office in alphabetical order. She was beginning to wonder if she could stand to spend a summer doing such routine and monotonous errands—after all, she mumbled to herself, "I am well on the way to becoming an engineer and would like to have some experience on an actual project. This internship has become so boring. Why can't I at least proof a plan or a report, or something that would use my skills and talents?"

Later that day Amy went to lunch with a fellow colleague. Sam was one of the lead engineers at a manufacturing plant in the area. As friends, they tried to get together every once in a while to catch up and brag about the projects that they could showcase. Amy sat and waited for Sam for 15 minutes before he arrived for their luncheon date. "I was beginning to think you forgot," Amy said in an annoyed voice. "Sorry, my summer intern was giving a presentation to the team about his project. He has so many ideas and concepts that we all lost track of time," Sam replied.

"What, on how to make copies more effectively?" Amy responded sarcastically. "No," Sam replied sharply. "He is from the Department of Natural Resources Pollution Prevention Intern Program. Some of his ideas are going to save us big bucks in the long run." Sam went on to explain how her company had applied to have an intern work for his firm. The intern's job was to first monitor how the company operates and then evaluate the processes used in terms of solid waste reduction, hazardous waste reduction, water conservation, water quality reduction or improvement, air quality improvement, energy reduction, and greenhouse gas emission reduction. "When our intern presented today, he had pinpointed the areas we could "cut some fat" out of our operations, what the upfront costs would be to implement some of the ideas, how long it take to realize some cost savings, and how much we could save in the long run! He is going to benefit our company greatly—it's simply amazing! Not to mention we will have a much better impact on the environment. Imagine, an intern saving us hundreds of thousands of dollars over the course of a year."

Case 12: Interns: An Underutilized Asset

Amy sat and pondered what Sam was telling her during the rest of the lunch. Sam noticed that Amy seemed distracted, but did not comment on her inattentiveness. By the time Amy arrived back at her office, she realized how much money she was potentially costing BPECG by not allowing her and the other summer interns to excel in those areas where they had knowledge and interest. She went straight into her office and shut the door, and once more examined the resumes of the selected interns, beginning with Christina's.

As she went through the "2009 Pollution Prevention Intern Program Case Summaries" that the Department of Natural Resources (DNR) representative left with her, she was astonished to see how the interests and skills of the engineering students had been properly matched with the organizational needs of diverse organizations drawn from the three economic sectors (private, public and non-profit). Amy found the metrics used by the DNR and EPA in assessing the impact which the interns had on the sponsoring organizations particularly intriguing. Of course, the interns had a firm grasp on the types of problems they were prepared to research since they were advanced undergraduate engineering students from colleges and universities within the state and they personally wanted to make a difference in the general areas of economic and environmental sustainability. Specifically, they understood that they would be gaining real-life, hands-on, experiential based knowledge—not just serving as office "handy-persons," as they went about their business of research and making recommendations that would improve the efficiency of operations and industrial processes.

As Amy read through the intern report, she was flabbergasted to learn that the cumulative savings realized from the intern recommendations in the areas of waste reduction (hazardous and solid), water conservation, and reduction/diversion of air pollutants and greenhouse gases, etc. was much higher than she could ever have imagined — $1,279,642. She also read with eagerness about the ten year history of actual savings (2001-2009) from the internship program and could hardly believe that $58,653,401 had been realized through cost saving measures recommended by the engineering students. In terms of reduction in water use alone, over one billion gallons had been realized and in the area of waste management, nearly 320 tons had been averted from the waste stream including over one million gallons of hazardous waste. Further reduction was found in mercury abatement (48,812 grams) and energy use in KWH (258,669,685) and in THERMS (16,576,117). Last, the intern recommendations for 2009, in tons of air pollution diverted for SO_2 (103), CO (282.27), NO_x (206.98), VOC (15.51), and PM (78.04) were acknowledged. In terms of greenhouse gases (GHG) diverted in tons the numbers were equally impressive: CO_2 (23,766), CH_4 (9,061), N_2O (3,987) and CFC (344).

She was anxious to learn more about some of the actual student projects and see how the interns contributed to pollution prevention, abatement and reduction, the types of waste streams reduced, and improvements they made on lowering operation costs. She singled out three projects that had been researched in public and non-profit organizations. She felt that if net efficiencies could be achieved in these sectors, it would be much easier to identify cost and energy saving measures in manufacturing and industrial environments.

Allen Memorial Hospital (AMH): A 85 year old hospital with about 820,00 square foot structure that cared for about 50,000 patients a year. AMH was like other hospitals in the state and produced vast amount of solid waste. The chemical engineering student, Meredith, was charged with reducing biohazard waste and conducting other waste management assessments. In the final analysis, she found that 13 percent of the waste stream was made of regulated medical waste — not the 3-5 percent suggested by the Centers for Disease Control and Prevention (CDC). She found innovative ways to reduce the stream by 38 percent and save the hospital $25,177 yearly: education of clinical staff, location of biohazard containers, and instructive signage. Also, she found ways to produce electrical savings by replacing incandescent bulbs with fluorescent ones and the use of LED exit signs. Further, she introduced a solvent recycling system that cut the cost of purchasing and disposing of *xylene* by 95 percent — a hazardous waste. The biohazard waste reduction plan that she developed will save AMH about $25,000 annually.

The City of Pella, Iowa: This city has operated its own municipal coal fueled power plant since 1911 and generated about 38 MW on site, augmented by 28 MW produced in its adjacent diesel powered plant. Andrew, a mechanical engineering student, assessed the performance level of the plant and analyzed ways that would produce water and chemical savings in the cooling and boiling operations. In an effort to reduce pollution, save energy, and reduce water consumption, he recommended boiler upgrades, variable frequency drives (VFD) for pumps and fans, cogeneration (biomass from adjacent manufacturing facilities), lighting upgrades, evaporator replacement, and insulation programs. The lighting upgrades will produce about $16,000 in annual savings for the city and if the cogeneration plan was implemented, the city would save approximately $829,000 a year.

Nebraska Medical Center (NMC): The Nebraska Medical Center is located in Omaha and is the largest hospital in the state. It has 14 buildings with two million square feet of space. It has a staff of 5,000 that complements 1,000 physicians. David, a mechanical engineering intern, assessed the way energy use could be reduced and found that a savings of $39,400 or a 695,400 KWH reduction could be realized on a yearly basis. Simply, T12 fluorescent bulbs were replaced with T8 fixtures, and by making changes that improved the lighting adequacy in hallways, offices and, among other areas, examination rooms, cost savings could be realized. By the replacement of older fluorescent technologies with new ones (T8), maintenance and inventory costs, as well as energy costs were sharply cut, in some instances up to 50 percent.

Amy had just had an "aha!" moment. Her idea of a successful internship experience had drastically changed. Under her direction, Amy created a work team and charged it with developing a plan outlining what interns might be assigned to do during their time at Braxston. For the first time, she solicited suggestions and ideas from the other lead engineers, interns, and other Braxston employees. She was on a mission to create a program that would not only provide a genuine, valuable engineering internship experience for the student, but one that would provide a healthy Return on Investment (ROI) for the Braxston Group.

Case 12: Interns: An Underutilized Asset

Questions and Instructions:

1. Analyze the abbreviated **Internship Handbook** which appears in **Exhibit 1**. Please note that it includes a component that deals with an introduction to undergraduate and graduate internship programs based on several guidelines provided by the national Association of Schools of Public Affairs and Administration (NASPAA); purposes of the Internship Program; the administration of the internship program; the academic component; placement of interns; work scheduling and hours; intern supervision; integration of interns into the organizational culture; intern and employer obligations; compensation; and internship evaluation.

2. Please examine the **Intern Evaluation Form** (see **Exhibit 2**) and determine if any additions, deletions or modifications are required. If so, please prepare an alternative form that you believe would more effectively evaluate the internship experience. Please discuss this form with members of your agency or department and based on their experiences with supervising and evaluating internship experiences, obtain their feedback.

3. A **Memorandum of Understanding** (MOU) is normally entered into between the academic institution and the partnering organization for a formal internship program (see **Exhibit 3**). Once more, examine the MOU and indicate if it has any deficiencies that should be addressed. Also, indicate those aspects of the MOU which you believe will add to the overall quality of the internship experience. Please be specific.

4. After reviewing Exhibits 1, 2, and 3, please prepare an internship or field experience for your own organization. The internships presented in the case study deal with the technical application of engineering principles to organizational processes and activities. However, given the background of students majoring in public administration, public affairs, and public policy, what kind of valid learning experiences would you be able to develop in your agency or department? Please be specific. Please discuss the prospects of having a well-developed internship program with others in your organization. Next, map out a plan that presents an intern description, including application and selection criteria, work/project assignment and supervision responsibilities, and among other components, a final organizational report. You may wish to include additional factors that would make up your "model of an idealized internship program." Please be specific.

Case 12: Interns: An Underutilized Asset

Exhibit 1. The State University Intern to Work Program

The State University Intern to Work Program

Universities and colleges that grant degrees in public administration and related fields (political science, management, sociology, etc.) usually require that students obtain practical field experience in one of the three sectors (public, non-profit, or private) prior to graduation. The actual experiential component is usually called an internship or field experience. In 1978, the National Association of Schools of Public Affairs and Administration (NASPAA) published its "Public Service Internship Guidelines," which membership institutions have found helpful.

Over the years, State University has drawn upon the philosophy, methods, and language of many internship programs in other colleges and schools, departments and programs in public affairs and administration, as well as academic and professional materials. Our aim is to provide prospective interns and intern supervisors in these different sectors with an overarching view of those orientations and practices which should guide our graduate and undergraduate experiential learning programs.

Internship Purpose:

The mission of the department is to bring "... the world into the classroom and classroom into the world." This can be done through a variety of experiential learning programs, especially an internship, in which students gain realistic exposure to complex, formal organizational and bureaucratic environments. This experience assists in developing an awareness of the internal dynamics of an agency or department and of the values and attitudes of its employees regarding their clients, superiors, and team associates. Thus, the internship becomes an essential component of the public service student's professional and academic education — a major building block in the formation of a professional degree.

State University's internship program provides a structured introduction to a practical learning experience. Throughout the experience, the student gets acquainted with "hands-on" work activities in a supportive learning environment. As such, the internship provides a needed bridge between the world of academia and the applied world of the public administrator. Students who have garnered such an experience are better able to assess which personal competencies they need to improve upon or develop — especially for those who have not worked in a major agency or department in one of the sectors.

The internship relationship is equally important in so far as the student, university and supporting agency all benefit from the experience. In brief, a collaborative, reciprocal, and mutually beneficial relationship is established between all those involved in the internship program. Interns bring to the program a comparatively high level of general skills in management, policy, methods of analysis, statistics, and economic and financial understandings. In an augmentative manner, the internship provides the sponsoring agency with a chance to diversify the mixture of its staff and assign research and evaluation projects that ordinarily might not be accomplished. The internship supervisor also interacts directly and regularly with the intern and becomes a participant in preparing future public managers in the complexity and uncertainty of competing values and roles which public administrators often find themselves.

For the department and university, the internship provides a critically important link to the professional community. The experiential learning program contributes to the overall quality of the educational experience at State University and establishes a connection between the academic department (professors and students), and managers/analysts in their effort to jointly provide a meaningful learning experience and actually use the "...world as a learning resource."

Internship Supervision:

Supervision, coaching and mentoring of the internship involves the agency manager and the internship coordinator from State University. Normally, the agency supervisor is designated by the sponsoring agency and is responsible for making work assignments, evaluating the work products/reports of the intern, and assessing the progress which the intern is making. The agency supervisor is asked to serve as a mentor or coach and discuss with the intern the essential factors associated with different management strategies and assessment approaches associated with the assigned duties and projects. It is expected that the intern will become, as more experience is acquired, a fully-functioning member of the sponsoring agency, and exercise a modicum of leadership, decision-making, and managerial skills. Once more, a joint relationship should be established between agency manager and internship so that in a spirit of "trust and confidence," a mutual assessment of one-another can take place and they can both develop an awareness of the knowledge, skills and abilities, of the intern and degree to which administration discretion and responsibility might be properly delegated. Of course, this process takes time and as the manager, intern and internship coordinator evaluate the experiential knowledge gained and the maturity developed.

This supervisory relationship is the lynchpin of the internship program. It requires the creation and maintenance of a reliable and regular open channel of communication between the three parties (intern, supervisor, and coordinator). Mutual interests and expectations must be candidly discussed along with making regular assessments of the progress and problems, if any, in the performance of the individual tasks (assignments) and projects which the intern is performing. In this type of open, honest communication and trusting environment, the intern may be most appropriately monitored and evaluated and the capabilities and limits of the intern established. After all, the intern is in the program to gain a valuable learning experience and be appropriately supervised and evaluated. Although there is no single best way to manage interns, there is a balance that can be established between near-continuous, close supervision or monitoring of all activities to virtual absence of guidance and supervisory attention to daily activities. It is advisable to establish joint goal-setting meetings between the intern and agency manager so that a discussion of the learning and performance objectives can be discussed and evaluated. These meetings should be followed by periodic regular work-progress reviews and an in-depth exit interview at the conclusion of the internship.

Since the intention of the internship is educational in nature, the agency is encouraged, to the extent possible and practical, to conduct an orientation session similar to the orientation given new hires, in which the intern is introduced to persons with whom they will be working (administrative support personnel) and a historical overview of the agency and its objectives. It is important to include the intern in all meetings related to the assigned activities and areas of responsibility. This requires that the intern becomes a recognized member of the work group and has the needed resources (facilities, desk, computer, etc.,) to do their work.

Learning Objectives:

Interns are expected to prepare statements of learning objectives at the beginning of their experience. These objectives should be mutually developed and agreed upon by the agency manager, internship coordinator and the intern. They become essential in providing a structure and in assessing the progress that the intern is making. The performance objectives that are developed will specify what the intern will do on the job and also form a basis for internship evaluation at the conclusion of the experience. The mutual understandings associated with this collaborative process are essential to the success of the experiential learning process. In brief, the learning objectives should identify what the intern is expected to be able to do as a result of the internship experience; address how the intern expects to acquire the knowledge, skills, or abilities identified as an objective; and how the intern will acknowledge and demonstrate that the objective(s) have been accomplished. These statements (objectives) should be precise, specific and unambiguous. Verbs such as write, identify, state, solve, and compare, are preferable to appreciate, familiarize and understand. Once the learning objectives and performance objectives are prepared and jointly agreed upon, the means by which they will be accomplished may be specified. For example, if one of the intern's learning objective is to be able to identify the allocation of human and financial resources in the agency, then, the intern and agency manager will jointly determine how this can be best accomplished (e.g., inspection of the budget, position allocation statement, conversations with agency administrators, etc.).

Additionally, as mentor, the agency manager should provide frequent feedback regarding the intern's job performance. This may take the form of informal comments and observations or the supervisor may schedule one or more work-progress review with the intern to serve as a helper, coach or facilitator. At the third or fourth week of the internship it is recommended that a joint meeting be scheduled between the intern and agency manager at which time the intern's learning and performance objectives are reviewed and assessed. At this time, the intern should be encouraged to discuss any performance problems that might be present and provide the supervisor with a self-assessment of the progress which is being made toward meeting the agreed upon learning and performance objectives. Periodically, during the internship, these joint meetings should be scheduled in which progress is assessed and administrative strengths and deficiencies can be addressed. At these meetings it is appropriate to also discuss career options and developmental strategies.

Intern and Employer Obligations:

There are a few essential intern obligations that must be met:
1. Secure the agency manager's and intern coordinator's consent to beginning and ending dates, hours of work, and vacations;

2. Develop written learning and performance objectives for the internship experience;

3. Perform the duties required by the employer in a responsible, professional and timely manner;

4. Evaluate the job experience in terms of the benefits and learning acquired; and

5. Complete the academic component of the internship program.

Employers are asked to:
1. Provide conscientious supervision (mentoring and coaching) and developmental consultation and communication;

2. Assist the intern in the development of learning and performance objectives;

3. Provide work experience that is appropriate to the preparation and sophistication of the intern and calculated to realize the intern's learning objectives;

4. Provide the intern with a constructive discussion of the intern's learning objectives and complete an exit interview upon the completion of the internship; and

5. Provide a written evaluation of the intern's performance, including recommendations for job performance and personal growth and development.

Case 12: Interns: An Underutilized Asset

Exhibit 2. Intern Evaluation Form

Intern Evaluation Form

Instructions: Using the form below, please provide an evaluation of the student who interned with your organization. The intern should be compared with other students of comparable academic level, with other personnel assigned the same or similarly classified jobs, or with individual standards (whichever you agreed upon). This information will assist the coordinator of the Professional Intern Program in determining the overall effectiveness of the internship experience and in grading the intern for academic credit. The department greatly appreciates your cooperation and assistance in this matter and this type of experience could not be provided if organizations like your own did not participate in the program.

A stamped, addressed envelope is provided for your convenience in returning this evaluation. If you have any questions, comments, or suggestions, please email or call me and I will immediately respond.

Part I: Ability and Application

Attitude Toward Work (enthusiasm, cooperativeness, willingness):

( ) enthusiastic; outstanding cooperation; tries new ideas; responds readily to constructive criticism
( ) responsive; cooperates well; meets others more than half-way; responds to constructive criticism
( ) usually cooperates; does not resist new ideas or constructive criticism
( ) uncooperative; resents new ideas and constructive criticism; displays little interest

Dependability (willingness to accept responsibility; to follow through):

( ) outstanding ability to perform with little supervision
( ) willing and able to accept responsibility; little checking required
( ) usually follows instructions; normal follow up
( ) refuses or unable to carry responsibilities; needs constant follow up

Quantity of Work (output of work; performance speed):

( ) works consistently and with excellent output
( ) works consistently with above average output
( ) maintains group average output
( ) below average output; slow

Writing Skills (organization, grammar, usage, punctuations, sensitivity to audience):

( ) outstanding
( ) above average
( ) average

Case 12: Interns: An Underutilized Asset

( ) below average
( ) no opportunity to observe

Relations with Others (ability to work in groups, interpersonal skills, sensitivity to others needs and to informal norms of the office):

( ) exceptionally well accepted; fits in, advice is sought
( ) works well with others
( ) gets along satisfactorily
( ) has difficulty working with others
( ) works very poorly with others

Initiative (ability to exercise self-reliance and enterprise):

( ) grasps situation and goes to work without hesitation
( ) works independently often; seldom waits for others
( ) usually waits for instructions; follows others
( ) does only what is specifically instructed to do

Quality of work (accuracy and effectiveness of work; freedom from errors):

( ) consistently good quality; errors are rare
( ) usually good quality; few errors, lateness
( ) passable work if closely supervised
( ) frequent errors; cannot be depended upon to be accurate

Attendance (reliability to be on the job):

( ) always can be relied upon to be at work on time; absent only when real emergency
( ) usually can be relied upon to be at work on time; explained absences occur occasionally
( ) comes in late with reasonable excuses; fairly frequent explained absences
( ) frequent unexplained lateness and/or absences

Speaking Skills (organization, sensitivity to audience, time constraints, vocabulary):

( ) outstanding
( ) above average
( ) average
( ) below average
( ) no opportunity to observe

Case 12: Interns: An Underutilized Asset

Job Knowledge (technical knowledge of job; ability to apply it):

( ) knows job thoroughly; rarely needs help
( ) knows job well; seldom needs help
( ) knows job fairly well; requires instructions
( ) little knowledge of job; requires constant help

Part II: Summary Evaluation

    A. Is this intern the type of employee you would consider hiring if he/she interviewed for a position?

( ) yes, definitely   ( ) no, probably not   ( ) not certain
( ) yes, possibly   ( ) no, definitely not

    B. If this intern were your student, what letter grade would you award for his/her work performance?

……F……D……C……B……A……

    C. Would you care to add any additional comments or observations concerning the job performance of the intern?

    D. What comments or observations would you care to make concerning the developmental needs of the intern if he/she is to be an effective manager?

(Please print)

Name of Intern: _____ Date Completed: _____

Name of Supervisor: _____

Job Title: _____

Agency or Organization: _____

Signature: _____

Case 12: Interns: An Underutilized Asset

Exhibit 3: Memorandum of Understanding (MOU) for State Professional Intern Program

Memorandum of Understanding (MOU) for State Professional Intern Program

Professional Intern Program

Department of Public Administration and Public Affairs

Date_____

Student's Name_____ Phone_____

Address_____ City, State, Zip_____

Employer_____ Internship Title _____

Intern's Site Supervisor & Title_____

Faculty Sponsor_____Deparment_____Phone_____

Beginning Date_____ Completion Date_____

Hours per week_____ Work Schedule _____

If credit is desired, Course Number & Title_____ Credit Hours____

Intern's Major Responsibilities:
_____
_____
_____

Learning objectives (be specific):
_____
_____
_____

Academic Requirements (journal, papers, reports, readings, meeting with faculty):
_____
_____
_____

Evaluation by faculty sponsor will be based on:
_____
_____
_____

Case 12: Interns: An Underutilized Asset

Type of supervision (daily, scheduled conference, conference as needed, or…):
_____
_____
_____

Service training and/or orientation to be provided by employer:
_____
_____
_____

Additional conditions agreed to:
_____
_____
_____

General Responsibilities of Intern and Coordinator

    A. The student agrees to comply with the policies of the employing organization, to attend all required orientations, in-service and staff meetings.

    B. The student will notify his/her work supervisor if unable to work as scheduled.

    C. The employer agrees to provide the student with orientation and supervision necessary to carry out the above specified responsibilities.

    D. The internship will not be terminated before the specified date by either the student or employer until the faculty sponsor has been notified.

This memorandum has been reviewed and agreed to by:

Student_____ Date_____

Faculty Sponsor_____ Date_____

Supervisor_____ Date_____

Each of the above will be provided with a copy of this agreement. The original will be kept on file in the Department of Public Administration and Public Affairs.

If major changes are made in any of the intern's responsibilities, student objectives, or academic requirements, all participants, including the Department of Public Administration and Public Affairs, must be notified in writing.

Case 12: Interns: An Underutilized Asset
Name:

Case Log and Administrative Journal Entry

This case analysis and learning assessment is printed on perforated pages and may be removed from the book for evaluation purposes.

Case Analysis:
Major case concepts and theories identified:

What is the relevance of the concepts, theories, ideas and techniques presented in the case to that of public management?

Facts — what do we know *for sure* about the case? Please list.

Who is involved in the case (people, departments, agencies, units, etc.)? Were the problems of an "intra/interagency" nature? Be specific.

Are there any rules, laws, regulations or standard operating procedures identified in the case study that might limit decision-making? If so, what are they?

Are there any clues presented in the case as to the major actor's interests, needs, motivations and personalities? If so, please list them.

Case 12: Interns: An Underutilized Asset

Learning Assessment:
What do the administrative theories presented in this case mean to you as an administrator?

How can this learning be put to use outside the classroom? Are there any problems you envision during the implementation phase?

Several possible courses of action were identified during the class discussion. Which action was considered to be most practical by the group? Which was deemed most feasible? Based on your personal experience, did the group reach a conclusion that was desirable, feasible, and practical? Please explain why or why not.

Did the group reach a decision that would solve the problem on a short-term or long-term basis? Please explain.

What could you have done to receive more learning value from this case?

13

Lingering 9/11 Concerns

by
C. Kenneth Meyer and Gina DeVoogd

Edward Greenwood, was a human resource generalist for the state's Medicaid program, and assigned to work in a satellite office of the agency the day the terrorists attacked the twin towers of the World Trade Center (WTC) and the mammoth, invulnerable Pentagon. These events changed his view on safety and ignited his concerns about his own security — something he never felt he had to deal with before, because he had always assumed that all was well on the shore and home fronts and America was free from outside attack. Today, however, he speaks with specificity and authority about failed and successful bombings in other parts of the world.

Since the September 11, 2001, date, Edward had a protracted interest in the type and magnitude of terrorist acts worldwide and in casual conversation felt comfortable reciting with ease the extensive litany of terrorist acts against American installations, ships and other interests, and incidents against countries allied with the United States worldwide. The problem Greenwood is facing now is not at such a grandiose level where he had to deal with the causes and effects of international terrorism. Instead, his present management dilemma was focused on Muhammad Qazsi, an employee who raised suspicions due to his behavior during the time that America came under attack.

When Edward Greenwood returned to the central office on September 12, 2001, Wednesday, the day after the fatal attacks in New York City and Washington, D.C., Nancy Sparks, the director of human resources told him that Muhammad Qazsi had been absent from work for three days and had failed to notify the office of his absenteeism from work. The audit manager, Jackie Price, a vigilant and detail oriented professional, looked up Muhammad's home telephone number, dialed it, but to no effect. She received a voice recording, she told Sparks, that stated "…the number dialed was no longer in service!"

Not easily dissuaded by a recorded message, she accessed Qazsi's employment file and discovered he was absent from work on the Friday last, and Monday and Tuesday — the three workdays that immediately preceded the terrorist attack. As Price continued to scour Muhammad's record, she was stunned to find that he was only able to work in the United States with the approval of the Immigration and Naturalization Services (INS), and his social security card specified this important and limiting restriction. Also, Jackie Price found out that not all of the required documents were garnered from Qazsi by the Office of Compensation and Benefits when he was first hired by the state.

Case 13: Lingering 9/11 Concerns

Upon learning the details, Nancy Sparks informed Edward Greenwood of her concern about Muhammad's employment status with the state. She said, "Muhammad's absence from work without permission is a serious problem in its own right." She went on to say, "What really troubles me is the state of current world events and the fact that we do not have the appropriate INS documents for Qazsi." She concluded, "This is potentially problematic if discovered and publicly revealed. We have a reputation to uphold and it is likely to be damaged by Muhammad Qazsi's behavior."

Edward Greenwood's interest in unearthing Qazsi's "real status" switched from one of general interest to that of suspiciousness. He observed that Mr. Qazsi had a good work history and that he had a reputation for showing up for work promptly and daily and for him to stop coming to work the week before the WTC tragedy raised serious doubts in his mind. The fact that he did not pick up his final check, that the INS had not sent his work permit to the office, and that he could not be reached by phone or mail was further disconcerting. Greenwood said to Sparks, "Muhammad's behavior is very suspicious. Do you think we should call the Federal Bureau of Investigation or the INS and have them check this situation out?" Sparks candidly responded, "It does look suspicious, but let's wait and see what happens!"

Edward Greenwood felt that Sparks' concerns were largely over issues of "personal survival" and she did not want her failure to get complete documentation from Qazsi to jeopardize her office or more importantly her own career. Sparks, however, informed Greenwood that the state's Attorney General had been contacted in an effort to engage in damage control over the missing INS documentation and she was told to secure, if possible, Muhammad's complete personnel file. She also told Greenwood that she had secured Qazsi's payroll check and would personally hold it until Muhammad showed up and the required exit interview had been concluded.

Greenwood requested the establishment of a time line on Muhammad Qazsi's employment status from September 11 onward. Jackie Price put together the following list of events that had transpired:

Timeline on Muhammad Qazsi's Contacts with the Medicaid Office

9-13-2001   Muhammad Qazsi called Jackie Price and asked for his last pay check and indicated he did not come to work because of concerns he had over the WTC attack. He said he would pick up his check on Friday, 9-14-2001. He also indicated he had relocated in town and did not have a phone number or address that he could provide presently. Qazsi was informed that the exit interview must be completed before he would receive his final payroll check.

9-14-2001   Muhammad Qazsi (MQ) did not come into the Medicaid Office as promised.

9-17-2001   No contact with MQ

9-18-2001   No contact with MQ

Case 13: Lingering 9/11 Concerns

9-19-2001   Jackie Price initiated contact with the International Students Office at the area community college and asked about Muhammad's Qazsi's student status, telephone number, and mailing address. Price was told that he was a student and that the other information could not be released.

9-20-2001   No contact with MQ

9-21-2001   No contact with MQ

The whereabouts of Qazsi raised additional concerns that Greenwood needed to address. State employees who separate, regardless of reason, must complete the exit interview, turn in their employee badge, and building keys. The badge and keys would enable the terminated employee to gain access to the several building that housed the Medicaid offices and if not secured would present a serious breach in security. Of course, Greenwood immediately contacted the Office of Information and Technology and the security department and had Qazsi's security and access codes revoked.

In an "off the record" impromptu meeting with Greenwood in the hallway, Sparks commented with anguish that if someone's name was Ali or Muhammad, they would be looked upon with a suspicious eye, although they might well be decent, patriotic and outstanding citizens of the United States. She also stated that racial and ethnic profiling was a real and present danger that threatened the civil and human rights of non-majority groups in America, and that this type of profiling would hardly take place if your name was Johnson, Nelson, Olson or Edwards, and that caution should not be thrown to the winds.

A full week had passed since the office had any contact with Qazsi. Then, on Monday of the following week, Muhammad called Sparks and indicated that his college courses and workload kept him from securing his check as promised. Sparks told him that he must bring with him the needed documentation and a telephone number and email address if she needed to contact him at the college. As in the past, Muhammad promised to bring the documents to her office the next day. Tuesday arrived and passed and Muhammad was once more a "no-show' in human resources. Diligently, Sparks left a message for Qazsi to call her, but received no call back or response.

Greenwood's suspiciousness continued to escalate and again he approached Sparks and said, "I really think we need to call the INS and let them know about Muhammad's activities. He is probably just a college student with other things on his mind, but I'm concerned about the fact that he has not shown up with the required documents and has not asked for his last check. Don't college students need money? Don't you think we need to report this incident and his behavior to someone?"

To Greenwood's chagrin, Sparks did not look up from the computer screen. She did not say a single word. What Greenwood had just stated had been completely ignored, or so it seemed.

Greenwood inquired as to what he should do next. On one hand, he knew how he would feel if a terrorist event did occur, especially if Qazsi was involved. He would feel particularly guilty if he had not reported him and his suspicious activities to anyone in the INS or in a position of governmental authority.

Case 13: Lingering 9/11 Concerns

On the other hand, he knew his office did not have the appropriate documentation on Muhammad and by contacting someone, he could get the department in serious trouble. He wanted to, as an act of last resort, discuss the matter with Spark's manager, but felt uncomfortable doing so for that meant he had to "jump the chain" and Nancy Sparks would certainly question his loyalty in the future.

Questions and Instructions:

1. Do you believe that Edward Greenwood's suspiciousness and paranoia about Muhammad Qazsi was justified, or was a not so thinly veiled example of "racial and ethnic profiling?" Please elaborate. Were the fears expressed by those in management positions justifiable from any perspective given the known facts of this case? Please explain.

2. If you were in Nancy Sparks' position, would you have approached the absenteeism issue similarly or differently? If not, why not? Is yes, justify your answer.

3. Generally, what documents ideally should have been present in Muhammad Qazsi's employment file when Jackie Price conducted an audit? Please make a checklist of required items.

4. Was the establishment of a timeline helpful in resolving this case? If not, what additional information would you have found helpful? Please explain.

5. In the final analysis, did Nancy Sparks accurately summarize in her impromptu discussion with Greenwood, how the situation would be managed if the person in question did not have what appeared to be an Arabic or Muslim name? Please discuss with your colleagues.

Case 13: Lingering 9/11 Concerns
Name:

Case Log and Administrative Journal Entry

This case analysis and learning assessment is printed on perforated pages and may be removed from the book for evaluation purposes.

Case Analysis:
Major case concepts and theories identified:

What is the relevance of the concepts, theories, ideas and techniques presented in the case to that of public management?

Facts — what do we know *for sure* about the case? Please list.

Who is involved in the case (people, departments, agencies, units, etc.)? Were the problems of an "intra/interagency" nature? Be specific.

Are there any rules, laws, regulations or standard operating procedures identified in the case study that might limit decision-making? If so, what are they?

Are there any clues presented in the case as to the major actor's interests, needs, motivations and personalities? If so, please list them.

Case 13: Lingering 9/11 Concerns

Learning Assessment:
What do the administrative theories presented in this case mean to you as an administrator?

How can this learning be put to use outside the classroom? Are there any problems you envision during the implementation phase?

Several possible courses of action were identified during the class discussion. Which action was considered to be most practical by the group? Which was deemed most feasible? Based on your personal experience, did the group reach a conclusion that was desirable, feasible, and practical? Please explain why or why not.

Did the group reach a decision that would solve the problem on a short-term or long-term basis? Please explain.

What could you have done to receive more learning value from this case?

14

A Hiring Dilemma: Recruitment from In-House Versus from Outside

by
Randy Edwards and C. Kenneth Meyer

The Law Enforcement Bureau of the state Department of Natural Resources (DNR) was comprised of nearly 100 full-time employees, including a chief, assistant chief, six district supervisors, a safety education programs supervisor and 86 field conservation officers, a training coordinator, a snowmobile/ATV program coordinator, a boating education program coordinator and an administrative assistant. There are also 42 seasonal water patrol and ATV enforcement officers.

One of the district supervisors was near retirement age and it was decided that it would be beneficial to hire his replacement early to allow an overlap whereby the outgoing supervisor could help train and familiarize the new, incoming supervisor with the day-to-day tasks of supervising the 14 full-time conservation officers and six seasonal officers in the 16 county district in the northern area of the state. The district budget was approximately $1,471,100.

As assistant chief of the law enforcement division of DNR, Charles McHenry led the selection panel. The interview team was comprised of three men and two women, the Conservation & Recreation division administrator, the assistant division administrator, the bureau chief of the Customer Service Bureau, the chief and assistant chief of the Law Enforcement Bureau). Obviously, the chief and assistant chief were experienced conservation officers, and all members of the panel were seasoned public servants with nearly 85 years of departmental experience and memory. The interviews were conducted on a Friday afternoon.

McHenry had a reputation for fairness and probity and was respected for being a stand-up kind of guy. He prided himself on being honest and his professional integrity was unassailable. He had earned the respect and trust of his colleagues over many years of service and the officers felt he represented their professional and personal interests always! As a career law enforcement officer he was troubled by what he came to believe was an avoidable tension that often surfaced between those in the department who saw the value of filling administrative positions from the outside and those who felt that internal hiring, when done for the right reasons and done properly, epitomized successful career succession planning. His passion for fairness soon was to be put to the test over the recruitment and selection of a public service executive 2 position (a district law enforcement supervisor).

Case 14: A Hiring Dilemma: Recruitment from In-House Versus from Outside

As they whittled down the long list of applicants to a short list of three, they engaged in a timely discussion while making their assessments based on the job description and job qualifications, as shown in **Exhibit 1, Vacancy Announcement, Public Service Executive 2**. As they rifled through the applications, they commented to one another on the subjectivity that was often found when they had to make equivalency ratings between the value given to education and that of relevant experience. The conservation and recreation division administrator laughingly stated that their task "…was like that of a sausage maker. If done right, the final outcome was delectable, but no one would want to eat it if they actually saw how the sausage was made." In short, it was considered to be an imprecise, subjective, and messy enterprise. Ultimately, three qualified finalists were interviewed for the position.

The final top two candidates, John Bevington and Mark Ramsey, varied substantially in terms of the type and years of law enforcement experience that they had garnered and their personal profiles have been abbreviated as follows.

John Bevington's Profile

The most senior of the candidates was John Bevington. He was relocating to the capital city from a large town on the western border of the state. John's wife, Gloria Quade, had just obtained her ultimate career goal as an administrative support staff person at Central State University, located in the capital city. John informed the interview panel that he had left his current position as police chief to enable Gloria to fulfill her own career goals. Coincidentally, for John, the DNR had recently posted the job vacancy for the district supervisor position which was housed in DNR's central office and also located in the capital city.

Bevington informed the panel that he had just resigned his position as Chief of Police of the city of St. John's Bay, a position he had held for seven years. John had excellent credentials and experience in the field of law enforcement and administration. His department was comprised of 161 sworn officers, 47 full time civilian employees and 25 part-time crossing guards, and he managed a $20 million budget. In addition, he directed law enforcement and crime prevention services for a city of nearly 100,000 people, that responded to about 140,000 annual calls for service yearly in a geographic area of 64 square miles. Under his watch, the department had received National Law Enforcement Accreditation during his third year as chief and was approved for re-accreditation a few months ago.

In the five years previous to becoming the police chief, he had served as the county sheriff in the same county, Alfalfa County, where he later became police chief. As sheriff, he managed a staff of 140 full time sworn and civilian personnel and a reserve deputy unit comprised of 30 sworn volunteers. The Sheriff's Department had a budget of nearly $9 million and two jails with a capacity to hold 210 inmates. Alfalfa County had a population of just over 190,000 citizens. John had run unopposed for a third, four-year term when he was recruited to fill the Chief of Police position, and he felt honored that he had been unopposed at the last election.

John also possessed a B.A. degree in Criminal Justice and Psychology from a private in-state college and was also a graduate of the F.B.I. National Academy for Police Executives. Overall, he spent 22 years working his way up through the ranks of St. John's Bay Police Department before running for Sheriff. Earlier, he spent three years in the U.S. Army as an infantry and military police officer.

Case 14: A Hiring Dilemma: Recruitment from In-House Versus from Outside

Committee Discussion

The selection committee felt that John Bevington had scored very high when he answered the panels' questions relating to general law enforcement, management, budgeting and supervisory matters. His 34 years of experience and achievements were impressive and much of this previous experience could be used in advancing the professionalism of the DNR officers.

The panel found it troubling, however, that when asked detailed questions about the DNR and the specific role and responsibilities of the district supervisor (and conservation officers), that Bevington was generally not conversant with the DNR. He freely admitted that he had little knowledge of either its main functions or its organizational structure. He added that his only experiential reference was from the limited camping and boating that he had done over the years, but that neither he nor his wife are avid outdoor enthusiasts. Further, he informed the panel that he had applied for several other job opportunities in the area.

Mark Ramsey's Profile

Conservation officer Mark Ramsey scored the second highest on the selection criteria. Ramsey's experience first began as a seasonal employee with the bureau where he worked in water patrol enforcement at one of the largest state lakes, Blue Angel Lake, before becoming a full-time, permanent employee with DNR. Additionally, he had several years of seasonal experience in the department's Wildlife Bureau trapping turkeys for relocation and working waterfowl check stations. Mark had a passion for and a good understanding of the state's natural resources. He was also an active hunter, angler, boater and had substantial experience working with several conservation stakeholder organizations — groups that respected and trusted his judgments. Overall, he had been a state conservation officer for eleven years and his experience was further bolstered by the bachelor's degree in biology that he earned from the state's major university.

During his tenure with the DNR, Mark had distinguished himself in a number of areas and had received numerous accolades from a variety of private and public entities. He was among the top performing officers in the bureau and had been recognized by one of the largest constituency groups as their selection for Outstanding Conservation Officer of the Year. The department had also twice recognized him for Outstanding Performance and Meritorious Service and he was routinely involved with making major arrests in the fish and wildlife areas.

In addition to being well liked, he was recognized by his peers for his extraordinary people skills and congeniality. Over the years, he was present at a number of fatal boating accidents and drowning cases and during these tragic events, had worked closely with the immediate family members and was known for his empathy. Family members had informed central office by letters of thanks and commendation for his kind demeanor, professionalism and compassion — traits which were also acknowledged the director of the DNR.

Case 14: A Hiring Dilemma: Recruitment from In-House Versus from Outside

Mark had a thorough understanding of state and federal fish and wildlife regulations and was up to date on the personnel and inner workings of the department and the Law Enforcement Bureau. He had attended a large number of in and out-of-state training sessions on a variety of conservation law enforcement topics.

Committee Discussion

Panel members knew that Mark had wanted to become a district supervisor and had worked hard to prepare himself for this promotional opportunity. They knew he had personally asked some of them about what he could do to best prepare himself for career succession, and he had followed their recommendation by taking the twelve mandatory management and supervision courses called the Applied Management Series (AMS).

The committee also noted that Ramsey had spent time with each of the district supervisors, the assistant chief and the chief himself, asking them questions about the role of the supervisor, and posed questions about the pros and cons of the position, what they liked, and how things could be made more efficient and effective. The panel knew from their own dealings with Ramsey, that he was the first to volunteer to come into the central office and fill-in when the current district supervisor was absent. This gave Mark an opportunity to experience first-hand what the supervisor did on a day-to-day basis and learn what was expected in a supervisory role.

The panel made special mention that Mark was selected to participate in the Certified Public Managers (CPM) program that was co-sponsored by the state and a local private college. Before he committed to the program, he personally talked to every DNR employee who had graduated from the program in order to get an insider's view of the breadth, scope and value of the program. During the interview he explained that he was nearing the completion of the seventeen-month program and expounded on the valuable things he had already gleaned from this professional training.

Comparative Panel Assessment

Upon the completion of the interview process, the panel agreed that John Bevington and Mark Ramsey comprised the short list of candidates. The panel had examined their application forms, resumes and asked probing questions that they had agreed to prior to the initiation of the interview process. Now that the personal interviews were conducted, the panel members sat in stone cold silence and waited for Division Administrator Avery to initiate the discussion — a discussion that would soon show a lack of consensus.

It was clear that John Bevington had the needed skills and superior experience lacking in Mark Ramsey and three of the members supported Bevington. Chris Avery, Division Administrator, said, "Bevington is clearly a tried, experienced, and skilled administrator and his package of traits would help the division and department move forward." The rest of the panel gave an affirmative nod for they too felt he clearly had a record of superior law enforcement activity and experience, especially in the area of administrative tasks and responsibilities.

Case 14: A Hiring Dilemma: Recruitment from In-House Versus from Outside

However, as textbooks and experienced leaders are apt to point out, consensus is difficult to reach and that was the case here. Several members felt that the group should move slowly and look more closely on the relative experience of the two candidates. Certainly, while John Bevington possessed some very impressive credentials and had many years of top level supervisory experience, would he be happy in this entry-level supervisory role? What about his experience in the field of conservation enforcement? Although some in the department took a generic view that law enforcement was law enforcement, they were in agreement that this was essential to the job. However, some felt that conservation law enforcement was different in many ways and often even foreign to officers from other law enforcement agencies, at least that had been their collective experience.

Paula Jones, Chief of Customer Service, argued that Bevington's budgetary responsibility would be only a small fraction of what he had worked with in his previous positions, and that he would often find himself taking orders and direction from others who had less experience in law enforcement. Donovan asked, "Will Bevington be able to adapt to this new order especially after having been the boss for so many years?" Again, these comments were met with skepticism by the panel as they paused to ponder the implications of what Donovan had asked.

McHenry broke the silence and said, "John had admitted that he had scant knowledge about the department or how it functions. Although he had a career of experience, he knew nothing about the role of the supervisory position in the DNR nor that of the officers that he would be supervising." Jones agreed and said this was a "... disconcerting fact." She added, "While John is clearly intelligent and capable, don't you believe that more consideration should be given to the need for knowledge of wildlife law enforcement and natural resource protection? Shouldn't this be necessary criteria for a conservation law enforcement *supervisor*?"

McHenry reiterated the major concern that the panel had voiced and asked again if knowledge and understanding of state and federal fish and wildlife laws with their respective nuances, along with the regulations related to all-terrain vehicle and snowmobile operation, boating, trapping and a myriad of other outdoor activities was imperative to success in this field. Then in a firm and assertive voice stated, "Hunting and fishing are highly regulated activities. It takes years to get up to speed on these many, detailed and complex topics and understand their specific applications."

When the panel discussed Mark Ramsey, it was clear that he lacked the budgetary and administrative experience, although the district office that he would work from was actually in the central office of the DNR, and just around the hallway from the budget and finance department. Avery said, "Given Mark's personality, these folks would be delighted to work with him to get him up to speed on division and department budgetary processes and procedures."

Arnold Smith, Chief of the Law Enforcement Bureau, agreed and further muddied the discussion by saying, "The department had been making every effort over the past few years to implement a variety of opportunities for career succession planning for supervisory positions." He added, "We all know that nearly one-half of our supervisory staff will be replaced over the next five years to retirement." Then he added, "Seminars are routinely conducted for those persons who desire to learn more about the roles of supervisors and expectations within the agency. In fact, all of the department supervisory staff are required to attend and complete the AMS program, and applications for the CPM program are growing every year."

A Hiring Dilemma

The panel agreed that the two finalists, Ramsey and Bevington, met equally the minimum requirements for the supervisory position. What had begun to bother them as the discussion unfolded was that Ramsey had been an outstanding, long-term employee who had done virtually everything he could to properly prepare himself for advancement. They wondered if it was fair to pass over him in preference to someone from the outside. And, more importantly what kind of message would this decision send to those who thinking about career progression in the department? Chief Smith stated, "It really bothers me that after an excellent employee gets nearly a dozen years of employment experience, training and professional development in this agency, that the lack of supervisory experience, when it is not specifically required in the job description, should carry so much weight."

After some further discussion, Chris Avery, seeing that consensus would not be found easily, instructed the team to study over the weekend the interview responses, resumes, and the position description as presented in **Exhibit 2**. He quickly added that a decision would be made on Monday morning! Then he concluded the meeting with the following admonition, "I want the candidate selection to be *unanimous*. After all, the group is hiring a *supervisor*."

The meeting was adjourned and a long, stressful weekend of soul searching began.

Monday Morning: Time to Hire

Members of the selection committee were convened around the massive conference table in the executive office and they began to discuss the implications of hiring from within versus hiring from without. McHenry began the discussion by saying, "We are all seasoned employees of the department and we have our own reasons for supporting candidates from the in-house pool rather than the outside pool. In order to kick off the discussion and get our views laid out on the table, I propose that we first list some of the reasons for hiring from inside. Later, we will list the reasons that are supportive of hiring from the outside. Basically, we will use a modified brainstorming process. When we make an argument, if you wish, you may follow it with a brief rationale. So, let's begin."

Elizabeth Donovan, Assistant Division Administrator, began, "I think that hiring from the inside is generally a good idea. It seems to me that it keeps the comfort levels of rank and file employees in the moderate range when an inside hire is made, especially when it is a supervisory position. New supervision brings with it a number of anxiety producing tensions." Jones retorted, "I agree. By promoting from within, we tend to get people who know the workforce, know and understand the kind of work we do, are familiar with the culture and politics of the DNR. That fact alone tends to shorten the learning curve, and makes the transition from supervisor to supervisor proceed more smoothly, quickly and with a minimum of disruption."

Case 14: A Hiring Dilemma: Recruitment from In-House Versus from Outside

Chief Arnold Smith joined the conversation and stated that he agreed with Donovan and Jones and added, "Promotions from within are good in the sense that they reward those employees who have distinguished themselves in their work and work ethic and see that their efforts have not gone unnoticed by higher management." He then said, "What incentive is there to succeed and move up the ladder if the bulk of management new hires come from outside the agency? I believe we can grow good candidates through our training programs and give them the chance to demonstrate that they have the right stuff when it comes to leadership. Don't you think that good leadership begets good leadership traits and behaviors in others?" Several good arguments had been presented and the group looked around the room as it once more fell into complete silence.

Donovan broke the silence and said, "I can see how bringing in a person from the outside might also be beneficial." She elaborated, "Outsiders often bring a fresh view to the workplace; they might have new ideas, an awakened sense of objectivity, and be steeped in more effective ways of doing things. Generally...well...they might just get management and employees out of their comfort zone and paying attention to the type and quality of work that is getting done. Although an outside hire can signal that it's not business as usual, they can truly be agents of change — and that is a good thing."

Avery joined Donovan with a "Yes," and added, "A new person can come into the job without any baggage, eliminating any preconceived notions or facts that people may have about an internal candidate. We should all keep in mind that if the DNR promotes employees that are average or below, this will reflect negatively on our decision-making ability and image we are attempting to create. We have seen it before and we will probably experience it again, that we cannot afford to send a message that only the mediocre need apply. That cannot be our standard."

Paula Jones had waited patiently as the others joined in the discussion and was caught up with what Avery had just said. She stated, "If I might put in my two cents worth, there is no question that it is difficult to build and sustain a competent, positive, innovative and exciting work environment with the same folks over a long period of time. Also, there may be those instances where we have no real "top-notch" internal candidates for a particular position. Of course, in that case, going to the outside is clearly the right thing to do for the betterment of the organization. Promoting people just because they have been in the division a long time or that they happen to be readily available is not a good practice in my view."

McHenry was more engaged in the discussion than during previous committee meetings. He said, "The very first question we have started asking candidates, particularly for supervisory positions, is, 'Specifically, what have you done to prepare yourself for this particular position?' This item can produce results that are very telling. Obviously, we are looking for folks who have tried to not only learn what they can about the specific responsibilities of the position, but also what they have done to truly prepare for career advancement such as taking classes, job shadowing, going to seminars, and the like. I thought we all were in agreement that the agency has attempted to find the right people, with the right skills, for the right job at the right time. Isn't this analogous to getting the right people on the bus as we learned in the book by Jim Collins, *Good to Great*? We know this is not an easy task but it is one of the most essential tasks that any leader can perform."

Case 14: A Hiring Dilemma: Recruitment from In-House Versus from Outside

McHenry's points were generally greeted with nods of appreciation and with a positive acceptance. Then, Chief Smith stated, "In the past, we sometimes hired with the understanding that what Avery just stated could be learned *after* they get the promotion. In my opinion, it's far too late by then. I want to hire supervisors who can come into the job with at least a basic, realistic and practical understanding of the major expectations and fundamentals of supervision, management and leadership. Effectively supervising, managing and leading employees is difficult, particularly when it comes down to those rare instances when disciplinary action must be taken. Many people want to be a supervisor until they get to that level. That's when it gets difficult and uncomfortable. Then this becomes a critical time for the organization and we need able supervisors who can actually do the right things."

Elizabeth Donovan, who had sat quietly and listened intently to her peers, seemed to be agitated with the tone and direction that the discussion had taken. She, like the others on the committee, had come up through the ranks. She assertively stated, "We know what moxie and skills are needed for this position in the northern district. Any new hire, from within or the outside would be assigned and encouraged to take advantage of additional training opportunities once they have been selected. But don't you agree with me that it's nice to see people who have a vision about their future and have taken the initiative and have the foresight to truly prepare themselves for the job they are applying for? At least in my mind's eye, it shows that they've really thought it through and that they are not applying simply because it is an opportunity for more pay and status, and that the position happened to open up at a convenient time."

Division Administrator Avery, now anxious to move the discussion forward, acknowledged the views of his colleagues and attempted to bring a sense of closure to their brief, but revealing, discussion. He said, "I firmly believe that we need to move beyond promoting people simply because they are very good at their current job. One's current job may have very little to do with the skills and competencies necessary to be successful and effective in the role of a supervisor and leader. Obviously, experience is a very valuable tool that will be gained once they're in the job. However, it's very refreshing, even rewarding, to hire people that are forward looking and have the drive, motivation and passion to become better. Being prepared shows real leadership potential in my book! We have all been there before, and frustratingly so, when we have interviewed candidates who have a poorly prepared resume, arrive at the interview knowing little about the position they seek or the organization they desire to join, and we have to spend precious time clearing up their inaccurate notions about the recruitment and selection process or about the tasks and responsibilities and requirements needed to meet the job. I can tell you that I have seen many crash and burn who, had they prepared, might have had a different lifetime of achievement in the DNR."

Case 14: A Hiring Dilemma: Recruitment from In-House Versus from Outside

Questions and Instructions:

1. In his book *Good to Great*, Jim Collins applies business principles to that of government. He focuses on getting the right employees in the organization, and contends that people are not an organization's most important asset rather getting the *right* people is. He emphasizes the need to get the right people on the bus, the wrong people off the bus, and the right people in the right seats on the bus. Utilizing Collins' perspective, which of the two finalists should be given a supervisory seat on the DNR bus? Please explain. Mark Ramsey b/c he has been preparing for this role. He has a knowledge of the wildlife aspect and John was unprepared showing little interest.

2. How does one effectively, fairly and accurately weigh and compare various degrees of practical experience in relationship to the expectations of a particular position? The practical experience has to be in the right place. For example, John has general law enforcement knowledge but this is wildlife specific. People voluntary come to parks and spend money so it takes a different kind of law enforcement.

3. Hiring from the outside can certainly be beneficial. What are some of the potential positive outcomes? Please provide some specific examples.
   Fresh Ideas
   Renewed look at processes
   Sends message that being a warm body in current org doesn't guarantee promotion.

4. What might be some of the negative ramifications of hiring from the outside in this particular case? Please provide several implications. Don't know what you're getting
   Low employee moral
   Training needed
   Mismatch b/w employee/employer

5. How much of a particular type of experience is "enough"? Is it possible to have too much experience for an entry level supervisory position? Is it possible that Bevington was overqualified for the position? Please explain. Yes it is possible b/c they could be biding time until a better position w/ more money. How much experience is enough depends on candidate. For example, my boss would say I have experience to take his position even though I don't on paper.

6. Specifically, what competencies, education and experience factors should be considered in this case? What other criteria might be considered? Why and more importantly, *how*?
   Degrees, Department Leadership training. Supervisory b/c employees are a whole different thing.

7. If you were a member of this interview panel, who would you have selected and for what reasons? Please be specific.
   Mark b/c an employee that prepares and works hard for succession should be rewarded.

Case 14: A Hiring Dilemma: Recruitment from In-House Versus from Outside

Exhibit 1. Vacancy Announcement, Public Service Executive 2 Position

STATE DEPARTMENT OF NATURAL RESOURCES

State Capitol Complex

VACANCY ANNOUNCEMENT 542*

PUBLIC SERVICE EXECUTIVE 2

(District Law Enforcement Supervisor Northern District)

Natural Resources Selective [450]

Salary Range $1,937- $2,996 BiWeekly (Pay Grade 32)

Office Location: **Ewald Office Building**

Travel, both within and outside of the district, and occasionally out-of-state will be required as well as some night, weekend, and work on holidays.

Work Responsibilities: Supervises the work of a professional staff of full-time conservation officers and part-time water patrol/ATV patrol officers by keeping time records, conducting performance evaluations, hiring, terminating, establishing work schedules and assignments, supervises training and administering department policies, procedures and collective bargaining contracts. Directs and monitors activities, progress and status of officers within the law enforcement district and conducts their respective annual performance evaluations. Establishes goals and assignments for staff. Reviews and approves reports of activities of subordinate staff; makes work distribution decisions and is involved in the grievance process. Reviews all reports submitted by subordinates. Makes budget and program recommendations for the district. Administers district cost centers and reviews and approves purchases of equipment, materials, and supplies. Processes and approves appropriate paperwork regarding travel vouchers, claims, AOs, and request for purchase orders. Attends various professional and intergovernmental meetings to increase knowledge of specific programs supervised, remain current on practices and procedures for field operations. Makes recommendations to bureau administration related to personnel matters, policies, procedures and programs. Prepares and maintains reports and files of activities supervised, does law enforcement work as time allows, and gives presentations as required.

Education, Experiences, and Special Requirements:

Graduation from an accredited four year college or university and experience equal to four years of full-time professional level work in program administration, development, management or operations;

OR

an equivalent combination of education and experience substituting experience equal to one year of full-time required work for one year (thirty semester or equivalent hours) of the required undergraduate coursework to a maximum substitution of four years;

OR

substitution of twenty-four (semester or equivalent) hours of graduate level course work in a special program curriculum such as Social Work, Law, Education, Engineering, or Public or Business Administration for each year of the required full-time experience to a maximum

substitution of two years;

OR

employees with <u>current</u> continuous experience in the state executive branch that includes experience equal to one year of full-time work as a Public Service Executive 1 or a comparable management level position.

Necessary Special Requirements:

This is a peace officer position and all applicants, if not already certified, must be eligible for enrollment in the State Law Enforcement Academy (SLEA) basic training program. The following information is a listing of those requirements as set forth by the Academy:

Law Enforcement Academy
CHAPTER 2
MINIMUM STANDARDS FOR LAW ENFORCEMENT OFFICERS

501—2.1(80B) General requirements for law enforcement officers. In no case shall any person hereafter be selected or appointed as a law enforcement officer unless the person:

2.1(1) Is a citizen of the United States and a resident of *the state* or intends to become a resident upon being employed; provided that, with the approval of the state law enforcement academy council, a city located on a state border that is within a standard metropolitan statistical area may allow officers to reside in an adjacent state within that statistical area upon written application by the agency administrator to the council showing substantial reason and documenting undue hardship. Railway special agents who are approved by the commissioner of public safety as special agents of the department shall be exempt from the states residency requirement.

2.1(2) Is 18 years of age at the time of appointment.

2.1(3) Has a valid driver's or chauffeur's license issued by the state. Railway special agents who are approved by the commissioner of public safety as special agents of the department and officers who are

Case 14: A Hiring Dilemma: Recruitment from In-House Versus from Outside

allowed to reside in an adjacent state within a standard metropolitan statistical area shall be required to possess a valid driver's or chauffeur's license.

2.1(4) Is not addicted to drugs or alcohol.

2.1(5) Is of good moral character as determined by a thorough background investigation including a fingerprint search conducted of local, state and national fingerprint files and has not been convicted of a felony or a crime involving moral turpitude. Moral turpitude is defined as an act of baseness, vileness, or depravity in the private and social duties which a person owes to another person, or to society in general, contrary to the accepted and customary rule of right and duty between person and person. It is conduct that is contrary to justice, honesty or good morals. The following nonexclusive list of acts has been held by the courts to involve moral turpitude: income tax evasion, perjury, or its subornation, theft, indecent exposure, sex crimes, conspiracy to commit a crime, defrauding the government and illegal drug sales. Various factors, however, may cause an offense which is generally not regarded as constituting moral turpitude to be regarded as such. The offenses of assault, domestic abuse, or other offenses of domestic violence, stalking, and any offense in which a weapon was used in the commission are crimes involving moral turpitude.

2.1(6) Has successfully passed a physical test adopted by the state law enforcement academy.

2.1(7) Is not by reason of conscience or belief opposed to the use of force, when necessary to fulfill that person's duties.

2.1(8) Is a high school graduate with a diploma, or possesses a GED equivalency certificate.

2.1(9) Has an uncorrected vision of not less than 20/100 in both eyes, corrected to 20/20. Has color vision consistent with the occupational demands of law enforcement. Passing any of the following color vision tests indicates that the applicant has color vision abilities consistent with the occupational demands of law enforcement:

Pseudoisochromatic plates tests such as but not limited to: Tokyo Medical College, Ishihara, Standard Pseudoisochromatic Plates, Dvorine, American Optical HRR Plates, American Optical.

Panel tests such as: Farnsworth Dichotomous D-15 Test or any other test designed and documented to identify extreme anomalous trichromatic, dichromatic or monochromatic color vision. Individuals with extreme anomalous trichromatism or monochromasy color vision, as determined through testing, are not eligible to be hired as law enforcement officers in the state.

2.1(10) Has normal hearing in each ear. Hearing is considered normal when, tested by an audiometer, hearing sensitivity thresholds are within 25db measured at 1000Hz, 2000Hz and 3000Hz averaged together.

2.1(11) Is examined by a licensed physician or surgeon and meets the physical requirements necessary to fulfill the responsibilities of a law enforcement officer.

Additional SLEA Requirements:

Applicants may have to:

- Take a mandatory psychological test (Minnesota Multiphasic Personality Inventory).
- Pass the National Police Officer Selection Test (POST) with a minimum score of 70 percent on each of the four sections of the exam. The four sections of the exam are math, reading, grammar, and writing.
- Meet minimum physical agility requirements. Physical agility testing has four different sections: sit and reach, one minute sit up, one minute push up, 1.5 mile run.

APPLICATION PROCEDURES:

Interested applicants must file an application for this position with the Department of Human Resources (DHR) by the close of business on March 31. Application forms may be obtained from any Workforce Development Office or from DHR's Web page. If you have a current application on file (less than 2 years old), you may call DHR and apply for one of these positions, or you may complete and submit the form following the vacancy announcement on DHR's Web page. You must include the job title and job vacancy number on all requests. Applications may also be faxed to DHR.

In addition to the DHR application, applicants MUST submit a brief letter of interest and a complete resume by the closing date to: Director, Department of Human Resources. Materials requested must be received by the closing date. Failure to follow these instructions will disqualify you from consideration for this position.

THIS STATE IS AN EOE/AA EMPLOYER

*Additions, deletions, and modifications have been made to the official document in order to provide a generic example rather than a state specific one. Other changes have been made to the original document for illustration of human resource management principles.

Case 14: A Hiring Dilemma: Recruitment from In-House Versus from Outside

Exhibit 2. Department of Human Resources Position Description

Department of Human Resources	
Position Description	
Position Classification: Public Service Executive 2	Class Title: Law Enforcement Supervisor
Agency: Department of Natural Resources	Position Number: 76421-001
Hours worked: Non-standard work week to include some nights, some weekends, some holidays, some over-night and some out-of-state travel as required. Full time – 40 hours per week min.	
Immediate Supervisor: Arnold Smith - Chief, Law Enforcement Bureau	

Time %	WORK PERFORMED
60 %	a) Provide supervision to 14 conservation officers and six seasonal officers in the 16 counties comprising the Northern District. Ensure that personnel practices, including hiring, firing, promotions, reclassifications, leaves of absence, work schedules and assignments, performance reviews and recognition, training, staff development and exit interviews are conducted in accordance with departmental policy, contractual language and Department of Human Resources processes and rules. Hear grievances at the first step; resolve work related problems, and administer other personnel related policies and procedures, including but not limited to EEO/AA, ADA, FMLA and FLSA; and approve use of sick leave and vacation. Ensure that position descriptions are rewritten as needed to reflect the changing needs of the organization, competencies required and the responsibilities inherent in all positions supervised. Ensure that training is scheduled for employees in accordance with agency and individual needs, and availability of funding. Conduct regular staff meetings. b) Establish and monitor staff performance plans. Assign duties to each staff person and monitor their performance. Determine the need to make staffing reassignments within the geographical district on a long and short-term basis. Prepare and conduct a formal performance appraisal for each employee within the section on an annual basis. Appraisals shall, at a minimum, include a review of competencies, a training and development plan, and appropriate performance goals for the subsequent appraisal period. The training and development plan will be developed in cooperation with each employee and be designed to facilitate the employee's ability to successfully meet or exceed the position's performance expectations and to enhance the employee's professional and personal stature. All new employees will have a three-month and a six-month performance appraisal. c) Serve in the capacity of a role model, and as such, demonstrate conduct exemplifying the department's guiding principles. Utilize management strategies that promote a culture that values diversity, respect for individual differences, teamwork, a customer focus, accountability, a results orientation and ethical business practices, as well as a culture that encourages employee

Case 14: A Hiring Dilemma: Recruitment from In-House Versus from Outside

	cooperation, pride and trust. d) Promote a work environment wherein employees are encouraged and empowered to suggest innovations and improvements to the bureau's programs and services, and to recommend creative and inventive solutions or courses of action to resolve complex problems or issues. e) Facilitate timely and effective communication throughout the bureau's sections to identify collaborative opportunities, minimize duplication of effort, and maximize staff and financial resources.
15 %	a) Assist with the development of annual goals and performance measures for the Law Enforcement Bureau (in conjunction with the bureau chief and assistant chief) that are consistent with the department's strategic plan. Incorporate those goals, means for measuring progress and mechanisms for reviewing and updating goals into the performance expectations for staff. b) Assist with the development and administration of the bureau's annual operating budget in conjunction with the bureau chief and assistant chief. Ensure that expenditures are consistent with the section's goals, the bureau's goals, the division's strategic plan as well as applicable rules, regulations and the Code. c) Make budget and program recommendations for district enforcement operations and administer all cost centers and a district-wide inventory. Review and approve requests for the purchase of equipment and supplies.
10 %	Attend various professional and intergovernmental meetings to increase knowledge of specific programs supervised, remain current on practices and procedures for field operations, and make recommendations to the central office staff related to personnel matters, policies, procedures and programs. Prepare technical articles for publication in professional journals and presentation at meetings.
10 %	a) Coordinate special field projects or operations and respond to requests from subordinates, other departmental personnel, other law enforcement agencies or private citizens regarding specific enforcement practices and problems. b) Carries out specialized high-level assignments involved in the general operating activities of the division, including acting for the assistant chief and chief of the Law Enforcement Bureau in their absences.
5 %	a) Review and evaluate data and make recommendations on facility needs, land acquisition and land development. Make recommendations for changing or improving facilities, lands, waters or enforcement programs. b) Perform other duties as assigned.

Case 14: A Hiring Dilemma: Recruitment from In-House Versus from Outside

	ADDITIONAL REQUIREMENTS: Identify the essential functions that must be performed by the incumbent, with or without reasonable accommodations for disabilities:
	a) Ability to obtain and maintain certification as a peace officer as required by the State Law Enforcement Academy. Ability to traverse, on foot, on uneven terrain in all sorts of weather conditions. Ability to fire both a shotgun and a handgun for qualification and protection purposes. This requires manual dexterity in both hands. Ability to load and unload (trailer/re-trailer) various sizes of boats at a boat ramp. Ability to lift 25 pounds. Ability to ride in or on and/or operate a snowmobile, all-terrain vehicle, boat, and a patrol vehicle (sedan/pickup/sport utility vehicle) for a minimum of four continuous hours under a variety of weather conditions, both day and night. Ability to perform up to bureau training standards and requirements. Ability to possess and maintain a valid driver's license. Ability to travel overnight and work some weekends and some holidays. Ability to enforce and interpret laws and be able to conduct criminal and other investigations. b) Broad knowledge base of DNR programs, policies, operational abilities and regulatory requirements; ability to communicate effectively verbally and in writing with constituents, legislators, Governor's staff, DNR staff, management personnel and other state and federal agencies; ability to work independently with consistent results and minimal supervision; ability to analyze organizational and operational problems and develop timely and economical solutions; ability to plan, organize, and effectively supervise the work of a subordinate staff; knowledge of the principles, techniques and trends of public administration, including financial management, labor relations and other resource management; ability to establish program objectives or performance goals and assess progress toward their achievement; ability to read and interpret complex federal and state laws, rules and regulations; capacity to adjust to change, work pressures or difficult situations without undue stress; ability to use PC based software at a moderate to advanced level. c) Must demonstrate initiative, a customer service and team orientation and display high standards of ethical conduct. Position is a full-time position and as such, requires regular attendance.

Case 14: A Hiring Dilemma: Recruitment from In-House Versus from Outside

Case 14: A Hiring Dilemma: Recruitment from In-House Versus from Outside
Name:

Case Log and Administrative Journal Entry

This case analysis and learning assessment is printed on perforated pages and may be removed from the book for evaluation purposes.

Case Analysis:
Major case concepts and theories identified:

What is the relevance of the concepts, theories, ideas and techniques presented in the case to that of public management?

Facts — what do we know *for sure* about the case? Please list.

Who is involved in the case (people, departments, agencies, units, etc.)? Were the problems of an "intra/interagency" nature? Be specific.

Are there any rules, laws, regulations or standard operating procedures identified in the case study that might limit decision-making? If so, what are they?

Are there any clues presented in the case as to the major actor's interests, needs, motivations and personalities? If so, please list them.

135

Case 14: A Hiring Dilemma: Recruitment from In-House Versus from Outside

Learning Assessment:
What do the administrative theories presented in this case mean to you as an administrator?

How can this learning be put to use outside the classroom? Are there any problems you envision during the implementation phase?

Several possible courses of action were identified during the class discussion. Which action was considered to be most practical by the group? Which was deemed most feasible? Based on your personal experience, did the group reach a conclusion that was desirable, feasible, and practical? Please explain why or why not.

Did the group reach a decision that would solve the problem on a short-term or long-term basis? Please explain.

What could you have done to receive more learning value from this case?

15

Other Duties as Assigned

by
C. Kenneth Meyer and Joy Zingler

Jenny Harris had an abiding interest in serving the public. Her interest in helping people started early on in her life as she helped organize volunteer projects that assisted those in financial and personal need in her community. Later on, in high school and college, she was known as a quiet, although assertive, young woman who lamented the fact that so many families, especially single mothers with younger children were not given adequate social, economic or psychological support from those who administered governmental programs such as Women in Need (WIN), USDA Food Stamps and Community Assistance, TANF and housing assistance.

As a maturing young adult who had been raised in a family that was considered reasonably middle-class by most standards, she developed a strong character and moral sense of what was right and wrong, good and bad, and just or unjust. For Jenny Harris it was wrong to neglect a vulnerable child or adult or to deny a family the right to affordable and safe housing and, of course, accessibility to health care.

The scenario that Jenny found the department caught up in began last year when Capital Housing Authority executive director, Sherry McGregor, told her staff that Housing and Urban Development (HUD) had to change how the housing subsidy for all families would need to be calculated. The new formula, she said would affect many who sought the help of the HUD office in seeking affordable rental housing assistance.

In addition, McGregor told her staff that their agency would have to cut back because of a reduction in funding from U.S. Housing and Urban Development. Therefore, she had gone ahead and devised a new formula that would enable the office to work within the new budgeting constraints. Jenny and her coworkers who dealt with vulnerable families, especially single parent, female headed families with children, were not consulted and asked to provide guidance on how the new payment schedule would affect their clients. As Jenny recounted later, "We were given no guidance on how to address the change in payment, except to say less money was available from HUD." Also, the executive director had little appreciation of how her decision would impact the lives of poorer families. This style of decision making was in character with Sherry's authoritarian leadership style and was augmented by her "bullying" behavior, emotional outbursts, and use of guilt as a means of controlling others.

Case 15: Other Duties as Assigned

Jenny had been a faithful, dependable, hard-working and conscientious employee for three years and during her tenure saw her immediate supervisor demoted to a housing specialist. Jenny was told that effective immediately, everyone was to report directly to McGregor. The administrative assistant, Jorge Rodriquez was terminated within his first year in the agency, although those he supervised felt he was personal, professional, and competent. Additionally, Sherry did not enforce the harassment policy. To the contrary, she often made discriminatory remarks, especially aimed toward Jenny by derogatorily commenting on body type and figure, religiosity, and moral sexual behavior. As executive director, McGregor had her own demons to reign in, but there was no one in the office positioned to address her offensive and intimidating behavior.

Eventually, the agency decided to build a new administrative office and solicited input from a few selected staff members. Some suggested that the facilities they operated out of were satisfactory and any new monies should be used to increase the availability of affordable housing for low income families, or refurbish existing housing units. But the executive director made the decision unilaterally to build a new administrative building. Unfortunately, however, McGregor was able to pull together enough money from various sources for new construction, but did not factor in the funds needed to pay for the contracted maintenance and custodial services.

To make things work, Kate, a full-time employee, was hired on a temporary basis to clean the offices, reception area, conference and rest rooms after normal working hours. This arrangement worked well, by all accounts, until the money ran out for contracted janitorial and cleaning services. Now, as Jenny reflected on a dilemma that would become very personal, she and the other housing specialists, on a rotational basis, were asked to clean the offices and public restrooms. Essentially, they were to provide janitorial services to the agency, even though they were not given any training for bloodborne pathogens or safety.

When McGregor was asked about these other duties as assigned, she said, "Clean the toilets as if they were your own." Of course, Jenny and some of the other specialists felt their newly assigned duties went well beyond their job descriptions and that their professionalism was being diminished. When Jenny objected, McGregor said, "That she had a choice to clean, be fired, or resign." When Jenny stood up to the director and said she would not clean the restrooms, McGregor reacted angrily. In turn McGregor asked Jenny if she would be at work the next day and Jenny said she would be and that she had no intention of resigning. At that point, she was bluntly told that she was fired and not to come back to work.

The choices that were given were unacceptable for Jenny and although she felt comfortable making the rooms tidy, she felt the toilet cleaning tasks she had been assigned to perform went well beyond what would normally be expected of one in her position. She wrote a letter to Executive Director McGregor and stated that she declined to perform the janitorial duties since they were not part of her job duties when hired and, furthermore, she argued presented potential health hazards.

Jenny felt she had been unfairly treated and wrote a letter to Tom Doe, chair of the executive board of Capital Housing Authority. The letter as shown in **Exhibit 1**, addressed McGregor's managerial and leadership style and her inability to manage complex financial accounts. It also addressed the housekeeping and janitorial duties she was obligated to perform and how she was dismissed. She also

Case 15: Other Duties as Assigned

asked to be reinstated, indicated how she had been harassed, and generally asked for protection from further abuse or retaliation. Simply, she wanted to do the job she was initially hired to perform.

Later on, Jenny sent another letter, as revealed in **Exhibit 2**, to Tom Doe revealing her disgruntlement with the Capital Housing Authority office and her fear of being further harassed and retaliated against should she return to work.

Final Disposition of the Case:

In the end, Jenny did not pursue her rights to a reinstatement hearing and with the aid of an attorney had her employment record changed to show that she resigned rather than having been terminated. Also, she asked that she be given a letter of recommendation that accurately reflected her good annual performance evaluations and her years of satisfactory performance. The executive board approved her request and the case was closed from Jenny's perspective. Her experience in the nonprofit sector had been distasteful and that was all she had to savor for her dedicated years of serving the public.

Questions and Instructions:

1. What does the case reveal about the overall organizational culture at the local Housing and Urban Development? Please elaborate.

2. In your opinion, did Jenny Harris have a right to object to being assigned custodial duties, especially public toilet cleaning tasks at HUD? Please be specific on what you would have done if placed in a similar situation.

3. Based on the case scenario, please critique her initial letter to Tom Doe, Exhibit 1, and indicate what you would have advised her to mention, delete, emphasize, or change.

4. If you had been treated like Jenny Harris was, would you have written the second letter to Tom Doe, as shown in Exhibit 2? Again, please indicate what was appropriate or inappropriate for her to write about in registering her complaints? Please be specific.

Case 15: Other Duties as Assigned

5. Would you have personally agreed to settle your grievance on the same terms as Jenny Harris did? If yes, why do you feel it was a fair resolution? If not, what would you have required as part of your settlement? Please specify in detail.

Case 15: Other Duties as Assigned

Exhibit 1: Letter to Tom Doe, Chairman, Executive Board

August 30, 2010

Tom Doe
Executive Board Chairman

Dear Tom,

I am requesting a hearing with the executive board regarding my termination from Capital Housing Authority (CHA) employment. I believe it is a wrongful discharge. I am requesting reinstatement. I submitted a letter to Sherry McGregor on Wednesday, August 30th stating that I respectfully declined to perform janitorial duties which included cleaning toilets. My letter to Sherry accompanies this request. After receiving the letter, Sherry gave me the impression that either I cleaned (including toilets) or I was to resign. When I did not clean, she came to my office and asked if I would clean. She appeared angry. I said no. She asked if I would report to work tomorrow and I said yes, and that I was not resigning. Penny was present at this time and also heard me tell Sherry that I thought the janitorial work should be contracted out and that no one in the office should be required to do it. At this point Sherry told me not to come back to work. She got me a box, told me to pack my stuff, give her my office key and leave. I received no information about my paycheck, accrued vacation, or COBRA rights.

I have volunteered to help with extra duties that are related to my work. For example, I have covered the front desk when needed. I accommodated Kate when her vacation time overlapped her monthly meetings for enrollment and briefings, handling this along with my regular workload, as well as covering for the administrative assistant when she needed to be away from the desk. I feel these actions demonstrate my willingness to volunteer for extra duties as needed.

I have been a faithful and loyal worker serving CHA for almost six years. I have received favorable reviews, yearly raises and bonuses when paid out. Last year, Sherry recommended me for admission to a Masters of Public Administration Program.

In addition to reinstatement, I request assurances that there will be no reprisals for my actions. For example, in the presence of staff members while planning the 2007 Christmas Party, I told Sherry I could not attend the weekend she suggested for the party because I was going out-of-town to attend a church retreat. She replied, "You bitch." I have no idea whether it was in jest or not, but it was inappropriate behavior. Furthermore, after we moved in the new office during the spring, while sitting in the conference room during lunch in the presence of Penny and others, Sherry graphically described sex acts from the X-rated movie "Debbie Does Dallas" in full knowledge that I am a religious person that finds this very offensive. I had to leave the lunch room. I never received an apology. I am afraid of retaliation.

I expect to have my current case load back, no verbal or psychological abuse, and no coalitions formed against me that make work difficult and forces me out. I simply want to do my job to the best of my ability, be respected, and get on with my career.

Sincerely,

Jenny Harris

CC: Sherry McGregor, Executive Director

Exhibit 2, Second Letter to Tom Doe, Chairman, Executive Board

September 5, 2010

Tom Doe
Executive Board Chairman

Dear Tom,

    To do my best at CHA (Capital Housing Authority), I also need to know that I can speak up about agency policy issues I feel strongly about without feeling afraid that I will suffer belittlement, have my feelings or suggestions summarily dismissed without counsel or explanations — or be fired.

    As I am sure you are aware, prior to Sherry's announcement that we needed to build a new facility; she changed the voucher program rules which reduced subsidy money to constituents. As an example, under Sherry's new rules, a single mother with a child under seven years old received less money to cover her rental unit expense. If she was renting a two bedroom apartment, she was forced to pay the difference or move. This obviously caused hardship. I understood the reason for the rule change was budget cuts or that we needed to save money. When Sherry announced we would spend our reserve money on a new building after subsidies had been cut, and that no money would be spent on building new housing projects or rehab, I felt compromised in my ability to work with clients.

    I received no explanation other than it would save us money and I worried that constituents would think we were benefiting at their expense. It appeared to me that we were, but I did not feel I could share my feelings with Sherry. I felt she would take offense, so I suffered emotional distress from not being able to talk with her about my feelings and from not knowing how to deal with complaints. Despite constituent outcry and complaints, nothing was done until the new building was completed in September of 2007 and staff had moved in. Then Sherry changed the rules back to the previous disbursement level. Again, I was never provided an adequate explanation that I could communicate to our constituents as to why we were changing the rules back after we built our new facility. I need assurance upon reinstatement that I can share my concerns without reprisal. I have and will enforce rules, but feel I have a right to assistance when forced to deal potentially major public relation issues. If Sherry fired me for not wanting to clean toilets, how could I go to her with any issue that questioned her judgment?

Respectfully,

Jenny Harris
1234 S 5th St

CC: Sherry McGregor, Executive Director

Case 15: Other Duties as Assigned

Case 15: Other Duties as Assigned
Name:

Case Log and Administrative Journal Entry

This case analysis and learning assessment is printed on perforated pages and may be removed from the book for evaluation purposes.

Case Analysis:
Major case concepts and theories identified:

What is the relevance of the concepts, theories, ideas and techniques presented in the case to that of public management?

Facts — what do we know *for sure* about the case? Please list.

Who is involved in the case (people, departments, agencies, units, etc.)? Were the problems of an "intra/interagency" nature? Be specific.

Are there any rules, laws, regulations or standard operating procedures identified in the case study that might limit decision-making? If so, what are they?

Are there any clues presented in the case as to the major actor's interests, needs, motivations and personalities? If so, please list them.

Case 15: Other Duties as Assigned

Learning Assessment:
What do the administrative theories presented in this case mean to you as an administrator?

How can this learning be put to use outside the classroom? Are there any problems you envision during the implementation phase?

Several possible courses of action were identified during the class discussion. Which action was considered to be most practical by the group? Which was deemed most feasible? Based on your personal experience, did the group reach a conclusion that was desirable, feasible, and practical? Please explain why or why not.

Did the group reach a decision that would solve the problem on a short-term or long-term basis? Please explain.

What could you have done to receive more learning value from this case?

16

City Bargaining

by
C. Kenneth Meyer, K. W. Greethurst, and John Donahue

The city of Park Wood faced a projected revenue decrease of ten percent for the next fiscal year. The following years did not look much better. Two plants had closed and no new jobs were on the horizon. New construction had slowed to a trickle. The city manager, Julia Rhines, struggled with putting together the next budget. The revenue decrease would have serious consequences but she wanted to preserve as many of the town's services as possible. She considered the options. Cuts to wages and benefits, while not impossible, would be difficult since virtually all city employees were under collective bargaining contracts that extended for at least two more years. That left the prospect of reorganizing departments, revising procedures, or even outsourcing some of the traditional government services, such as waste management, road maintenance, and engineering.

Park Wood had a sizeable public workforce of over five hundred employees including police, fire, sanitation workers and public works. Five major unions represented the town's employees: American Federation of State, County and Municipal Employees (AFSCME); the American Federation of Government Employees (AFGE); the International Brotherhood of Teamsters (IBT); the Fraternal Order of Police (FOP); and the International Association of Fire Fighters (IAFF). These labor organizations knew money was going to be tight at city hall and they knew enough about the workings of city government to know that sooner or later they would be hit with the prospect of layoffs or some other changes. Rumors of layoffs or reorganization were already flying amongst the workers even though City Manager Rhines had not made any recommendations to the city council. The unions worried about the effects any changes might have on their respective bargaining units and the delivery of public services. In private, they were concerned that any reorganization or changes to job descriptions would only set the stage for even more concessions in the future. Regardless, they elected not to approach the city manager or the council with their concerns but would wait to see what developed.

Thus City Manager Rhines and her assistants were confronted with fiscal as well as policy and human resource concerns. After many long hours of crunching numbers and reviewing city organizations, they settled on a plan which they were convinced would preserve the most public services while minimizing the impact on public employees. They would seek a ten percent increase in contributions that supervisory and managerial personnel made to their health insurance plan and there would be no cost of living (COLA) increase for them during the upcoming budget year. Employees would be asked for a two percent increase in their health insurance contributions and forego, for one year, any COLAs provided for in their union contracts. By doing so, the city manager's office was confident they could avoid any employee layoffs and buy valuable time within which to research the opportunities for reorganization of city departments and increasing efficiencies as a long-term fix to declining revenues and preservation of jobs and services. They realized that any combination of jobs, cross-training, or reengineering could lead to recruitment problems and higher wages/salaries and that they might end up losing the benefits of any enhanced efficiency. They further realized that future privatization might be seen as a double-cross. But those were all issues to be dealt with down the road.

Rhines felt that it was essential that she secured and maintained the support of the employees if she was to be successful. While she did not consider herself "anti-union" she was convinced that, in this case, the unions would be a major impediment to the changes she saw as not only critical, but inevitable. She reflected on why 38 percent of public employees were organized compared to only nine percent of their private sector counterparts. She had heard many of the standard fare reasons for the decline of private sector union membership. There was the historic "union busting" incident during President Ronald Reagan's presidency where he fired air traffic controllers after their Professional Air Traffic Controllers Association (PATCO) union led them out on strike in violation of federal law. The 13,000 air traffic controllers expressed a three pronged set of needs: a 32-hour workweek, better retirement package, and $10,000 pay raise — across the board. When they were ordered to return to work, only 1,650 complied and the other 11,350 were terminated. There was the popularity of building new manufacturing plants in "Right-to-Work" states with a legacy of weak unionization. There was the outsourcing of manufacturing and textile production to lesser developed countries which eliminated millions of jobs once held by a largely unionized workforce. She had heard the stories about how some younger workers were turned off to unionization because they knew little about the history of collective bargaining in the United States and failed to appreciate the part unions played in getting many labor, safety and wage protection laws passed (the very protections which now led many young workers to conclude they did not need a union). Then, there was the fear of costly strikes and of being permanently replaced by a strike-breaker. Finally, there was the concern among some union workers that their unions were corrupt and had lost solidarity and the aggressive spirit that went with it.

Rhine mused that it was much easier for non-federal public employees to organize since most already had strict state statutes in place to protect them from unlawful discharge in general and from retaliation for union activity in particular. Many argued that these laws were more effective than even the National Labor Relations Act (NLRA) that applied only to private sector employees. Moreover, most did not have the right to strike but did have the protection and comfort of final and binding interest arbitration to settle contract disputes.

In any event, Rhines had to act and felt she needed to do so quickly. She wanted to be fair and treat the workers with dignity and respect. She knew the city could not avoid the unions but she was convinced that if she got her message out to the employees first then they would likely support the concessions and not be swayed by the unions even if they opposed her plan. She wanted them to know exactly what was being proposed and the rationale behind it without her message first having to go through any union filters. After gauging their response, she would decide whether to approach the city council and ask their approval to confront the unions.

Case 16: City Bargaining

Rhines' staff prepared a letter, explaining her proposal, to be given to each employee on payday. Rhines' also planned to conduct short, shop floor, meetings with employees where she would explain her plan and answer questions. She would solicit employee input. She would ask certain sympathetic supervisors to try to "talk up" the proposal directly with employees. She hoped to avoid any arguments with union stewards or officers and any who became disruptive would be politely asked to leave. She was convinced she had everyone's best interests in mind and did not believe she was out of line inasmuch as the unions would be officially notified and given an opportunity to bargain at the appropriate time should the city council approve her recommendations.

Questions and Instructions:

1. Most state labor statutes that apply to state, county and municipal employees are patterned after the National Labor Relations Act (NLRA). The NLRA proscribes certain conduct on the part of employers and labor organizations and these unlawful acts are called Unfair Labor Practices (ULP). List the types of conduct considered ULPs on the part of employers and then list the types of conduct considered ULPs if engaged in by a labor organization.

2. Briefly compare your own state code dealing with public employee relations (public collective bargaining) with the provisions of the NLRA.

3. How is "interest arbitration" utilized to resolve contract issues? Please elaborate.

4. Did Rhines engage in bad faith bargaining even though she saw her mission as simply communication of her position? Please explain.

5. What impact, generally, do you believe collective bargaining has on job redesign, reengineering, privatization of the public sector and the "nuts and bolts" issues of recruitment, selection, promotion, training, and termination? Please elaborate.

6. If you were in Julia Rhines' position, what would you do first to tackle the budget shortfall and why? Please explain.

7. Please consult the literature of labor relations and collective bargaining and verify or refute the reasons that Rhines believes has contributed to the decline of unionization in the private sector.

8. Why is there a growth of public employee unionization and what are the immediate and long-term implications for the management of the public sector? Please discuss.

Case 16: City Bargaining

Name:

Case Log and Administrative Journal Entry

This case analysis and learning assessment is printed on perforated pages and may be removed from the book for evaluation purposes.

Case Analysis:
Major case concepts and theories identified:

What is the relevance of the concepts, theories, ideas and techniques presented in the case to that of public management?

Facts — what do we know *for sure* about the case? Please list.

Who is involved in the case (people, departments, agencies, units, etc.)? Were the problems of an "intra/interagency" nature? Be specific.

Are there any rules, laws, regulations or standard operating procedures identified in the case study that might limit decision-making? If so, what are they?

Are there any clues presented in the case as to the major actor's interests, needs, motivations and personalities? If so, please list them.

Case 16: City Bargaining

Learning Assessment:
What do the administrative theories presented in this case mean to you as an administrator?

How can this learning be put to use outside the classroom? Are there any problems you envision during the implementation phase?

Several possible courses of action were identified during the class discussion. Which action was considered to be most practical by the group? Which was deemed most feasible? Based on your personal experience, did the group reach a conclusion that was desirable, feasible, and practical? Please explain why or why not.

Did the group reach a decision that would solve the problem on a short-term or long-term basis? Please explain.

What could you have done to receive more learning value from this case?

17

Doing the Zoo

by
C. Kenneth Meyer and Pamela Pepper

For those who affectionately call themselves Marquettians, it seems like ancient history now since Mr. Bernard Ignatius Bird gave $150,000 to the city of Marquette in the 1960s to build a zoological garden for children. The city has undergone massive changes during the past four decades and has become a bustling financial and insurance services city boasting a population of nearly one-half million citizens. The children's zoo had its grand opening a few years later and was tagged by the locals with a parochial label — Birdland Zoo. This was done in respect for and recognition of the zoo's generous benefactor!

The zoo was initially designed around nursery rhyme themes and it featured a castle with all of the obligatory trappings (*Chemin de ronde*, drawbridge, gun port, murder hole, parapet, turret, tower, and moat), Noah's Ark, Monkey Island, Barnyard Haven, and "Getting to Know You" (animal petting area), and a fully operational miniature train with brightly colored logos that were strategically placed on the freight, tanker, and flat cars representing paid advertisements from area businesses and corporations.

Marquette built, managed, operated, and maintained all facilities, grounds and other activities related to the zoo. The city also placed a director to oversee the zoological operations and hired professional zookeepers to care for and manage the animals and their exhibitions.

Nearly two decades later, a proactive group of civic and business leaders formed the Birdland Zoo Foundation as a 501(c)(3) organization, and formed a successful private-public partnership with the city of Marquette. Then, the community citizens approved a $1.8 million bond referendum and conducted a community-wide capital campaign that raised an additional $1.4 million. With this record of successful fund raising activities, the old zoo was closed and the renovation began for a new zoo that would open in four years.

For four years the zoo underwent a face lift with major transformation and the brand new 22 acre Birdland Zoo opened its doors once again to the public. It was designed by a local landscape architectural firm that used professional zoo planning consultants, and featured a zoo geographic theme with spacious, naturally landscaped outdoor environments for animals and visitors. During the next 17 years, the zoo hosted more than 3.6 million visitors, averaging 214,525 visitors per year.

Case 17: Doing the Zoo

During those seventeen years, several additional renovations took place under the direction of the zoo director, Mark Thomas. In the first ten years, three special event pavilions were added and the White-handed Gibbon exhibit opened. Shortly thereafter, the William and Linda Mist Great Cats Exhibit opened and it featured tigers, lions and snow leopards. Next came the Richard and Lucy Bird Discovery Center — the zoo's first all indoors exhibit. Most recently, the zoo embarked on an effort to appeal to a wider audience and sponsored numerous events and functions in newly built covered special events area.

About two years ago, the foundation board of directors assumed operations of the zoo and signed a two year 28E agreement with the city of Marquette. It was thought, that at the end of this period, it would be determined if the foundation should take over the operation and management of the zoo, or whether the zoo should be closed. In brief, the zoological staff was to remain as employees of the city with the exception of those positions that were already with the Birdland Zoo Foundation in the important areas of membership, marketing, and fundraising.

Within in a few months of signing the 28E agreement, the first zoo CEO, Barry Jones, was hired and his goal was to expand the outreach of the zoo by increasing attendance and gate receipts, thereby placing the zoo on a more financially stable footing. Jones had previously worked in the cable television business and had been a part of the local buyout by a major media franchise. He was self-declared as being financially independent and did not need to work, but, nevertheless, took on the task of revitalizing the zoo using the business acumen he had developed during his many years of corporate management.

18 months after Barry Jones assumed the helm, it became evident to the city of Marquette that the foundation had been successful in its venture and a new 28E agreement was signed — this time for 20 years. All staff became employees of the foundation and no longer city employees, except for those who had been employed by the city for 20 years or more.

Marquette kept some employees under its direction since it still owned the land and wanted to make sure that the property was used as provided in the 28E agreement. However, it was understood that if a municipal employee separated from their position that the job would be eliminated and the Birdland Zoo Foundation was authorized to hire their replacement. Mark Thomas served as an overseer of the zoo and kept his city employment status. He served in a supportive position as the zoo transitioned from a wholly-owned municipal operation to a nonprofit 28E organization.

The new CEO, Barry Jones, immediately leaped into action putting his ideas into place. With a major goal of bringing the budget into balance, he raised the price of general admission for all visitors, increased the membership fees, and created a plan to increase the number and diversity of special events which, in turn, would boost attendance levels and lead to financial independence. However, he was strong willed and single minded and refused to listen to the admonitions of the staff to move at a slower pace and get to know the place before implementing such drastic changes.

The ideas that Jones had for special events included after hour, adult only zoo parties; adult only alcoholic beverages were optional at corporate sponsored and zoo initiated events; zoo concerts held on the grounds; and family weekends which kept the zoo opened longer on select Friday evenings. These changes, he argued, would increase revenue receipts and zoo attendance went up. His basic motto was simply to "Throw everything at the wall and see what sticks!"

Several weeks went by and everything at the zoo had been uneventful, when Jones came into the office with an idea to build partnerships by pairing up with other cultural organizations in the region. He wanted two other organizations to merge with Birdland Zoo and he would then lead all three organizations. He thought it was ridiculous for each organization to have staff in the areas of marketing, fundraising, and accounting and to his way of thinking, these redundancies affected their financial sustainability. Although he had not discussed his idealized plan with the other affected organizations, in casual conversation he would constantly compare the zoo to the less than stellar operations of the agencies he wanted to combine.

He also had several other ways that he felt would enable him to get a handle on the budget. First, he immediately hired several fundraisers who had records of success working for nonprofit organizations. By being a "Dr. Jeckel, Mr. Hyde," he drove out of her job Marge Carlson, a senior experienced employee, who had previously done political fundraising, for the organization. He stated publicly that she was too old and too connected to the old city mentalities associated with zoo operation to be an asset to the zoo as it underwent dramatic change. His second fundraiser, Max Bright, had been on the marketing staff and came to the zoo with an extensive background in media. Max, however, was no longer needed to handle marketing functions and Jones, therefore, placed him in fundraising.

Interpersonal matters became more complex at the zoo when Jones hired Samantha Cummings as the key fundraiser and gave her the first major assignment of terminating Max Bright, who he said was inefficient and lacked the zeal and enthusiasm required for successful job performance.

On her first day of work, Samantha felt she had finally landed in a zone of comfort that would enable her to mature professionally. She was struck by the cacophony of sounds that erupted from the zoo. On this winter day, she was early for work and as she entered the grounds the sun had just broken over the horizon, arousing the birds from their slumber and the animal kingdom began to stir and call out for their territorial recognition. She knew in her heart that this was the right job for her as she bounded with zeal and enthusiasm toward the office complex.

Samantha worked hard and used the contacts she had developed in the corporate and nonprofit sectors over many years, and was able to build some rather large endowments. Despite her success at fundraising, she found it personally difficult to work with Jones who she characterized as being "mercurial," like a thermometer when dealing with zoo exhibitions and activities. Later, in talking with her close friends about the mess at the zoo, she said he was all about "giddy up and whoa," making a decision and then changing his mind. This caused uncertainty in the attitudes and behaviors of the professional staff. Samantha said, "Personally, I don't have a clue on which way to turn." To make matters even worse, he recoiled when questioned by the staff on trivial to serious matters and said he would run Birdland Zoo in the only way he knew that would work — his way!

The scenario at Birdland Zoo continued to play out, albeit with many ups and downs. It hit rock bottom with Samantha when he asked her to remove his own name from a list of minor donors and place

Case 17: Doing the Zoo

it among those who had contributed large sums of money to the zoo. He indicated that he had examined the salaries of other executives in the nonprofit cultural sectors and found that he was not paid at the same level. Thus, he rationalized that the difference in his pay should be considered, in all fairness, as a gift to the zoo.

Emotionally drained and physically exhausted from dealing with Barry Jones, Samantha went home night after night and compared Jones to Scarlett O'Hara in the classic movie *Gone with the Wind*. Although Scarlett said she would lie, steal or kill if she had to in order to protect her home, Samantha was no Scarlett O'Hara and was not ready to do this for the zoo to make her CEO look good. On the way to her car, she crossed the park and in the distance she heard the faint howl of the grey wolves and coyotes that were housed in the Western Animal Collection and the haunting sound of a White Owl that had taken up residence in the park. Now, more than ever, she realized that zoological gardens exist not only for recreation, but for education, research, and conservation purposes.

Questions and Instructions:

1. What other measures would you have recommended to bring in more money for the zoo? Please elaborate.

2. Should all organizations regardless of their public, private and non-profit status, be held to the same standard of conduct in the areas of ethics, financial accounting, and management? Please explain. Should executive directors like Barry Jones be permitted to do whatever they wish with having little or no accountability to the Board of Directors? Please explain.

3. If you had been on the Board of Directors of Birdland Zoo, would you have held the executive director to a higher level of accountability? Please elaborate.

4. If you were faced with Samantha's dilemma on recognizing her boss on the donor wall, what would you have done? Please be specific. How would your decision have impacted future fundraising activities? Please be specific.

5. How should an employee handle the kind of ethical problem Samantha encountered with her executive director? What would you have done if were on the zoo's staff? Please elaborate.

Case 17: Doing the Zoo
Name:

Case Log and Administrative Journal Entry

This case analysis and learning assessment is printed on perforated pages and may be removed from the book for evaluation purposes.

Case Analysis:
Major case concepts and theories identified:

What is the relevance of the concepts, theories, ideas and techniques presented in the case to that of public management?

Facts — what do we know *for sure* about the case? Please list.

Who is involved in the case (people, departments, agencies, units, etc.)? Were the problems of an "intra/interagency" nature? Be specific.

Are there any rules, laws, regulations or standard operating procedures identified in the case study that might limit decision-making? If so, what are they?

Are there any clues presented in the case as to the major actor's interests, needs, motivations and personalities? If so, please list them.

Case 17: Doing the Zoo

Learning Assessment:
What do the administrative theories presented in this case mean to you as an administrator?

How can this learning be put to use outside the classroom? Are there any problems you envision during the implementation phase?

Several possible courses of action were identified during the class discussion. Which action was considered to be most practical by the group? Which was deemed most feasible? Based on your personal experience, did the group reach a conclusion that was desirable, feasible, and practical? Please explain why or why not.

Did the group reach a decision that would solve the problem on a short-term or long-term basis? Please explain.

What could you have done to receive more learning value from this case?

18

Printing, Politics and Personal Preference

by
Andrew Zalasky and C. Kenneth Meyer

Sunnyside General Hospital (SGH) was a municipally owned facility in Jersey Lake, an affluent community of about 100,000 residents, comfortably nestled in the coastal hills 40 miles north of a major urban center with a population nearing 850,000.

Gina Baxter, the Marketing Director at SGH, had served in her position for nearly a decade when Fred Colton joined the hospital as vice president of outreach services. Colton came from an area of the country in which there was stiff competition between healthcare providers in their search for patients, and he firmly believed in the necessity of establishing a recognizable "brand name" if SGH were to be successful in the rapidly changing healthcare market in Humboldt County. He frequently went out of his way during staff meetings to point out the interconnectivity between brand name and product and stated that "…facial tissues and Kleenex, athletic shoes and Nike, light bulbs and General Electric, and computer software and Microsoft were just as inseparable as bread and butter, peanut butter and jelly, bacon and eggs, and racing and NASCAR at the colloquial or parochial levels of association." Of course, the staff knew full well that brand name identification is powerful phenomenon in the marketing arena.

Gina Baxter did not readily submit to Colton's hard-driving tactics, but reluctantly, although inevitably, saw the value in strengthening image and awareness — even in the absence of any serious local or regional competition. Upon direction from Colton, and under the leadership of Baxter, SGH implemented a new general health publication, *HealthWise*, to showcase the wonderful facilities, competent staff and top-notch physicians they were offering to the Humboldt economic region.

In keeping with SGH's standard operating procedure, Baxter used a procurement process to select local printers to produce, prepare for distribution, and mail the new publication which was sent to approximately 75,000 households that comprised the Humboldt Metropolitan Statistical Area.

Three local companies with established printing, publication and distribution histories promptly responded to the Invitation-to Bid (ITB) that set out the objectives, specifications and audit requirements that Baxter had prepared with the help of SGH's Department of Public Relations and media staff in consultation with the Department of Finance and Budgeting. Together they had touched base with the major phases involved in ITB preparation. They had considered the alternatives to contracting-out; compared in-house versus private-service delivery; wrote the objective and performance indicators; and developed the penalties and incentives. Additionally, they prepared the ITB with an emphasis on how responsive the bidder was to the ITB proposal; their fiscal, staff, and facility capacity; experience and reputation; and the total cost and cost per unit. They also knew that to successfully administer the contract, it had to be monitored and that a number of audits needed to be performed, pre-audit to post-audits, as well as a due diligence analysis and report completed on the firm that received the award.

Interestingly, although predictably so due to their similar size and technological sophistication, the three firms that responded to the ITB submitted quotes that were almost identical to one another. Polytech Print Shop (PPP) submitted the lowest acceptable bid and was awarded the contract. With the contract complete, Gina and her staff directed their attention and energies on producing the publication, and based on Colton's recommendation they outsourced the design work to Cosmos Design (CD), a company that was well known nationally for its fantastic imagination and artistic boldness.

Cosmos Design was based in Washington Heights, a suburb adjacent to the city where Colton previously was employed. Colton had become familiar with Cosmos Design's graphic and artistic capabilities after conducting a fair amount of business with them over the previous years. Also, he had established a professional and social friendship with principals of the firm, and knew they could be trusted with meeting all of the contractual obligations. Fred informed Baxter that he was confident that Cosmos would deliver a product that would stand out and capture the reader's interest and attention. As the project unfolded, Baxter found out that Fred Colton had not exaggerated his belief in the company and what he said about CD proved to be the case.

The first publication drew rave reviews and exceeded the expectations of the SGH's CEO and Board of Directors. Some local design firms; however, were less-than-enthused to learn that the publication had been outsourced to a company located in another state. The local competition felt that SGH, as a municipally operated and financed hospital, should buy and contract local whenever possible.

Despite these rumblings, the new publication soon became the centerpiece of an aggressive marketing campaign steered by Baxter and carried out by the marketing staff at SGH. In the beginning, there were a number of growing pains since the staff found the issues of copy, design, style and format, and so on to be not only new but strangely creative. Since the staff was inexperienced with the "revolutionary new designs," as stated by one design artist, it was expected that a few scheduled dates might not be met, and that proved to be true. Indeed a few issues did not meet the targeted publication and mailing dates. Although these discrepancies did not draw attention from the greater regional community, since they were not privy to this insider information, Colton noticed the irregularities and he did not like what he saw. As a close supervisor, perhaps even a micro manager, he brought the scheduling problem to Baxter's attention and in a matter of fact way told her, "Fix it and get on schedule now!"

In managing the sundry of operations and activities, if one part of the production cycle is missed, it has a cascading effect on the others. Gina knew this fact well and her anxiety spiraled upward as she began to experience this problem. She was in a real bind and Colton was not the managerial type who had empathy for those who could not meet the established deadlines. On one hand she was working with local printers who she acknowledged were not as sophisticated or upscale as those she was working with in Washington Heights. She told her best copy editor that the local contractors required more lead time than

Case 18: Printing, Politics and Personal Preference

Cosmos Design, and this put added pressure on the staff to have the final draft of the publication in the hands of the printer at least one month or more before the distribution date. Although she never publicly revealed her true sentiments, she felt the local printers were backward and pedestrian in their approaches to printing and design. Knowing how "deadly" serious this kind of remark might be if it became public, she garnered the strength and resilience to keep her thoughts to herself knowing full-well that her own survival in the organization was at stake.

The production process was made even more difficult and problematic with Cosmos Design being on the other side of the country. Thus, the marketing staff did not have the luxury and convenience of running the corrected proofs across town for a quick turnaround time. Alternatively, they had to compile the changes in a document that was emailed to Cosmos Design, which in turn had to decipher and make sense out of the changes, make the needed modifications, additions and corrections, and email the corrected proof to SGH. The distance factor usually added two or more days to the actual production cycle each time changes were noted and made. Laughing inappropriately to herself, she wondered if the cutting age artistry and design was worth all the problems it had caused, especially since she would have been able to get reasonably good work produced locally.

Being a steadfast manager, Baxter and her staff worked through all of the distance and scheduling nuances and attempted to make the best of a bad situation. Overtime, improvements were regularly made to the publication and the community continued to express positive feedback. Fred Colton, as was his demeanor, continued to maintain a scrupulously close eye on the publication and became uneasy when the upcoming fall edition, once again, failed to meet the deadline for publication.

During his weekly meeting with Baxter he told her in no uncertain terms, "We need to talk about *HealthWise*." He then stated, "You are well aware that this publication is once more behind schedule and that is unacceptable. We have raised the performance bar in this organization and it's vital that you and others meet the timelines we've laid out. You must get a handle on this problem and get it corrected! This type of continued tardiness reflects poorly on SGH and diminishes what I am attempting to establish as a brand name. Simply, we meet the expectations we have established among the clientele and community we serve at this hospital and there is no room for failure.

Baxter was surprised by Colton's directness. She had just hired a new staff member after having had a six-month vacancy in the department and was working closely with him to perfect the publication process. Consequently, this process of carefully orienting and training a new associate caused the publication to lag behind the established schedule, but Gina knowingly understood the importance, in the long run, of teaching the right way to do things now so that it would pay huge dividends down the road.

Gina looked into Colton's eyes and said, "I realize it's a bit behind schedule Fred. But I want to be sure we're doing it the right way now so I don't have to steer the process every time. The delay isn't anything the public will notice and it won't impact any of the programming we have scheduled up to now."

"That doesn't matter," Fred snapped. "I need to know exactly what the holdup is."

Case 18: Printing, Politics and Personal Preference

Once more, Baxter set about carefully detailing and explaining the publication and production process — the sort of things that can and often do go wrong; the distance factor; the predictable and unforeseen delays, the communication problems; staff turnover and lead time for printing. Colton listened intently to the scenario that Baxter had presented and jotted a number of key words onto the small notebook he customarily brought to staff meetings. In her heart, Baxter felt she had held the door wide-open to his intervention, by reiterating the litany of problems and uncertainties and that Colton would tell her how to solve the problem since she apparently was not up to the task herself. To her surprise, Colton summarily concluded the meeting and said in a strident voice, "The contract with Cosmos Design has worked well. We should explore the need to find a printer who is not in our own back yard. We cannot afford to sacrifice our reputation when it comes to meeting deadlines."

"I can see the benefit in moving the job to someone who can turn it around more quickly," Gina replied. "But we have to keep in mind that politically, this may not be a good move. If we move a big job like this out of Humboldt the local printers will take notice and we will be faced with a fire-storm of controversy."

"We can't worry about what may happen politically," Fred sternly replied. "We have to meet our timelines and I know Harper Printing can get the job done. They did it for me when I was in Havensville, and we never experienced this comedy of problems that you just articulated. We'll meet this afternoon and put together a new ITB, and we'll see if the local printers can match what Harper can provide."

Upon leaving the meeting and returning to her office, Gina felt a tug-of-war going on in her mind. She knew that Fred Colton was close friends with the lead account representative at Harper Printing and she knew that the ITB process would result in better pricing and quicker turnaround from Harper than the local contractors. She also had a firm understanding of the local political undercurrent and had worked with community-based printers for ten years, and the fact they also edited and printed the local papers was worrisome. Aptly, she recalled the admonition of Will Rogers, a humorist and writer who often stated something to the effect of not picking a fight with someone who buys ink by the barrel. SGH would now find out firsthand if contracting out-of-state would prove to be mightier than the pen!

Case 18: Printing, Politics and Personal Preference

Questions and Instructions:

1. Do Fred Colton's recommendations reveal a conflict of interest? If so, why?

2. Should Gina Baxter be concerned about the political "fallout" if a quicker turnaround is obtained from an outside printer? Please be specific.

3. If Harper Printing does receive the print job, how should Gina communicate the news to the local printers? Should she "massage" the message to try to maintain some semblance of political harmony? If so, how might she do it?

4. If Gina Baxter is accurate in her assessment that the community is not aware of mail dates and programming is not affected by a later-than-expected delivery, is the established timeline an important one or merely "bureaucratic" one? Please justify your response.

5. Could Fred Colton have presented this change in work process differently to allay Gina's fears of political fallout? How?

6. Which article(s) in the Statement of Conflict of Interest Policy (see Exhibit 1 below) do you believe directly pertain to the issues raised in this case? Please elaborate. In answering this question, you might consult the website of the National Institutes of Health Blue Ribbon Panel on Conflicts of Interest Policies, http://www.nih.gov/about/ethics_COI_panelreport.pdf.

Case 18: Printing, Politics and Personal Preference

Exhibit 1: Sunnyside General Hospital Conflicts of Interest Policy

ARTICLE I - STATEMENT OF POLICY

Trustees, officers, key employees (administrative staff and department directors) and medical staff members with administrative responsibility to Sunnyside General Hospital (SGH) shall exercise the utmost good faith in all transactions touching upon their duties to SGH. In their dealings with and on behalf of SGH, they shall be held to a strict rule of honesty and fair dealing between themselves and SGH. Acts related to SGH duties of such interested persons shall be for the best interests of SGH. Such persons shall not accept any gifts, favors, or hospitality that might influence their decision making or actions affecting the institution. They shall not use their positions or knowledge gained therein so that a conflict might arise between the interests of SGH and those of the individual.

In accordance with state law, any person who serves or is employed by SGH shall not engage in any outside employment or activity which is in conflict with the person's official duties and responsibilities. As set forth in the Code of Sunnyside, an unacceptable conflict of interest shall be deemed to exist in situations where:

A. The outside employment or activity involves the use of SGH's time, facilities, equipment, and supplies or the use of the badge, uniform, business card, or other evidences of office or employment to give the person or member of the person's immediate family an advantage or a pecuniary benefit that is not available to other similarly situated members of the general public;

B. The outside employment or activity involves the receipt, promise, or acceptance of money or other consideration by the person, or a member of the person's immediate family, from anyone other than SGH for the performance of any act that the person would be required or expected to perform as part of the person's regular duties or during the hours during which the person performs service or work for SGH.

Other activities may present actual or potential conflicts of interest, and shall be disclosed in accordance with this policy.

ARTICLE II - DEFINITIONS

1. Interested Persons: Any trustee, officer, key employee or medical staff member with administrative responsibility to SGH who has a direct or indirect financial interest as defined below, is an interested person. If a person is an interested person with respect to SGH or any of its related entities, he or she is an interested person with respect to SGH.

2. Financial Interest: A person has a financial interest if the person has, directly or indirectly, through business, investment or family:

a. An ownership or investment interest in any entity with which SGH has a transaction or arrangement, or

b. A compensation arrangement with SGH or with any entity or individual with which SGH has a transaction or arrangement, or

c. A potential ownership or investment interest in, or compensation arrangement with, any entity or individual with which SGH is negotiating a transaction or arrangement.

Compensation includes direct and indirect remuneration. Interested persons are also subject to the Code of Sunnyside ("Gifts Accepted or Received"). Trustees and employees are also subject to the Code of Sunnyside ("Interest in Public Contracts").

ARTICLE III - PROCEDURES FOR DISCLOSURE OF TRUSTEE CONFLICTS OF INTEREST

1. Duty to Disclose -- In connection with any actual or potential conflict of interest, an interested person must disclose the existence and nature of his or her financial interest to the trustees considering the proposed transaction or arrangement. Such disclosure shall include any relevant and material facts known to such person about the contract or transaction which might reasonably be construed to be adverse to SGH's interest.

2. Determining Whether a Conflict Of Interest Exists -- After disclosure of the financial interest, the interested person may be asked to leave the board meeting while the financial interest is discussed and voted upon. The remaining board members shall decide, by majority vote, if a conflict of interest exists. If a conflict of interest exists, such person shall not vote on, nor use his or her personal influence on, nor participate in the deliberations with respect to such contract or transaction. The foregoing requirement shall not be construed to prevent the individual with a possible conflict from briefly stating his or her position on the matter, or from answering pertinent questions from other members of the board, since his or her knowledge may be of assistance to them in their deliberations. If the interested person is a trustee, such person may be counted in determining the existence of a quorum at any meeting where the contract or transaction is under discussion or is being voted upon.

3. Procedures for Addressing the Conflict Of Interest -- The chairperson of the board may, if appropriate, appoint a disinterested person or committee to investigate alternatives to the proposed transaction or arrangement. After exercising due diligence, the board shall determine whether SGH can obtain a more advantageous transaction or arrangement with reasonable efforts from a person or entity that would not give rise to a conflict of interest. If a more advantageous transaction or arrangement is not reasonably attainable under circumstances that would not give rise to a conflict of interest, the board shall determine by a majority vote of the disinterested trustees whether the transaction or arrangement is in SGH's best interest and for its own benefit and whether the transaction is fair and reasonable to SGH, and shall make its decision as to whether to enter into the transaction or arrangement in conformity with such determination.

4. Violations of the Conflicts Of Interest Policy -- If the board has reasonable cause to believe that an interested person has failed to disclose actual or potential conflicts of interest, it shall inform the interested person of the basis for such belief and afford the interested person an opportunity to explain the

alleged failure to disclose. If, after hearing the response of the interested person and making such further investigation as may be warranted in the circumstances, the board determines that the interested person has in fact failed to disclose an actual or potential conflict of interest, it shall take appropriate disciplinary and corrective action.

5. Minutes of the Board Shall Contain – (a) The names of the persons who disclosed or otherwise were found to have a financial interest in connection with an actual or potential conflict of interest, the nature of the financial interest disclosed, any action taken to determine whether a conflict of interest was present, and the board's decision as to whether a conflict of interest existed. (b) The names of the persons who were present for discussions and votes relating to the transaction or arrangement, the content of the discussion, including any alternatives to the proposed transaction or arrangement, a record of any votes taken in connection therewith, the interested person's abstention from voting and participation, and whether a quorum was present.

ARTICLE IV - ANNUAL STATEMENTS

Each trustee, officer, key employee and medical staff member with administrative responsibility to SGH shall annually sign a statement which affirms that such person: has received a copy of the conflicts of interest policy; has read and understands the policy; has agreed to comply with the policy; understands that SGH is a public entity that must engage exclusively in activities which accomplish one or more of its public purposes; and discloses any known actual or potential conflicts of interest. All forms will be reviewed by the board officers. The Board of Trustees delegates to the president and CEO the administration of this policy with respect to SGH employees.

ARTICLE V - PERIODIC REVIEWS

To ensure that SGH operates in a manner consistent with its public purposes, periodic reviews shall be conducted by SGH personnel or by outside consultants. The periodic reviews shall be conducted at least annually and, at a minimum, shall include the following subjects:

A. Whether compensation arrangements and benefits are reasonable and are the result of arm's-length negotiation.

B. Whether acquisitions of other provider services result in inurnment or impermissible private benefit.

C. Whether partnership and joint venture arrangements conform to written policies, are properly recorded, reflect reasonable payments for goods and services, further SGH's public purposes and do not result in inurnment or impermissible private benefit.

D. Whether agreements to provide health care and agreements with other health care providers, employees, and third party payers further SGH's public purposes and do not result in inurnment or impermissible private benefit.

Case 18: Printing, Politics and Personal Preference
Name:

Case Log and Administrative Journal Entry

This case analysis and learning assessment is printed on perforated pages and may be removed from the book for evaluation purposes.

Case Analysis:
Major case concepts and theories identified:

What is the relevance of the concepts, theories, ideas and techniques presented in the case to that of public management?

Facts — what do we know *for sure* about the case? Please list.

Who is involved in the case (people, departments, agencies, units, etc.)? Were the problems of an "intra/interagency" nature? Be specific.

Are there any rules, laws, regulations or standard operating procedures identified in the case study that might limit decision-making? If so, what are they?

Are there any clues presented in the case as to the major actor's interests, needs, motivations and personalities? If so, please list them.

Case 18: Printing, Politics and Personal Preference

Learning Assessment:
What do the administrative theories presented in this case mean to you as an administrator?

How can this learning be put to use outside the classroom? Are there any problems you envision during the implementation phase?

Several possible courses of action were identified during the class discussion. Which action was considered to be most practical by the group? Which was deemed most feasible? Based on your personal experience, did the group reach a conclusion that was desirable, feasible, and practical? Please explain why or why not.

Did the group reach a decision that would solve the problem on a short-term or long-term basis? Please explain.

What could you have done to receive more learning value from this case?

19

Employee Health Benefits

by
Nichelle Miedema and C. Kenneth Meyer

It was Monday morning, early Monday morning and Erin Mills, the director of the Department of Human Resources of Horizon Place, sat at her desk and mulled over in her mind the many things she had just finished reading about alternative health care benefits. Erin had searched the academic, professional, and trade journals with care and worried about the limited coverage plan that Horizon Place made available to its employees. The thoughts about what should be done in the rapidly changing area of health care benefits raced through her mind during the weekend and interrupted her sleep. Now she was exhausted and had to devote her full energies to coming up with a plan that would be beneficial to the organization and its members and meet her fiduciary responsibilities.

To expedite the planning process, she sent a hastily written email to the HR staff and asked that each member come to the Thursday meeting at 9:00 a.m. prepared to discuss "current, innovative and best practices in employee health care benefits." The time leading up to the meeting seemed to literally dissipate. There was so much to be done and so little time to do what was needed. As Erin entered the room, a quiet hush came over the group, as they turned their attention to the front of the room. She noticed the animated discussion that her co-workers were having and the fact they too seemed interested in the subject of the meeting, and that was a good sign in her opinion.

As she scanned the room, and gave a hearty, "Good morning!" she noticed that Margaret Mason, a charter employee and one of the benefits counselors was not in her customary place. It was important that Margaret be there and hear the discussion in its entirety for she was the "go to" person on the current health care benefits plan and as its major architect felt it was the "best and most viable option for the agency." Margaret knew Horizon Place and was involved in designing much of what was now in the Organizational Handbook. She was a "lifer" and always put the interest of Horizon Place first and foremost. In Margaret's opinion, their employee health care benefit plan was just fine.

Mills promptly called the meeting to order and as she began to list some of her concerns, Margaret came into the conference room with a clearly marked "Benefit Portfolio" and wedged herself in between several others on the corner of the far end of the table. She had not brought to the meeting any supplemental material. Such was not the way she customarily behaved. Erin proceeded, nevertheless, and outlined some of the strengths and deficiencies of the current health benefits plan and noted that employer and employee contributions were based on factors such as marital status and number of dependents. In a sign of courtesy and deference, she also asked Margaret to describe the benefits connected to each plan.

Case 19: Employee Health Benefits

Mason placed her open folder in front her and described in assiduous detail each benefit plan. She stated, "The agency currently offers a three-tiered plan. The first plan costs the employee the least, provides less coverage in case of catastrophic illness; requires the highest co-pay for office visits and prescriptions; and, requires the employee to pay a higher yearly deductible for inpatient hospital care. In addition, the employee is required to stay within a certain preferred provider organization or the out-of-pocket costs rise." Mason noted that this plan had been most popular with the younger, healthier, and single employees. She continued her outline and said, "The other two plans require the employee to make higher monthly contributions, has lower co-pays than the first plan, and the yearly deductibles are nearly 50 percent of the first plan." She was quick to mention that, "The more expensive plans provide greater benefits for catastrophic or chronic illness."

When Mason finished summarizing each plan, she gratuitously stated that the health care benefits at Horizon Place were comparable and competitive with other operations of the same size.

Mills thanked Mason for her summarization and then opened the floor for general discussion of the present plan. Sensing that the discussion would be a sensitive one, the staff was not eager to join the debate. As silence completely filled the room, everyone looked around for someone to say something.

Megan, a financial counselor, nervously began to talk. She stated that the current plan, although deemed inadequate by some, was costing Horizon more than it could afford given its current receipts of revenue, and if nothing else changed, the employer contribution was projected to rise 10 percent by next fiscal year. She also indicated that traditionally the agency had raised the employee contribution share as it cut benefits to make it more affordable. She said, "This is customarily the case in many organizations faced with the spiraling cost of health care — we are not alone in facing this edge of the knife."

With the silence broken, Greg Sim, a benefits counselor and a close working associate of Mason, recited some interesting findings based on his own research. He said that The Robert Wood Johnson Foundation reported that the numbers of employees able to afford their company's health care plans would decrease as the population grew, and that the accompanying increase in the cost of health care would make purchasing health care benefits impossible for lower income employees. He further suggested that the problem was exacerbated since the annual pay increases were not keeping up with the annual increases in health care costs. As he cautiously turned and faced Margaret, he said "Several Horizon employees have refused benefits and some others were considering dropping their benefits in order to save money."

Mills picked up on what Greg had stated and said, "Ditto."

Mills began to feel that the staff was opening up and was ready to lay it all out on the conference table in a frank and honest manner. She asked if anyone had ideas that would assist employees and simultaneously contain agency health care costs. She opened the discussion by stating that some companies were thinking about dropping medical plans for their retirees. She stated, "Elderly retirees are a major drain on the insurance plans as this cohort tends to have more medical needs and their illnesses tend to be more catastrophic in nature." Sim bounced around in his seat and quickly disagreed with Mills. He said the current employees would come to the gate with "pitch forks in hand" if this happened since they were hired under the premise that they would receive health care benefits upon retirement. Sim's view was reinforced by Jeffrey Moody, the agency's chief recruiter. He indicated that retirement benefits were a major factor in recruiting talent to Horizon Place, and he gently cautioned the group to realize that the agency was not able to match the pay scale of the private sector and that providing excellent benefits was one way to attract potential hires to the agency. In response, Sim further engaged the discussion and suggested that retirees pay a nominal monthly fee for their health benefits, in lieu of being terminated.

Sim enlarged the debate by saying that he believed, "The real problem is the cost of prescriptions rather than the retirees." He suggested that rather than their traditional solution of raising premiums to employees and cutting coverage benefits, they try to address the administrative processes regarding selection and administration of their coverage providers. He had researched a company that provided technology based vendor responses. "In the past," he said, "they had tried to analyze and compare vendors of insurance benefits on their own. One company provided the vendor analysis for them by utilizing an online process for immediate qualitative and quantitative analysis of vendor proposals. It disclosed all fees associated with health care costs, and evaluated service delivery while comparing it to the actual terms of the contract." He further noted that it is difficult for Horizon Place, like its counterparts, to research and engage in health care benefit comparisons. He believed that by purchasing this service they would save time and money, and overall, make a much better decision regarding the employee's benefits package. "In the final analysis," he stated, "all parties involved would benefit — especially the employees and the employer."

Mason, who had sat attentively during the previous discussion, now asked for the floor and said that she and the previous HR director had done the bulk of the research on the current plan. She added, "The agency's financial resources would be better spent on programming needs in other departments."

Realizing that the discussion was getting off track, Megan refocused the debate and reinforced Sim's contracting-out idea. She told her colleagues that she had researched some alternate benefit delivery methods and came across what is termed "comprehensive service delivery" under the administration of an outside service provider. Under this arrangement, the service provider would customize the delivery plan to the specific employee base of Horizon Place, and the plan would serve the employee throughout the employee cycle from hire to retire. She chuckled and said, "Imagine this; the entire plan would be administrated via the Web." The first step is to move the benefit plan online. Then, the employee would become responsible for accessing the site and selecting those services they needed or felt were most beneficial. By outsourcing this service, it would remove the in-house cost of administrative processes, offer personalized and flexible services to the employee, and streamline the hiring process. In turn, the savings in resources would allow the agency to contribute more financially to the employee benefit package. Mason nodded knowingly toward Smith, and then continued to voice concerns over the cost of the service, and among other things, the loss of administrative control over the health care service provision. Megan retorted that more outcome data would be made available as that was a complimentary service provided by the contracted vendor. In addition she said, "Regular employee and administrative reports would be made to the company executives regarding the quality of the service."

Moody then mentioned he had recently heard that some credit card companies had begun to offer insurance debit cards with all benefit information encoded on the cards. This information could be easily accessed by merely scanning or reading the card at the point of care, thereby eliminating certain administrative costs. Not surprisingly, his colleagues had not heard of this service, but felt it might merit further inquiry.

Mills turned to the two newest members of the team and asked for their suggestions or ideas. Mackenzie Morgan, a new graduate from a well-respected accounting school, had sat quietly during the discussion, but looked like she had something to say. Sydney Powers, a recent business school graduate, brought to the meeting the research she had accumulated on health care issues and had been waiting patiently to present her idea.

Morgan spoke first. She told the group that she had researched various employee contribution options and had prepared a worksheet where the major options were displayed for comparison purposes. She asked the group to review the several designs that she distributed. Most of the group nodded affirmatively that they were familiar with Flexible Spending Accounts and preferred providers. Morgan, however, indicated that she was most excited about Point of Services plans, such as the Health Savings Accounts (HSA) and Health Reimbursement Accounts (HRA). She explained that these services operate under the assumption that employees will control their benefits as consumers of health care plans offered by their employers. As she explained, "The traditional tiered and cafeteria plans would become more complex as the employee purchased as much coverage as they wished or could afford to have." In turn, the employer provided a basic set of core benefits and the employee was given the option of adding on those benefits or protections that they valued.

She went on to explain how some of these services would work and be beneficial to the agency as well as the employee. There are three components to the HRA: the Health Care Reimbursement Account, the Individual Responsibility Gap, and traditional health insurance. Each employee receives a health care reimbursement account to which the employer allocates a specific number of health care dollars each year. Employees use these funds to pay for all health care costs up until the point that the account is exhausted. If the employee does not use all of the funds, a portion of the allocation can be rolled over to the following year. Once the account is exhausted the employee reaches what is called an individual responsibility gap where they pay for health care costs until they reach the point where the traditional health insurance benefit covers the remaining benefits. Erin asked how this would be a savings to the agency and what would be the limitations. Morgan explained that it is a zero balance pass through account to the employer. The agency funds the account on actual needs rather than prepaid premiums and accounting line items reserving funding for employee insurance benefits. The limitation is that the agency may have to choose a different insurance provider to meet the requirements of the HSA service provider.

Sim did not like the idea of the employee responsibility gap. He wanted to know how this would benefit the employee and what limitations might the employee face. Again, Mackenzie was prepared with an answer for him. The employee benefits from the plan because up until they exhaust the HSA they have no medical expenses at all. The account also covers vision, dental, and chiropractic services. In addition, some of the funds will roll over to the next year if not used. The HSA account is typically enough money that the majority of employees will not exhaust their funds. The individual responsibility gap is not so cost prohibitive that someone experiencing more medical needs than usual in a given year would not be able to manage. The drawback to the employee is that in a service like this, while the insurance coverage

Case 19: Employee Health Benefits

is extensive if an employee reaches this level of the benefit plan, the out of pocket cost to the employee is more than traditional health care plans.

Megan was warming up to Morgan's information and asked her to explain some of the other research she had found. Morgan then explained Health Reimbursement Accounts. These accounts are very similar to flexible spending accounts. In this plan, the employee estimates at the beginning of each fiscal year approximately how much out of pocket health care costs they anticipate for the following year. They then agree to have a certain amount of money removed from their paycheck each month prior to taxes being taken out. That money is then placed into an account which can be accessed only for specified medical purposes. Typically these medical conditions are not covered by the current health care plan or the funds are used for co-pays and deductibles.

The employee must fill out forms and return them to the vendor to receive reimbursement. Sim suggested that it might be beneficial to look into Jeff's insurance debit card idea to avoid all of the administrative costs of the middle person if the group decided to implement this plan.

Morgan had one last piece of information she wanted to share with the group. She recently read of several large companies going to employee health care plans that involved premium sharing scaled to salary. Under this system, employee's health care pre-tax premium increases will be based on their rank and base salary level. In the case she had researched administrative staff and low-level management saw no increase in premiums while top level executives became almost 100% responsible for their premiums. This was a large private company. The program would have to be adapted to meet the needs of their nonprofit agency but she thought the idea had merit. She stated that she realized this was a radical idea and that many people in the room would see increases in their premiums if this happened. However, if as Sim mentioned previously, many employees were denying health insurance because they could not afford it this might be a way to make it more affordable to some of their lower wage employees. Mills looked around the room and saw many thoughtful looks on the faces of the group but no one raised a comment yet.

Sydney then brought her plan to the table. She explained in a humble way, that the cost of health plans is directly related to the number of claims made by employees. As health care costs increase in the medical community and the number of claims continue to rise, the cost to employers and employees would simultaneously increase. She suggested that the best way to reduce the number of claims was to practice prevention. Sydney cited several studies done by major research universities — findings that nearly 80 percent of diseases in the United States were preventable. She also suggested that the HR department take a proactive approach toward reducing the number of claims by providing and emphasizing the promotion of disease prevention among the employees. She suggested that a health plan be implemented that rewarded employees for participating in preventative health care. She explained the process as follows: First, Horizon Place would assess onsite health care needs by, among other things, providing an ergonomic analysis of the offices and workspace. This in turn, would help reduce orthopedic claims associated with back pain, neck and headaches, and repetitive use injuries. Second, Horizon Place should contract with a benefit service provider that would work closely with personal physicians in identifying potential long-term health risks based on each employee's current health behaviors. As she explained, she had already identified several vendors who provided health coaches to employees identified as having specific conditions which require prevention or maintenance and care managers who assist employees in coordinating support services when a team of health care professionals was required. As she spoke, the group listened with interest and surprise at what Sydney had revealed.

When everyone thought that Sydney had exhausted her recommendations, she suggested a corporate wellness program. She stated that, "Many companies and public agencies had begun to implement these programs and there was significant research that revealed long-term savings in employer health care costs. Typically these programs provide each employee with a health risk appraisal. There is a psychometric tool which asks the employee to self-report health behaviors in areas such as amount of physical exercise, typical diet, hours of sleep, alcohol and drug consumption, smoking habits, use of seat belts, frequency of doctor and dentist checkups, and indicators of stress from different sources. These assessment inventories help the employee identify areas of concern which might lead to preventable diseases. Then, aggregate data may be provided to the employer, and a profile of employee health risks can be better assessed." In response to a number of questions, Sydney noted that some companies have gone as far as to also offer free biometric screenings such as weight measurements; cardiovascular; strength; and flexibility testing; body mass index; body fat testing; blood cholesterol screening; stool analysis; mammograms; and skin cancer screenings. She reassured the group that, "Individual results are made available to the employee and in some instances aggregate data may be supplied to the agency if employee confidentiality is ensured."

The group was inquisitive about Sydney's recommendations, and in their desire to know more details, interrupted her with questions as she attempted to fully explain her health plan. For instance, Moody wanted to know how this individual and aggregated information would directly benefit the agency, and if the employee could choose to have the health information remain personal and confidential or whether the agency was just footing the bill for more health care services. Someone else asked what the agency would do with the grouped data and how that would drive down health care costs. Sydney answered their questions directly and then said, "With the overall health assessment we will generally know the health status of our employee base, but where do we go from here?" She then explained that with the added awareness of potential employee health risks, Horizon Place could implement programming to assist in employee health preventative techniques. She stated, "Even if an employee chose not to disclose, the plan would give immediate feedback to the employee once the health risk assessment was completed. And, if requested, the employee could elect to have educational materials, exercise regimes, etc., suggested by the director of the agency's wellness program."

Megan queried Sydney on the cost to the agency and questioned her about the long-term return on investment (ROI). Sydney was prepared for these questions since she had read about and recorded some of the major metrics found in her literature review. She knew that ROI would be an important part of the debate and she had prepared herself in this area.

Sydney reminded the group that the mission of their organization was to provide services and promote safety in underserved populations. She felt as if she might be overstepping her position as a recent hire in the agency, but she had been asked to comment and present suggestions. "One of the best ways to communicate Horizon Place's vision is to live it," she opined. And then, without naming names, she reminded the group that several employees were dangerously obese and many were smokers. She knew she was going out on a limb because at least one person in the room was a regular smoker. In addition, due to their client population, all of their employees dealt with significant on the job stress daily. Finally, because resources were limited, she said many employees were using ergonomically incorrect chairs and work stations. She then iterated an interesting supporting statistic: "The number of claims for back injuries alone went up 28% last year for Horizon Place." She suggested that if the agency promoted wellness among the employees by providing a safe workplace, resources for improved health care, access to fitness and nutrition classes, and health screenings they would be living their mission. She also cited several cases of well-known large corporations who reported large returns on their wellness investments by providing preventative health care to their employees. "One study," she said, "had reviewed 30 articles examining comprehensive work-site health promotions programs. In total, the research reviewed had examined more than 293,000 experimental subjects and comprised more than 120 years of formal study. All but two of the thirty studies examined provided evidence of cost savings." She asked the group to keep in mind that employee illness affects more than just the agency's cost for providing health benefits. "Employees out on sick leave are not productive and valuable resources must be used to cover their time away from the job," she said.

Sydney had now become quite self-conscious about the amount of time she had consumed during the meeting and wondered if her co-workers would value what she had to say. "Nevertheless," she thought to herself, "I have gone this far, why not complete what I have to say." She concluded by stating, "If we improve working conditions in the office work areas we may decrease our number of worker's compensations cases, and if we keep our employees healthy we will decrease the chances of incurring the costs associated with employee disability. A less measurable return on the investment, but equally important, is the level of employee satisfaction and productivity. A healthy and happy employee may be a more productive employee."

Erin looked at the clock and realized it was time for the meeting to adjourn. She thanked everyone for their contributions and asked that they consider all of the ideas that had been presented. She concluded the meeting by thanking everyone for their suggestions and ideas, and indicated that she wanted to introduce the new employee health benefit plan to the board of directors at next month's meeting. She scheduled another meeting for the following week and began drafting an outline for the "New Plan."

Case 19: Employee Health Benefits

Questions and Instructions:

1. Of the many options presented by the employees of Horizon Place, which ones do you think are most feasible? Please explain.

2. List the major options and then outline the major advantages and limitations of each option.

3. Compare and contrast the key elements of the "traditional plan" with the different options brought to the meeting, especially those presented by Sydney.

4. Which of these plans is most beneficial to the employer? The employee? Is there a win-win plan among the various options? Please explain.

5. If you were in Erin Mills' position, which plan do you believe the government board would be most likely to consider and adopt? If this were a private company, would you select a different option? What if Horizon Place was a large government agency? Please explain.

6. Are there any other alternatives or options that might satisfy the demand for improved health care benefits without increasing costs to either the employee or the employer? Please be specific.

Case 19: Employee Health Benefits

Case 19: Employee Health Benefits
Name:

Case Log and Administrative Journal Entry

This case analysis and learning assessment is printed on perforated pages and may be removed from the book for evaluation purposes.

Case Analysis:
Major case concepts and theories identified:

What is the relevance of the concepts, theories, ideas and techniques presented in the case to that of public management?

Facts — what do we know *for sure* about the case? Please list.

Who is involved in the case (people, departments, agencies, units, etc.)? Were the problems of an "intra/interagency" nature? Be specific.

Are there any rules, laws, regulations or standard operating procedures identified in the case study that might limit decision-making? If so, what are they?

Are there any clues presented in the case as to the major actor's interests, needs, motivations and personalities? If so, please list them.

Case 19: Employee Health Benefits

Learning Assessment:
What do the administrative theories presented in this case mean to you as an administrator?

How can this learning be put to use outside the classroom? Are there any problems you envision during the implementation phase?

Several possible courses of action were identified during the class discussion. Which action was considered to be most practical by the group? Which was deemed most feasible? Based on your personal experience, did the group reach a conclusion that was desirable, feasible, and practical? Please explain why or why not.

Did the group reach a decision that would solve the problem on a short-term or long-term basis? Please explain.

What could you have done to receive more learning value from this case?

20

Was Her Privacy Violated?

by
C. Kenneth Meyer and Gina DeVoogd

Cynthia Martin worked in the Licensing Division of Clay County Treasurer's office. Cynthia's department was made up of 15 customer service representative, one administrative assistant, and one manager. The department handled a heavy work load averaging 1,500 license applications per day.

The problem started, it seemed, innocently enough. Cynthia Martin left work at 1:00 p.m. to take Madison, her daughter, to the doctor. Cynthia told her friends, Sarah and Bonnie, her peer service representatives, that Madison had a doctor's appointment. In short, Madison had complained about having stomach pains for the better part of a week and the pain seemed to be getting worse.

Not able to identify the source of Madison's discomfort, her pediatrician, Dr. Harold Kash, referred her to a gastrointestinal specialist and she was able to schedule an appointment for the same afternoon. The pediatrician was concerned that the pain was related to Madison's appendix and that she might be a candidate for an emergency appendectomy.

Cynthia, not realizing how complicated Madison's case was, scheduled only two hours of paid-time-off (PTO) time to be away from work. She knew the office as going to be busy, and knew she wouldn't be able to make it back to work by quitting time. Therefore, she called her manager Peggy Wells on the way to Madison's next doctor's appointment.

Erica, the administrative assistant, answered the phone for Peggy and received Madison's call. Cynthia said, "Hi Erica. I need to speak with Peg." Erica replied, "Sorry Cynthia. Peg just left for a meeting. Can I help you in any way?"

Then Cynthia said, "Yes. Please tell Peg that I won't be making it back to work this afternoon. Madison was referred to a specialist for her stomach pains. The doctor thinks she might need an appendectomy. It seems that her abdomen is tender to the touch. I'll keep you posted." Erica replied, "No problem. Tell Madison we are thinking about her. I'll pass your message on to Peg."

When Erica hung up the phone, she sent an email to Peggy Wells, and copied the other members of the department. The email read, "Cynthia called. She will not return to work today as her daughter was referred to a specialist. Thanks, Erica."

Case 20: Was Her Privacy Violated?

Sam Dunkin, a human resource specialist in the department, received a phone call the same afternoon from one of Cynthia's co-workers indicating that she felt the office had violated the Health Insurance Portability and Accountability Act (HIPAA) and Cynthia's right to privacy.

Questions and Instructions:

1. Was HIPAA and Cynthia Martin's privacy violated in your opinion? Why or why not? Please elaborate.

2. Do you feel Erica handled the message appropriately? What would you have done similarly or differently? Please be specific.

3. What action, if any should Sam Dunkin take? Please explain.

Case 20: Was Her Privacy Violated

Name:

Case Log and Administrative Journal Entry

This case analysis and learning assessment is printed on perforated pages and may be removed from the book for evaluation purposes.

Case Analysis:
Major case concepts and theories identified:

What is the relevance of the concepts, theories, ideas and techniques presented in the case to that of public management?

Facts — what do we know *for sure* about the case? Please list.

Who is involved in the case (people, departments, agencies, units, etc.)? Were the problems of an "intra/interagency" nature? Be specific.

Are there any rules, laws, regulations or standard operating procedures identified in the case study that might limit decision-making? If so, what are they?

Are there any clues presented in the case as to the major actor's interests, needs, motivations and personalities? If so, please list them.

Case 20: Was Her Privacy Violated?

Learning Assessment:
What do the administrative theories presented in this case mean to you as an administrator?

How can this learning be put to use outside the classroom? Are there any problems you envision during the implementation phase?

Several possible courses of action were identified during the class discussion. Which action was considered to be most practical by the group? Which was deemed most feasible? Based on your personal experience, did the group reach a conclusion that was desirable, feasible, and practical? Please explain why or why not.

Did the group reach a decision that would solve the problem on a short-term or long-term basis? Please explain.

What could you have done to receive more learning value from this case?

21

New Direction for the Department of Personnel

by
Anthony Moody and C. Kenneth Meyer

It was a very exciting time for Marietta Petersen, a workforce planner for a department within a large state agency. She was "tuned-in and turned-on" to the latest rumors concerning the dynamic new director that the state had recently hired, and she felt that it was just too good to be true that the director might actually listen to the employees and consider their suggestions for reinventing the Department of Personnel.

During the last four months Rachel Matthews' name had become synonymous with change and she was certainly pleased that the rumors had come true. Indeed, an experienced, competent professional women and personnel specialist in charge was more than she could have ever imagined the state might hire. After all, the director's position in the past had always been used by the governor to reward the party regulars and, of course, to reinforce the maxim "to the victor go the spoils" associated with winning the statewide race. Additionally, Marietta always took every opportunity to keep up on current changes impacting the field of human resource management, and she very much wanted to see changes made within the state that would result in creating efficiency, effectiveness and equity, while simultaneously providing for a more competitive workforce.

Marietta felt that human resource management within the state system was made difficult because of the entrenched bureaucracy and its perceived resistance to change, and the popular view that government service was not a noble, desirable calling. Indeed, she had heard it said many times, "Those who work for the government can't find a job anywhere else." She also knew that many felt that government employees were mindless, incompetent, and uninformed laggards that excelled in ripping off the state and who were lazy in their work habits and indifferent to the customer, and this angered her. To further complicate matters, the enduring limited budgetary resources and unavailability of funding for implementing cutting edge human resource management (HRM) programs and policies raised their ugly heads with unwelcome regularity. She also knew that the time to play catch-up had arrived and now the state must come to grips with its history of benign neglect of the physical infrastructure, as well as its insensitivity to investment in the human resource infrastructure. All of these problems had added up to create a mountain of a problem and cumulatively they now extracted a high price. There seemed to be some truth in the adage, she felt, that "There is no such thing as a free lunch!" She also learned over the years that many agencies and departments of state government felt they were inadequately staffed, trained, and had to work with obsolete technology and equipment. To further complicate matters, virtually no resources or programs existed to deal with the essential area of management development.

Case 21: New Direction for the Department of Personnel

Marietta Peterson discussed her concerns with the co-workers in her department and she quickly realized that she was not the only employee who had registered concern about the direction that state government needed to take. She learned from others that the recruitment and selection processes were slow and burdensome and the classification and compensation system had not kept pace with the market; evidence began to trickle-out, revealing that there was no pay for performance plan, and that the current job descriptions were grossly antiquated. One supervisor remarked, "Job descriptions are about as relevant to the tasks people perform as Marx is relevant to capitalism." Also, Marietta found out that nearly 60 percent of the state employees had reached the zenith of their pay range, and there was no place for them to go financially. Another problem area she discovered was associated with the obsolete and cumbersome Human Resource Information System (HRIS) database and the absence of a strategic workforce planning initiative. To make matters even worse, she learned that during the past year there were 658 grievances that led to 36 arbitrations in the general area of labor-management relations. Marietta felt that current personnel policies didn't lead to cost-effective management decisions and that the true cost of managing the peoples' business must be somehow hidden in the budgetary process.

While attending night classes at a local university, Marietta overheard a conversation among several fellow graduate students. They were talking about Rachel Matthews: "What's happening in state government?" "Rachel Matthews is!" As the conversation progressed, Marietta's continuing interest in the new director grew. Matthews was taking the Department of Personnel in a direction she personally agreed with and, furthermore, she knew that Matthews had previous experience in managing a neighboring state's job training program and served as the director of department of personnel. She had also worked in human resource management for a large corporation. Things were now beginning to happen quickly, especially since the new governor was elected and this key personnel position was filled in a manner that symbolized the changing of the guard. Their loss is our gain, she thought, and we better get prepared for an interesting journey. For Marietta, Matthews had become a professional role model and she envisioned the day when she too would become certified as a human resource professional.

Rachel Matthews was convinced that the governor and his staff were committed to change and improving the quality of state services. While Matthew was originally hesitant about taking on the monumental task of directing the future of the state's human resource function, she did not hesitate to implement a continuous process for improvement. One of the governor's chief advisors remarked that the governor was very impressed by her progress, but more so at her courage to take chances and make changes.

Drawing upon current management philosophy, Matthews embarked upon a "100-day plan" to gather information, often times firsthand, from internal and external customers of the Department of Personnel. She intended to gather relevant information to better assist the governor in achieving his vision for state government: Revitalize the state's human resource infrastructure to better serve the department's customers: *State Government Employees.*

Several weeks had passed and Marietta was in the break room filling her coffee mug as usual, when she saw a copy of Matthews' "100-Day Plan." This day, she abstained from her normal routine, and actually took a break. As she began to read the report, thinking one of the upper-level managers must have left it accidentally for others to see, she began to believe that change could actually take place. The

Case 21: New Direction for the Department of Personnel

plan began to identify what was right with state government, and what was wrong. Surprisingly, most of the items Marietta felt were wrong were also identified by those who participated in the many focus groups that Matthews had conducted statewide. The areas detailed for dramatic improvement were revealed, and plans for action were developed.

- ☐ Redesign the recruitment and selection system
- ☐ Initiate a training-focused leadership academy
- ☐ Implement labor-management committees
- ☐ Redesign the job classification system
- ☐ Redesign pay plans and pay policies
- ☐ Develop and implement a strategic workforce plan
- ☐ Redesign the performance management system
- ☐ Create a health advisory council
- ☐ Reengineer the state's retirement computer system

As with any strategically minded leader, Matthews identified potential problem areas that could impede the progress of the plan. She bifurcated the forces that had to be considered into the following categories:

I. Internal Forces

i. State government is heavily unionized, with 81percent of the executive branch covered by a collective bargaining agreement.
ii. The average age of the state employee is 44, and interest in retirement options could create shortages in personnel and organizational knowledge.
iii. Turnover and retirement rates will most likely rise. Managers who participated in the focus groups stated that recruiting, hiring and retaining employees with specialized skills was becoming more difficult, partly due to pay and benefit disparities between the public and private sectors.

II. External Forces

i. Record low unemployment both nationally and within the state had placed pressure on state government to compete with other employers for the most sought after talent. An increase in retirement rates, coupled with the current compensation structure, plus the fact that it took, on the average, 51 days to hire a new employee, contributed to the overall low productivity levels.
ii. Public trust and confidence in state government was low, yet higher than that of the national government, coupled with the public perception that government had become overly bureaucratic and non-responsive to citizens' individual needs.
iii. The negative public perception of government employees also impacted the ability to obtain the best and brightest within the applicant pool. Governance was further complicated by taxpayers who demanded increased services at ever increasing higher levels of quality, but who were unwilling to adequately fund these initiatives.

Case 21: New Direction for the Department of Personnel

Marietta knew from direct experience that these conditions had existed for a long time, yet they had never been openly addressed by the prior administration. On her way back to her workstation, Marietta saw the 44-page report on several of her coworkers' desks. What seemed like an unlikely find, and an insight into secret management initiatives, turned out to be an open presentation of the facts and plans of the new Department of Personnel. The report prominently listed the department's Web page and it had been made public to all who had an interest in state government. For Marietta, it seemed too good to be true.

Six months from the initiation of the "100-Day Plan," Marietta was pleasantly surprised to receive a copy of a Department of Personnel publication called *Personnel Matters*. This newsletter outlined the 100-day report, and informed the department's customers on the progress of the personnel changes.

- ☑ *Initiate a Training-Focused Leadership Academy.* State agency leaders had begun training in cooperation with a local university.

- ☑ *Redesign the Recruitment and Selection System.* Five months after the release of the "100-Day Plan," the governor signed a bill, prepared as a cooperative effort between the governor's office, the legislature, union representatives, agency employees and the Department of Personnel, that passed both the house and the senate, *unanimously*. The law allowed for a streamlined hiring process. Vacancies for positions are now announced through state and private websites, newspapers, colleges, etc. Applications are then screened through the Department of Personnel, and referrals go through to the hiring managers. This new change eliminated the maintenance of certification lists for every job class, and the mailing of hundreds of notices to people on job classification lists, regardless of their interest in any particular opening. Application, recruitment and selection duties were delegated directly, if requested, to the hiring agency by the Director of Personnel.

- ☑ *Redesign the Performance Management System.* The new law provided for the creation of a performance management system to help make decisions related to promotion, salary increases, layoffs and other personnel decisions.

- ☑ *Redesign the Job Classification System.* Several professional level positions were excluded from the merit system, thereby providing for increased accountability.

- ☑ *Implementation of Labor-Management Committees.* Given the number of employee grievances that had been filed, this was top on the governor's priority list. More than 30 training sessions were jointly conducted by the Public Employment Relations Board (PERB) and the Federal Mediation and Conciliation Service (FMCS). Labor union representatives and the Department of Personnel partnered in establishing the committees.

- ☑ *Redesign Pay Plans and Pay Policies.* One more step was added to the pay scale.

- ☑ *Miscellaneous Benefits Expanded.* A Deferred Compensation Match Trust Fund (DCMTF) was authorized, educational assistance was expanded, and job applicants could be reimbursed for interview expenses.

Case 21: New Direction for the Department of Personnel

As Marietta reviewed the progress that had been made, she felt proud of Matthews' accomplishments, especially the major changes she had initiated in such a short period of time. While on her watch, the process for improvement of state government personnel management had begun and she also knew that many local governments were carefully watching what Matthews and the Department of Personnel had done. Perhaps, she thought, the reinvention ideas brought to the state level of government would begin to stalk the city halls and county court offices and that government might be eventually seen as being both efficient and effective. "Just maybe," she wondered, "could governments at all levels be able to function as well as their private sector counterparts?" "If government is managed effectively," she mused, "might it not overtake the private sector in terms of both measurements of productivity and efficiency?" Now she could answer the question herself about "What's happening with state government?" And for once she felt perfectly comfortable in retorting that "Rachel Matthew and the Department of Personnel is what's happening!"

Questions and Instructions:

1. There are a number of human resource management issues and challenges that exist in the case. If you were in Director Matthews' position, how would you deal with an aging workforce, employee burnout, and the cumbersome recruitment, hiring and retention programs she inherited? Please be specific. How would you deal with employee benefits to create a more competitive workplace? Please elaborate.

   [Handwritten notes: Aging Workforce - Benefits for family (All 3) Training System — Flexible Schedule New Pay Plans]

2. In personnel administration, the topics of building and maintaining a diverse work force, incorporating performance based appraisals and compensation plans, and enriching employee development and training programs, while achieving high levels of productivity during an era of scarce financial resources and funding, are frequently mentioned as problematic. Do you think these topics deserve more attention or are they passing fads? Explain.

3. What key issues are involved when management begins to redesign or re-engineer government? What issues are associated with the creation of labor-management committees? What does the National Labor Relations Board (NLRB) have to say about the delicate roles unions and labor management committees play in the contemporary workplace? Does this facilitate or stifle management innovation and the participation of rank-and-file employees in decisions affecting the conditions of employment and pay? Explain.

Case 21: New Direction for the Department of Personnel

4. How likely is it that Rachel Matthews' initiatives and successes in the Department of Personnel will translate into the reversal of public sentiment about the overall attractiveness of state government employment?

5. Do you think that state employee morale will increase because the changes she has promulgated? If so, in what way? Please be specific.

6. Now, after having provided answers to the above questions, please visit the following website http://das.iowa.gov/about_DAS/100-Day_Report_2007.pdf and read the "100 Day Plan." With the added information provided in the report, does it change your initial reasoning on questions 1-4? If so, in what way?

Case 21: New Direction for the Department of Personnel

Case 21: New Direction for the Department of Personnel
Name:

Case Log and Administrative Journal Entry

This case analysis and learning assessment is printed on perforated pages and may be removed from the book for evaluation purposes.

Case Analysis:
Major case concepts and theories identified:

What is the relevance of the concepts, theories, ideas and techniques presented in the case to that of public management?

Facts — what do we know *for sure* about the case? Please list.

Who is involved in the case (people, departments, agencies, units, etc.)? Were the problems of an "intra/interagency" nature? Be specific.

Are there any rules, laws, regulations or standard operating procedures identified in the case study that might limit decision-making? If so, what are they?

Are there any clues presented in the case as to the major actor's interests, needs, motivations and personalities? If so, please list them.

Case 21: New Direction for the Department of Personnel

Learning Assessment:
What do the administrative theories presented in this case mean to you as an administrator?

How can this learning be put to use outside the classroom? Are there any problems you envision during the implementation phase?

Several possible courses of action were identified during the class discussion. Which action was considered to be most practical by the group? Which was deemed most feasible? Based on your personal experience, did the group reach a conclusion that was desirable, feasible, and practical? Please explain why or why not.

Did the group reach a decision that would solve the problem on a short-term or long-term basis? Please explain.

What could you have done to receive more learning value from this case?

22

Betting on Family Life

by
Lance Noe and C. Kenneth Meyer

The message from the local AFSCME union was clear, "Benton City Casino is UNFAIR to working families who wish to maintain a good family life." These signs were placed on the windshields of all patrons who parked in the Benton County Casino parking lot. What sparked the controversy was a change in the shift rotation for the all-night gambling center. Employees were told that they were now required to work staggered shifts. Previously, workers were assigned one of three regular shifts. As employees moved up the seniority ladder, they could apply for the shift of their choice. The director of human resources was facing a recruiting crisis and was struggling to find enough employees to fill the over-night shift. Thus, he proposed to management that a staggered shift would give everyone a chance to enjoy a "good" shift while eliminating the hiring problems that were crippling the operation. With the new plan, everyone was rotated through all shifts four times each year, like it or not.

Marcus Grimly, a long-time employee at the casino and who had an above average employment record, upon being notified that he would be rotated through the all-night shift, immediately contacted his union steward and filed a grievance citing his illness and how he was protected under the Americans with Disability Act (ADA). He claimed that fluctuating blood sugar levels affected his ability to perform his assignment in the over-night shift. Another grievance was filed by an employee who claimed she couldn't drive at night and needed to be accommodated by remaining on the day shift. Others complained that family life was now going to be in a constant state of flux, with parents now unable to find permanent childcare. Of even more concern was the expected impact that a constantly changing work schedule would have on family life.

Questions and Instructions:

1. Because Benton City Casino is owned and operated by the city, is there a special obligation to family and community life that impacts this issue? Does the city have a moral obligation to ensure that family life is protected and children are raised in the most stable environment possible? *From a recruitment standpoint it will be difficult to hire new staff knowing they will be rotating.*
73% of workers are willing to put family above career.
I believe there is a moral obligation to the families, but it is lawful.

Case 22: Betting on Family Life

2. What issues, ADA and otherwise, are impacted by the move from a fixed to staggered shift schedule?

   Health issues w/ sleep on a constantly changing schedule.
   Driving tired.
   ~~Safety for evening workers,~~
   Family - Babysitter, marriage, children,

   Workers other scheduled activity, such as higher education.

3. What is the most equitable way to deal with operations that require employees to be on duty 24 hours per day? Please elaborate.

   The way it was being handled previously, but add a pay differential to make it more attractive to work @ night. As they become more senior allow the choice of shift, but if there is a $1/hr pay differential they may see more staying on nights.

Case 22: Betting on Family Life

Name:

Case Log and Administrative Journal Entry

This case analysis and learning assessment is printed on perforated pages and may be removed from the book for evaluation purposes.

Case Analysis:
Major case concepts and theories identified:

What is the relevance of the concepts, theories, ideas and techniques presented in the case to that of public management?

Facts — what do we know *for sure* about the case? Please list.

Who is involved in the case (people, departments, agencies, units, etc.)? Were the problems of an "intra/interagency" nature? Be specific.

Are there any rules, laws, regulations or standard operating procedures identified in the case study that might limit decision-making? If so, what are they?

Are there any clues presented in the case as to the major actor's interests, needs, motivations and personalities? If so, please list them.

Case 22: Betting on Family Life

Learning Assessment:
What do the administrative theories presented in this case mean to you as an administrator?

How can this learning be put to use outside the classroom? Are there any problems you envision during the implementation phase?

Several possible courses of action were identified during the class discussion. Which action was considered to be most practical by the group? Which was deemed most feasible? Based on your personal experience, did the group reach a conclusion that was desirable, feasible, and practical? Please explain why or why not.

Did the group reach a decision that would solve the problem on a short-term or long-term basis? Please explain.

What could you have done to receive more learning value from this case?

23

AIDS in the Public Workforce

by
C. Kenneth Meyer and Lance Noe

The "Plague of the Millennium" is how Robert Hoyt referred to the pandemic known as Acquired Immune Deficiency Syndrome (AIDS). Hoyt, as director of the state's Bureau of Personnel, was well versed on most of the statistics pertaining to the growth and pervasiveness of AIDS in the United States and around the world. Although still prevalent among intravenous drug users and homosexuals, AIDS was disproportionately found in the Black and Hispanic communities, and especially among younger persons. The disease was taking on an ominous characteristic as data revealed its presence in over 100 nations of the world and the fact that it was rapidly accelerating within the heterosexual community, and especially among younger women.

He was particularly shocked, however, by what he had recently read in the Sunday paper when he learned that President Thabo Mbeki of South Africa stated that the biggest killer on the African continent was poverty rather than AIDS. But more disturbing than this was Mbeki's position that poverty caused AIDS, rather than the dominant belief held by scientists worldwide that the HIV virus caused AIDS! Hoyt understood that poverty presented its own unique set of living, housing, and occupational characteristics and risks, and he could see how it might at least be linked to AIDS as part of a matter of lifestyle. However, Hoyt's concern immediately deepened when he read that children born in Botswana in 2010 are projected to have a life span of about 29 years and about 30 years in Swaziland, 33 in Namibia — the lowest in 100 years — and that these statistics for sub-Saharan Africa were not far removed from what the life expectancy was during the 14th century plague in Europe. As he continued to pour over the pages dealing with the 13th International Aids Conference that was held in Durban, South Africa, he further learned that spokespersons for the United Nations AIDS projected a HIV infection rate of 20 percent in South Africa, and a 36 percent and 26 percent among adults in Botswana and Zimbabwe, respectively. He wondered if the world would stand idly by and let nearly one-quarter of the people who live in this largely forgotten continent die of a disease that showed some response to treatment in the developed and industrialized world. "How can this be tolerated," he mused. "Something needs to be done to speed up the approval of drugs that will attack this vicious killer," he thought, "and which leaves literally a generation of children without parents in Africa."

"Comparison. Yes, comparison was needed now to put this plague into perspective," he thought. What is happening in the United States in contrast to the hot beds of AIDS internationally? He went on the Internet and learned that the U.S. Centers for Disease Control and Prevention (CDC) revealed an HIV infection rate decline of nine percent between 1994 and 1998. He was alarmed that the drop among older women largely influenced the overall decline, but that the infection rate had nearly doubled for those in their early 20s. Further, the CDC estimate that nearly 40,000 new HIV cases are reported yearly in America and that these are disproportionately found among the age groups that make up the work-a-day-world. But there was also a ray of sunshine in the stories he read that the HIV infection rate in America was down from the highest levels of nearly 100,000 new cases yearly that characterized the 1980s.

The questions Hoyt had about the HIV virus and AIDS literally jettisoned from his mind. For sure, he had many more questions than there were consistent and reliable answers. He sought information on how the treatment of AIDS patients might result in higher health insurance premiums for state government as well as for the society at-large. He thought about the AIDS problem and how it would affect Medicaid and the tax rate. Of less concern to Hoyt was its impact on the cost of life insurance since life insurers could adjust premiums on a periodic basis. He wondered about the constitutionality of health insurance vendors testing for the AIDS virus based on their belief those insurers costs would cause them to become financially insolvent. With the AIDS related medical costs soaring into the tens of billions of dollar each year, and life insurance payments for AIDS victims project to exceed $100 billion by the early part of the millennium, Hoyt realized that his organization needed to start a planning process that would develop appropriate public personnel policies.

More specifically, the crisis which Hoyt now faced dealt with the hiring and retention of employees who were found to have the HIV antibody, which indicated prior exposure to the AIDS virus. The civil rights issues were substantial ones and pertained to informed consent, authority, primary rights, privacy, confidentiality, the need, as well as the right to know, and the Fifth Amendment rights of protection against self-incrimination. Hoyt sought advice from Joe Bauer, a personnel analyst and an employee of good standing in his office for five years, who was just diagnosed with having AIDS. Although Bauer was a discreet employee, Hoyt was sure that he should take action to protect Bauer's associates and co-workers and to educate them and other state employees on the risk of contracting AIDS from sources other than contaminated needles, sexual behavior, and blood transfusions.

Questions and Instructions:

1. What programs, if any, should be developed by the Bureau of Personnel to deal with state employees who test positively for the HIV virus? Please outline the details of the program.

Case 23: AIDS in the Public Workforce

2. Should employees who have AIDS be treated differently from those who may have other contagious diseases, such as hepatitis or tuberculosis? Please explain.

3. Does an employer illegally discriminate when he refuses to hire a person with AIDS? Please give the rationale for your decision.

4. Should Joe Bauer's co-workers be informed of his diagnosis or should these matters be left confidential? Elaborate. How do you believe the Americans with Disability Act pertains to the protections of those with AIDS?

Case 23: AIDS in the Public Workforce

Case 23: AIDS in the Public Workforce
Name:

Case Log and Administrative Journal Entry

This case analysis and learning assessment is printed on perforated pages and may be removed from the book for evaluation purposes.

Case Analysis:
Major case concepts and theories identified:

What is the relevance of the concepts, theories, ideas and techniques presented in the case to that of public management?

Facts — what do we know *for sure* about the case? Please list.

Who is involved in the case (people, departments, agencies, units, etc.)? Were the problems of an "intra/interagency" nature? Be specific.

Are there any rules, laws, regulations or standard operating procedures identified in the case study that might limit decision-making? If so, what are they?

Are there any clues presented in the case as to the major actor's interests, needs, motivations and personalities? If so, please list them.

Case 23: AIDS in the Public Workforce

Learning Assessment:
What do the administrative theories presented in this case mean to you as an administrator?

How can this learning be put to use outside the classroom? Are there any problems you envision during the implementation phase?

Several possible courses of action were identified during the class discussion. Which action was considered to be most practical by the group? Which was deemed most feasible? Based on your personal experience, did the group reach a conclusion that was desirable, feasible, and practical? Please explain why or why not.

Did the group reach a decision that would solve the problem on a short-term or long-term basis? Please explain.

What could you have done to receive more learning value from this case?

24

The Sweet Smell of a Good Appearance Policy

by
Lance Noe and C. Kenneth Meyer

John Kimmer, director of personnel, didn't look forward to dealing with the complaint he received about Chris Drapeir, the newest trainer to join Good Mission Community Training Center. Earlier in the year, Good Mission, a nonprofit agency, responded to a United Way Invitation to Bid (ITB) for a computer training program that would serve four low-income neighborhoods in the city of Clear Lake.

It was a day of jubilation when the $150,000 grant was awarded to Good Mission, yet Kimmer realized that information system trainers were difficult to not only locate and hire, but nearly impossible to retain, especially in an economy that was literally begging for employees who possessed the requisite computer skills and abilities. Kimmer also was conversant with the nearly one-million job vacancies that existed nationwide in the area of computer specialization and he knew it was a seller's market in this area. "If only his clients could learn the requisite skills needed to enter this burgeoning area, their lives and those of their families could be changed," he thought.

The theory of Adam Smith waltzed through his mind and for the first time the "supply-demand" economic equation took on a new meaning. Still, the statistics dealing with the percent of communities in the United States that were linked to the Internet spelled out a long-term problem that had to be addressed if all citizens, regardless of socio-economic and racial/ethnic status were to have accessibility to the tools that would enable them to become full participants in the global e-commerce and e-service society. He also realized that those with higher levels of education, professional status, and income were in all likelihood already connected to the Net, and notion of digital divide had real meaning in his city.

The latest complaint to reach his desk, however, centered on Chris Drapeir. Chris graduated from the local community college with a degree in computer software and training and everyone's first impression was that Chris was extremely competent, energized, and fully dedicated to the goals of Good Mission. Kimmer reflected on what a great interview he initially had with Chris, and how his strong educational base, coupled with extensive experience in the "real world," had made the hiring decision an easy one. However, one unfocused issue stood out in Kimmer's mind as he revisited the steps that were involved in hiring Chris. He wondered if he had overlooked any personal characteristics that would negatively impact Chris' potential to be successful as a trainer with Good Mission. "Was I too hurried to fill the position," he asked himself. Kimmer had mentioned in passing to some of the other trainers that "Chris surely wears a unique fragrance," but he left it rest at that. He also recollected that during the interview that he had pointed-out in a subtle manner, the appearance policy, which included language about dress and general cleanliness. Kimmer was always adamant that he made it clear to new hires that image was important that they represented Good Mission Community Training Center to the public. The standard was set high: trainers are to dress, groom, and present themselves in a professional manner consistent with the expectations of the community.

Unfortunately, the first site assigned to Chris was a community center for retired persons, many who had maintained their membership in a long time local community based social club. The more active social club members also regularly attended many of the city council meetings and prided themselves on having the "ear of local elected officials." Kimmer thought that this might be a bad first assignment, as this group was known to be very particular about the services they receive. Sure enough, the head of the community center called to report, "This person you sent to us smells funny and we don't like it!" Kimmer apologized and said he would speak to Chris about it before the next session.

The next day Kimmer met with Chris. The normal pleasantries were passed and eventually he transitioned into explaining the appearance policy. Chris sat nervously through the counseling session and wondered why the appearance issue was being singled out for special attention. After all, compliance with organizational standards for style and dress had never been brought up before and, previously, Chris had worked in many other environments without complaint. Kimmer recognized Chris' nervousness and after several minutes had elapsed finally told Chris of the specific complaint. Chris responded with astonishment and disbelief over what had been brought-up and was at first embarrassed and then became very angry. "The fragrance I have on is especially designed to promote a professional atmosphere. It is not only expensive but is imported from France. Besides, smell is something that is very personal and I find the fragrance you are wearing today to be rather strong." Kimmer, now angered by the response to what he thought was a rational statement sharply responded, "We at Good Mission demand that to you promote a little more professionalism and a whole lot less atmosphere!"

Questions and Instructions:

1. Should there be a different expectation for appearance policies based on "representing the firm" versus working in-house? If so why? If not, why not? Elaborate.

2. The appearance policy doesn't refer to fragrance. Please write a policy dealing with fragrances. Should the standard for fragrance differ for men versus women?

3. Why have policies dealing with cosmetics, deodorants and fragrance, recently drawn more attention? Who may be adversely affected by such policies? Explain.

4. Would you have handled this situation differently? Be specific.

Case 24: The Sweet Smell of a Good Appearance Policy

Name:

Case Log and Administrative Journal Entry

This case analysis and learning assessment is printed on perforated pages and may be removed from the book for evaluation purposes.

Case Analysis:
Major case concepts and theories identified:

What is the relevance of the concepts, theories, ideas and techniques presented in the case to that of public management?

Facts — what do we know *for sure* about the case? Please list.

Who is involved in the case (people, departments, agencies, units, etc.)? Were the problems of an "intra/interagency" nature? Be specific.

Are there any rules, laws, regulations or standard operating procedures identified in the case study that might limit decision-making? If so, what are they?

Are there any clues presented in the case as to the major actor's interests, needs, motivations and personalities? If so, please list them.

Case 24: The Sweet Smell of a Good Appearance Policy

Learning Assessment:
What do the administrative theories presented in this case mean to you as an administrator?

How can this learning be put to use outside the classroom? Are there any problems you envision during the implementation phase?

Several possible courses of action were identified during the class discussion. Which action was considered to be most practical by the group? Which was deemed most feasible? Based on your personal experience, did the group reach a conclusion that was desirable, feasible, and practical? Please explain why or why not.

Did the group reach a decision that would solve the problem on a short-term or long-term basis? Please explain.

What could you have done to receive more learning value from this case?

25

Leave it to Bereavement

by
Lance Noe and C. Kenneth Meyer

As the final draft of a letter was submitted to Barb Rosen, Director of Human Resources for her approval and signature, she sighed with relief that this issue was finally laid to rest! What should have been an easy interpretation of a blue-collar union contract rule turned into a fierce internal battle with cultural overtones. "I hope we did the right thing here," she remarked while signing the letter.

One month earlier, Max Buckman, Director of Parks and Recreation for Scottsville, was completely frustrated by D. Mawisa, a Parks and Recreation Maintenance I employee who had left the country and missed eight consecutive days of work. In an angry tone of voice he stated to Barb and others within hearing distance in the Human Resources office, "I am sick and tired of these guys from other countries going home for long visits whenever they feel like it and believing they should be paid for it at the same time." While Barb didn't appreciate the tone of the comment, she had to agree that some foreign-born nationals didn't seem to appreciate the notification requirements and limits on leave for family issues, such as illness and death. Barb expressed her frustration to Kevin Clark, the Labor Relations Manager, "Why do we spend days arguing over these contracts when most of our employees just do what they want to do anyway?"

D. Mawisa, a recent immigrant to the U.S., was by all accounts doing a great job with Parks and Recreation in a Maintenance I position. However, six months into the job, he called the office from overseas to explain that his sister died and that he would be back in a week. This was allowed by the blue-collar contract which allows 40 hours of bereavement leave for an immediate family member. By definition, an immediate family member is defined as: parents, sister, brother, spouse, son, daughter, employee's grandparent(s), mother-in-law, father-in-law, grandchildren, stepchildren domiciled in employee's household, and persons determined "in loco parentis" (in the place of the parent) by the director of the Human Resources Department.

In Mawisa's case, however, a week turned into eight days and the subsequent information called in to the office by his spouse didn't match the final information he provided upon his return to work. Mrs. Mawisa called the office on the sixth day of her husband's absence and stated that her husband couldn't return due to illness; then, on the seventh day she called stating that he couldn't return due to passport problems. When Mr. Mawisa returned to work on the ninth day, he claimed that while home for the funeral of his sister, a second sister died resulting in the need for an additional 40 hours of bereavement leave.

Case 25: Leave it to Bereavement

Upon hearing this request, Parks and Recreation Director Buckman sought approval to terminate Mr. Mawisa. "Two sisters dying within three days of each other — give me a break!" Max complained to anyone in human resources who would listen. The second death claim, especially in light of the last minute calls claiming sickness and passport troubles, did seem incredible. However, Barb Rosen convinced Buckman that he should "play it straight" and request the documentation allowed for by the contract. "We fought hard for the language allowing management to request documentation in certain cases. Let's use the contract to deal with this issue, not our emotions," she reasoned with him.

Both Buckman and Rosen were surprised to receive official documentation in the form of two government death certificates a few days later. Apparently, Mr. Mawisa had thought to request official documentation while on his trip. When they sat down to look at the materials, they quickly found the documentation was not in English. Rosen, now determined more than ever to follow the "rules of the game," now had to find someone who could translate the documents into English. Fortunately, Paulette, a secretary who primarily dealt with pension and retirement, once lived in Mr. Mawisa's home country, so a meeting was arranged.

While it looked like one of the documents supported his claim, the second death certificate seemed to show that a cousin, not a sister, had died. Cousins are not in the contract, so his documentation appeared not to support his claim. However, in a follow up meeting with Mr. Mawisa, he repeatedly claimed that in his home country, a cousin is often considered to be a "sister" in the family. "You don't understand our culture, we are as close to our cousins as to our brothers and sisters," Mr. Mawisa told bewildered Barb Rosen and a skeptical Max Buckman. This claim was further supported by the translator, although she repeatedly said that she did not want to take sides and was merely there to read the documents and translate them into English.

Max wanted to hold firm. "He called our bluff by submitting foreign documentation, but we then called his bluff by going to the trouble of finding a translator. I say we still have a good case to fire him." Barb however wanted to learn more about the cultural values of his home country and she spent added time talking with Paulette, about family values in that country. She also went on-line and accessed the U.S. Department of State's Web pages for foreign countries. There she found a great deal of information on Mawisa's country's spoken languages, its history, culture, and economic and political system. She also found the information on cultural and religious practices to be useful.

The results of the meeting and subsequent final action are recorded in the letter to Mr. Mawisa from Barb Rosen, Director of Human Resources, Scottsville.

Dear Mr. Mawisa:

On October 1st, you sent me a letter in which you stated that the Parks and Recreation Division did not allow bereavement leave for the full-time period you were in your home country to attend funeral services for two sisters who died a few days apart. According to your letter, the division did not approve your leave because of the difference in the last name of your sisters raising questions regarding the claim that both were in fact your sisters.

Case 25: Leave it to Bereavement

I contacted Parks and Recreation who provided me with the following information related to the events that lead to their decision. On September 27th, the day you were due back from an initial five day bereavement leave due to the death of your sister, the division reported that they received a call at 6:30 a.m. from Mrs. Mawisa who said that you were sick and would not be reporting for work. She was advised that per division policy, the employee must personally call the division unless unable to do so due to extenuating circumstances. The division reports that they did not receive a call from you on that day.

The following day, Mrs. Mawisa came into the office and reported that you were experiencing passport troubles and could not leave your home county to return to the U.S. Mrs. Mawisa was then told of the dock in pay policy that would be implemented per the blue-collar contract agreement. On Thursday, September 30th, you reported for work and explained that while in your home country for the funeral of your sister, a second sister passed way delaying your stay and that you were requesting a second week of bereavement leave. The division explained that in order to be granted bereavement leave, documentation establishing the relationship with the employee can, per the blue-collar contract, be required. At this time they asked for such documentation, which you subsequently provided. The documentation was not in English, but it was initially determined by an employee of Scott County, who served as a translator, that the documentation did not establish the sister relationship between you and both persons represented on the death certificates.

Due to the unique nature of the certificates, we arranged a meeting with you to clarify the issue. In that meeting we agreed that the first certificate showed that the deceased parents were Mr. A. Mawisa and Mrs. M. Suruses also both deceased. The death certificate for the second person showed her parents to be Mr. R. Mawisa and Mrs. J. Lormara. You then stated that Mr. A Mawisa was your father and Mr. R Mawisa is your uncle — meaning the second person was your cousin, not your sister. Based on this information and the fact that no single parent appears on both documents, you have only established that one of the persons was your sister.

Therefore, we recommended to the division that you be granted 40 hours of bereavement leave in accordance with the Blue Collar Bargaining Agreement (Article 11 Bereavement Leave, Section 1) and not 80 hours as you requested. However, I am also recommending that the division allow you to use emergency annual leave for September 27, 28, and 29 which will be deducted from your annual leave total even though the proper procedure was not followed in requesting such leave. In future if you do not accurately follow the procedural requirements of the contract, you will be subject to appropriate disciplinary action.

As you can see, much effort has been expended in response to your claim. We regret the losses you and your family have suffered.

Sincerely,

Barb Rosen, Director of Human Resources

Cc   Parks and Recreation-Division Director
       Human Resources-Labor Relations Manager

Case 25: Leave it to Bereavement

Questions and Instructions:

1. Assess the actions recommended by Paula Rosen. Did her recommendations result in an action that was fair to all parties? If not, who was ill-served by her recommendation? Please elaborate.

2. Should leave policy take into account differences in cultural values and traditions? If so, how would you incorporate these values and traditions into policy?

3. As you read the case study, what was your reaction to the events leading to Mr. Mawisa being asked to provide documentation? What did you think motivated the initial claims of sickness and passport troubles? Please discuss.

4. What do you believe is important to know about the international and multi-cultural dimensions of human resources management? Does culture really make a difference? Explain.

Case 25: Leave it to Bereavement

Case 25: Leave it to Bereavement
Name:

Case Log and Administrative Journal Entry

This case analysis and learning assessment is printed on perforated pages and may be removed from the book for evaluation purposes.

Case Analysis:
Major case concepts and theories identified:

What is the relevance of the concepts, theories, ideas and techniques presented in the case to that of public management?

Facts — what do we know *for sure* about the case? Please list.

Who is involved in the case (people, departments, agencies, units, etc.)? Were the problems of an "intra/interagency" nature? Be specific.

Are there any rules, laws, regulations or standard operating procedures identified in the case study that might limit decision-making? If so, what are they?

Are there any clues presented in the case as to the major actor's interests, needs, motivations and personalities? If so, please list them.

Case 25: Leave it to Bereavement

Learning Assessment:
What do the administrative theories presented in this case mean to you as an administrator?

How can this learning be put to use outside the classroom? Are there any problems you envision during the implementation phase?

Several possible courses of action were identified during the class discussion. Which action was considered to be most practical by the group? Which was deemed most feasible? Based on your personal experience, did the group reach a conclusion that was desirable, feasible, and practical? Please explain why or why not.

Did the group reach a decision that would solve the problem on a short-term or long-term basis? Please explain.

What could you have done to receive more learning value from this case?

26

Madison County's Zero Tolerance of Harassment and Discrimination Directive

by
C. Kenneth Meyer and Lance Noe

Maggie Jones mused over the statistics she had just read concerning the attitudes of military members toward gays and lesbians. She wondered if the "don't ask, don't tell, don't pursue" policy that was put into place in 1993 by President Clinton's administration would stand the resistance it was receiving, especially from male soldiers. In any event, the data had been gathered, the analysis made, and the Department of Defense (DOD) acknowledged it had a problem.

As human resources training specialist, she had literally heard and seen it all when it came to discussing and valuing differences. The treatment of African-Americans, Asians, and Hispanics always raised questions about the legacy of racism, segregation, and separation, and most recently, the issues of "one nation, one people, one language," were on the front-burner. She dealt with the stereotypical attitudes about women — that they were too emotional "because of their special kind of hormones"; that they preferred male bosses over their female counterparts; that it was common knowledge that women are only in the workplace as "babes," "gals," or "girls," and were primarily interested in getting a man who would be, in the final analysis, the real bread-winner and family provider. Yes, she had heard it all! And to complicate things even further, she now had to deal with the biases of age, religion, and appearance.

Now, the brutal murder of a young male soldier in the 101st Airborne Division at Fort Campbell, Kentucky, who was thought to be gay, raised new questions. The media had reported that gays were often harassed at Fort Campbell and taunted verbally and by body language gestures; movement of hands, eyes, and general physical demeanor. The graffiti in the barracks and other public places left no doubt that some soldiers hated those who they perceived to have a different sexual orientation than their own. Some soldiers felt that political correctness (PC) had gone awry with the differentiation that was made in their diversity training between sexual preference and sexual orientation. They were sure that gay soldiers actually preferred being homosexual — it was that simple and that easy to understand, and "that was that." Discrimination and harassment of homosexuals was rampant at Fort Campbell and the high discharge rate of gays and lesbians there, in contrast to other military installations of similar size, pointed to an overall organizational climate of intolerance and rejection that reached a low point at the installation when the young soldier was slain. Of course, the DOD had sent in its inspectors and interviewed several thousand soldiers and civilians in an attempt to assess the magnitude of anti-gay attitude and behavior.

Case 26: Madison County's Zero Tolerance of Harassment and Discrimination Directive

She recounted in her mind that they had found harassment to be commonplace and that it was often manifested in terms of comments and gestures and other forms of mistreatment and abuse.

Maggie Jones wondered how she would develop an anti-harassment training plan for her own county—a county that was largely urban with a diverse population. She found the expression of negative attitudes as revealed in recent local newspaper and media editorials about the influx of Somalians, Haitians, Bosnians and Guatemalans to add further evidence that a culture of intolerance existed in America. She knew these attitudes and beliefs had to be addressed, but how was she to do it without turning-off a group of employees that by most conventional standards were considered caring and compassionate people. Would she take a strident, aggressive approach to the needed training? Would she lay it all on the line in terms of what she personally felt, ideas that were mostly supported by the academic literature? And, there was no room to set this complex set of issues aside for she had to deal with the directive she recently received from Carolyn Fong, the county manager for Madison County.

The directive said that Madison County had "…a zero-tolerance for all forms of harassment, violence and discrimination. Supervisors would be held accountable for the actions of their subordinates who engaged in intimidating, hostile, abusive, or violent behavior against other employees, clients, customers, or vendors." The directive left no room to wiggle. It was a tall order and she knew that her own professional reputation would clearly be placed on the firing-line.

Questions and Instructions:

1. If you were Maggie Jones, what would comprise the key elements in your anti-harassment action plan? Please list in the order that these important elements would appear in your comprehensive action plan.

2. Do you believe the employees of Madison County should be queried about their attitudes toward gays and lesbians? What about the complimentary issues of race, age, gender, religion, national origin, and social-economic status or class? Is this information needed for the development of your comprehensive action plan? Please elaborate.

3. In the final analysis, do you believe that discriminatory attitude and behavior directed against gays and lesbians can be changed? What key issues do you expect the trainees to raise? List some of them. How would you personally deal with the belief that some hold that homosexuality is unnatural, immoral, and that homosexuals can be transformed into healthy heterosexuals? Please discuss.

4. Does a "zero-tolerance policy against intolerance," violate the premise of tolerance in American civic culture? Please elaborate and give examples.

Case 26: Madison County's Zero Tolerance of Harassment and Discrimination Directive

Name:

Case Log and Administrative Journal Entry

This case analysis and learning assessment is printed on perforated pages and may be removed from the book for evaluation purposes.

Case Analysis:
Major case concepts and theories identified:

What is the relevance of the concepts, theories, ideas and techniques presented in the case to that of public management?

Facts — what do we know *for sure* about the case? Please list.

Who is involved in the case (people, departments, agencies, units, etc.)? Were the problems of an "intra/interagency" nature? Be specific.

Are there any rules, laws, regulations or standard operating procedures identified in the case study that might limit decision-making? If so, what are they?

Are there any clues presented in the case as to the major actor's interests, needs, motivations and personalities? If so, please list them.

Case 26: Madison County's Zero Tolerance of Harassment and Discrimination Directive

Learning Assessment:
What do the administrative theories presented in this case mean to you as an administrator?

How can this learning be put to use outside the classroom? Are there any problems you envision during the implementation phase?

Several possible courses of action were identified during the class discussion. Which action was considered to be most practical by the group? Which was deemed most feasible? Based on your personal experience, did the group reach a conclusion that was desirable, feasible, and practical? Please explain why or why not.

Did the group reach a decision that would solve the problem on a short-term or long-term basis? Please explain.

What could you have done to receive more learning value from this case?

27

A Proud Tradition of Affirmative Action

by
Lance Noe and C. Kenneth Meyer

Governor Maria Aura looked pleased and smiled broadly when she awarded the Department of Economic Development (DED) with the annual "Governor's Affirmative Action Award." This annual award is given to those agencies and departments of state government who best demonstrated excellence in achieving the goals of promoting equal opportunity employment practices and increasing diversity in state employment. During the well-attended presentation ceremony and dinner, the governor stated that the state had a long history of breaking down barriers that promote unequal representation in both private and public employment. She further proclaimed, "Our state leads the way in challenging employment practices that hold people fast to the sticky floor of gender, racial, and disability stereotyping. Our state is committed to shattering the old hiring and promotion practices. We welcome the bright sunshine of affirmative action to improve opportunity for all qualified persons in our state." This public statement drew much applause from those in attendance — the media, party notables, state leaders, and department executives.

In her remarks she reminded the guests of the state's current affirmative action program and said it was designed to set the standard for affirmative action programming in the state's public and private sectors. The program, she noted, not only sets goals for diversity and provides a system for measuring and assessing accountability, but also determines if progress is being made. "We have traveled far, but still have more challenges ahead, so tonight let us agree to continue down the road to complete equality and opportunity for all citizens in our state. Tonight we recognize the Department of Economic Development as a leader in this mission," she said, while simultaneously presenting the large wall plague to the department director.

Standing in the back of the dining hall, several mid-level managers of the Department of Economic Development were amused by what she had declared and snickered to each other, "Imagine the praise we would receive if our department actually reflected the diversity of the state!"

The state affirmative action program featured the following components:

1. Each department must submit a plan that addresses remedial hiring goals and the timetable for reaching their goal. Hiring goals are set utilizing the Equal Employment Opportunity Commission's (EEOC) "Guidelines on Affirmative Action Appropriate under Title VII of the

Civil Rights Act of 1964," as amended 44 CFR 4422 (November 21, 1991), 29 CFR 1608. This standard holds that hiring goals should match the ***proportional availability*** of qualified women, minorities, and persons with disabilities in a given category of work. If a state agency employs a lower percentage of diversity from the available qualified workforce pool, the agency is said to be in a condition of "underutilization" and additional affirmative action is needed.

2. Each department must submit an annual progress report to the Affirmative Action Compliance Board (AACB) which compiles the reports and creates the annual State Report on Equal Employment and Affirmative Action.

3. If the underutilization condition is found to exist, then a short-term and long-term plan must be developed to balance the workforce.

4. Additionally, a qualitative review of employment practices policy is to be completed to evaluate the potential for discrimination or underutilization of diversity that currently exists in the labor market pool.

Using these guidelines, the Department of Economic Development developed a program to address their underutilization levels. In assessing their hiring practices, they discovered that they had relied primarily on hiring from the private sector persons who recently retired or sold a business. This resulted in a workforce that reflected the workforce pool of the 1960s and 1970s when white males dominated the private sector management positions. By changing their hiring practices and through more extensive recruitment at public and private university campuses, they were able to improve the diversity of their department moving them from "underutilization" status into short-term compliance. Last year, some employees who were reaching retirement age were offered attractive incentives to separate early, which in turn, opened positions for new hires that were being recruited from the university ranks. However, some of the local university programs didn't seem to offer the level of diversity expected by the director of employment. In spite of this situation, talented persons were found and recruited to fill the open positions.

The overall employment profile of the state revealed the following characteristics:

- Twenty-two percent of the state agencies were in full compliance with diversity standards for women, minorities, and persons with disabilities;

- Forty-percent of the state agencies (including those in complete compliance) were compliant in at least two of the three categories of diversity;

- Half of the state agencies that set short-term remedial goals for hiring women met their goal;

- Half of the agencies that set short-term remedial goals for hiring minorities met their goal; and

- Five percent of agencies that set short-term remedial goals for hiring persons with disabilities met their goal.

Case 27: A Proud Tradition of Affirmative Action

Interestingly, the Department of Economic Development lacked compliance in all three categories (women, minorities and persons with disabilities) prior to the current year. Goals were set and the results of their affirmative action program are as follows:

Department of Economic Development			
Benchmark Year			
Total Workforce	Total Females Employed	Under-utilization	One Year Goal
250	75	25	10
	Total Minorities Employed	Under-utilization	One Year Goal
	20	4	2
	Persons w/disabilities employed	Under-utilization	One Year Goal
	20	5	2
Results: Year One			
Total Workforce	Total Females Employed	Remaining Under-utilization	One Year Goal
250	85	15	Met
	Total Minorities Employed	Remaining Under-utilization	One Year Goal
	25	1	Exceeded
	Persons w/disabilities employed	Remaining Under-utilization	One Year Goal
	22	3	Met

Questions and Instructions:

1. In the case-study, "underutilization" is determined by examining the diversity in the current qualified workforce pool in the state. The hiring goal is set so every agency maintains that level of diversity and no more. It does not assess under representation within the qualified workforce compared with the general population. How does this program impact employment diversity?

2. The Department of Economic Development did not reach full utilization, but did reach or exceed their one-year goals. What approach is appropriate in both the short and long-term to reach affirmative action goals in a given organization?

Case 27: A Proud Tradition of Affirmative Action

3. The Department of Economic Development reached their one-year hiring goals by meeting the exact number required in two categories and exceeding the goal by one in another. Does this result suggest that a "soft goal" is really just another term for "hard quota"? Do goals help or hurt in the quest for increased diversity?

4. How would you assess the progress of the state in improving diversity of their workforce?

5. What recommendations, if any, would you make to modify the affirmative action program for this state?

6. What is the current status of affirmative-action program in America? Why have states such as Florida, Texas and California taken diverse routes to overcoming the past practices of historical discrimination?

7. What do you envision as the future for affirmative action and why has it become such a contentious issue in public policy debate? Please elaborate.

Case 27: A Proud Tradition of Affirmative Action

Case 27: A Proud Tradition of Affirmative Action
Name:

Case Log and Administrative Journal Entry

This case analysis and learning assessment is printed on perforated pages and may be removed from the book for evaluation purposes.

Case Analysis:
Major case concepts and theories identified:

What is the relevance of the concepts, theories, ideas and techniques presented in the case to that of public management?

Facts — what do we know *for sure* about the case? Please list.

Who is involved in the case (people, departments, agencies, units, etc.)? Were the problems of an "intra/interagency" nature? Be specific.

Are there any rules, laws, regulations or standard operating procedures identified in the case study that might limit decision-making? If so, what are they?

Are there any clues presented in the case as to the major actor's interests, needs, motivations and personalities? If so, please list them.

217

Case 27: A Proud Tradition of Affirmative Action

Learning Assessment:
What do the administrative theories presented in this case mean to you as an administrator?

How can this learning be put to use outside the classroom? Are there any problems you envision during the implementation phase?

Several possible courses of action were identified during the class discussion. Which action was considered to be most practical by the group? Which was deemed most feasible? Based on your personal experience, did the group reach a conclusion that was desirable, feasible, and practical? Please explain why or why not.

Did the group reach a decision that would solve the problem on a short-term or long-term basis? Please explain.

What could you have done to receive more learning value from this case?

28

Competition from Behind Bars*

by
C. Kenneth Meyer and Lance J. Noe

Hale Tesh, mayor of Kinross, read the article titled "Securing a Captive and Attentive Workforce" in the *Modern Manufacturer Monthly* trade magazine with disgust. The article was promoting the advantages of hiring prisoners and placing them in training programs to develop their skills in fabricating custom parts for obsolete machinery; building utility cargo trailers; manufacturing mobile homes, boats, birdhouses; and even electric harness assemblies for auto manufacturers. Also touted as desirable was the new trend of utilizing prisoners in service areas, such as telemarketing, hotel reservations and airline service agents. The magazine also boasted of the trend to utilize prison labor as an ideal new way for moderate-sized businesses in rural communities to maximize profits and cut costs. Employers pay an hourly wage only. No workers' compensation. No unemployment. No health insurance. No benefits. And best of all, the state will build your factory!

Tesh thought to himself, "If that new 'young genius/CEO,' Jordan Klean, at the *Tractor Works* reads this, he will jump at the chance to sell all of us out."

Tesh was referring to the head of the new management team that had recently taken over the city's largest employer — the Soil Handler Tractor Works. The new team was headed by Jordan Klean, the 34-year-old grandson of the founder, who vowed to "find new and innovative ways to clean up the books" and increase the value of the blue chip stock firm.

The Tractor Works, as it is referred to by the locals, had always provided high-paying, secure jobs for the city of Kinross for several decades. As long as one was a hard worker, showed-up on time, and religiously obeyed the orders of "Old Man Klean," Tractor Works took care of the rest — including training, housing, benefits, and a liberal pension plan. The implicit promise underpinning the psychological contract that existed between the employer and employees entailed employees giving Tractor Works an honest 40 hours of work per week and in return the company would take care of each employee and their family. It was a paternalistic organization and the men that ran it were committed to keeping the image they had created over the years of being tough-minded, and family-centered, yet fair. But, times had changed all of this and the attention was now focused sharply on the bottom line.

Case 28: Competition from Behind Bars

The change in attitude was evident when Jordon Klean "updated" the company mission statement from "...we are committed to feeding the world by building the best equipment in the world..." to "...we are committed to increase shareholder value and become the world's largest equipment builder."

Prior to his election as mayor of Kinross, an old industrial river city of 88,000 people, Tesh worked for 20 years on the line at Soil Handler Tractor Works. Now into his third year as mayor, he was facing a crisis. It was just announced that the state government was building a metal fabricating factory for Lynnfort Manufacturing in his community. The town was in an uproar.

Tesh heard many complaints such as, "What if many of these prisoners decide to stay in Kinross after they have served their time in the 'Big House' and are released? When convicts are trained in a modern factory setting that uses the most modern, state-of-the-art technology, including laser-guided assembly and welding processes and computerized work stations — all paid for, naturally, with my tax dollars, once released, they will also want our jobs and our homes. How is my law-abiding son or daughter supposed to get a job at the Tractor Works when they are up against a highly-trained welder from the prison factory? Can't the union at Tractor Works do something about this? Would someone please clue me in as to why the state is willing to train prisoners at Lynnfort Manufacturing that will take away any chance that our children might have to work at Tractor Works in the future? By chance, although it may now seem ridiculous, what if Jordon Klean wanted to convert Tractor Works into a prison factory?"

Mayor Tesh had also received numerous calls from his constituents concerning the prison labor issue. Some of the messages left on his answering machine were very supportive of providing opportunities for rehabilitation and others were angry at the mere prospect of prison laborers taking on jobs that otherwise might go to those who wished to work in the private sector.

One irate citizen stated, "They did their crime, now let them do their time!"

Another citizen said, "All the state needs to do is to lock 'em up and let 'em rot — rehabilitation of those crooks is the last thing that they need."

One citizen complained that the prison training program was just another new way in which the criminals were being coddled by society.

Still others felt that if they would find the Lord through their rehabilitation program, it made the program worth the investment and the risk. Claiming that "God acts in mysterious ways." Some even said they would volunteer to work in the prisoner training programs if they were located within an easy commute.

In meeting with the state officials and representatives from Lynnfort, Tesh took little comfort when he learned workers would be paid the average prevailing wage of the communities where the companies and businesses were located. This meant that the hard-working Kinrossians would still make good union wages —wages that were only slightly less than those paid by Tractor Works. Granted, federal law mandated that should the labor market become saturated with workers, the prison industry would be forced to shut down or hire non-inmate workers, and this provided some sense of comfort and security.

Still, Tesh was skeptical, "You mean to tell me that these guys will be making as much as me in there? Why, that is more than 90 percent of the law-abiding citizens in Kinross make who don't work at Tractor Works, and that's not fair. Some of my neighbors working retail or light construction just scrimp by on near minimum wage. I'll be willing to bet that some of them will be trying to figure out a way to get thrown into jail to get a promotion!"

The next morning while driving his car to work, he muttered to himself and queried aloud why the state would pay $3.4 million to build the factory, and then lease it to Lynnfort for $1 per month so they would have ready access to a "permanent" workforce — an incarcerated population that did not have to be paid benefits. "We in Kinross are going to become second-class citizens to the prisoners in the state penitentiary," Tesh thought. "These prisoners are becoming part of the 'jet set,' and the rest of us remain embedded in the 'Chevrolet set.'"

Hale also knew that if the economy headed "south," that the prison jobs would be given to regular workers who had been displaced by an economic recession. Yet he was also familiar with the fact that families tend to join their imprisoned loved ones and add a host of new problems to the cities that provide lockups, jails, prisons, and prisoner-release or training programs. And, worse, Hale thought, "These families have a tendency to stay on even when the prisoners are relocated or returned to regular prison duty!"

The Unions Respond

The labor union Local 814 at Tractor Works was joined by several other area unions (including the major public employees' unions and AFL-CIO) and they were ready to take action against the new plant. The workers had "had it up to their eyeballs" and something had to be done. If they didn't give a loud voice now to the issue of prison labor, they would have yet another "nail driven into the coffin" of their collective future.

The union leadership could feel that the sentiments among the community and the membership ran strong and deep. They knew that the issue would generate a strong reaction when their statement was placed on the floor for debate and approval. They felt comfortable this time that they had done the necessary background research and they were ready to answer any question raised from the floor. In brief, they were ready to "rumble" when they confidently walked to the lunchroom and posted the next meeting time, date, and agenda on the union board.

One leader turned to the union secretary, John Harvey, and said, "All the arrangements are in order for a large turnout and it's about time that we show the world what solidarity is all about. What say you?"

Case 28: Competition from Behind Bars

On the plant floor of Tractor Works, some of the workers had stewed all week long about the prison labor problem. Their anxieties, fears and anger were further fueled by what their "brothers and sisters" said was happening in different parts of the country.

"Was the proposed program just one more thinly disguised attack by the state on the union movement?" the workers opined.

The meeting announcement reported that the union officials had been in contact with the national office and had received assistance in preparing a statement on prison labor that would be submitted to the director of the Department of Correction, and that a news release was ready for distribution to the statewide media if their unified report was approved.

The statement read in part: "Consider the following: A hot climate where men are shackled together in work gangs; those refusing to be subjected to such degradation are chained to a hitching post where they stand in the sun for hours. A place where workers receive between 15 and 50 cents per hour for the 4.6 million hours they work each year, with no workers' compensation or benefits — only in a third world country you say? No, private-sector businesses are profiting from this growing source of cheap manpower, and the government applauds the use of a "Made in the USA" label on prison production for private profits. It is a fact that prisoners in some facilities, who refuse to work, lose credit for "good time" and any chance at work release. In one state, prisoners refusing to work are locked in their cells for 23 hours a day and are referred unfavorably or even blackballed for parole."*

Although the announcement was unusually long this time, it instructed the membership that a copy of the International Labor Organization Convention #105 statement, that condemned the use of forced prison labor (as displayed in **Exhibit 1**) had been placed in their mailboxes. The full text of the Unified Report was made available on their website and those who took the time to read it noted that clear distinctions had been made between what constituted working and training.

The rank-and-file members found the differences between training and work to be pitifully simple. One member, Mary Klinesmith, a tool and dye maker, with many years of seniority felt that everyone knew that *training* enabled a prisoner to more easily make a successful transition into mainstream society, while *working* was what inmates do as part of their punishment as dished out by the guards.

After the meeting was called to order and the roll read, a motion was quickly made from the floor to approve the leaders' letter and send it on to the state's correction administrator. The membership discussed the prison labor program and the union stewards were unusually sensitive to projecting the notion that, on a philosophical basis, they had no objection to prisoners earning some money that might be paid in the form of restitution to victims or victims' families. But they protested the suggestion that restitution was the driving force behind the use of prison labor. The facts on restitution had been easily collected by the secretary and the membership was informed that only $1.7 million out of the nearly $530 million dollars that was annually given to victims out of the Justice Department's Office for Victims of Crimes fund actually came from prison labor — the rest came from corporate fines.

Case 28: Competition from Behind Bars

At one of the tables in the union hall, a member told his coworkers, "Corporate criminals who are found guilty of pilfering millions from victims were not required to work while in prison for wages to repay victims." He laughed as he quipped, "I wonder if the executives at Arthur Anderson and ENRON know this?"

For Mary Klinesmith, however, this was not a time to be funny or humorous. She had worked hard to get into the union and she valued the wage and benefits she had earned and the quality of life it helped her provide as a single mother for her three children. When she stood up to address her peers, it became apparent that she had placed a great deal of thought into the prepared statement that she read.

"Work is important to us and we get our identity from the work we do. Our work becomes an extension of who we are and by using prison labor — our new slave labor in America — it devalues our self-worth and diminishes our self-esteem. All of you know that we have as workers only one source of real power, the right to withhold the value derived from our labor. Prison labor is exempt from the rules of contract negotiation and the collective bargaining activities performed by our union. The use of prison labor compromises the ultimate tool we have available in dealing with management — the right to strike. We can stop working, but prisoners can't. This is America! What are they trying to do to us? Many of us as loyal Americans have served in the military and helped make this country truly safe for democracy. This is certainly some form of recognition that we get in return for being proud, law-abiding Americans who earn a decent wage for a decent hour of labor! Now, we have to compete with pedophiles, thieves, and murderers! We don't ask for much, but can't we have the dignity back that we have all earned as workers?"

As Mary sat down, her remarks were met with thunderous applause and whistles. She had made it clear that work was important and that the union would not succumb easily to state-sponsored programs that jeopardized the welfare and future of unionized employees.

Exhibit 1. International Labour Organization Convention #105 Abolition of Forced Labour Convention, 1957

PREAMBLE

The General Conference of the International Labour Organization, Having been convened at Geneva by the Governing Body of the International Labour Office, and having met in its Fortieth Session on 5 June 1957, and

Having considered the question of forced labour, which is the fourth item on the agenda of the session, and

Having noted the provisions of the Forced Labour Convention, 1930, and

Having noted that the Slavery Convention, 1926, provides that all necessary measures shall be taken to prevent compulsory or forced labour from developing into conditions analogous to slavery and that the

Case 28: Competition from Behind Bars

Supplementary Convention on the Abolition of Slavery, the Slave Trade and Institutions and Practices Similar to Slavery, 1956, provides for the complete abolition of debt bondage and serfdom, and

Having noted that the Protection of Wages Convention, 1949, provides that wages shall be paid regularly and prohibits methods of payment which deprive the worker of a genuine possibility of terminating his employment, and

Having decided upon the adoption of further proposals with regard to the abolition of certain forms of forced or compulsory labour constituting a violation of the rights of man referred to in the Charter of the United Nations and enunciated by the Universal Declaration of Human Rights, and

Having determined that these proposals shall take the form of an international Convention, adopts the twenty-fifth day of June of the year one thousand nine hundred and fifty-seven, the following Convention, which may be cited as the Abolition of Forced Labour Convention, 1957:

Article 1

Each Member of the International Labour Organization, which ratifies this Convention undertakes to suppress and not to make use of any form of forced or compulsory labour —

(a) as a means of political coercion or education or as a punishment for holding or expressing political views or views ideologically opposed to the established political, social or economic system;

(b) as a method of mobilizing and using labour for purposes of economic development;

(c) as a means of labour discipline;

(d) as a punishment for having participated in strikes;

(e) as a means of racial, social, national or religious discrimination.

Article 2

Each Member of the International Labour Organization which ratifies this Convention undertakes to take effective measures to secure the immediate and complete abolition of forced or compulsory labour as specified in Article 1 of this Convention.

Source: C105 Abolition of Force Labour Convention, 1957, http://www.ilo.org/.

Prison Labor: A Booming Business

Tesh felt better now! The meeting was successful and the vote came out the right way. On his way home, he could not get out of his mind that 38 states had authorized the use of prison labor by private employers in intrastate commerce, and that prison industry sales had exceeded $9 billion last year. What still annoyed him, however, was that many prisoner produced products would be exported proudly and stamped with the "Made in the USA" label and that states had already begun to advertise their prison industries. In conducting the background research, he had uncovered an advertisement that he had posted on the union board alongside the meeting announcement.

CORRECTIONAL ENTERPISE SERVICES — Highly motivated and reliable workers; customized to meet your company needs; bring work back to our state from overseas — hire our prison-based workforce.

He was proud that he had taken the time to post it alongside of the meeting announcement.

"Maybe, just maybe," he chuckled to himself, "the announcement would help energize the membership to get off their butts!"

Right now, however, he was prepared to taste the victory and was so happy that the union had stuck together and had given their unanimous approval of the letter. As he traveled down the road, he reflected on the discussion that some of the members had concerning what constituted a "successful" prison firm. When asked from the floor, Jim Hanson, one of the strongest stewards in the shop, stated that facilities with a low turnover — meaning states with mandatory sentencing and minimum-security prisons located close to maximum security sites — are considered to be the most successful.

Hanson had also stated, "This is needed in case prisoners behave well and are then moved to a lower security site. It would be bad news for the firm should the new prison be located away from their factory."

He had passionately stated during the meeting that companies that hire prison labor really seek "lifers," because they represent a stable work force and that hiring preferences at some firms are given to prisoners with mandatory terms of five years or more — which raises the question of work as a form of rehabilitation for quick and successful reentry into society.

As Tesh turned off State Highway 43 and headed down the last stretch of highway that would take him home, he recalled the words of Mary Klinesmith that evening, "Rewards for productivity are inexpensive for the firm and include fast food lunches and other prison luxuries that are inconsequential outside of prison life."

He remembered what she said about court rulings on prison labor and that they were "not covered under minimum wage, pension, unemployment compensation, workers' compensation, collective bargaining, or any other laws designed to insure worker rights in the U.S."

Tesh thought this made perfect sense from the corporate perspective and thought how pathetic our society had become that we had arrived at the point where, as one company executive stated, "We now have secured a workforce that we don't have to worry about showing up for work or suing us courtesy of

Case 28: Competition from Behind Bars

the state!" As he recounted what he had read and heard about the use of prison laborers, he knew that he and the union were on the right side of this issue.

*Case, in part, was adapted from material presented in "Prison Labor: Are We Heading Back to the Future?" prepared by the Public Employee Department, AFL-CIO.

Questions and Instructions:

1. Discuss the merits of creating a work environment for persons in prison. Do the benefits outweigh the costs? Is there an overriding factor in this policy that makes a cost versus benefit argument inappropriate? Please elaborate.

2. Does the prison work system, as described in this case, violate the International Labor Organization Statement? Please elaborate.

3. What role does the union play in this issue? Should unions unite to fight against prison labor? Why do you think that unions would be concerned with this issue?

4. From a human resources management perspective, what are the major implications associated with hiring prisoners to perform governmental work, such as maintenance or new construction of government buildings or campuses? As a personnel specialist, would you consider the hiring of prisoners for any line of work in your organization on site? Please be specific and provide a rationale for your answer.

5. If the money earned by the prisoners working in the "private sector" would be used for victim restitution, child support, taxes and per diem meal and lodging expenses, would your attitude toward the prisoner training program change? Please explain.

6. What are some of the implications for the personnel department who hire those who are reentering society after serving time in prison? Would you consider hiring a convicted felon in your line of government work? Would you find it objectionable to work with a felon? Please elaborate and give several reasons why you would or would not hire a convict who had met his or her sentencing obligation.

Case 28: Competition from Behind Bars

Case 28: Competition from Behind Bars
Name:

Case Log and Administrative Journal Entry

This case analysis and learning assessment is printed on perforated pages and may be removed from the book for evaluation purposes.

Case Analysis:
Major case concepts and theories identified:

What is the relevance of the concepts, theories, ideas and techniques presented in the case to that of public management?

Facts — what do we know *for sure* about the case? Please list.

Who is involved in the case (people, departments, agencies, units, etc.)? Were the problems of an "intra/interagency" nature? Be specific.

Are there any rules, laws, regulations or standard operating procedures identified in the case study that might limit decision-making? If so, what are they?

Are there any clues presented in the case as to the major actor's interests, needs, motivations and personalities? If so, please list them.

Case 28: Competition from Behind Bars

Learning Assessment:
What do the administrative theories presented in this case mean to you as an administrator?

How can this learning be put to use outside the classroom? Are there any problems you envision during the implementation phase?

Several possible courses of action were identified during the class discussion. Which action was considered to be most practical by the group? Which was deemed most feasible? Based on your personal experience, did the group reach a conclusion that was desirable, feasible, and practical? Please explain why or why not.

Did the group reach a decision that would solve the problem on a short-term or long-term basis? Please explain.

What could you have done to receive more learning value from this case?

29

Life at Quality Care House

by
C. Kenneth Meyer and Gina DeVoogd

Emily Hyde has been a faithful employee at Quality Care House (QCH) for about a decade. She was passionate about her duties there and felt a strong connection between her work and the way she led her life. She had witnessed how so many in her field had attempted to separate their work from the essential ingredients of living: eating, recreating, loving, playing, and enjoying. She felt that her education had at least exposed her to some major psychological theories such as Sigmund Freud's "Will to Pleasure," Alfred Adler's "Will to Power," and Viktor Frankl's "Will to Meaning." Emily felt a strong kinship with Frankl because in her own way she had found values that were not only meaningful internally, but were worth pursuing. In her own pedestrian way of looking at life, she felt that the will to meaning was born within one's soul and, if that was the case, then nobody could take away her ultimate freedom to choose her attitude toward living. And, in her case, early on in her life, she had begun to realize her own shortcomings and yet loved herself as she loved and forgave others. She made progress in finding her own sense of meaning and it included the enduring values of justice, fairness, mercy, empathy, love, and compassion.

QCH, she imagined, was like literally a million other "half-way houses," and "assisted living arrangements" that dotted the urbanscape. Her clients were people in need of assisted living and were placed in community neighborhoods where they might have a reasonable chance of living a "normal" life — whatever that meant. Organizationally, QCH had many homes that were scattered across a multiple state area. In brief, each home had a maximum of four clients who were assisted by two full-time caretakers. Clients were selected and designated to a home based on their level of development — essentially their ability to function in society, take care of their personal hygiene, and live in a social system similar to a family unit.

QCH promoted as it core philosophy the value of family living and as such it became a home for those who lived there. The residents in turn lived out their days doing what the traditional nuclear family was largely thought to have done fifty years earlier in the United States. That is, they ate breakfast, lunch and dinner together, as a family seated around a table. Their activities for the day were planned in advance and the family members looked forward to their "outings" as they were called. The activities were by and large routine in nature, but oftentimes challenged their physical and mental abilities. For Emily, her charges were persons who had challenges mentally and developmentally and she found the label of "mental retardation" and "crippled" repugnant! In short, QCH was a house with four bedrooms, a kitchen, living room and several bathrooms. Each person had a separate bedroom and their own private space, when needed.

Emily was the lead caretaker during the second shift. She enjoyed working from 3:00 p.m. to 11:00 p.m. because it gave her flexibility in the mornings to pursue her own personal and recreational interests. Although Emily had hours that gave consistency and continuity to her shift, her care-partners varied as they were assigned from one home to another based on need and attendance behaviors. Emily was supervised by Marion Burns who had many years of social work experience tucked under her belt. For the most part, her long tenure had worn well with Marion and on her sleeve she wore the interests and needs of the residents. Each week she visited QCH and checked with the residents and, of course, with Emily on their situations. Emily liked Marion Burns and the feelings of respect and good will seemed to vibrate sympathetically between them. Burns was always friendly and promoted excellent care for the "household" and praised the way that Emily treated and related with her "family."

Initially, Rex, a 20-year-old male resident of QCH, followed Emily around the house and repeatedly told her how much he loved her. It was not uncommon for him to repeat the mantra, "Love, I love, I love you---you, you, you." In medical terms, this condition is known as *echolalia*. In family situations, Rex told his associates of the fantasized love he had for Emily and she for him. Eventually, he began to further fixate on the idea of getting married to Emily, and he told his colleagues at dinner that was his only desire. In a courteous, respectful way, Emily responded to the group with a polite smile and said she "…loved all of them equally," and would not be getting married to Rex or anyone else in the household. Although she felt uncomfortable about Rex's newly found attraction, she knew this sort of behavior often is manifested in the environment in which she labored.

Rex's infatuation with Emily was not disquieted by the way that Emily responded to his overtures of love and romance. A week or so later when Emily arrived at the home to begin her shift, when as usual, the residents asked for and were each given a hug. Customarily, members of the home would ask Emily for a hug and in a "therapeutic" manner she would respond with warmth and care. However, when she gave Rex a hug he responded by grabbing her breasts. Although the contact was brief, she acted in a mature, professional manner and took Rex aside from the group and explained that touching her breasts was inappropriate and it was "ok" if he loved her, but only in a "friend to friend" way—not in a "boyfriend-girlfriend" manner. Rex seemed to understand what Emily had explained and they both went about their routines as if nothing had happened.

Emily thought her "little talk" with Rex was having the intended and desired effect and a week or so went by without a repeated, inappropriate, incident. Then, one night as Emily was checking on the residents in their bedrooms, she bent over to reach the water glass on Rex's nightstand and move it to a place where it would not be spilled during the evening. As she leaned to reach the glass, Rex reached up and pulled her off balance and she fell on top of him. He wrapped his arms around her and attempted to kiss Emily's lips. Emily sternly told him to "stop" and "…never to do that again!"

Emily, of course, understood the cognitive and developmental difficulties that she was expected to professionally and competently handle on a daily basis. Accordingly, she documented Rex's sexual interest and behavior and charted it in her daily report.

Case 29: Life at Quality Care House (QCH)

When Marion Burns made her next weekly supervisory visit, Emily told her about Rex's infatuation, inappropriate language, and aggressive sexual advances (attacks), and asked for her experienced advice about how she might treat Rex in the future. During her conversation, Emily specifically asked for training in "self-defense" so she might protect herself from Rex or from any other future attack. Marion responded with concern and deep appreciation for Emily's request and said that she would see what kind of training the parent organization might provide. As they parted, Marion assured Emily that Rex's behavior was probably "…just a brief infatuation," and that it would end as time went on.

Rex's affection toward Emily did not subside. He continually told her he loved her and when she looked at him he responded by "blowing kisses at her!"

Three weeks passed since Emily and Marion talked about Rex's "attachment" problem. Then, as Emily was helping Rex get dressed, he spontaneously reached out and pinched her breasts. In pain, Emily reacted to the pinches by slapping Rex on the face. He then released her.

Dutifully, Emily once more admonished Rex and she immediately reported the incident to her supervisor. In an apologetic and humble demeanor, Emily told Marion that the slap was a "reflex action" to the pain and that she had no intent to either hit Rex or cause him any pain, harm or personal injury. Accordingly, as procedure called for, Marion reported the incident up the chain to Raymond Hills, the director of Quality Care Homes, Incorporated. In turn, he dispassionately terminated Emily with dispatch and indicated that her response was inappropriate, unethical, unlawful, and "unnecessary." Later, Raymond Hills told his colleagues about the incident and said he only learned after the termination had been effected, that Rex had previously sexually assaulted Emily.

Emily was astonished and humiliated by her termination. She now wondered how she should respond to QCH's long goodbye. Yet, she remembered the story of Viktor Frankl's imprisonment at Auschwitz and Dachau concentration camps and that the will to meaning comes from within — not from the outside. She had the freedom to choose her response. Now, would she respond with anger, indignation and rage, or were her better instincts directing her to forgive herself, forgive others and let understanding, love and a positive disposition characterize her attitude. After all, Emily was merely seeking in her life to become a decent, honest, person who served others.

Case 29: Life at Quality Care House (QCH)

Questions and Instructions:

1. Was Emily Hyde a victim of sexual harassment? If yes, please explain and if not, why not?

2. Did Marion Burns handle Emily Hyde's earlier reports of sexual assaults adequately? Please explain.

3. If you had been placed in Raymond Hills' position, how would you have dealt with the problem of Emily Hyde striking a vulnerable person — one of her charges? Please explain.

4. What kind of training, if any, would have been appropriate for "care pairs" working at Quality Care Home to have formally received? Please elaborate.

Case 29: Life at Quality Care House

Case 29: Life at Quality Care House
Name:

Case Log and Administrative Journal Entry

This case analysis and learning assessment is printed on perforated pages and may be removed from the book for evaluation purposes.

Case Analysis:
Major case concepts and theories identified:

What is the relevance of the concepts, theories, ideas and techniques presented in the case to that of public management?

Facts — what do we know *for sure* about the case? Please list.

Who is involved in the case (people, departments, agencies, units, etc.)? Were the problems of an "intra/interagency" nature? Be specific.

Are there any rules, laws, regulations or standard operating procedures identified in the case study that might limit decision-making? If so, what are they?

Are there any clues presented in the case as to the major actor's interests, needs, motivations and personalities? If so, please list them.

Case 29: Life at Quality Care House (QCH)

Learning Assessment:
What do the administrative theories presented in this case mean to you as an administrator?

How can this learning be put to use outside the classroom? Are there any problems you envision during the implementation phase?

Several possible courses of action were identified during the class discussion. Which action was considered to be most practical by the group? Which was deemed most feasible? Based on your personal experience, did the group reach a conclusion that was desirable, feasible, and practical? Please explain why or why not.

Did the group reach a decision that would solve the problem on a short-term or long-term basis? Please explain.

What could you have done to receive more learning value from this case?

30

The Expectant Mother

by
Gina DeVoogd and C. Kenneth Meyer

Robert Miller, supervisor of the mail department at Mount Pleasant Hospital, contacted Sophie Stanton, Human Resources Manager, to hire a temporary employee to replace mail sorter Jessica Robinson. Jessica had been approved to leave the office for a 6-week period to have a pre-scheduled medical procedure. Robert requested a temporary employee for an 8-week period. Further, he requested the temporary employee work in the office with Jessica for two weeks to learn the mail sort position prior to Jessica leaving for her medical procedure. He stated: "A week or so on-the-job-trading (OJT) is worth many days of orientation and classroom training."

Stanton contacted Kent and Company, the local temporary agency that was customarily used by the hospital. After performing the normal, but obligatory, background check and documents that Mount Pleasant Hospital required, Kent and Company sent Paula Jacobson to assist with the mail sort.

Two days after Paula started working with Jessica Robinson to learn the "ins and outs" of sorting and delivering the mail, Robert Miller again contacted Sophie Stanton. Robert said to Sophie, "Paula is very smart and learning the mail room work quickly. However, Paula is not going to work out in our department. Sadly, she is an 'expectant mother'."

In response, Stanton asked Robert, "Has Paula indicated to you that she is expecting a baby and that she will not be able to fulfill the assignment we requested?"

Robert replied, "No. However, she looks as if she could deliver the baby any day and I need someone who can work the entire period that Jessica is going to be away from the office. This is a mail room, not a delivery room."

Case 30: The Expectant Mother

Questions and Instructions:

1. Should Robert discuss with Paula her expected delivery date and explain the requirements of the temporary assignment? Please explain.

2. Based on the maternity and discrimination laws, what options are available for Mount Pleasant Hospital to pursue? Do you believe the hospital can end Paula's temporary assignment because of her pregnancy? After all, the hospital requested someone to fill Jessica's position for an 8-week period. Can the hospital end Paula's assignment if she is performing well in the job they requested her to do? Please explain.

3. What responsibility does the temporary agency have in this situation? Should the temp agency have sent someone to fill the Mount Pleasant Hospital assignment if they knew the temporary employee would not be able to fulfill the entire assignment period? Please elaborate.

Case 30: The Expectant Mother
Name:

Case Log and Administrative Journal Entry

This case analysis and learning assessment is printed on perforated pages and may be removed from the book for evaluation purposes.

Case Analysis:
Major case concepts and theories identified:

What is the relevance of the concepts, theories, ideas and techniques presented in the case to that of public management?

Facts — what do we know *for sure* about the case? Please list.

Who is involved in the case (people, departments, agencies, units, etc.)? Were the problems of an "intra/interagency" nature? Be specific.

Are there any rules, laws, regulations or standard operating procedures identified in the case study that might limit decision-making? If so, what are they?

Are there any clues presented in the case as to the major actor's interests, needs, motivations and personalities? If so, please list them.

Case 30: The Expectant Mother

Learning Assessment:
What do the administrative theories presented in this case mean to you as an administrator?

How can this learning be put to use outside the classroom? Are there any problems you envision during the implementation phase?

Several possible courses of action were identified during the class discussion. Which action was considered to be most practical by the group? Which was deemed most feasible? Based on your personal experience, did the group reach a conclusion that was desirable, feasible, and practical? Please explain why or why not.

Did the group reach a decision that would solve the problem on a short-term or long-term basis? Please explain.

What could you have done to receive more learning value from this case?

31

Managerial Succession

by
C. Kenneth Meyer and Gina DeVoogd

Austin Ford, director of operations in the Metropolitan Transit Authority (MTA), had a real dilemma. During the past few months, he had received many complaints about Annie Tate from her co-workers. Annie managed the customer service department — a position she held for only eight months. Austin knew that Annie had to be removed from her current management position and reassigned to a non-management position. She had discovered while pursuing her undergraduate degree in management that there were many ways to place a person on the path to career succession, but the literature was limited as to how to deal with the emotionally charged idea of actually demoting someone without damaging their self-esteem or deadening their motivation and morale.

Austin began sizing up his staff and identifying some others who might make a good replacement for Annie. Austin wanted someone who was smart, flexible, would treat employees fairly, and someone who was able to keep up with managerial responsibilities associated with the position. He also wanted to promote someone who was a good communicator, fair, and made good decisions.

The first employee who came to mind was Maggie Smith. Maggie was well liked as a manager and she had managed several areas in the authority during her ten years of service. Maggie excelled in opening a customer service satellite office for the MTA. Indeed, she had successfully hired and trained the new staff consisting of 12 employees. Currently, Maggie was in the Claim and Process Control Department. When Maggie started managing that area, she had major attendance issues with the staff. The department had been using archaic procedures initiated by an earlier administration and no one questioned changing them to make the tasks more efficient and jobs more easily accomplished. Maggie put together project teams to look at the functions of the department and in a few months her unit exceeded the goals established for the production of claims and mail processing. Also, and importantly, attendance issue that once plagued the department was no longer problematic. In fact, some of the other departmental managers who had also experienced a high level of absenteeism "picked Maggie's brain" in an attempt to find out what she had done to turnaround the attendance rate. Austin felt that although Maggie had been in the department for less than a year, he was confident that she was the right choice to head up the customer service department.

Maggie Smith was called into the director of operations office. Austin Ford asked Maggie to leave the management position in Claims and Process Control and move to customer service. Austin told her that his current manger, Annie Tate, was going to be shifted to a non-management position in a different department due to the many complaints he had received about the way she had led the department and handled personnel issues. Additionally, Austin told Maggie this assignment would represent a "tough fix" in a department that had run amuck, but he had faith that she would be able to size up the problems quickly and made the needed corrections in both attitude and in operation.

The complaints Austin received ranged from Annie showing preferential treatment by going to lunch with specific staff members, to Annie regularly attending after-hour parties with several of the staff members. This behavior caused some of the staff to feel that she had given special treatment in job assignments and responsibilities, and had unfairly scored some employees high on the annual employee performance evaluations. One employee explained that she fell asleep at her desk because of the medication she had taken to help manage pain associated with a broken ankle. Annie, rather than awaking her gently, shook her shoulder and yelled at her in front of her co-workers. Needless to say, the employee reported that she felt like dirt and she was embarrassed to have eye contact with her peers for several days.

Two others complained that Annie refused to handle work issues related to staff errors and told employees who came to her with their concerns to "...consult, confer and provide feedback to each other." Austin also recalled on several instances where the assistant director became angry because Annie failed to complete timely mandatory governmental reports, and when completed, they were filled with errors.

The first day on the job in the customer service department, Maggie noticed that many of the employees did not speak to one another. The employees who spoke to one another were usually at each other's desks and they whispered rather spoke in a normal audible level. Maggie learned from Emily, a team member, that staff members with the department were pitted against one another. Annie had empowered the employees to give each other feedback on errors found in their work and that the feedback was not given or shared in a professional manner, producing hard feelings.

On the second day in the department, Maggie opened her email and quickly scrolled through the list of incoming mail. To her surprise, she had received an invitation from one of her new employees inviting her to birthday party which was to be held at a sports bar on Sunday afternoon. She also was astonished to open another email that invited her to attend a Pampered Chef party the next weekend hosted by a staff member in her department.

Maggie noticed that Emily had been charged with managing the vacations of all staff members and that she would approve some and not others. Emily mentioned to Maggie that she was going to meet with one team member and discuss the excessive amount of time that she had been away from work during the last performance period.

At the end of first week in her new assignment, Maggie had already received about 25 suggestions from Joshua Blakely, a customer service representative, on how to improve the department and the changes that should be made in the processing and control operations.

Case 31: Managerial Succession

Maggie understood that the employees in her department worked in a high stress environment due to the constant changes that were being made by those in the human resource department and finance and accounting departments, as well as those which were coming down from the U.S. Department of Transportation (DOT) and its corollary department at the state level. Her staff had to simultaneously deal with all of these changes and the fallout from a previous, failed administration.

Questions and Instructions:

1. What attributes would you have looked for in selecting the person who was to head up the Customer Service Department? Please list and give the reason for each trait.

2. Would you have accepted the invitation to the birthday party or to the Pampered Chef party? If yes, why would you have accepted and if no, why not?

3. Had you been placed in Maggie Smith's position, how would you have sized up the organization and prepared yourself for what dilemmas you were to encounter in a department that had a failed manager? Please explain.

4. Do you believe Austin Ford acted properly by detailing the reasons why Annie Tate was being demoted and transferred to another department? Do you think it violated any right that Annie Tate might have toward privacy and confidentiality? Please explain.

Case 31: Managerial Succession

Case 31: Managerial Succession

Case 31: Managerial Succession
Name:

Case Log and Administrative Journal Entry

This case analysis and learning assessment is printed on perforated pages and may be removed from the book for evaluation purposes.

Case Analysis:
Major case concepts and theories identified:

What is the relevance of the concepts, theories, ideas and techniques presented in the case to that of public management?

Facts — what do we know *for sure* about the case? Please list.

Who is involved in the case (people, departments, agencies, units, etc.)? Were the problems of an "intra/interagency" nature? Be specific.

Are there any rules, laws, regulations or standard operating procedures identified in the case study that might limit decision-making? If so, what are they?

Are there any clues presented in the case as to the major actor's interests, needs, motivations and personalities? If so, please list them.

243

Case 31: Managerial Succession

Learning Assessment:
What do the administrative theories presented in this case mean to you as an administrator?

How can this learning be put to use outside the classroom? Are there any problems you envision during the implementation phase?

Several possible courses of action were identified during the class discussion. Which action was considered to be most practical by the group? Which was deemed most feasible? Based on your personal experience, did the group reach a conclusion that was desirable, feasible, and practical? Please explain why or why not.

Did the group reach a decision that would solve the problem on a short-term or long-term basis? Please explain.

What could you have done to receive more learning value from this case?

32

Crossing the Ethical Divide

by
Jack Fellers and C. Kenneth Meyer

The antique "New England" clock ticked slowly on the mantle. Brock looked back and forth from the nearly empty glass in his hand to the clock. He had hoped that a refreshing drink would bring some comfort and perhaps some insight. He glanced again at the clock: 2:00 a.m. It seemed like days had passed since the events of the past evening unfolded. He had tried to sleep, but sleep did not come easily this night. "Perhaps, just perhaps, this was a bad dream and that it would dissipate as he awakened." He wondered to himself about what had happened and wished that things could go back to the way they used to be, back to the good years. But, as he thought about it, he realized that things had been going downhill for some time — tonight, he realized that he had gone over the cliff.

Brock Throckmorton was, in everyone's eyes, the epitome of success. He had a thriving professional career that spanned more than 20 years of having progressive responsibility and heightened personal achievement. He had a great family life and was actively involved in many corporate, professional and community activities. His peers and neighbors respected him and if truth be known, envied his successfulness. Mostly, in his circle of close associates, he was known as a team player, an ethical professional, and a devoted family man.

Brock began his career as a sales representative for a regional heavy equipment company. He quickly moved up in the organization as his sales success led him to more promotions and eventually to work for a Fortune 500 company. He continued to climb the corporate ladder, earned an MBA, and ultimately topped off his career having risen to the rank of vice president of marketing. At first, all was well as sales continued to climb, new talent was recruited, innovative new products were released, and recognition and rewards came his way. But Brock was not in the career field that he had idealized while in college and wanted to be engaged in work that had a socially responsible mission. He often said to his wife that he wanted to work for a nonprofit organization that would enable him to return something of value to the community and to society. That dream came true when he was hired to work in one of the largest nonprofit organizations in the state.

He took to his new position and duties "like a duck takes to water." It all seemed so natural for him to devote his considerable talents and expertise in generating funds and grants that would help serve those who he said, "had virtually lost their voice in society."

Case 32: Crossing the Ethical Divide

However, for the last several consecutive quarters things have not gone well for Brock. A new rival appeared on the scene, not one of the traditional competitors, but an upstart, a new nonprofit that was heavily utilizing technology to help add and keep clients in a way that Brock had never seen before. His organization spent hours studying this upstart, hired consultants to evaluate their processes and even hired away some of their lower level talent at high salaries and wages. But all of this was of no avail. Brock's ability to generate new contributions continued to slide as his competition was coming on strong. He was feeling a tremendous amount of pressure from the CEO and the Board of Directors, and was unable to explain to them what had happened, what had gone wrong. Nothing he tried seemed to work. The competition seemed to beat him to every potential contract, and seemed to have an uncanny way of determining their needs and settling in on what would be considered a comfortable contribution. Brock had reached the end of his rope. That led up to the events of tonight.

What Brock did know from the analysis of the other organization was that they had some new strategy, some new way of using technology to obtain enormous amounts of client information using the Web and then storing this information in large databases. They would then "sweep" those databases to put the key information into a data warehouse. Subsequently, they used data mining techniques to "go against" the data warehouse to provide information to use in delivering their services to their clients and contributors. Their employees could browse through that data on the organization's Intranet and target key clients easily. As a result of this new strategic information system, coupled with a new and innovative Client Relationship Management System (CRMS), many of Brock's contributors switched over to this new startup. Brock realized that the only way to compete was to get his hands on some of that data. But first, he had to figure out what they were doing and how they were doing it. Failure to discover their successful methods and techniques would mean that his organization would be adversely impacted financially and that could even mean job loss—including his own position.

Earlier in the evening, Brock had been sitting in his study, staring blankly at the computer screen. Startled by the doorbell, he got up to answer the door. To his surprise, it was Jeremy, a fifteen-year-old adolescent neighbor. Jeremy was infatuated with Brock's daughter Sara. Unfortunately for Jeremy, Sara and her mother had left earlier in the evening for a couple hours of shopping at the Riverside Mall. Jeremy, however, was in a chatty mood and Brock needed a distraction, so he invited him into the house. As they chatted, Brock remembered what Sara had said about Jeremy being some kind of computer genius and that he had gotten into trouble several years ago by hacking into several computer systems. Brock thought about asking Jeremy if he knew anything about the competitor Brock was dealing with. Then, he had an idea. Maybe if he framed it as a challenge he could get Jeremy to try to hack into the upstart's computer systems and find out what they were doing.

Brock thought about the implications of asking an adolescent to do something that he knew was patently wrong. Jeremy noticed that Brock was distracted and asked if something was bothering him. In a moment of desperation, Brock playfully challenged Jeremy to see if he could break into the other organizations' computer systems. He teasingly stated to Jeremy that this organization "…had bragged that no one ever could get into their systems!" The gauntlet was down. "I've heard you're good with computers, but probably not that good!" The challenge was taken. Jeremy at once went at the computer with a gleam in his eye and with purposeful intent. This was a dare and Jeremy had the ability to measure up to the challenge.

Case 32: Crossing the Ethical Divide

Brock stood and watched in amazement as Jeremy easily bypassed one security measure after another. "Primitive!" he heard him exclaim. Brock realized that what the information technology (IT) people had been telling him about their own systems was true: that someone who really knows what they are doing can break into nearly any conventional computer system. Once Jeremy entered the system and printed the data Brock wanted, he continued to search through the complicated system. Startled by the tune on his cell phone, Brock admonished Jeremy to "Get out before we get caught!" Jeremy, however, was fascinated with what he was finding and made a startling discovery. Most of the data the competition was collecting was being acquired in an illegal way, through highly sophisticated and complex methods. As Brock looked through the data, he realized that they were also collecting information about his own organization and the other state-based and regional nonprofits that they were in competition with. "It's all beginning to make sense," Brock mused to himself on how the new startup had been successful in hitting the ground and capturing a lucrative donor base.

Jeremy, who had been caught up in thrill of the moment, began to sense that there was more than just a casual challenge at hand. He looked up at Brock and saw the fear in his eyes as sweat began to roll down Brock's cheek. He wondered what had just transpired; breaking into systems had always been a fun challenge, but this time he had sensed that maybe he had gone too far. As Jeremy got up to leave, Brock kept saying over and over again that, "This will be our secret, and whatever you do, don't tell anyone and stay away from the computer!" As Brock ushered Jeremy out the door he realized that he had just crossed a line he had stubbornly refused to cross during his twenty-year career.

Now, sitting in his den alone, he once more was captivated by the ticking clock; he wondered out loud about what was he to do next? His options were pretty bleak. If he did nothing, the other nonprofit would continue to roll over his own and perhaps jeopardize the future of other nonprofits in the region. He asked himself if his own career security was being placed on the line and if he might even lose his job. Further, he realized that he could not turn them in anonymously or "blow the whistle" publicly. He had looked at it from every angle and he was not without his own blame and guilt. He was caught in a classic prisoner's dilemma and there was no easy way for him to be extricated from the problem that was of his own adventure and making. He reasoned, "I can turn them in, but to do so, I will have to explain to authorities not only what Jeremy and he had found, but how the sensitive information was discovered."

The clock continued to move ever more slowly and as the pendulum moved from left to right producing its natural, rhythmic sound. Brock knew he must move quickly or forever hold his voice. If the new startup realized that someone had broken into their system, and that their database had been compromised, they might hire a forensic specialist to track and identify who had penetrated their fire wall. Although it was clear that his competition had collected and stored information that had been unlawfully gathered and mined without the consent of the clients, vendors, contributors or donor organizations, Brock realized that he was not without blemish and fault himself. Time was of the essence and he had to make a decision and he had to make it now. Then he rationalized in his own doubting and skeptical mind, "Who knows what else they might do in terms of collecting and using illegally obtained, proprietary information."

Case 32: Crossing the Ethical Divide

Questions and Instructions:

1. What unethical or illegal actions have taken place in this case and by whom?

2. If you were Brock, what would you do? Remember, you cannot turn the other company in anonymously. You either have to "go public" or say nothing. There is no middle ground. How did you reach your conclusion; what process did you go through?

3. Based on your response to question two, what are the likely consequences of your actions (i.e., what will happen to you, Jeremy, your organization, your competitor)?

4. If you were Brock, what could you have done differently? If you were Jeremy, what would you do now?

Case 32: Crossing the Ethical Divide

Name:

Case Log and Administrative Journal Entry

This case analysis and learning assessment is printed on perforated pages and may be removed from the book for evaluation purposes.

Case Analysis:
Major case concepts and theories identified:

What is the relevance of the concepts, theories, ideas and techniques presented in the case to that of public management?

Facts — what do we know *for sure* about the case? Please list.

Who is involved in the case (people, departments, agencies, units, etc.)? Were the problems of an "intra/interagency" nature? Be specific.

Are there any rules, laws, regulations or standard operating procedures identified in the case study that might limit decision-making? If so, what are they?

Are there any clues presented in the case as to the major actor's interests, needs, motivations and personalities? If so, please list them.

Case 32: Crossing the Ethical Divide

Learning Assessment:
What do the administrative theories presented in this case mean to you as an administrator?

How can this learning be put to use outside the classroom? Are there any problems you envision during the implementation phase?

Several possible courses of action were identified during the class discussion. Which action was considered to be most practical by the group? Which was deemed most feasible? Based on your personal experience, did the group reach a conclusion that was desirable, feasible, and practical? Please explain why or why not.

Did the group reach a decision that would solve the problem on a short-term or long-term basis? Please explain.

What could you have done to receive more learning value from this case?

33

The Downward Spiral of Founder's Hospital

by
C. Kenneth Meyer and Alison Lemke

Frank Jahoda had been a hospital and health care administrator for nearly twenty-five years. He began his career in the field of finance and business administration, but soon was viewed as not only a "quick study" but also one who had a penchant for asking the right questions. Jahoda prided himself as being a competent team leader who could size up a problem quickly and turn what was destined to fail into success. Those who worked with Jahoda considered him pragmatic and an effective team player and turnaround manager. He loved, as he often said "…to demonstrate the there are many routes to success, and that listening to and trusting co-workers are two signposts that cannot be missed on the journey." Sure enough, Jahoda felt that his rapid rise through the administrative ranks of a large hospital were part luck and he would say it was "…merely being at the right place at the right time," but those who knew him well largely discounted his self-deprecation and said he was able to formulate a vision, communicate it and build an environment on interpersonal trust. Therefore, when he was hired as a consultant for Founder's Hospital, he came with a set of credentials that were beyond reproach and his trademarks of honesty and integrity were embedded in his *persona*.

Frank Jahoda was hired as a consultant by Melinda Wise, Interim CEO, to assess and objectively report on what he was told constituted "…failed board oversight, mismanagement, low physician and staff morale, and declining public confidence in Founder's Hospital." Melinda Wise was an experienced health care provider in her own right with many years of nursing under her belt at Founder's Hospital and a laudable track record as head nurse in several other regional hospitals.

He knew that Founder's, as it was usually called, was facing same difficulties and he learned from his grapevine connections, that things had gone awry. Frank had a track-record of being brought into situations were failure was an ongoing state of affairs, but he would reserve passing judgment until he had spent a week or so interviewing the hospital board of directors, hospital employees, the administrative team and, of course, the physicians, nurses, and allied medical professionals.

In making his rounds he met an allied health care employee who had a calm demeanor and responded to his queries with what he concluded were "carefully scripted, independently mature, and objective observations." In the course of his interview, he asked Cheryl Elmore if she would put into her own words what had transpired at Founder's and do so in a chronological order. Frank was not surprised when he received the following statement:

Case 33: The Downward Spiral of Founder's Hospital

Hospitals do not operate in a vacuum! Citizens of Pearl Valley are concerned about the recent developments at Founder's Hospital. They learned that a prominent physician group sent a statement of non-support for Harold Alexander the hospital's CEO, alleging fiscal mismanagement, poor physician/administration relationships, obsolete management practices in the Department of Human Resources and the Office of Accounting, Finance and Management (OAFM), and on-going operating losses. The hospital has in rapid succession gone through three failed CEO's: Bill Jones, resigned in 2000; Ralph Hays, resigned in 2005; and Gary Ward, resigned in 2008. All three executives lost the confidence and support of the physicians but the community was told that they resigned for reasons other than the loss of confidence.

As Jahoda made his rounds, he probed, listened, and reflected on what he had been told by the many stakeholders. He learned, for instance, that recently, some hospital employees had joined forces with the physicians and had reiterated the list of complaints and grievances presented by the physicians through an active letter writing, email and blogging campaign. By sending their stories to the local newspaper, they had not only gone public, but had upped the "ante." A careful reading of the letters and emails shows complaints on the following topics:

- premature and short-sighted management practices among the ranks of the administrative team;
- plummeting employee morals and job satisfaction;
- inhumane treatment of employees by the human resources director;
- precipitous decline in patient care services while nurse to patient ratios were increased;
- decline in nursing staffing while experiencing a dramatic increase in middle-management positions;
- favoritism and cronyism practiced by the Board of Directors, who are close social friends with the CEO, CFO and director of human resources; and,
- long-term permanent hospital employees who felt they must submit to administrative prerogatives or face certain retaliation.

According to the rumor mill, some board members were bewildered to learn that upper managers were ruthless with employer service, although Jahoda found all of the recent CEO's seem to be congenial and "outwardly nice." He felt it was reasonable to believe that Founder's recent financial difficulties were somewhat related to poor Medicare and Medicaid reimbursements and an increase in the percentage of uninsured patients — problems that apparently were not aired in the administrative meetings with the board. Upon meeting with the Board of Directors, Frank wrote in his notebook the following remarks:

- Board members who were friends with members of the hospital's administrative team were stunned by the outpouring of dissatisfaction and the complaints that were published in the newspaper.

Case 33: The Downward Spiral of Founder's Hospital

- Accusations of conflict-of-interest among board members seem to be somewhat unfair since members stated they were unaware of the widespread unhappiness in the hospital and local healthcare community.

- Board members had been repeatedly reassured by the two most recent CEO's and by the administrative team that the hospital was basically in "fine shape," and that the financial problems could be easily fixed. They were also told that the negatively expressed from a selected few low performing, disgruntled employees should not be given much credence or veracity. And these few disaffected employees needed to be "weeded out" from the ranks of the valued employees if the hospital were to be successful.

Frank reflected on what he had been told from the various stakeholders and began to put together his report. He wrote the following, preliminary statements. Of course, he was just beginning to see the full picture of what was taking place at Founder's Hospital. He reflected on his interviews and made the following points that would be used in his final report.

- Founder's Hospital [FH] has a long history of operation dating from 1920's and is considered to be a treasured, local asset.

- FH kept current by adding new services, updating and expanding the facilities as required by population growth and hospital/clinical utilization rates.

- FH has a solid reputation for being a compassionate, personalized, and competitive center that provides an excellent standard of care.

- FH has a history of investing in new diagnostic and treatment equipment to provide high-quality patient care.

- Several years of patient surveys demonstrate high levels of satisfaction with physicians, hospital services, and health care employees.

- During the last decade, FH has experienced an increase in the number of uninsured patients, higher number of patients covered by Medicare and Medicaid--both programs have a record of providing inadequate reimbursement based on Diagnostic Related Groups (DRG) in contrast with private insurers, thus producing substantial patient cost-shifting.

- FH has experienced increased competition for hospitalization services from larger, metropolitan hospitals in the regional delivery area.

- Controversy exists among the board over the compensation package established for the position of CEO, CFO, and HR director. Founders Hospital is a 501(c)(3) not for profit organization and is housed in a governmental (municipal) owned facility, thereby not exempting it from publicly revealing the pay for its top executives as reported with the IRS 990 form. Legal counsel indicated the presence of State's Attorney General's opinion that stated, in effect, that since the city owned the hospital, but did not give it ongoing operating funds, it was not obligated to release salary information. Bonuses for executives are given at the end of the fiscal year and based on financial results, and approved by the Board of Directors.

- Physicians and Board of Directors are engaged in the development of a new strategic plan.

- The new strategic plan retained the long-standing mission statement for FH's "...to meet community needs by providing compassionate, personalized health services."

- The CEO and administrative team appear to place great emphasis on meeting the twin goals of growing net revenues and managing expenses in order to remain competitive. This is perhaps due to the private sector backgrounds of the executives.

- Salaries for clinical staff are benchmarked below the salaries for similar job classifications in other area hospitals.

- A new Information System (IS) has been installed with costly computer software. The new system is generally viewed as being cumbersome and time-consuming for clinical and nursing staff to use, thus resulting in decreased time for direct patient care, and increased job dissatisfaction for care givers.

- Patient satisfaction survey for 2009 revealed an "alarming" decline in availability of nursing staff, food quality, room cleanliness, and other important hospital services and amenities.

- Hospital employees and physicians are dissatisfied with the administration of the hospital and have ventilated their grievances publicly.

Frank Jahoda had now completed interviewing hospital stakeholders and had to settle in and write a report of his findings and recommendations. He had ample "evidence" that the rapid turnover of executives at the highest levels had left its own "DNA" on administrative leadership, oversight, accountability, transparency and management continuity. Frank understood that emotions had been "rubbed raw" in the physician and health care ranks and that it would take more than the one time application of a magical "happy lotion" to assuage these disgruntled and alienated feelings. He also understood that his findings would be presented to the Board of Directors in several weeks and that what he presented would not please all stakeholders. He realized that based on his past consulting experiences that some would want to know what had gone wrong at Founder's Hospital and who was to blame and others would worry about its survival. And, of course, some would want the problems identified and quickly remedied. Realistically, Frank thought to himself, there was no "silver bullet" in his armory that would immediately solve this management scenario and enable Founder's to heal quickly.

Case 33: The Downward Spiral of Founder's Hospital

Questions and Instructions:

1. What do you think might be the effect of the public airing of grievances on the part of the hospital employees and physicians? Do you think "going public" on the issue was justified? Why or why not?

2. Did the Board of Directors exercise adequate and appropriate oversight of their community hospital? Why or why not? Please elaborate. What role should the board play for a public or non-profit hospital? Please be specific.

3. What are some internal management issues that are raised in the case study? Did these internal management issues contribute to the difficulties this hospital was now facing? Please explain.

4. Do you think the emphasis upon financial performance, as reflected in the hospital's strategic goals and its awarding of bonuses to executives based on financial performance, is appropriate for a public hospital? Why or why not?

Case 33: The Downward Spiral of Founder's Hospital

5. Do you think hospitals like Founder's should be allowed to shield the salaries of their executives from public view? Why or why not? If you were a member of the public who believed this information should be made public, but you were unable to gain access to the information, what steps would you take next? Please explain.

6. What does it mean to manage a hospital "for the public good" with regard to financial performance and community benefit? Please comment.

Case 33: The Downward Spiral of Founder's Hospital

Case 33: The Downward Spiral of Founder's Hospital
Name:

Case Log and Administrative Journal Entry

This case analysis and learning assessment is printed on perforated pages and may be removed from the book for evaluation purposes.

Case Analysis:
Major case concepts and theories identified:

What is the relevance of the concepts, theories, ideas and techniques presented in the case to that of public management?

Facts — what do we know *for sure* about the case? Please list.

Who is involved in the case (people, departments, agencies, units, etc.)? Were the problems of an "intra/interagency" nature? Be specific.

Are there any rules, laws, regulations or standard operating procedures identified in the case study that might limit decision-making? If so, what are they?

Are there any clues presented in the case as to the major actor's interests, needs, motivations and personalities? If so, please list them.

257

Case 33: The Downward Spiral of Founder's Hospital

Learning Assessment:
What do the administrative theories presented in this case mean to you as an administrator?

How can this learning be put to use outside the classroom? Are there any problems you envision during the implementation phase?

Several possible courses of action were identified during the class discussion. Which action was considered to be most practical by the group? Which was deemed most feasible? Based on your personal experience, did the group reach a conclusion that was desirable, feasible, and practical? Please explain why or why not.

Did the group reach a decision that would solve the problem on a short-term or long-term basis? Please explain.

What could you have done to receive more learning value from this case?

34

Daughter Dearest: Nonprofit Nepotism

by
Ben Bingle and C. Kenneth Meyer

Dan Grayson felt physically and emotionally spent and was ready for a "time-out" from his daily office routines. He was a self-identified "workaholic" with broad experiences and knew the "ins-and-outs" of his position. He was never given a project that he did not relish taking on and this orientation would soon become problematic. Accordingly, as the number of projects under his purview grew, he became stretched and stressed. Thus, it came as no surprise that he would wait with an expectation of "hurried anticipation" for the Christmas-New Year break, a week of paid time-off.

Generally, Dan enjoyed his position as program director for the Credit Builders Association (CBA) – a national 501(c)(3) nonprofit organization which provided training and resources for low-income clients with credit problems. He loved the fact that he was able to help vulnerable people establish credit worthiness and create a lasting impact in the lives of others. Although national in scope, CBA featured a staff of only ten employees, which caused Tina Murphy, the CBA executive director, to often refer to the tight knit group as a "family."

While Dan Grayson did not consider his associates as being part of his own family, he did enjoy the cordial and caring working relationships he had established with them. He considered the organizational culture of CBA to be inviting, warm and flexible, but he was not terribly comfortable with its lack of structure and standardization — attributes of formalization he preferred. For example, although organizational policies governing hiring and procurement (purchasing) were in place, they were essentially "cut and pasted" from examples downloaded from the Internet. Elementary, but sufficient, they were used to pass muster for a national audit that CBA underwent several years earlier. The audit required mandatory written policies for the different functions and phases of human resources management and budgeting and financial administration. However, the executive director and the Board of Directors did not look at them as being much more than "window dressing" — in short, as one director quipped, "CBA will comply until we die." And, noteworthy, organization decisions were rarely made on the substance of the policies that had been "boiler-plated." Dan often laughed to himself about CBA not being policy bound.

Dan had five years of experience with CBA national in the Prairie Island office, and was the most tenured staff member other than Tina Murphy, the executive director. As a trusted and valued co-worker, Tina relied upon him completely and sought out his advice and assistance when making hiring decisions, developing strategic partnerships, and when confronting organizational difficulties. When asked to help,

Case 34: Daughter Dearest: Nonprofit Nepotism

Dan would sometimes joke with Tina and say, "This isn't in my job description and it is certainly above my pay grade," and then they would "knowingly" smile at one another.

Dan had a few projects to wrap-up before he left for the holidays. First and foremost, he had to prepare the agenda for the upcoming staff meeting that was scheduled at the end of the week. He would be meeting with staff from CBA's other branch offices and they would present their quarterly progress reports. Then, they would have a "holiday lunch," exchange some gifts, and head back to their offices to ready themselves for the anticipated weekend. Dan especially looked forward to "putting his feet up" and taking off some well-deserved time.

The staff meeting had gone off without a hitch. As Dan and his colleagues were gathering their materials, logging off from their laptops and placing them in the carrying cases inscribed with the CBA acronym, Tina Murphy nervously cleared her throat and said, "Excuse me, I have a couple of things I would like to cover that were not on the agenda."

Taken back, all eyes and attention turned to her as she slowly rose from her chair and began to speak in an authoritative voice. She informed her associates about a commitment she entered into with Banker's Loan and Trust (BLT) and how exited she was about the new partnership. She said, "CBA would gain access to new revenue sources and much needed credit lines which would enable CBA to help qualified clients get reasonably low interest rates on their loans without meeting the 'normally' expected, higher credit scores."

Tina did not appear to be conversant with all of the details surrounding the newly formed agreement and did not itemize any of its positive or negative implications. However, she indicated that CBA would be moving ahead with the project because it opened some doors that were previously closed, and would ultimately serve as a good source of unrestricted revenue. She further stated, as her eyes darted around the conference table, that they would need to "Immediately staff-up for the new venture and make a new hire." Then, to everyone's astonishment she told the group that she had made the hiring decision and Mandy Murphy would be joining the staff and heading up the new initiative. While she elaborated, her staff responded with blank stares and stony silence as no words or eye contacts were exchanged. Then, she intoned with a raised voice, "I realize that the decision to hire my daughter may raise questions, but please know that I have thoroughly discussed this appointment with Mandy and I guarantee you that there will be no conflict of interest. Initially I had some reservations about this hire, but as I talked it over with Mandy, it became obvious she was a great candidate and a good fit for the organization. Also, time is a factor if we want to capitalize on the BLT project. To reiterate, and I can't say this more emphatically, there will be no conflict of interest or preferential treatment. As you get acquainted with Mandy, you will come to know that she is a perfect fit with our culture and staff."

The staff began to fidget nervously with the unpacked paperwork they had received during the staff meeting as she wound down her remarks. Tina then asked if there were any thoughts or concerns on the matter and since none were raised, she thanked them for their attention and wished them a joyful holiday season. Of course, how could anyone express their concerns or reservations at this juncture? After all, the issue at hand was the hiring of the boss's daughter!

Case 34: Daughter Dearest: Nonprofit Nepotism

After a period of uncomfortable silence — a quietude that seemed to last for an eternity—Tina gleefully closed the matter and said: "Ok, I just wanted to make sure that everyone was aware of what we have going on. I know Mandy looks forward to working with you. Who's ready for lunch? I'm excited that we will have the opportunity to share some quality time together before we go our separate ways."

Dan carpooled to the restaurant with two of his closest associates, in stark silence. As they waited to be seated, it was obvious that everyone was trying to erase from their minds what they had just heard at the staff meeting. Accordingly, they began to "chit-chat" about their holiday plans and upcoming schedules.

Dan sat down at the elongated table that had been set by the restaurant staff, and as he arranged his napkin and adjusted his tie, Tina came to him and leaning over whispered in his ear, "Just give Mandy a week and she will show you why I hired her for the job. She'll be great!"

Once more, Dan could not believe his "lying" ears. Tina had singled him out in front of the entire staff in order to inform him of her daughter's greatness. Dan wondered if Tina actually thought that he was the only staff member who would question Mandy's hiring, and, if that was her belief, she had totally lost her footing in reality.

"What a way to begin a vacation," Dan muttered to himself, as he drove back to the office. As he reflected on what had just transpired, he began to feel "sick to his stomach." Dan knew there were no specific state laws against nepotism, but he could not fathom why this hire differed so much from past CBA hiring decisions. In the past, Tina never made a hire without first consulting him. This time, the position was not advertised to ensure a large candidate pool from which to select, hiring was done before the funding had been established, and a detailed recruitment and selection process had not been satisfied.

The more Dan assessed what Tina had done, his upset stomach turned into psychological disgust. He had a "*de ja vu*" moment as he recalled a conversation that Tina had initiated six months earlier when she told him that Mandy had been actively looking for a job the past year without much luck! Obviously, Dan reasoned further, Tina knew this decision would reverberate throughout the organization. Why else would she have taken the time to ask him to give Mandy a chance? Had Tina sprung this on the CBA staff right before the holiday lunch, and their week off from work as a premeditated strategy? Or, were these factors purely coincidental with the side effect that any ill feeling would undoubtedly "cool" with time? Had Mandy submitted a resume? Was she qualified for the task at hand when a position description had not yet been written? And, what would happen if the partnership with BLT failed? These questions should be probed, but who would risk jeopardizing their relationship with Tina by asking them?

As Dan entered the city limits of his home town, he thought about the awkwardness of the next staff meeting. Knowing that Mandy lived in a city on the Atlantic coast, would she relocate or telecommunicate from a remote office located in her home? Would she be provided a subsidy for a residential office with a computer, printer, Internet connection and the accompanying supplies? Would CBA authorize air travel to attend staff meetings at the home base? And Dan could not resist thinking about the first staff meeting in which Tina and Mandy would be jointly present. Would this "mother-daughter banquet" have greater future repercussion on the CBA staff, organizational culture, and balance

Case 34: Daughter Dearest: Nonprofit Nepotism

sheet? These questions would be answered in the course of time, but now Dan was tired and he had just had the "wind taken out of his sails." Then, Dan had a final "entertaining" notion as he pulled into his garage, "With the holidays coming up is there any better way to show love for a daughter then to hire her?"

Questions and Instructions:

1. Is there any substance to Dan Grayson's questioning of Tina Murphy's hiring decision and the way it was done? Please explain.

2. Please identify the implications, positive and negative, associated with nepotism? Please elaborate.

3. Assess the manner in which Tina Murphy announced the new hire? Was her decision premeditated or coincidental to the "holiday" staff meeting?

Part 2, Continuation of the Case Study

Dan Grayson enjoyed his vacation despite all that had transpired earlier in the CBA office and although he wanted to place the nepotism issue to rest, it seemed to pop-up as his visits with friends and family members drifted towards work. The twin emotions of shock and disbelief were commonly shown by others when Dan told them about the recent CBA hiring decision. The circumstances surrounding the hiring and the blatant disregard for the Equal Employment Opportunity Act sentimentalities and laws would surely have to be dealt with later.

With the holiday behind him, Dan returned to his office and everything again seemed normal: mountains of paperwork to process, dozens of unanswered telephone calls, hundreds of emails, some important and some that would have been better off if blocked. Nevertheless, one email he received came from a close colleague simply stated "Get a load of this!" Attached to the email was a document entitled Credit Builders Association Conflict of Interest Policy, as displayed in **Exhibit 1**.

Case 34: Daughter Dearest: Nonprofit Nepotism

Exhibit 1. Credit Builders Association Conflict of Interest Policy

> **Definition: Organizational Conflict of Interest**
>
> A conflict of interest arises when a director or employee involved in a decision-making capacity is in the position to benefit, directly or indirectly, from hi/her dealings with CBA or entities and/or individuals conducting business with CBA.
>
> Examples of conflicts of interest include, but are not limited to, situations in which a director or employee of CBA:
>
> 1. Negotiates or approves a contract, purchase, lease, or other legally binding agreement on behalf of CBA and has a direct or indirect interest in, or receives personal benefit from, CBA or the individual providing or receiving the goods or services;
>
> 2. Employs, endorses the employment of, or approves the employment of, on behalf of CBA, a person who is an immediate family member of the director or employee; and,
>
> 3. Sells products and/or services offered by CBA in competition with CBA.
>
> **Conflict of Interest Violations**
>
> Violations of this policy, including failure to disclose conflicts of interest, may result in termination of a director, executive director, or member of senior management (at the direction of the audit committee) or employee (at the direction of the executive director or chair of the audit committee).

Pressed for time given the backlog of communication he had on his desk, Dan quickly read the attachment and it appeared that Tina Murphy's decision to hire her daughter was a direct violation of the CBA policy and was "punishable" with termination. Yet, he felt charitable toward his director since she had never referenced this policy in discussing organizational decisions and may not have known that her new hire violated CBA policy. More problematic and troublesome to Dan was the prospect that the concern over nepotism had spread more generally throughout the office and this was "not a good thing!"

Fighting the urge, Dan Grayson finally opened his Internet browser and typed the words "workplace nepotism" into the search field. He wanted to become more informed about the consequences, legalism, and the pros and cons related to nepotism. He knew that nepotism had its proponents and detractors in industry and commerce. It was considered to be one of the many ways that perspective employees get prepared to join organizations and along with education, training, internships, apprenticeships, and other means of enhancing vocational aptitude was an "effective" way of socialization and anticipatory assimilation. Whatever the case, push had come to shove and Dan and others would have to come to terms with CBA's newest employee.

Case 34: Daughter Dearest: Nonprofit Nepotism

Questions and Instructions:

1. In consideration of the CBA conflict of interest policy as shown in Exhibit 1, what responsibilities, if any, does the CBA Board of Directors share in this case of nepotism? Please explain.

2. Did the conflict of interest policy preclude the hiring of Mandy Murphy? Please explain.

3. What are some of the considerations that the executive director should have weighed before hiring an immediate family member? Please elaborate. Would you have made a similar decision of you were filling Tina Murphy's shoes? Why or why not?

Case 34: Daughter Dearest: Nonprofit Nepotism

Case 34: Daughter Dearest: Nonprofit Nepotism
Name:

Case Log and Administrative Journal Entry

This case analysis and learning assessment is printed on perforated pages and may be removed from the book for evaluation purposes.

Case Analysis:
Major case concepts and theories identified:

What is the relevance of the concepts, theories, ideas and techniques presented in the case to that of public management?

Facts — what do we know *for sure* about the case? Please list.

Who is involved in the case (people, departments, agencies, units, etc.)? Were the problems of an "intra/interagency" nature? Be specific.

Are there any rules, laws, regulations or standard operating procedures identified in the case study that might limit decision-making? If so, what are they?

Are there any clues presented in the case as to the major actor's interests, needs, motivations and personalities? If so, please list them.

Case 34: Daughter Dearest: Nonprofit Nepotism

Learning Assessment:
What do the administrative theories presented in this case mean to you as an administrator?

How can this learning be put to use outside the classroom? Are there any problems you envision during the implementation phase?

Several possible courses of action were identified during the class discussion. Which action was considered to be most practical by the group? Which was deemed most feasible? Based on your personal experience, did the group reach a conclusion that was desirable, feasible, and practical? Please explain why or why not.

Did the group reach a decision that would solve the problem on a short-term or long-term basis? Please explain.

What could you have done to receive more learning value from this case?

35

Entrepreneurialism or Exploitation

by
C. Kenneth Meyer and Amy Cowan

Herbert Fairfield's gloomy disposition changed to one of zeal and enthusiasm as he read the local newspaper account of how several cities had begun to use "ex-cons" and homeless persons to provide services related to public custodial, maintenance, repair and construction jobs. The article specifically addressed how ex-convicts were used to plant trees, refurbish sidewalks, groom boulevards, clean up neighborhoods, and even make furniture for municipal uses. Fairfield had bought into this idea many years earlier and felt that city governments could be operated more efficiently, effectively and "better" than they were in many cities that he had worked in and visited during his twenty-five years of service to the state's League of Counties and Municipalities (LCM).

As he read the newspaper he gave pause to reflect upon what he had learned in the early 1990s about governmental change or transformation. Although the ideas presented then were fresh, they now seemed ancient and obsolete by contemporary management standards. He laughed to himself about the need to have "smarter," more transparent, responsive, accountable and fair government today and he wondered if that was what he thought to be synonymous with the "good government" practices. He also recalled the litany of concerns that earlier writers, such as Dwight Waldo, Aaron Wildavsky, David Osborne, Ted Gaebler, Tom Peters and a host of others had identified in their seminal contributions to the public administration and public policy literature. As his mind began to race, he felt the resurgence of the passion he once had for innovation and change. He once more became "fired up" about what was being done in Summit Grove, a city of nearly 200,000 people. He liked the challenge of making government relevant, flexible, efficient, ethical, risk oriented, results and mission driven, creative, and entrepreneurial. He said, "Everything has its time in history and that time has arrived for thinking outside the tube."

As a corollary, Herbert wanted the same employment chances to be available for the city's sizeable homeless population as well as for ex-convicts. He told his peers, "Cleaning and sweeping city streets, mowing grass, planting trees and shrubs, or mopping floors in City Hall or the numerous municipal buildings, may not seem too exciting or enriching to the average person but take, for example. Jasper Knoll's experience. Jasper led a pretty normal life until his late teens when it began to change for the worst. He began and continued to occasionally use illegal drugs, then stole a bicycle for the evening to cruise the loop downtown and was arrested by the local police. Jasper's decision to break the law did not include that part of the equation that dealt with behavioral consequences. As the scenario unfolded, Jasper was not only arrested, but then booked into the Cotton County Jail, eventually convicted, and then sentenced to several years in lockup. For people like Jasper, the opportunity to clean and sweep streets, plant trees or mow grass offers him a chance to get a new lease on life, get a fresh breath of air, and rekindle a sense of hopefulness."

Herbert began looking closer at what was taking place in Summit Grove. Summit Grove shared many financial characteristics with it neighboring cities: reduced tax revenues, home foreclosures, loss of jobs, and generally a tightened budget. As the city examined ways it could cut costs, maintain acceptable levels of city services, and complete city projects that had been postponed too long, it created a work program specifically designed for inmates of the Cotton County jail.

The city of Summit Grove desired to become part of the pathway to successful employment for ex-convicts enabling them to garner gainful work experiences and pay while under the supervision of the state's Department of Corrections (DOC). The inmates involved in the work program had to qualify as "trustees," meaning they had to meet the standards for trustworthiness. Accordingly, the criteria, status, and processes for inmate participation were established by the city. The warden, Jeremiah Golfman, would make sure that inmates who worked outside the prison walls were not only qualified for participation, but that they would be adequately supervised. Golfman thought that common sense should drive the policies and procedures would be established. Inmates had to meet strict eligibility standards for the program: the inmate presents a minimum security risk, inmate must volunteer themselves for the work; and those charged with serious crimes against persons or property (rape, child molestation, murder, robbery, etc.) would be denied participation.

In addition to the basic qualifiers, the jail established a multiple check-off system to minimize risk and maximize program successfulness. First, inmates had to be approved by the jail's shift supervisor who had daily contact and knowledge of the inmate's behavior. Thus, those with disciplinary problems were automatically disqualified. Second, the booking department reviewed the inmate's record and examined such factors as parole holds and open charges in other jurisdictions. Also, inmates who had medical problems that prohibited them from working were identified and then denied participation. Last, the warden would review the inmate's entire record to ensure that his decision was in complete compliance with all laws, regulations and rules, and only when all qualifications had been fully met, would inmates be assigned to the work program. This was a risky new venture, Golfman thought, and he could not afford to place the citizens of Summit Grove in physical harm or jeopardy. As he explained later, it was essential to reduce the public's exposure to risk (public safety), and to help ensure the overall success and veracity of the program. After all, as Warden Golfman warned, "One bad apple can destroy the whole program, resulting in program cancellation."

Setting up the qualifications for the work program seemed to be rather straightforward and simple once completed. Voluntary participation, background checks, and an assessment of the inmates overall fitness to participate had been established. What seemed to be far more difficult, however, were the "sticky" questions concerning inmate compensation and the potential for public employee labor replacement. In terms of compensation, the "Goldilocks Paradox" presented itself: "How much is too little, just right, or too much?" Will pay be required and, if so, should the prevailing minimum wage prevail? Should homeless persons be compensated and inmates not paid? And, yet more difficult to answer was the question related to pay and volunteerism. After all, volunteers do not get paid for

Case 35: Entrepreneurialism or Exploitation

voluntary work and if inmates and the homeless are volunteering their services, should they be treated just like other citizens who volunteer?

In terms of the work program's impact on city and county workers, it was clear that volunteer labor should only be used to augment, not replace permanent laborers. In discussing the program with city, county and union officials, it was determined that the program should make certain that no public employees lost their jobs to either the homeless or to the inmates. On the other hand, the question remained as to whether or not volunteer laborers should be used in lieu of contracting out activities and projects to the private sector or to faith based programs. And when money was saved due to the volunteer efforts, should the financial savings be redirected toward programs for the "needy" or for projects that would enhance the city/county facilities or properties? These questions needed to be answered if public support was to be garnered and opposition arguments to the program diffused.

To Warden Golfman the program had to be designed to meet the twin goals of providing a service to the community and also providing work therapy. He understood that those who participated in similar regimes elsewhere had a heightened feeling of self-esteem, felt more productive, experienced a greater freedom of movement, valued hard work and the ability to get outside the prison and, importantly, experienced a sense of personal responsibility. For some, these were emotions they had never experienced. The literature on this kind of work program also suggested that inmates had a chance to develop positive attitudes and relationships that would eventually translate into self-improvement, economic independence and sustainability.

Questions and Instructions:

1. Should municipalities, cities, towns and counties look to inmate and homeless work programs to lighten their budgetary problems? Please be specific.

2. Remuneration or pay is a potential "deal breaker" for the work program. Should homeless workers be compensated for their work on public activities and projects? Please explain. What about incarcerated persons who participate in work programs? Please explain.

Case 35: Entrepreneurialism or Exploitation

3. Public safety concerns, real or perceived, will be central to the policy debate. What safety concerns do you believe are likely to arise from the different quarters of society, such as the general public; public employee organizations; private maintenance and construction businesses; and, victim center public interest groups? Please elaborate.

4. If inmates are paid, should the earnings be offset by allocations to prison administration and operating costs, victim restitution funds, or their obligations, when applicable, for child support? Please be specific.

5. What mandatory personal and program eligibility requirements should be satisfied for homeless worker participants? Please explain. And, what essential criteria should be satisfied for the inmate participants? Please explain. Should the mandatory and essential eligibility requirements be the same or should they differ by strata? Please elaborate.

6. How would you go about ensuring that the public safety and welfare would be protected, especially given the stereotypes or images often associated with inmates and homeless persons? Please discuss.

7. During a period of financial scarcity and tight budgets, how would the costs associated with providing competent professional supervision, management, orientation, and training be handled? Please elaborate.

Case 35: Entrepreneurialism or Exploitation

Case 35: Entrepreneurialism or Exploitation
Name:

Case Log and Administrative Journal Entry

This case analysis and learning assessment is printed on perforated pages and may be removed from the book for evaluation purposes.

Case Analysis:
Major case concepts and theories identified:

What is the relevance of the concepts, theories, ideas and techniques presented in the case to that of public management?

Facts — what do we know *for sure* about the case? Please list.

Who is involved in the case (people, departments, agencies, units, etc.)? Were the problems of an "intra/interagency" nature? Be specific.

Are there any rules, laws, regulations or standard operating procedures identified in the case study that might limit decision-making? If so, what are they?

Are there any clues presented in the case as to the major actor's interests, needs, motivations and personalities? If so, please list them.

Case 35: Entrepreneurialism or Exploitation

Learning Assessment:
What do the administrative theories presented in this case mean to you as an administrator?

How can this learning be put to use outside the classroom? Are there any problems you envision during the implementation phase?

Several possible courses of action were identified during the class discussion. Which action was considered to be most practical by the group? Which was deemed most feasible? Based on your personal experience, did the group reach a conclusion that was desirable, feasible, and practical? Please explain why or why not.

Did the group reach a decision that would solve the problem on a short-term or long-term basis? Please explain.

What could you have done to receive more learning value from this case?

36

An Instance of Racial Bias

by
C. Kenneth Meyer and Jeff Geerts

Union City advertised for an administrative assistant-receptionist who could type forty-five words a minute and be proficient in a variety of software programs, such as Microsoft Word. The advertisement required that the applicant be pleasant, well-groomed, and willing to perform housekeeping duties. The advertisement stated that the salary was negotiable, depending on experience.

Among the applicants was Lani Kolini, a male Iranian and naturalized citizen who lived in Union City. He was thirty years old and a college graduate. While at college, Kolini held office in several social and honor organizations. He had received no job offers upon graduation.

Kolini was interviewed by Roger Clark, the city manager. Clark, a staunch patriot, served in the Vietnam War and was still active in the army reserve and veteran's organizations. He was in his late-fifties and the father of four boys. Although Clark had an uncanny way of letting everyone know he was the boss on all decisions, he got along well with city employees.

Kolini appeared for the interview with a small, well-groomed beard. When asked about the beard, he explained to Clark that he wore it because he wished to preserve his cultural heritage. Clark then questioned him about his connections with his native country and why he became a citizen of the United States. Kolini refused to answer the questions because he felt they were not job-related. Clark then told Kolini that if he were hired he would be expected to "perform some housekeeping duties" and "dress up the office." Kolini informed Clark that he always tried to be well groomed and pleasant but preferred not to wear a suit and tie or be someone's personal maid.

Kolini left the interview feeling that Clark had not treated him as a serious applicant for the position. He told his wife that the interview had been biased because he had not been questioned about his excellent credentials.

Kolini was not hired. Instead, Clark hired Rebecca Schlick, a 21-year-old high school graduate with two years' experience as a receptionist-data entry person at a local Hilton Hotel. She had minimal secretarial skills but was attractive and had a winning personality.

Case 36: An Instance of Racial Bias

Questions and Instructions:

1. List several reasons why you would have hired Kolini for the job.

2. List several reasons why you would not have done so.

3. What advice would you give Kolini regarding his next job interview and why? Please explain.

4. Does an employer have a duty to hire an overqualified applicant rather than one who is minimally qualified? Please be specific.

5. What legal remedies are available to Kolini? Please explain.

6. Does sexual discrimination extend to males in jobs that may have been traditionally held more often by women? Please explain, for instance, the implications associated with reverse discrimination.

7. What advice would you give Roger Clark concerning the questions he asked Kolini?

Case 36: An Instance of Racial Bias
Name:

Case Log and Administrative Journal Entry

This case analysis and learning assessment is printed on perforated pages and may be removed from the book for evaluation purposes.

Case Analysis:
Major case concepts and theories identified:

What is the relevance of the concepts, theories, ideas and techniques presented in the case to that of public management?

Facts — what do we know *for sure* about the case? Please list.

Who is involved in the case (people, departments, agencies, units, etc.)? Were the problems of an "intra/interagency" nature? Be specific.

Are there any rules, laws, regulations or standard operating procedures identified in the case study that might limit decision-making? If so, what are they?

Are there any clues presented in the case as to the major actor's interests, needs, motivations and personalities? If so, please list them.

Case 36: An Instance of Racial Bias

Learning Assessment:
What do the administrative theories presented in this case mean to you as an administrator?

How can this learning be put to use outside the classroom? Are there any problems you envision during the implementation phase?

Several possible courses of action were identified during the class discussion. Which action was considered to be most practical by the group? Which was deemed most feasible? Based on your personal experience, did the group reach a conclusion that was desirable, feasible, and practical? Please explain why or why not.

Did the group reach a decision that would solve the problem on a short-term or long-term basis? Please explain.

What could you have done to receive more learning value from this case?

37

What Should it Be? CEO or Executive Director

by
Angela Moody, C. Kenneth Meyer and Garry Frank

Joan Yamamoto was passionate about children and felt that their quality of care was a reflection of how they were valued by society. She often recounted with genuine fondness how much satisfaction — even happiness and joy — that she received as a care giver. Her day to day counseling and administrative duties were not without their idiosyncratic irritations, but she always hung on to a deeply engrained belief that hope would defeat despair, courage would trump fear; and, that peacefulness was preferable to conflict — whether among adolescents, adults, or for that matter, even nation states. In brief, she had dedicated her life to helping children and she was proud to be an employee with the Hope for Boys Center (HBC).

The Hope for Boys Center was a regional 50l(c)(3) nonprofit organization that was originally designed to provide essential services and help to boys in need of assistance (care) and a safe place to live while they faced their "issues." Sixty years ago, HBC opened its doors and at that time it provided educational opportunities, long-term living arrangements similar to those that were historically given by orphanages, and other residential-educational programs. As a regional center, HBC did not have the stature or funding of a Boy's and Girl's Town. Nevertheless, it was respected by social workers, psychologists, and the juvenile justice system for the overall quality of services it provided to adolescent boys.

For its first twenty-five years of operation, HBC utilized an organizational model that was commonly associated with the educational system of the day. Accordingly, it had a superintendent who was in charge of the overall operations and who reported to a board of directors. The professional staff were trained educators in several fields, and the house parents provided supervision and care during the evening hours. Later, HBC went through a number of changes. The majority of the residential staff was employed by the local school district. Then, the board of directors decided to add a mental health component to deal with clients in need of counseling and psychological therapy outside of the normal school hours. Thus, the superintendent model remained the design of choice for the agency with the administrative and professional staff on the payroll of the local school system and subject to its rules, regulations and standards. Later on, and more recently, HBC became a private, not for profit organization and as such, hired and paid its own social workers, psychologist, and sundry mental health employees.

During the last thirty-five years, Gordon White served as the superintendent of HBC. He was a legendary figure in the organization and was well liked and trusted for putting the interests of the boys

Case 37: What Should it Be? CEO or Executive Director

above everything else. As in most cases where incumbents are successful and have served for many years, it was inevitable that he would eventually decide to resign, although the board of directors was reluctant to accept his letter when that time came.

In accepting White's resignation, the board gave him the title of superintendent *emeritus*. They also decided that the time was ripe to revisit the leadership model at HBC and determine if a new model would be more *apropos*. The board acknowledged that the programs offered at HBC had fundamentally changed over the years from being entirely focused on educational and residential living to therapeutic programs in which education had become secondary. Therefore, they reasoned, the superintendent model had served them well over the years, but it was no longer typical of the organizational structures currently in most comprehensive residential treatment facilities. Secondly, the superintendent had dual roles to perform administratively: to manage the staff hired by HBC and to manage those who fell under the purview of the local school district. Also, there were two different sets of personnel policies, two employee unions, and the board had limited control over the decisions made by the superintendent. Now, with the departure of Gordon White, the board felt it was an opportune moment to examine the organization design, make appointments to a search committee, develop a position description, and in earnest begin its search for a new HBC director.

The search committee accepted its charge of hiring Gordon's replacement, and despite the objections of White, promptly contracted with an executive search company and began its efforts to identify and attract at least six experienced and qualified candidates for the advertised position of chief executive officer. A seventh candidate, Sylvia Hyde-Watson, was an internal candidate for the position. Although she had the required educational degrees, and had been a prime mover in the forward momentum of HBC, she lacked experience as an executive leader. The executive search firm did not place her among the top six candidates to be interviewed by the board and she was considered as a long shot for the position.

With Gordon White's retirement and the six candidates found unsatisfactory in one regard or another, the board felt they should fill the vacancy with Charles Grayson, a recently retired superintendent of the local school district. The board reasoned that a temporary hire was better than hiring a permanent executive director who was not the right fit. With Grayson in place, the board requested that the search committee review the policies and criteria it had initially established, and then go through the steps required to complete their task of searching for the right person to head HBC.

Sylvia Hyde-Watson had confided in her associates that she wanted to be the new executive director, but since the executive search committee had dismissed her from the search with little doubt that they had made the appropriate decision, she felt her chances were now "null and void."

The board asked a candidate who had been placed on the initial list to return for a second interview and to Sylvia's astonishment, surprise and utter amazement, asked her to sit for an initial interview. Sylvia was anxious to meet with the board, explain how her vision for HBC dovetailed with the center's mission statement, and explore with them her views of transformative leadership. In the back of her mind, however, she felt she was being mined for ideas of what kind of leader HBC needed to move ahead with its 21st century agenda. To her chagrin, she was nearly overwhelmed with delight when the search committee recommended her to the board and stated, "She had exactly the desired characteristics and qualities that they were looking for and was the right person for the position." In turn, the committee asked the executive search firm to conduct a Profile XT and the General Management-in-Basket test with Hyde-Watson. As expected, Sylvia passed the tests easily and the board, in a unanimous decision, offered her the job as executive director.

Sylvia held the top position in the organization as executive director, but she wondered why she was given a title other than that officially advertised and posted. She asked the hiring committee why she was not hired as the chief executive officer (CEO). Orville Mead, the board president told her that she did not have the tenure of the interim CEO and that she had not yet earned the title of CEO. Mead further explained that although the board had not established the exact or specific parameters for the position, it felt that the CEO designation was premature given her relative inexperience. In addition, he suggested that a CEO had a more strategic role in steering an organization — especially for a for-profit, private firm in which he was most familiar. Last, Mead told Sylvia that she was a rising star and would be saddled with directing HBCs activities for the first year and then, with the needed experienced garnered, the board would revisit the title associated with her present position.

Hyde-Watson however, questioned Mead further and asked on what criteria his definition of CEO was based. He responded in a voice of indifference that his definition was a commonly accepted and global one, at least in the private sector. Although he suggested it might not be a perfect fit, he felt comfortable that the board had acted rightly in changing the title from CEO to executive director. He then summarized his definition by giving the following example. He said, "A CEO is to a president, like an executive director is to the vice president in their respective worlds of work." This analogy only complicated matters in Sylvia's mind for she had been promoted from the second in command in her agency (vice president) to the top of her agency (president).

Sylvia realized that her attempt to reconcile the title in question was a losing battle, at least with Mead. The decision had been made and it was now immutable. Yet, she continued to wrestle with the feelings she harbored, that her gender may have had more to do with the board's decision than her level of experience!

Case 37: What Should it Be? CEO or Executive Director

Questions and Instructions:

1. Orville Mead, the president of the board, said he used a common definition of CEO from his world of business. Do you believe that his rationale is appropriate for private, public or nonprofit organizations? Please explain.

2. If you were selected to head a 501(c)(3) organization, would you prefer the title of executive director or chief executive officer? Please explain.

3. Please contact at least three nonprofit organizations in your community and identify the various titles given to executive leadership. Are there any commonalties? Please explain.

4. Do you think Sylvia Hyde-Watson thinking that she was a victim of gender based discrimination is justified? If yes, please justify your decision and accordingly do the same if you find no basis for discrimination.

5. In a number of universities today, there are indications that some academic departments are moving away from the traditional designations of department chairperson or department head to that of executive director. Similarly, it is now more common to find a president of a university to carry the dual title of president and chief executive officer. What do you see as the major implications, if any, of these recent changes in the kingdom of official titles? Please explain.

Case 37: What Should it Be? CEO or Executive Director
Name:

Case Log and Administrative Journal Entry

This case analysis and learning assessment is printed on perforated pages and may be removed from the book for evaluation purposes.

Case Analysis:
Major case concepts and theories identified:

What is the relevance of the concepts, theories, ideas and techniques presented in the case to that of public management?

Facts — what do we know *for sure* about the case? Please list.

Who is involved in the case (people, departments, agencies, units, etc.)? Were the problems of an "intra/interagency" nature? Be specific.

Are there any rules, laws, regulations or standard operating procedures identified in the case study that might limit decision-making? If so, what are they?

Are there any clues presented in the case as to the major actor's interests, needs, motivations and personalities? If so, please list them.

Case 37: What Should it Be? CEO or Executive Director

Learning Assessment:
What do the administrative theories presented in this case mean to you as an administrator?

How can this learning be put to use outside the classroom? Are there any problems you envision during the implementation phase?

Several possible courses of action were identified during the class discussion. Which action was considered to be most practical by the group? Which was deemed most feasible? Based on your personal experience, did the group reach a conclusion that was desirable, feasible, and practical? Please explain why or why not.

Did the group reach a decision that would solve the problem on a short-term or long-term basis? Please explain.

What could you have done to receive more learning value from this case?

38

The "Pink Slip" Support System

by
C. Kenneth Meyer and Charles Stewart

La Donna McKnight religiously read the *Wall Street Journal* (WSJ) on a daily basis and usually spent a good portion of her weekends absorbed in the Weekend Edition of the *New Work Times* (NYT) — her paper of choice and the nation's "newspaper of record."

As she turned the pages of the WSJ, she was amazed to read about the financial failures of banks (large and small), investment houses, security firms, insurance companies, Fannie Mae and Freddie Mac, and a myriad of other corporations. They had fallen into disarray and were either in a state of insolvency, Chapter 11, receivership, bankruptcy, or had been acquired, consolidated, or merged with other corporations. As she read the paper, she was astonished by the amount of federal dollars that were loaned to failed businesses in the form of bailout loans or payments. Paradoxically" she thought it was quiet strange that the records of who got what, when, were, why, and how much was not more transparent. "Indeed," she told her colleagues at work on Monday morning, "the waning days of 2008 were filled with accounts of billions of dollars that were 'coughed' up from the coffers of the federal government and the billions turned into trillions, in fact, nearly nine trillion dollars."

She read on with interest the op-ed written by a *Nobel laureate* economist who felt the funding for bail and buy-outs from the federal treasury would not become worrisome until another ten trillion or so dollars had been distributed to those who sought federal monies sufficient to salvage their enterprises. She thought her feelings were typical in that she realized that the economy had reached an acute level of financial instability both domestically and worldwide. And, according to the daily diet of news, the United States was in the midst of an economic recession that was unmatched since the "good ole days" of the Great Depression. Yet, the special interests that converged on the new financial "Wall Street," the federal city, were taking a number at the "bailout counter" and queuing-up: the big two U.S. automobile manufacturers (Chrysler and General Motors), state and local governments, a variety of insurance companies, in short, corporations big and small that needed a loan to bridge the troubled waters they were crossing.

What really irked La Donna was the insurance company — American International Group (AIG) — that solicited and was granted nearly $185 billion dollars or an amount approximately equal to 25 percent of the total Department of Defense (DOD) budget for fiscal year 2009. In addition, she complained that the money was turned over to AIG hardly without a word of public discussion or congressional debate. Accordingly, she wanted to have, like most of her colleagues, more public transparency and accountability for the federal dollars.

Further, as she read about the economic meltdown, she wondered why the various sectors of the economy had been treated differently. She said, "'Wall Street' interests were bailed out with ease and 'Main Street' businesses had difficulty getting the financial assistance and loans they required for survival." She asked herself if this was just one more example of upper-class economic interests trumping the interests of the working and middle-classes — the blue and white collar workers in the old, Midwestern, and formerly heavily industrialized cities. The rhetorical question she posed was succinctly answered in her own mind's eye. "Yes, layoffs will follow and bankruptcy would be the best cause of action for some of the corporations and businesses that failed to change, innovate, and adapt to the new world economic order. There should be no such thing as 'too big to fail.'"

As La Donna tossed these complex economic and political notions around in her head, she focused more closely on the national unemployment rate that had edged over nine percent and the nearly twelve percent unemployment rate present in her own backyard. These statistics, she mused, did not bode well for the future. In fact, bringing the matter closer to home, how would her own regional area deal with the prospect of having the only remaining automotive parts manufacturing plant shut down in her city? She further wondered if push came to shove and demands for automotive products were severely reduced or even eliminated, what would be the economic future of hundreds of non-unionized workers.

Unfortunately, La Donna had only a short time to wait before her fears became a reality and Grand Prairie was hit with one of the largest plant closings in its history.

Grand Prairie's largest remaining manufacturing company, ACME Automotive, Inc., announced that it would be closing its aging plant doors and moving its production to a new facility it had constructed several years earlier in Mexico. ACME's CEO Duane Butler cited escalating labor costs, high state and local governmental taxes, and excessive health care costs as the main economic factors on which the closure decision was predicated. The aging, obsolete plant was a non-union shop that employed nearly 350 workers, mostly in the parts manufacturing and assembling business. Butler regretfully informed the employees that due to the serious national recession and the precipitous decline that the industry expected in parts orders, that only those workers with critical job skills would be considered for transfer to one of two remaining U.S. operations. He further stated that layoffs would be across the board.

La Donna worked for the Region 4 Economic and Planning District and understood that ACME would need to comply with the Worker Adjustment and Retraining Notification (WARN) Act. This 1989 federal law she read, provides protection to employees, their families, and communities by requiring employers to give affected employees and the state and local representatives notice 60 days in advance of a plant closing or mass layoff. She examined the provisions of the act that made it applicable to employers with one-hundred or more full-time employees and downloaded the section on which she now needed to review and fully understand. She jotted down the following provisions of WARN and prepared to discuss them with her immediate supervisor, Jack Schwabe, the director of the 4th Economic and Planning District. She wrote in an abbreviated form these bulleted points:

Case 38: The "Pink Slip" Support System

- WARN is applicable to employers with 100 or more full-time employees;

- A 60-day notice of layoff is required when plant closings include 50 or more employees over a thirty-day period or layoffs of 50 to 499 employees equaling 33 percent or more of the workforce at a single site;

- Notification must be given to affected employees, union representatives (if applicable), and to the chief elected officials in the jurisdiction(s) — usually a mayor or county chair; and

- Important exception: Plant closure related to a natural disaster is not covered by WARN.

Shortly after La Donna had met with Jack Schwabe, he was notified by ACME that all employees had been notified of the plant closing. In addition, Mayor Randy Holbrook and County Chair Jake Lester and had also been officially given a formal letter of plant closing notification.

STOP: Please answer questions 1 to 3.

Questions and Instructions:

1. If you were in La Donna's position, how would you begin to prepare for the massive layoff at ACME? Please explain.

2. To what extent would you work with agencies and programs available at the city, county, and state levels, and also with ACME Corporation? Please elaborate.

3. What resources could you bring to the employees of ACME? Please list these resources and indicate how they would be helpful to ACME employees and the city of Grand Prairie.

Case Continuation: Second Part

La Donna McKnight had never directly experienced a plant closing and layoff of this size. In fact, none of the earlier plant closings or downsizing she was involved with had more than 30 to 40 employees and none of them met the threshold for WARN compliance.

Case 38: The "Pink Slip" Support System

She wondered how the city, county and planning district might be helpful to ACME employees as they prepared to be laid-off. Although she had some knowledge of the state's unemployment agency, she did not have a firm grasp of what role it might play, if any, in this situation, other than certifying worker eligibility for unemployment insurance.

Accordingly, she spoke with Miles Meier, Director of Human Resources for ACME, and he informed her that they had been contacted by the state's Office of Workforce Development (OWD), and told of the Workforce Investment Act of 1998 (WIA). In short, he stated, "This federal law was passed to consolidate, coordinate, and improve employment training, literacy, and vocational rehabilitation programs in the United States, and for other purposes." Meier also told La Donna, and to his surprise, that he had learned that a "one-stop" career center needed to be established that provided employee access to seventeen (17) different federal funding sources. As he spoke with the representatives of the local OWD, he was also told that a customer cannot enter a wrong door for services since they are all present behind the same door! Then, he was asked if he wanted to meet with the WIA representative and workforce development staff and consider hosting a "Rapid Response Event."

This was great news for Miles Meier and he promptly set up a joint meeting at the ACME plant for all affected workers. Not surprisingly, the meeting was heavily attended and the orientation provided by the OWD office was complete insofar as it presented an overview of all services that would be made available at the "one-stop" shop. The workers were informed that they were covered under WARN and, as such, were automatically eligible for all OWD services.

Applications were handed out to those in attendance and they were asked to complete and return them while on-site. Appointments were also scheduled for affected employees to meet an OWD designated career advisor. Further, at the briefing, staff members from the unemployment insurance office were present and they helped employees complete their applications for unemployment benefits. Most employees were impressed by the promptness of the governmental response and pleased that a process was beginning to take shape to help their transition, hopefully, to new jobs or careers.

Several weeks had passed since the OWD "one-stop" shop had been set up and La Donna had heard nothing but positive things about its operation from the mayor and county chair. She decided to see for herself and made an unannounced visit to actually observe firsthand the operation of the one-stop office. She was amazed, even shocked, at what she found! As she left the shop, she picked up a brochure that OWD had prepared for general distribution and it listed the funded services, as shown in **Table 1**.

La Donna scanned the list and thought to herself that she had never heard of many of the funded services before. She was informed that although OWD provided considerable funding to her planning district, that the marketing and advertisement budget for OWD had been severely cut. In the midst of her discussion, one OWD staff member told her, "We rely nearly exclusively on word-of-mouth or person-to-person advertising to get the word out. We know the programs should be better communicated, but without money, eligible program participants will more than likely be passed by. We're doing the best we can with a bad situation."

Case 38: The "Pink Slip" Support System

Table 1. Services Funded and Provided Through the "One-Stop" Office

WIA Funded:

- Personal interest inventories and other assessment tests
- Resume writing laboratory
- Access to local, state and national job listings
- Workshops on how to look for a job
- Personalized career advisement and job coaching
- Funding for training at local colleges and technical schools
- Subsidized employment opportunities such as on-the job training (OJT)
- Support services to attend training, such as child care assistance
- Access to phones, faxes, and the Internet for job seeking services

Adult and Community College Funded:

- English as second language classes
- GED classes
- Student loan and financial aid counseling
- Short-term remediation classes, including computer literacy
- Literacy programs

Wagner-Peyser Act Funded:

- Unemployment insurance
- Trade Adjustment Act training funds
- Special training and job placement opportunities for veterans

Department of Rehabilitation Funded:

- Specialized services for people with disabilities, including funds for training and specialized work opportunities
- Funds to assist employers with making Americans with Disabilities Act (ADA) accommodations
- Support services, such as the purchasing of assistive technology and equipment

Community Services Block Grant (CSGB) Funded:

- Weatherization assistance
- Access to food and clothes banks
- Emergency shelter
- Utilities payment subsidies

Case 38: The "Pink Slip" Support System

- Ride service for those without transportation or needing accessible transportation

Title V Funded:

- Specialized services to people age 55 and older, including funds for training and specialized work opportunities.

Satisfied that what she had just observed was every bit as good as what she had been briefed by her associates, she returned to the planning office and told her co-workers the following, "There is a rich menu of services offered at no-cost to the affected workers. One-stop said it all! The services that are needed immediately, such as resume writing and application for insurance and assistance were in place; and, long-term services for those that remained unemployed — funds to pay the cost of utilities — were also in place."

STOP: Please answer questions 4 to 7

Questions and Instructions:

4. Please contact your local WIA Office or Workforce Development Office and secure for your class members, brochures, pamphlets, and other information that address the services they provide when plants are closed down.

5. As shown in Table 1, there are many services that the Workforce Development Office provided in this case. Which ones do you feel would be most important (helpful) to the wide range of employees who were terminated at ACME? Please elaborate.

6. Are there any services that you would want added to the "one-stop" shop that are not mentioned in the case study? If so, who should provide these additional services: ACME, WIA, the 4th Economic and Planning District, Grand Prairie, the county, or the state? Please be specific.

7. Of the many services that were made available to ACME workers, which ones, if any, were you familiar with prior to reading Table 1. Services Funded and Provided Through the "One-Stop" Office? Please explain.

Case 38: The "Pink Slip" Support System

Case Continuation: Third Part

It did not seem possible to La Donna McKnight and Mayor Randy Holbrook that nearly two full years had passed since ACME had closed its door and hundreds of employees were left searching for their next employment. The boarded up ACME plant with its chained parking lot, remained as ugly reminders of an economy that, at least for Grand Prairie, had "crashed and burned." Although they both remained impressed by the type and quality of services provided by OWD, they realized that many employees remained either underemployed or unemployed, or in total frustration had just plain surrendered to their economic fate of joblessness.

The planning district and city had not been idle during this period and had been engaged in a vigorous effort to bring green collar jobs to Grand Prairie. The vacant ACME facilities with its cavernous warehouse space and office complex were ideally suited for the production of photo-voltaic panels. In fact, they had received a few "nibbles" from some of the premier manufacturers—one American and the other based in Germany. They were genuinely excited that their regional area might experience a surge of employment if they could negotiate a deal with either of the interested parties. The city was prepared to march ahead with a tax abatement plan and provide Tax Increment Financing (TIF), if necessary, but they shared a collective worry that it might take more than these traditional inducements if they were to "snag" a green collar company.

Satisfied with the services they had previously received from OWD during the ACME plant closure, they wondered about what kind of support, if any, they might receive from the same office if the local economy began to rebound, especially with the prospects of bringing a photovoltaic manufacturing center to Grand Prairie.

Once more they contacted OWD and were informed that there were many services that would be made available to a new company if brought into their midst and that most of the support would be available at no cost. These following services would be funded and provided by OWD:

- Multiple application distribution and collection points throughout the region using a network of partner organizations;
- Preliminary assessments of job applicants;
- Application screening services;
- Video interviewing of prospective employees;
- Accessibility to pools of hundreds of people looking for work at the regional and national level;
- Coordination with "one-stop" shops throughout the United States in order to help identify skilled laborers who were ready to move to the Grand Prairie area;
- Subsidized employment opportunities, such as on-the-job training (OJT);
- Incumbent worker training that would assist in upgrading persons already employed;

Case 38: The "Pink Slip" Support System

- Access to a wealth of needed, important information to the employer, such as Equal Employment Opportunity (EEO) and Occupational Safety and Health Administration (OSHA) regulations and statistics;

- Access to numerous state grant opportunities available to support training and infrastructure costs; and

- Community college funded grant and loan writing assistance, for the development and instruction of customized on-site training programs, and the development of business classes and workshops.

Excited by what they had learned, they incorporated many of these support services into the economic and planning portfolio that they had prepared for new industry and business solicitation.

Questions and Instructions:

8. If you were in any of the creative and entrepreneurial "green collar" businesses, which of the services listed above would be most important in attracting your business to Grand Prairie? Please explain.

9. Are there other programs that you believe to be essential if a green collar industry and labor force are to become more than a mere fantasy of economic development enthusiasts? Please elaborate.

Case 38: The "Pink Slip" Support System

Name:

Case Log and Administrative Journal Entry

This case analysis and learning assessment is printed on perforated pages and may be removed from the book for evaluation purposes.

Case Analysis:
Major case concepts and theories identified:

What is the relevance of the concepts, theories, ideas and techniques presented in the case to that of public management?

Facts — what do we know *for sure* about the case? Please list.

Who is involved in the case (people, departments, agencies, units, etc.)? Were the problems of an "intra/interagency" nature? Be specific.

Are there any rules, laws, regulations or standard operating procedures identified in the case study that might limit decision-making? If so, what are they?

Are there any clues presented in the case as to the major actor's interests, needs, motivations and personalities? If so, please list them.

Case 38: The "Pink Slip" Support System

Learning Assessment:
What do the administrative theories presented in this case mean to you as an administrator?

How can this learning be put to use outside the classroom? Are there any problems you envision during the implementation phase?

Several possible courses of action were identified during the class discussion. Which action was considered to be most practical by the group? Which was deemed most feasible? Based on your personal experience, did the group reach a conclusion that was desirable, feasible, and practical? Please explain why or why not.

Did the group reach a decision that would solve the problem on a short-term or long-term basis? Please explain.

What could you have done to receive more learning value from this case?

39

Language Has Meaning

by
C. Kenneth Meyer and Jeff Ritzman

James Bly was deeply honored to join the Sacagawea County Fire Service (SCFS). Bly came up through the ranks as those firefighters who preceded him had done. He studied hard, passed the mandatory civil service examination, and advanced quickly to the rank of captain. His career succession did not go as smoothly as he would have liked and hit a few bumps along the way that nearly derailed his advancement. Bly, however, was a tough minded survivor and he earned his "stripes" as a reconnaissance officer fighting an unpopular war in the jungles of Southeast Asia. Thus, when he was investigated for creating and supporting a hostile work environment the charges were unfounded and eventually dropped.

Bly was humiliated by the unfounded charges and chalked it up as another example of "sour grapes" by disgruntled workers who did not like his take-charge, hands on, "in your face," "leading from the front" style of management. There was little doubt that Bly gave a preferential ear to those in rank who were loyal and who over time had earned his trust. Some of his peers discussed his leadership orientation in private and felt that he had normally rejected out of hand input from female co-workers or as he called them "his worker bees." Nevertheless, regardless of the fact that he called those of lesser rank subordinates, he had some personal traits that served him well and he was able to move with some alacrity from one high profile position to another. He always thought he was a quick study in understanding change and felt that the pace of change in firefighting and emergency medical service (EMS) units was fast. He often quipped to his friends that he had no clue on how his career would end.

What should have turned out to be an honorific day for Bly became his worst nightmare. His trouble began when he was asked by Margot Farnsworth, Chair, Sacagawea County Board of Supervisors, to give the inaugural address at the dedication of the new County Fire Service Training Center (CFSTC), and to wield the ribbon cutting scissors. He was always sure of himself in being able to write a speech and deliver it with some zest, especially if he was "psyched-up" or "pumped-up" and in the company of prestigious political figures. And at the ceremony, he understood that the state's governor and two U.S. senators would be there for the dedication and he was politically astute enough to realize that they collectively took pride in being able to deliver the financial pork (earmarking of funds) that made the center happen.

Farnsworth was a successful county politico in her own right and had a reputation for taking progressive stances on civil rights and liberties and on most human resource issues — especially on valuing people as workers and taking a zero tolerance stance toward all manner of discrimination. She

Case 39: Language Has Meaning

also was instrumental in hiring Chris Young, an Asian male, as a recruiter for the fire service. Young quickly, although quietly, earned a reputation as a dynamic representative of the department and increased the number of women and minority applicants for firefighter and paramedic positions by over 250 percent in his short, two-year tenure.

In her introductory remarks, Farnsworth stated, "Success is in the pudding. In the last class that graduated from the Fire Service Training Academy (FSTA), there were seven women and eleven minority candidates that graduated out of a class of seventy, and we have Chris Young to thank for his efforts in this area."

Next, James Bly was introduced as the new director of the SCFSTC and he thanked Supervisor Farnsworth for her generous and nice remarks. He praised her and the other supervisors for their excellent leadership for reigning in the cost of government. Then, in a strong and deliberate voice he began his short speech that went something like this:

> Dear distinguished guests, ladies and gentlemen and fellow firemen. This is a great day for Sacagawea County and especially for the men who have served it honorably by putting on the military and fireman's uniforms and answering their call for service. Those men who have protected our freedom and liberties by fighting in foreign conflicts also answered the call of protecting our citizens here in Sacagawea County on a daily basis. I am deeply honored to head the new training center and work with this dedicated group of men who have built over the years a proud tradition that we are recognizing and honoring today.
>
> The tiered incident command system (ICS) in which SCFS is a full participant takes no back seat to any firefighting service in the United States and stands ready to help our weaker, sister agencies reach their full potential.
>
> The proud and distinguished tradition that was established by these men and their predecessors is now faced with the prospects of being eroded. Outside influences threaten to diminish the strong and deep current that has characterized our river of tradition and pride. If these influences are not stopped, the course of this proud river will be forever altered and changed. We must carefully weigh the ideas of change that come from sources that get close to a burning fire only when they prepare their artichoke *quiche*.
>
> My Sacagawea fire fighter brothers, I pledge as director of this training center to hold on to our proud tradition and stand fast against those forces that might threaten our cohesiveness. It is essential that we protect those values that our fathers and grandfathers did to make our service strong and that they be perpetuated. The citizens of this country deserve no less than the best efforts our brother firemen can provide. We will embrace those tried and true tactics that have enabled us to fight and suppress fires, rescue those who are in trouble, preserve human life and protect the property of the hardworking citizen of Sacagawea County.

Case 39: Language Has Meaning

James Bly's speech was followed by a standing ovation from some of the senior firefighters who had previously served in one or more of Bly's squads, especially those who were military veterans. Bly's speech, however, was viewed quite differently by Farnsworth.

The next morning, Farnsworth filed a complaint against Bly with the chief of the fire service. She said she was offended by his remarks and claimed they contained sexist and racist innuendo. And, she charged, that his remarks contained a thinly veiled and unwarranted criticism of the new recruiter, Chris Young.

The fire service, accordingly, initiated an internal investigation, conducted interviews of all SCFS members who were at the dedication ceremony, including all the probationary members of the recent graduating class from the Fire Service Training Academy. The initial complaint prompted a second investigation since the Full Disclosure Act for Police, Firefighters and Paramedics had taken effect having passed through both house of the state legislature on a straight party line vote. The new law had been supported by several organized national labor organizations and it allowed any police officer, firefighter or paramedic who had been disciplined to have complete access to all investigative files, notes and witness statements from a variety of sources (citizens, co-workers, and supervisors).

During the conduct of the investigation, two of Bly's superiors recalled the speech and stated that they believed it might have been offensive to some members of the SCFS who were female or members or of minority status, but not blatantly so. The probationary employees stated that they did not hear the speech or that they were not really "tuned" into Captain Bly's remarks. Some said they were more concerned with the tidiness of their uniforms and were nervous about going on stage and accepting their diplomas. In the end, no one who was interviewed could vouch for what was said or not said.

Because the witnesses were not in agreement as to the actual content of James Bly's speech, he received verbal counseling from his immediate supervisor and was ordered to write a formal letter of apology to Margot Farnsworth with the understanding that it would NOT be released to the media. Bly retained his assignment as director of the Fire Service Training Center.

Questions and Instructions:

1. Based on the evidence present in this case, how do you think James Bly was treated fairly or unfairly? Please elaborate. Is there any evidence that "bullying" is taking place in the workplace described? If so, explain.

    I think he was treated fairly and the punishment was in accordance w/ the act.

    The worker bees thing seems off to me. Don't care much 4 that language, but I hear it a lot w/ senior leaders. "I'll have the ladies send you that".

Case 39: Language Has Meaning

2. Since Margot Farnsworth was the complainant in this case, what do you think of Bly's remarks, as she understood them? Please be specific.

   I would imagine the foreign wars, brother fireman comments are what she took offense to.

3. What might have been going through the minds of the probationary firefighters when they were interviewed, especially since they said that they had really not paid attention to Bly's speech? Please speculate.

   I don't want to bad mouth the person I'm about to work for/with.

4. What impact do you believe the Full Disclosure Act for Police, Firefighters and Paramedics might have had on this investigation? And, what do you think will be the long-term impact on getting to the facts in any future investigation? Please elaborate.

   I think it turns into no one wanting to say anything because it's not anonymous.

5. Do you believe that the Full Disclosure Act for Police, Firefighters and Paramedics might have a chilling effect on the public, supervisors, and coworkers when they know that if they file a misconduct complaint against an authority figure or a supervisor, he or she will be able to read their statement word for word? Please elaborate. Should the identity of complainants be kept anonymous? Please explain your answer.

   They should be anonymous b/c fear of retaliation.
   It is good to be able to see the full case against you and the different perspectives of everyone.

6. Explain the difficulties Chris Young might have in recruiting women and minorities in an environment characterized by a "good-old-boy" syndrome? How might this organizational culture be changed? Please explain.

   The language is what needs to be addressed first. Things like firefighter instead of firemen. Family instead of brothers. Diversity traing across the board b/c I would imagine that these are perspectives that are not even thought of.

Case 39: Language Has Meaning

Case 39: Language Has Meaning
Name:

Case Log and Administrative Journal Entry

This case analysis and learning assessment is printed on perforated pages and may be removed from the book for evaluation purposes.

Case Analysis:
Major case concepts and theories identified:

What is the relevance of the concepts, theories, ideas and techniques presented in the case to that of public management?

Facts — what do we know *for sure* about the case? Please list.

Who is involved in the case (people, departments, agencies, units, etc.)? Were the problems of an "intra/interagency" nature? Be specific.

Are there any rules, laws, regulations or standard operating procedures identified in the case study that might limit decision-making? If so, what are they?

Are there any clues presented in the case as to the major actor's interests, needs, motivations and personalities? If so, please list them.

Case 39: Language Has Meaning

Learning Assessment:
What do the administrative theories presented in this case mean to you as an administrator?

How can this learning be put to use outside the classroom? Are there any problems you envision during the implementation phase?

Several possible courses of action were identified during the class discussion. Which action was considered to be most practical by the group? Which was deemed most feasible? Based on your personal experience, did the group reach a conclusion that was desirable, feasible, and practical? Please explain why or why not.

Did the group reach a decision that would solve the problem on a short-term or long-term basis? Please explain.

What could you have done to receive more learning value from this case?

40

A $5,000 Anonymous Phone Call?

by
C. Kenneth Meyer and Garry L. Frank

Jim Johnson began work with the Health Facilities Program in December and after an orientation period became one of five environmental health sanitarians whose responsibility was to survey licensed medical facilities within the state to determine their compliance with licensure, Medicare and other regulations. He was also responsible for providing part-time consultation to hospitals and nursing homes. Each survey team consisted of a registered nurse and an environmental sanitarian. The nurses were mostly mature, gray-haired women, while the sanitarians, although relatively young, tended to appear straitlaced and serious. Johnson, on the other hand, had curly brown hair that almost touched his shoulders, a pierced left ear; he wore faded blue jeans, and sandals. In addition he had a colorful Dungeons and Dragons tattoo on his right forearm.

Johnson's supervisor was Tom Blake. "I'm a little concerned about Jim's effectiveness as a surveyor-consultant," he said to Frances Maner, his administrative assistant. "I'm afraid many of the people he will be working with will classify him as a worthless bum because of his casual way of dressing."

"But, Tom," countered Maner, "You know he was the most-qualified applicant we interviewed. We both agreed he was intelligent and that there was a great deal of promise hidden under his unorthodox appearance."

"I know," Blake said, "but he doesn't dress professionally."

Johnson learned quickly and soon showed ample confidence and poise. He was fully capable of performing surveys after he had been on the job three months and showed potential for being a good consultant. Six months after being hired he attended a university for an intense, one-month specialized training course required of all health-facilities personnel conducting surveys under the Medicare and Medicaid programs. When Johnson returned, Blake noticed a marked improvement in his written reports and felt certain his survey activities would also show an improvement. After accompanying Johnson on two surveys, Blake decided he was doing as well as, or better than, any other sanitarian under his supervision.

Case 40: A $5,000 Anonymous Phone Call?

One morning, while Blake was expressing his satisfaction in Johnson's work to Maner, she reminded him of his earlier reservations. "I know," he confessed, "but Jim has really proven himself, and now he has my full confidence." "I think Jim will be the best sanitarian on our staff in a few years," Maner agreed. "Just wait and see."

A year after Johnson had been in the hospital and nursing-home program, Blake was called into the program director's office. Larry Dandurand, the program director, and Ralph Andrews, the chief inspector, were there, both looking upset.

"I received an interesting, although anonymous, phone call yesterday that I think deserves our attention," Andrews said. "It concerns one of the staff members, Jim Johnson."

Johnson was stationed in a district office in the eastern part of the state, sharing it with two other health department staff members, neither of whom was in the same program. Andrews said that the caller complained of all three persons engaging in horseplay while in the office, although this was not often since they were seldom there between 8:00 a.m. and 5:00 p.m. Andrews said, "The caller phoned because he thought the central office should know about it."

"I tried to explain that because our staff was involved in survey activities they had to spend quite a bit of time away from the office," Andrews said. The caller was quite persistent, insisting there was more productive work done by the inhabitants of a cemetery than done by the health department employees. Andrews said the caller ended the conversation with an accusation that Johnson was the worst offender and that he also was associating with undesirable persons, including habitual drug users.

Blake proposed that the episode be ignored since the caller had refused to identify himself, but Dandurand made it clear that he had no intention of letting the matter drop and since Blake was Johnson's supervisor, it was his responsibility to gather the relevant facts. Andrews suggested that Blake make discreet inquiries to substantiate the information given in the phone call. The idea of going behind Johnson's back to determine the accuracy of the phone call was repugnant to Blake. "Suppose I talk to Jim and ask him pointblank if what the caller said is true?" Blake asked.

"Fine," said Dandurand, "but let's get this thing cleared up right away."

After returning to his office, Blake tried to clarify the whole situation in his mind. He knew that Johnson did not spend any more time in his office than necessary. In fact, he recalled many unsuccessful attempts to reach him during his scheduled office hours. When he had talked to Johnson about his absence from the office, Johnson admitted that he had some problems in disciplining himself to observe normal office hours. Realizing that he was very young to be placed in a field office without direct supervision, Blake chalked up the irregular office hours as the price the program had to pay for running a decentralized operation. Besides, Johnson was getting the job done and that was the important thing. But Blake was upset that one of his sanitarians had been criticized by an anonymous phone caller.

Case 40: A $5,000 Anonymous Phone Call?

The following week Blake visited Johnson at his office and related the whole story to him. "As far as I'm concerned your work is excellent and that anonymous phone call is of no consequence as far as your performance is concerned," Blake explained. He made it clear, however, that the program director was upset over the whole matter and that as a state employee, Johnson would be closely scrutinized by the public.

Johnson was shocked. "Was it really an anonymous phone call or are you intentionally withholding the caller's name?" he inquired.

"Ralph Andrews took the call and he assured us he tried to get the caller to identify himself, and I believe him," Blake said.

Then Johnson admitted that earlier he had had problems keeping office hours but that in the past two months he had really tried to be in the office when not doing surveys. Blake knew this was true, since he telephoned all of the sanitarians at least once a week and during the period Johnson had always been there. Johnson said also that he did have two cousins who had been convicted of using drugs and that he saw both of them frequently. Johnson declared, "If the state is going to dictate who my friends have to be or the way I have to look, they can take this job and shove it."

"Jim, I assure you nobody in our office is trying to choose your friends," Blake said. "Whom you associate with is none of the state's business. What I really want to do is forget that phone call completely, but I did want you to know about the director's reaction, since it may have a bearing on your advancement potential in the Health Facilities Program." Blake looked Johnson straight in the eye and said, "As far as your personal appearance is concerned, it's a fact of life that external appearance affects the public's opinion about the quality of the work we do. Success is not always measured in terms of hard work and productivity."

At the end of the conversation, Blake felt that Johnson had accepted the discussion constructively, but two months later Johnson resigned. Blake telephoned him to find out the specific reasons for this resignation. He learned that Johnson was not leaving state government for a larger salary and, in fact, had no other job lined up. Johnson explained, "I just wanted to try doing something other than working for the state, and I guess I should make that change now, while I'm still young."

Blake asked him if the anonymous call had anything to do with his resignation, and Johnson said that it had helped him to make the decision but was not a primary reason. Blake urged Johnson to change his mind and stay with the program, but after a long discussion he felt that Johnson's mind was made up and the resignation was irrevocable.

After working with Johnson for a year and a half, Blake was certain that the telephone call had far more to do with his resignation than he had admitted. If the phone call could be considered the primary reason Jim resigned, Blake told himself, then it cost the state at least $5,000 in money lost training Jim for the job.

Case 40: A $5,000 Anonymous Phone Call?

Questions and Instructions:

1. Since the phone call was anonymous, should it have been given any consideration at all?

2. How could the substance of the phone call be verified or disqualified by a discreet investigation? If the caller's information could not be substantiated, would it have been necessary to tell Johnson anything at all?

3. Would it have been wise for Blake to transfer Johnson to the central office where he would have had the benefit of direct supervision?

4. Should more emphasis have been placed on the observation of normal working hours when Blake became aware of Johnson's work schedule?

5. If you were Blake and had time to reflect on this incident, what policy recommendation would you suggest to prevent this type of problem from occurring in the future? Should the central office consider having a definite number of hours or specific time during the day when field personnel should be in the office? What are the implications of this type of policy?

6. Is it possible that Johnson's appearance was beneficial in his employee-client relationship? What should be said or done about an employee's personal dress or appearance?

7. Is a supervisor responsible not only for informing an employee of undesirable attitudes or behavior but also for designing a plan to correct or improve them?

Case 40: A $5,000 Anonymous Phone Call?

Case 40: A $5,000 Anonymous Phone Call?
Name:

Case Log and Administrative Journal Entry

This case analysis and learning assessment is printed on perforated pages and may be removed from the book for evaluation purposes.

Case Analysis:
Major case concepts and theories identified:

What is the relevance of the concepts, theories, ideas and techniques presented in the case to that of public management?

Facts — what do we know *for sure* about the case? Please list.

Who is involved in the case (people, departments, agencies, units, etc.)? Were the problems of an "intra/interagency" nature? Be specific.

Are there any rules, laws, regulations or standard operating procedures identified in the case study that might limit decision-making? If so, what are they?

Are there any clues presented in the case as to the major actor's interests, needs, motivations and personalities? If so, please list them.

Case 40: A $5,000 Anonymous Phone Call?

Learning Assessment:
What do the administrative theories presented in this case mean to you as an administrator?

How can this learning be put to use outside the classroom? Are there any problems you envision during the implementation phase?

Several possible courses of action were identified during the class discussion. Which action was considered to be most practical by the group? Which was deemed most feasible? Based on your personal experience, did the group reach a conclusion that was desirable, feasible, and practical? Please explain why or why not.

Did the group reach a decision that would solve the problem on a short-term or long-term basis? Please explain.

What could you have done to receive more learning value from this case?

41

A Campaigner for Equal Rights

by
C. Kenneth Meyer and Lance Noe

Dawson Bryan had worked ten years in the building-construction trade in Parkhurst when he joined the Code Enforcement Department of the city as a code-compliance inspector. In just a few years he had been promoted up through the ranks from compliance inspector, to safety officer, assistant director of the department, and, last year, he was named director.

By city ordinance, the duties of the department were to inspect construction, alteration or remodeling of any buildings and the installation of electric wiring, gas and water lines, plumbing, and air conditioning; to act as designee of the county health department for the enforcement of health provisions in the city code; and to enforce housing, safety, and sign regulations.

A big, burly man, Bryan took a no-nonsense attitude toward his job and the 15 employees in the department. Tact was not a word in his vocabulary. When he gave instructions, he was inclined to shout as he had done when working outdoors in the building trade. The men in the department were used to his high-decibel communication and paid no attention to it. On the whole, the department was well managed, was strict in enforcing the codes despite being understaffed, and worked very well as a team. It was an all-male enclave in a city government that since the adoption of an equal-opportunity and affirmative-action ordinance had been increasingly infiltrated in recent years by female employees in departments like street cleaning and maintenance that had never seen them before.

The male stronghold in code enforcement was breached when the Department of Personnel sent Bryan a new compliance inspector grade I named Kate Grunwald. Bryan immediately got on the telephone to protest to Martin Everest, director of personnel, that the work of inspection was so specialized that no woman could handle it. Everest replied that Grunwald was fully qualified, in fact better qualified than some of the male inspectors because she had studied electrical engineering in a university for two years and only three or four of his present staff had any college work. "Anyway," Everest said, "read Articles III and IV of our union contract dealing with nondiscrimination and affirmative action. You'll see why we were glad to hire Grunwald." (See **Exhibit 1**). Bryan replied he did not need to read a book to learn that a woman in his department meant trouble.

Kate Grunwald was not the type to ask for any special favors on the job. She had quit the university after two years when she married and her husband, a petroleum-engineering senior, had taken a job in Saudi Arabia. Five years later their marriage ended in divorce and Grunwald, who gained custody of their son, was irregularly employed for a time in construction work, where she encountered difficulty because she was a woman. She had noted the subordinate position of women in the Iranian society and had suffered from gender bias on the job in the United States. She therefore became an ardent activist in the women's movement and took part in rallies and demonstrations of the National Organization for Women (NOW) in support of the Equal Rights Amendment (ERA). She had adopted a belligerent attitude toward what she perceived as gender bias.

On the job, Grunwald was first assigned to checking on complaints, most of them reports of health nuisances, and not on routine inspection of the electrical wiring, gas and water lines, and plumbing in new construction that she considered herself best qualified to do. She was reliable and competent, and Bryan could not find any reasonable fault with her work. Nevertheless, the relationship between the two might be accurately described as restrained hostility.

After Grunwald had been six months on the job, a vacancy occurred for a grade II compliance inspector. She mentioned to Bryan that she intended to apply for the job, but he tried to discourage her by saying she ought to have more experience before seeking a promotion. Nevertheless, Grunwald submitted an application to the personnel department. When asked for a report on her work, Bryan told Everest, the personnel director, that she was doing all right as far as he could see, but disrupted the peace of the department by expressing her views on women's rights and ERA and had taken time off during a busy spring-inspection season to attend a regional conference of NOW. "All the more reason for promoting her," Everest said. "We don't want a bunch of women libbers picketing city hall on her behalf."

A few months after receiving her promotion, Grunwald decided to apply for another vacancy in the department, that of safety officer, a supervisory position with a higher salary. She was dissuaded from doing so by Bryan on the basis that two other compliance inspectors with more seniority were already applicants. A year later the safety officer position became vacant again and Grunwald, against the advice of Bryan, applied for it.

A week later she obtained sick leave, but it was soon revealed publicly there was nothing wrong with her health: television news reports showed her in the forefront of a large crowd demonstrating for passage of the ERA on the steps of the state capitol. A resolution approving the ERA was being debated in the legislature and was the focus of national attention. Women's rights leaders from around the state and country had gathered to push for a favorable vote in the legislature, motion-picture and television celebrities urged adoption at rallies on the capitol steps and in newspaper and television interviews and supporters filled the statehouse corridors and legislative offices lobbying for the measure. Grunwald did not miss a day taking part in this activity.

When she returned to her job, Bryan angrily told her she had no business taking sick leave to engage in political activity, which was forbidden in the city charter. Equally angry, Grunwald told Bryan that he was a sexist and that most city departments were in violation of the equal-rights and affirmative-action provisions of the charter in respect to the employment of women. The only political activity forbidden in the city charter, she said, was a prohibition against employees taking part in city elections.

Case 41: A Campaigner for Equal Rights

A few days after this confrontation, the most heated that had taken place between Grunwald and Bryan, she learned that she had not received the promotion to safety officer.

Shortly afterward, Grunwald filed a complaint with the Equal Employment Opportunity Commission alleging that she had been passed over for promotion on grounds of gender discrimination. She charged that she had been discouraged from seeking promotions by the head of her department and that she was a victim of discrimination when she failed to get promoted when she had applied for a higher position. She also questioned the qualification of a male who, she alleged, was given the job of safety director without applying for it. She cited her department head's criticism of her support for the ERA as prima facie evidence of discrimination. She asked for advancement in position equal in pay and authority to past positions she had sought and for assurances there would be no retaliation resulting from her complaint.

Questioned by a newspaper reporter about her complaint, Grunwald said, "Women are not hired by the city for managerial positions on an equal basis with men. I'm interested in seeing more women selected as department heads. I'm going all the way with this complaint for the good of all women."

Questions and Instructions

1. Was the personnel director remiss in failing to do more than tell Bryan to read the union contract clauses on affirmative action to help prepare for the acceptance of a woman in the Code Enforcement Department?

2. What decision do you think the Human Rights Commission will reach on Grunwald's complaint under the Civil Rights Act of 1964? (See Exhibit 2).

3. Is the fact that Grunwald took sick leave to lobby for the ERA sufficient grounds for a reprimand or denial of a promotion?

Case 41: A Campaigner for Equal Rights

4. Do you think Grunwald was right in going directly to the EEOC with her complaint instead of seeking redress through grievance procedures outlined in the city's contract with the American Federation of State, County, and Municipal Employees Union? Explain.

5. Do you think Grunwald would make a good department head or supervisor?

Case 41: A Campaigner for Equal Rights

Exhibit 1. Union Contract Articles on Civil Rights

Article III

Non-Discrimination

Section 1. No employee or an individual being considered for employment shall be favored or subjected to discrimination by management or by the Union because of race, creed, color, gender, or national origin, relationship with any person or persons, or political or union activities, other than those prohibited by this Agreement.

Section 2. Management and the Union agree not to interfere with the right of employees to become or not to become members of the Union and further, will urge the employees that there will be no discrimination or coercion against any employee because of Union membership or non-membership.

Article IV

Section 1. The City and the Union are committed to the concept and practice of equal employment opportunity as a necessary component of merit principles, which is a phase of affirmative action.

Section 2. The Affirmative Action commitment will be supported by positive and aggressive practices and procedures, which will insure non-discrimination and equal-employment opportunity for racial and ethnic minorities, the disadvantaged, and women in securing admission in the City employment force and promotional opportunities at all job levels.

Section 3. The general objectives of the City and the Union in affirmative action practice will be:

   a. to engage in continuous planning and monitoring of the effects of practices in order to eliminate and prevent the occurrence of arbitrary, discriminatory practices and policies related to employment, membership and promotions; and
   b. to take positive steps to solicit applicants for employment and membership from minority groups and women's organizations.

Case 41: A Campaigner for Equal Rights

Exhibit 2. Excerpt from Civil Rights Act of 1964

Title VII — Equal Employment Opportunity

Discrimination because of race, color, religion, gender or national origin

Section 703

a. It shall be unlawful employment practice for an employer —

   1. to fail or refuse to hire or to discharge any individual, or otherwise to discriminate against any individual with respect to his compensation, terms, conditions, or privileges of employment, because of such individual's race, color, religion, gender or national origin; or

   2. to limit, segregate, or classify his employees in any way which would deprive or tend to deprive any individual of employment opportunities or otherwise adversely affect his status as an employee, because of such individual's race, color, religion, gender or national origin.

b. It shall be an unlawful employment practice for an employment agency to fail or refuse to tend to deprive any individual of employment opportunities or otherwise adversely affect his status as an employee, because of such individual's race, color, religion, gender, or national origin, or to classify or refer for employment any individual on the basis of his race, color, religion, gender or national origin.

c. It shall be an unlawful employment practice for a labor organization —

   1. to exclude or to expel from its membership, or otherwise to discriminate against, any individual because of his race, color, religion, gender or national origin;

   2. to limit, segregate, or classify its membership, or to classify or fail or refuse to refer for employment any individual, in any way which would deprive or tend to deprive any individual of employment opportunities, or would limit such employment opportunities or otherwise adversely affect his status as an employee or as an applicant for employment, because of such individual's race, color, religion, gender, or national origin; or

   3. to cause or attempt to cause an employer to discriminate against an individual in violation of this section.

d. It shall be an unlawful employment practice for any employer, labor organization, or joint labor-management committee controlling apprenticeship or other training or retraining, including on-the-job training programs, to discriminate against any individual because of his race, color, religion, gender or national origin in admission to, or employment in, any program established to provide apprenticeship or other training.

e. Notwithstanding any other provision of this title, (1) it shall not be an unlawful employment practice for an employer to hire and employ employees, for an employment agency to classify, or refer for employment any individual, for a labor organization to classify its membership or to classify or refer for employment any individual, or for an employer, labor organization or joint labor-management committee controlling apprenticeship or other training or retraining programs to admit or employ any individual in any such program, on the basis of his religion, gender or national origin in those certain instances where religion, gender or national origin is a bona fide occupational qualification reasonably necessary to the normal operation of that particular business or enterprise, and (2) it shall not be an unlawful employment practice for a school, college, university or other educational institution or institution of learning to hire and employ employees of a particular religion if such school, college, university or other educational institution or institution of learning is, in whole or in substantial part, owned, supported, controlled or managed by a particular religion or by a particular religious corporation, association or society, or if the curriculum of such school, college, university, or other educational institution or institution of learning is directed toward the propagation of a particular religion.

f. As used in this title, the phrase "unlawful employment practice" shall not be deemed to include any action or measure taken by an employer, labor organization, join labor-management committee, or employment agency with respect to an individual who is a member of the Communist Party of the United States or of any other organization required to register as a Communist-action or Communist-front organization by final order of the Subversive Activities Control Board pursuant to the Subversive Activities Control Act of 1950.

g. Notwithstanding any other provision of this title, it shall not be an unlawful employment practice for an employer to fail or refuse to hire and employ any individual for any position, for an employer to discharge any individual from any position, or for an employment agency to fail or refuse to refer any individual for employment in any position, or for a labor organization to fail or refuse to refer any individual for employment in any position if —

   1. the occupancy of such position, or access to the premises in or upon which any part of the duties of such position is performed, or is to be performed, is subject to any requirement imposed in the interest of the national security of the United States under any security program in effect pursuant to or administered under any statue of the United States or any Executive order of the President; and

   2. such individual has not fulfilled or has ceased to fulfill that requirement.

h. Notwithstanding any other provision of this title, it shall not be an unlawful employment practice for an employer to apply different standards of compensation, or different terms, conditions, or privileges of employment pursuant to a bona fide seniority or merit system, or a system which measures earnings by quantity or quality of production or to employees who work in different

Case 41: A Campaigner for Equal Rights

> locations, provided that such differences are not the result of an intention to discriminate because of race, color, religion, gender, or national origin, nor shall it be an unlawful employment practice for an employer to give and to act upon the results of any professionally developed ability test provided that such test, its administration or action upon the results is not designed, intended, or used to discriminate because of race, color, religion, gender, or national origin. It shall not be an unlawful employment practice under this title for any employer to differentiate upon the basis of gender in determining that amount of wages or compensation paid or to be paid to employees of such employer if such differentiation is authorized by the provision of section 6(d) of the Fair Labor Standards Act of 1938, as amended (29) U.S.C. 206(d)

Case 41: A Campaigner for Equal Rights

Case 41: A Campaigner for Equal Rights
Name:

Case Log and Administrative Journal Entry

This case analysis and learning assessment is printed on perforated pages and may be removed from the book for evaluation purposes.

Case Analysis:
Major case concepts and theories identified:

What is the relevance of the concepts, theories, ideas and techniques presented in the case to that of public management?

Facts — what do we know *for sure* about the case? Please list.

Who is involved in the case (people, departments, agencies, units, etc.)? Were the problems of an "intra/interagency" nature? Be specific.

Are there any rules, laws, regulations or standard operating procedures identified in the case study that might limit decision-making? If so, what are they?

Are there any clues presented in the case as to the major actor's interests, needs, motivations and personalities? If so, please list them.

Case 41: A Campaigner for Equal Rights

Learning Assessment:
What do the administrative theories presented in this case mean to you as an administrator?

How can this learning be put to use outside the classroom? Are there any problems you envision during the implementation phase?

Several possible courses of action were identified during the class discussion. Which action was considered to be most practical by the group? Which was deemed most feasible? Based on your personal experience, did the group reach a conclusion that was desirable, feasible, and practical? Please explain why or why not.

Did the group reach a decision that would solve the problem on a short-term or long-term basis? Please explain.

What could you have done to receive more learning value from this case?

42

Sick Leave or AWOL

by
C. Kenneth Meyer and Garry L. Frank

Paul Kahoe had been employed five years by the Federal Aviation Administration (FAA). He joined as an Air Traffic Control Specialist (Station) GS-7 upon receiving an honorable discharge from the United States Air Force, where he had been an air traffic controller. His first assignment with the FAA was with a Flight Service Station (FSS) in Arkansas. After three years he was transferred to another station in Nebraska. His performance was satisfactory and he was advanced to the grade of GS-11.

The previous year on August 21 Kahoe submitted a request to his team supervisor, George Wiesener, for annual leave plus an additional period of leave without pay from September 15 to November 1. In an accompanying letter he explained that he wished to "join a select expeditionary force in the capacity of production consultant" for a journey to the Marshall Islands to locate the wreckage of the airplane flown by the famous aviator Amelia Earhart, lost in the Pacific in 1937. He himself had contributed $20,000 to the project.

His supervisor, Wiesener, was also the watch-scheduling officer responsible for coordinating annual leaves for station personnel. Normal procedures called for all controllers to submit their leave schedules between January and March. Based on the requests, the watch schedule was made out for the year. Any requests submitted after March 1 were approved only if the watch schedule could be covered.

After checking the schedule for the period, Wiesener informed Arthur Lightner, the station supervisor, of Kahoe's request. He explained that it could not be accommodated without creating an overtime situation. He added that 14 days of the six-week period presented especially difficult operational problems. Lightner called the regional office to determine if overtime would be allowed in this instance. He was advised that it could not be authorized — that overtime could be given only to cover previously authorized annual leave, sick leave and training.

Informed by Wiesener that his request was denied, Kahoe became upset and said he might resign to go on the expedition and hope to be reinstated on his return. Following the conversation, Wiesener documented it on a Memorandum for Record (MFR).

Wiesener heard nothing more about the leave until September 12 when, talking with Fred Summers, a friend and co-worker of Kahoe, Summers asked, "Have you gotten Kahoe's watch covered?"

Case 42: Sick Leave or AWOL

Wiesener asked him to elaborate and Summers replied that Kahoe was taking sick leave and would go on the Marshall Islands expedition. Disturbed by this information, Wiesener telephoned Dr. Edward Perth, the flight surgeon for the station, to ask for advice on how to handle the situation if Kahoe were to request extended sick leave. He was advised, if this should happen, to make no decision until receiving supporting medial information from Kahoe's physician. A release would have to be requested from Kahoe for Dr. Perth to review his medical records. As before, Wiesener prepared a memorandum of the conversation. He gave the information on Kahoe to Lightner and received an outline on how to handle the situation should Kahoe ask for sick leave. Kahoe was to be told that a detailed medical statement was required, and it might be necessary for an FAA medical examiner to confirm the stated health condition.

Early on the morning of September 17 Kahoe called in sick. That afternoon he came into the station and handed Wiesener a letter signed by Dr. Fleming Peterson. The letter itself was not dated but bore a notarization dated September 17. The letter stated, "Paul Kahoe is a patient of mine. I have examined him and consulted Dr. Charles Atkinson in Omaha. It is my opinion that he should be placed on sick leave until further notice." Wiesener asked Kahoe how much sick leave he would need and was told "a couple of months." Wiesener informed Kahoe of the procedure that had to be followed for the leave request to be approved or disapproved, explaining that this would take a few days.

Wiesener again consulted Lightner, who advised him to inform Kahoe that his sick leave was disapproved until his medical records could be reviewed. Kahoe was to be assigned to administrative duties at the station pending review of the request. Seeking to get in touch with Kahoe to inform him of the decision, Wiesener called his home three times, leaving word on an answering machine for him to return the calls.

On the third call, he stated that the sick leave was disapproved until the medical condition could be verified. The next day both Wiesener and Lightner went to Kahoe's home to acquaint him with the decision about the request for sick leave and found no one there. On returning to his office Lightner wrote Kahoe a letter explaining the situation and his attempts to reach him by telephone and a personal visit. Kahoe was told to return to work or he would be considered AWOL until he justified his sick-leave request. Later in the day the mail brought a letter from Kahoe releasing his medical records, but Lightner's letter to him was returned the next week stamped "unclaimed."

Kahoe's medical history as reported by his physician, Dr. Peterson, related that on August 24 Kahoe on an office visit had complained of heart problems and of feelings of anxiety and depression. Dr. Peterson had examined him but found nothing physically wrong. On a second visit by Kahoe on September 7, Peterson found him still nervous and depressed and was told he was unable to sleep or concentrate. The doctor prescribed a mild medication for sleep and suggested that he obtain a sick leave.

Kahoe returned to Dr. Peterson's office on September 14 and reported that the medication did not seem to be doing any good. He was placed on stronger medication and advised to return if there were adverse side effects. Kahoe saw Peterson again on September 17 and since no undue symptoms had developed was told to check back in about two weeks. The doctor stated that he could find no obvious cause for depression and that the amount of leave time Kahoe might need was indeterminable. He planned to reevaluate Kahoe's condition when he returned in two weeks. His diagnosis was that Kahoe suffered

Case 42: Sick Leave or AWOL

from anxiety, neurosis and depression. On October 4, Dr. Perth wrote Dr. Peterson requesting information on the reevaluation and received the reply that Kahoe had not kept the appointment and that attempts to reach him at his house had been unsuccessful.

Kahoe finally got in touch with the station on October 22 when he reported for duty. Asked when he had returned to the area, he stated that it was on October 19 but he had not reported then because he knew he needed a release from Dr. Peterson, which he had obtained on October 22. Dr. Peterson had completed a form covering the leave from August 22 through October 22 and wrote Dr. Perth on October 22 that Kahoe was released to full active duty on that date, seemed to be recovered, had taken no medication for ten days and had probably suffered an anxiety spell with mild depression which had abated. No future problems were foreseen.

On returning to work, Kahoe was assigned administrative duties. He declined to inform Weisener and Lightner of his whereabouts during his absence, asserting that it was not relevant. During an investigative discussion on November 1, however, he admitted that he had taken the trip to the Marshall Islands.

Questions and Instructions

1. As regional personnel consultant for the FAA, you are assigned to review the case involving Kahoe and to make recommendations to Lightner on what action to take. Explain the recommendations you would make. You find there are four courses open to the station supervisor:
    1. He can take no action at all, returning Kahoe to full duty under the assumption that the sick leave was approved and therefore the matter is closed.
    2. He can consider Kahoe as having been AWOL and suspend him without pay, perhaps for the same number of days he had been AWOL.
    3. He can find that Kahoe is guilty of infractions of rules but that his offense is not so serious that he should lose his job; he can be retained in the FSS but at a reduced GS grade.
    4. He can decide that Kahoe's offense is so serious that action should be instituted to terminate his employment.

Case 42: Sick Leave or AWOL

2. Write a summary of the case analyzing the factors that should be taken into consideration in arriving at a conclusion as to what should be done about Kahoe. Analyze the four choices listed in question 1 and give reasons why you would accept or reject each of them.

Case 42: Sick Leave or AWOL

Case 42: Sick Leave or AWOL
Name:

Case Log and Administrative Journal Entry

This case analysis and learning assessment is printed on perforated pages and may be removed from the book for evaluation purposes.

Case Analysis:
Major case concepts and theories identified:

What is the relevance of the concepts, theories, ideas and techniques presented in the case to that of public management?

Facts — what do we know *for sure* about the case? Please list.

Who is involved in the case (people, departments, agencies, units, etc.)? Were the problems of an "intra/interagency" nature? Be specific.

Are there any rules, laws, regulations or standard operating procedures identified in the case study that might limit decision-making? If so, what are they?

Are there any clues presented in the case as to the major actor's interests, needs, motivations and personalities? If so, please list them.

Case 42: Sick Leave or AWOL

Learning Assessment:
What do the administrative theories presented in this case mean to you as an administrator?

How can this learning be put to use outside the classroom? Are there any problems you envision during the implementation phase?

Several possible courses of action were identified during the class discussion. Which action was considered to be most practical by the group? Which was deemed most feasible? Based on your personal experience, did the group reach a conclusion that was desirable, feasible, and practical? Please explain why or why not.

Did the group reach a decision that would solve the problem on a short-term or long-term basis? Please explain.

What could you have done to receive more learning value from this case?

43

What Color is Your Coded Message?

by
C. Kenneth Meyer and G. Joseph Sample

Brian Seymour, the director of the research department at Great Falls Hospital, had arrived at work at the usual obligatory time. He had a routine and pattern about his life and often said, "It is as convenient to be ten minutes early as inconvenient to be ten minutes late." Today, however, was no typical day.

Everything had gone perfectly well and the traffic was less than usual and his commute had gone "alarmingly smoothly." Seymour accessed his office through the emergency room and, as was his custom, he greeted those who were on duty with a courteous politeness and hardy good morning! Shortly after he had settled into his office and began performing the tasks he had scheduled for the day, he noticed an unusual situation as he walked past a window en route to his filing cabinet. It was 8:15 a.m. on Tuesday morning and a police car was parked directly in front of the doors leading into the annex that housed the hospital research and education center.

Seymour stopped quickly and then stepped backwards so that he could get a good view of what was taking place from his fifth floor office location. It struck him as being odd that several police officers were pulling back the shrubbery and looking into the bushes that were tightly nestled against the main entrance to the annex. He wondered if they were searching for someone or something. He patiently watched the police activity and after several minutes of intense searching, they returned to their squad car, turned off the emergency lights, and went about their business. In turn, Seymour, proceeded to the filing cabinet, filed the folders he was carrying, and noticed that some of them were not filed alphabetically.

The cause for alarm had receded in his mind and once again he went about answering his emails. He heard a loud noise outside his window and this time he noticed that there were several squad cars and hospital security vehicle that were strategically parked near the hospital entrance. He watched with contained curiosity for nearly 30 minutes only to be interrupted by a senior research fellow who asked him why security had blocked all the entrances to the hospital. His colleague explained that admission to the building was being denied to all but those who wore security badges. Doubtful about what was transpiring, he stepped out of his office and told those who had congregated to continue with business as usual until further notified. Calmly, he told the staff that he would personally alert them in case of an impending emergency and that they had nothing to worry about.

Case 43: What Color is Your Coded Message?

At 11:00 a.m., nearly three hours after he first noticed police officers at the hospital, Seymour and the rest of his staff received the following email from the hospital's head of security. It read, in part, as follows:

Today, the Emergency Communications Center (ECC) received a call from the city's police department regarding a possible situation involving the hospital campus. The information was given to public safety officers who responded appropriately and secured the main entry points to the hospital.

I want to take a moment to thank all of our staff, patients, and visitors who may have been re-directed during this time. We had tremendous support and appreciate everyone following the directions given by the public safety officers during an incident such as this. At this time, the city police have the situation under control and facility has been secured.

A number of Seymour's staff expressed concern over the approach that was used to communicate a potential security problem in the workplace. Much of the discontent was directed at Seymour, although he had not been notified by senior management of any security concerns. However, the situation became tenser when a number of employees went on the Internet and found information from local media sources about the incident that had taken place on their campus. To their chagrin, they discovered that the local media had posted that the police had been called by a man, the father of a recently fired hospital employee, about a concern that his son was going to the hospital with a gun and that no other information was available at this time. This information infuriated the employees! They questioned why they had not been better informed of the danger and wondered aloud about what they could have done to better protect themselves had this person actually entered the hospital with the intention of doing harm. They would have liked to have a description of the potential offender and who, if anyone, was the intended target of his retaliation or revenge.

At this stage there was little Seymour could do for his associates. He tried to assure them that the situation was under control and that he was confident that communication would be better in the future. He continued to promise them that he would provide information should he be informed of anything else that might be transpiring. But he, like the rest of the employees, received the following email at 4:20 p.m. from the vice president of human resources:

This morning, our Emergency Communications Center (EEC) received a call from the (city) police department regarding a potentially harmful situation involving an employee and our hospital campus. The information was given to Public Safety Officers who responded appropriately and quickly secured our main entry points.

During this time, visitors and patients were not allowed in or out of the building. Employees could enter if they had proper identification, but had to stay in the building until the incident was cleared. This is our normal operating procedure for these kinds of occurrences.

Public Safety is following up with (city) police regarding this morning's incident. The individual was apprehended by (city) police and is in custody. It is likely that you will hear more information on the

Case 43: What Color is Your Coded Message?

news. Please remember that this incident has been resolved with regard to the security of our campus and we have resumed normal operating procedures.

Thank you to all our staff, patients and visitors who responded with tremendous support and understanding during this incident. Thanks also to our public safety officers and other staff for planning for such an incident.

Nearly one month following this incident, another incident at the research center occurred, but with much less fanfare. During this incident, a receptionist, on her way to lunch, stopped in the research office and asked, "Do you know we're in lock-down?" The administrative assistant in the research office learned that apparently a threat had been made to the hospital administration office, which was located next to the research office. The administrative assistant — the only person in the office at that particular time — closed the office door, and left the building for a long lunch.

Shortly after this latest incident, the manager of the safety department sent an email to all hospital staff informing them of new procedures regarding special emergency situations. A "Code Yellow" would be added to the Emergency Preparedness Manual (EPM), and it would outline what employees should do when it was implemented. Along with this impending policy, employees were informed that a new communication plan would also be forthcoming. There would be email communication and an intranet posting immediately whereby all employees would be told about what was transpiring and the precautions that should be taken.

Questions and Instructions:

1. In this case, what are some of the key concerns that management should have addressed well before the two incidents addressed in the scenario took place? Please elaborate.

2. To what extent should emergency planning and security preparedness involve representative members of the various areas of the hospital? Please be specific.

3. If you were Brian Seymour, what actions, if any, do you think he should have taken after he observed the officers searching through the campus foliage? Why? Please explain.

4. Please review a safety and security policy from a local hospital. Next, compare and contrast what has been identified as essential security factors on the basis of the case discussion with the main components of your local hospital's policy statement.

Case 43: What Color is Your Coded Message?

Part 2. After questions 1 through 4 have been discussed, proceed to the second part of this case study.

Brian Seymour thought about the situation that Great Falls Hospital had just faced. He reflected on the use of the different color schemes and sounds that he had observed in use in a variety of different organization and work settings. He observed that codes are used to indicate or signal many categories of safety, emergency or danger. Sometimes, like the codes associated with the storage of chemicals, they indicate the type and dangerousness: red, flammable; blue, hazardous to health if ingested or inhaled; yellow, reactive and oxidizing reagent (when combined with air or water); white, corrosive, and gray, only moderately dangerous. Sometimes we develop riddles and jingles, such as "red next to yellow will kill a fellow." Often, he mused, different types of sounds are used to indicate the severity of a storm or severe weather, or an ambulance that is transporting a patient to the hospital. The codes used for trains, barges, and seafaring vessels are distinctive in their meaning as well. And, most people know what Code Blue means in a hospital or clinic setting — that a patient is in need of immediate resuscitation.

The more Brian Seymour thought about the coding system, the more he realized the variety and significance of the symbols used. As he explained to the members of his team, The Department of Homeland Security (DHS) utilizes a color scheme to indicate the potential for terrorist acts or threats, and banks and other financial centers that deal directly with the public, have their own set of codes or signals indicative of security or theft situations.

He mentioned, "Television and radio signal towers change their coded colors to indicate weather conditions and our highways are filled with signage, lighted and otherwise, that alert pedestrians and drivers alike with the colors of red, yellow and green." One of his colleagues was quick to add, "Color and other codes are used to inform us on a range of topics, from thermometers used in outdoor grilling to the combination of colors in the hydrometer that are used by the brew master in measuring the alcohol level in beer or liquor; likewise, the mechanic, uses a similar device to measure the antifreeze level in the cooling systems of our cars and trucks." In short, as Seymour came to know first-hand, coded messages had become a part of our daily living and that we all depend upon them for our safety.

Question and Instructions:

5. For Great Falls Hospital, what code or warning sign would you recommend? Explain. What is your rationale? Please elaborate.

6. What advantages do you think are connected with "color codes" versus "the use of sounds? Please list several of the advantages and limitations associate with color and with the use of sounds.

Case 43: What Color is Your Coded Message?

Case 43: What Color is Your Coded Message?
Name:

Case Log and Administrative Journal Entry

This case analysis and learning assessment is printed on perforated pages and may be removed from the book for evaluation purposes.

Case Analysis:
Major case concepts and theories identified:

What is the relevance of the concepts, theories, ideas and techniques presented in the case to that of public management?

Facts — what do we know *for sure* about the case? Please list.

Who is involved in the case (people, departments, agencies, units, etc.)? Were the problems of an "intra/interagency" nature? Be specific.

Are there any rules, laws, regulations or standard operating procedures identified in the case study that might limit decision-making? If so, what are they?

Are there any clues presented in the case as to the major actor's interests, needs, motivations and personalities? If so, please list them.

325

Case 43: What Color is Your Coded Message?

Learning Assessment:
What do the administrative theories presented in this case mean to you as an administrator?

How can this learning be put to use outside the classroom? Are there any problems you envision during the implementation phase?

Several possible courses of action were identified during the class discussion. Which action was considered to be most practical by the group? Which was deemed most feasible? Based on your personal experience, did the group reach a conclusion that was desirable, feasible, and practical? Please explain why or why not.

Did the group reach a decision that would solve the problem on a short-term or long-term basis? Please explain.

What could you have done to receive more learning value from this case?

44

Problems with Volunteer Workers

by
C. Kenneth Meyer

Under the New Federalism concept initiated by Ronald Reagan, and furthered by subsequent Republican administrations whereby the national government was to reduce or discontinue funds for services considered the responsibility of state governments, the state Department of Public Welfare was forced to cut drastically the agency budget for administering educational programs for children with disabilities. This created a crisis for Reginald MacArthur, director of one of the agency's facilities located in a small university town.

MacArthur considered a high staff-client ratio necessary for the proper implementation of his facility's programs. Although no staff positions actually were eliminated, no additional people could be hired and no vacancies created by resignation or retirement could be filled. The crisis was heightened when 16 children with disabilities were transferred to the facility's case load from another state agency. MacArthur applied to the director of the Department of Public Welfare for emergency assistance but did not expect any help for several months if at all.

Because of the facility's location in a university town and the nature of its services, it received many well-meaning offers of volunteer help. These offers often came from students with considerable training in special and adaptive education. In the past, MacArthur tended to make only limited use of these volunteers, assigning them to duties as aides and custodians with few chances for carrying out actual instruction and training. Recently, volunteers had received special development training from the department as ombudsmen on behalf of the clients.

In view of the existing financial crisis, MacArthur decided that he would have to place greater reliance on volunteers if he was to provide adequately for the additional children. He reviewed a large number of volunteer applications and selected two people whose backgrounds seemed the most appropriate.

One was Sharon Bowers, a graduate student in special education who expected to receive her degree within the next six months and said she hoped to work with children with disabilities. She was bright and enthusiastic and established immediate rapport with both the children and the professional staff members on her introductory meeting with them. She appeared to be reliable and responsible and was recommended in glowing terms by former employers. Under the circumstances, MacArthur would be inclined to offer Bowers a full-time paid position, but at the moment she was available for only about two hours every afternoon.

The other person chosen was Alice Pearson, a socially prominent local woman with a degree in elementary education. Although she had not taught for several years and her experience had been entirely with normal children, she had excellent local recommendations and several useful political connections. She was able to devote between 15 and 20 hours a week to the program. After being introduced to the group with which she would be working, however, she seemed overwhelmed with the magnitude of the children's handicaps.

While fitting Bowers and Pearson into the program, MacArthur received a request from Professor Paul Corkin, a faculty member of the university's Department of Education, to include the children in a study that would attempt to measure their educational development and achievement over a 12-month period. Since the study was designed to evaluate the teaching methods used by agency professionals, MacArthur felt that participation was almost a necessity. Negative results might reveal areas where program content should be improved while positive results would probably benefit the program. The study required that some of the children and their assigned staff workers spend several afternoons each week in a controlled experimental environment where they would be periodically tested.

MacArthur juggled his staff schedules to take best advantage of the volunteer help within the time limits imposed. This required having Bowers and Pearson work together with a group of five children during the period of the experiment. Pearson was also available to supervise during the lunch hour when the agency was particularly short-handed. Since the experiment was scheduled to start immediately, MacArthur was able to provide only a brief orientation session before the volunteers began their duties.

Several weeks passed before Professor Corkin had has first conference with MacArthur. He reported that during the experiment he had noted a great deal of antagonism between the two volunteers, Bowers and Pearson. They were barely civil to each other and competed for the children's attention. The children seemed to sense the conflict, and as a result were nervous, easily upset and generally uncooperative. The atmosphere was adversely influencing the outcome of the experiment. The professor revealed that Bowers had announced to him her intention of quitting. He was ready to abandon the study unless some change was made.

Further investigation by MacArthur revealed that Bowers was doing an outstanding job. She had developed warm relationships with all the children with whom she worked. Pearson had largely overcome the initial feelings aroused by the contact with the severely disabled, and was almost always able to be on hand when the agency was in critical need of additional help. She had also proved to be a valuable link with the local community and was engaged in fund-raising activities that would benefit the agency. Although she did not relate to the children as well as Bowers, she could be depended on to keep order.

MacArthur knew that his paid professional staff members were spread as thinly as possible. Altering schedules now would be nearly impossible. He also realized that community volunteers provided valuable services and financial support to the agency that he would hate to lose. He could not afford to offend members of this group yet knew he must do something to resolve this problem.

Case 44: Problems with Volunteer Workers

Questions and Instructions:

1. In such a sensitive program dealing with children with disabilities, do you think MacArthur is justified in attempting to make greater use of volunteer workers, who, despite their best intentions, might harm their young charges?

2. In view of the described situation, what do you think MacArthur can do to save the experimental program?

3. If it came to making a choice between Bowers and Pearson, which do you think MacArthur should keep in the program? Why?

4. What should be MacArthur's overriding concern in resolving the problem?

5. Discuss various choices open to MacArthur as they affect the facility's long-term and short-term well-being.

Case 44: Problems with Volunteer Workers

6. What functions would an ombudsman for children with disabilities perform?

7. Should different supervisory approaches be used for volunteer employees in contrast with paid employees? Explain.

8. How can MacArthur make better use of Pearson's and Bowers's skills and talents?

Case 44: Problems with Volunteer Workers
Name:

Case Log and Administrative Journal Entry

This case analysis and learning assessment is printed on perforated pages and may be removed from the book for evaluation purposes.

Case Analysis:
Major case concepts and theories identified:

What is the relevance of the concepts, theories, ideas and techniques presented in the case to that of public management?

Facts — what do we know *for sure* about the case? Please list.

Who is involved in the case (people, departments, agencies, units, etc.)? Were the problems of an "intra/interagency" nature? Be specific.

Are there any rules, laws, regulations or standard operating procedures identified in the case study that might limit decision-making? If so, what are they?

Are there any clues presented in the case as to the major actor's interests, needs, motivations and personalities? If so, please list them.

Case 44: Problems with Volunteer Workers

Learning Assessment:
What do the administrative theories presented in this case mean to you as an administrator?

How can this learning be put to use outside the classroom? Are there any problems you envision during the implementation phase?

Several possible courses of action were identified during the class discussion. Which action was considered to be most practical by the group? Which was deemed most feasible? Based on your personal experience, did the group reach a conclusion that was desirable, feasible, and practical? Please explain why or why not.

Did the group reach a decision that would solve the problem on a short-term or long-term basis? Please explain.

What could you have done to receive more learning value from this case?

45

Pressing a Harassment Suit

by
C. Kenneth Meyer

After several jobs with various small and unprofitable business firms, Mae Fiedler was pleased to be employed as a records clerk in the Union City Police Department. Here she had regular working hours, sick-leave pay, vacations, and health insurance, security she had not before enjoyed.

A disadvantage, however, was that she was frequently embarrassed by the indecent language used by her predominantly male coworkers and by their talk laced with sexual references. Noting this, the police officers often teased her by commenting on her appearance and by making suggestive remarks about wanting to be alone with her. A confrontation occurred one day. While walking along a hallway, Fiedler was stopped by three officers — Ernest Foster, Robert Aquinaldo, and Leslie Madison — who not only spoke indecently to her but touched the upper part of her body. Fiedler broke away from them and entered the records room. Looking back to see if they were following her, she saw Foster unzip his trousers and wave what she thought was his penis.

Fiedler reported the incident to Chief of Police Oscar Flanagan, as well as the indecent talk that went on in her presence. Although Flanagan promised to look into the matter, he told Fiedler that the officers were only having fun and meant no harm. But when the officers discovered that Fiedler had complained to the chief, they chided her for being a prude and posted pornographic pictures on a bulletin board of naked women bearing her name.

Seeking a way of stopping the harassment, Fiedler went to the city's Women's Resource Center for advice. Although the counselor assigned to Fiedler's case was sympathetic, she was not optimistic in regard to a favorable outcome. She explained that it was difficult to substantiate charges of sexual harassment and that most court cases failed. Unfortunately, she continued, the cases were unsuccessful because administrators were averse to taking action, coworkers were reluctant to cooperate for fear of losing their jobs or chances of promotion, evidence satisfying legal requirements was difficult to obtain, and the complainant was sometimes treated as the one on trial. "It takes time, money, and energy to follow this type of case through to the end," the counselor said. "Are you willing to initiate action you may lose? If so, we can give you moral support and recommend an attorney to represent you. But the decision is up to you."

Case 45: Pressing a Harassment Suit

Fiedler told the counselor that she would think the matter over. Two days later, however, when the department refused to view the incident as one of sexual harassment, she made up her mind to pursue the case. As a result of an investigation by Chief Flanagan, Officer Foster was suspended for three days without pay for "excessive horseplay," and Officers Aquinaldo and Madison received only written reprimands. The opinion of the department was that there had been no indecent exposure. The object displayed before Fiedler was a fake rubber penis that Foster had been displaying to other officers as a joke.

On the advice of the Women's Resource Center counselor, Fiedler went to the district attorney to file a criminal complaint. He questioned her in such detail that she felt, as she had been warned, like an accused person undergoing cross-examination. The district attorney refused to take action against the officers, saying that Fiedler was making too much of what was nothing more than a harmless prank. He told her that the officers' actions were not punishable crimes, and that she did not have adequate proof for conviction.

Angered by the district attorney's view, Fiedler consulted a lawyer recommended by the Resource Center, Amanda Arnold. Subsequently, she filed a claim for damages against the city under a state tort claims act. Arnold's petition requested $100,000 in damages for violation of Fiedler's right of privacy. It declared that Foster "intentionally exposed himself, knowing that Fiedler was looking at him" and that Fiedler had the right to be free of "such oppressive, insulting, and degrading behavior."

Shortly after filing the claim, Fiedler received written notification of her transfer from the police department to the city's garbage department to fill a new position at the sewage treatment plant where collection trucks were unloaded. Believing that this action was taken in retaliation for her suit, Arnold filed a complaint with the Equal Employment Opportunity Commission (EEOC). It alleged sexual harassment and requested that the city rescind the transfer. Fiedler's fight became even more difficult when the EEOC denied the request for investigation because of lack of time. It said, however, she had the right to sue city officials in federal court.

After more than three months of frustration, Fiedler brought suit in the United States District Court, asking $500,000 in actual damages and $2 million in punitive damages. The petition cited the failure of the city to respond properly to Fiedler's initial complaint to Chief Flanagan and to her $100,000 claim for damages, and the failure of the district attorney to take proper action. The petition also asked the court to direct the city to reinstate Fiedler in her position as a records clerk in the police department, to order an end to the harassment, and to require the city to issue a statement against sexual harassment of women.

Case 45: Pressing a Harassment Suit

Questions and Instructions:

1. In an age of sexual freedom, pornographic publications, plays, motion pictures, video cassettes, and male and female nude dancers entertaining in nightspots, did Mae Fiedler take too seriously the actions of the police officers?

2. Could Fiedler have handled the situation at work differently to improve her relationship with the officers, or was her choice of action the most effective one?

3. Do the Civil Rights Act of 1964 and the Directive on Sexual Harassment issued by the Equal Employment Opportunity Commission, even if followed, provide enough protection for employees who find themselves in a situation like that of Fiedler's? (See Exhibits 1 and 2).

4. Are the options available to employees who believe themselves victims of sexual harassment too complex and legally restricted to make it worthwhile to seek remedial action?

5. What punitive action should law codes provide against supervisors who take no action to stop harassment of employees by coworkers?

6. Which type of harassment is more difficult to deal with, the one which the victim suffers in the workplace or that which occurs in the effort to obtain redress?

Exhibit 1. Excerpt from Civil Rights Act of 1964

TITLE VII — EQUAL EMPLOYMENT OPPORTUNITY DISCRIMINATION BECAUSE OF RACE, COLOR, RELIGION, SEX, OR NATIONAL ORIGIN

Section 703.

a. It shall be an unlawful employment practice for an employer—

1. to fail or refuse to hire or to discharge any individual, or otherwise to discriminate against any individual with respect to his compensation, terms, conditions, or privileges of employment, because of such individual's race, color, religion, sex, or national origin; or

2. to limit, segregate, or classify his employees in any way which would deprive or tend to deprive any individual of employment opportunities or otherwise adversely affect his status as an employee, because of such individual's race, color, religion, sex, or national origin.

b. It shall be an unlawful employment practice for an employment agency to fail or refuse to refer for employment, or otherwise to discriminate against, any individual because of his race, color, religion, sex, or national origin, or to classify or refer for employment any individual on the basis of his race, color, religion, sex, or national origin.

c. It shall be an unlawful employment practice for a labor organization —

1. to exclude or to expel from its membership, or otherwise to discriminate against, any individual because of his race, color, religion, sex, or national origin;

2. to limit, segregate, or classify its membership, or to classify or fail or refuse to refer for employment any individual, in any way which would deprive or tend to deprive any individual of employment opportunities, or would limit such employment opportunities or otherwise adversely affect his status as an employee or as an applicant for employment, because of such individual's race, color, religion, sex, or national origin; or

3. to cause or attempt to cause an employer to discriminate against an individual in violation of this section.

d. It shall be an unlawful employment practice for any employer, labor organization, or joint labor-management committee controlling apprenticeship or other training or retraining, including on-the-job training programs, to discriminate against any individual because of his race, color, religion, sex, or national origin in admission to, or employment in, any program established to provide apprenticeship or other training.

e. Notwithstanding any other provision of this title, (1) it shall not be an unlawful employment practice for an employer to hire and employ employees, for an employment agency to classify, or refer for employment any individual, for a labor organization to classify its membership or to classify or refer for employment any individual, or for an employer, labor organization, or joint labor-management committee controlling apprenticeship or other training or retraining programs to admit or employ any individual in any such program, on the basis of his religion, sex, or national origin in those certain instances where religion, sex or national origin is a bona fide occupational qualification reasonably necessary to the normal operation of that particular business or enterprise, and (2) it shall not be an unlawful employment practice for a school, college, university, or other educational institution or institution of learning to hire and employ employees of a particular religion if such school, college, university, or other educational institution or institution of learning is, in whole or in substantial part, owned, supported, controlled, or managed by a particular religion or by a particular religious corporation, association, or society, or if the curriculum of such school, college, university, or other educational institution or institution of learning is directed toward the propagation of a particular religion.

f. As used in this title, the phrase "unlawful employment practice" shall not be deemed to include any action or measure taken by an employer, labor organization, joint labor-management committee, or employment agency with respect to an individual who is member of the Communist Party of the United States or of any other organization required to register as a Communist-action or Communist-front organization by final order of the Subversive Activities Control Board pursuant to the Subversive Activities Control Act of 1950.

g. Notwithstanding any other provision of this title, it shall not be an unlawful employment practice for an employer to fail or refuse to hire and employ any individual for any position, for an employer to discharge any individual from any position, or for an employment agency to fail or refuse to refer any individual for employment in any position, or for a labor organization to fail or refuse to refer any individual for employment in any position, if—

1. the occupancy of such position, or access to the premises in or upon which any part of the duties of such position is performed, or is to be performed, is subject to any requirement imposed in the interest of the national security of the United States under any security program in effect pursuant to or administered under any statute of the United States or any Executive order of the President; and

2. such individual has not fulfilled or has ceased to fulfill that requirement. Notwithstanding any other provision of this title, it shall not be an unlawful employment practice for an employer to apply different standards of compensation, or different terms, conditions, or privileges of employment pursuant to a bona fide seniority or merit system, or a system which measures earnings by quantity or quality of production or to employees who work in different locations, provided that such differences are not the result of an intention to discriminate because of race, color, religion, sex, or national origin, nor shall it be an unlawful employment practice for an employer to give and to act upon the results of any professionally developed ability test provided that such test, its administration or action upon the results is not designed, intended, or used to discriminate because of race, color, religion, sex, or national origin, It shall not be an unlawful employment practice under this title for any employer to differentiate upon the basis of sex in determining the amount of the wages or compensation paid or to be paid to employees of such employer if such differentiation is authorized by the provisions of section 6(d) of the Fair Labor Standards Act of 1938, as amended (29) U.S.C. 206(d).

Exhibit 2. Directive on Sexual Harassment Issued by the EEOC

Section 1604.11 Sexual harassment.

a. Harassment on the basis of sex is a violation of Sec. 703 of Title VII. Unwelcome sexual advances, requests for sexual favors, and other verbal or physical conduct of a sexual nature constitute sexual harassment when (1) submission to such conduct is made either explicitly or implicitly a term or condition of an individual's employment, (2) subdivision to or rejection of such conduct by an individual is used as the basis for employment decisions affecting such individual, or (3) such conduct has the purpose or effect of unreasonably interfering with an individual's work performance or creating an intimidating, hostile, or offensive working environment.

b. In determining whether alleged conduct constitutes sexual harassment, the Commission will look at the record as a whole and at the totality of the circumstances, such as the nature of the sexual advances and the context in which the alleged incidents occurred. The determination of the legality of a particular action will be made from the facts, on a case by case basis.

c. Applying general Title VII principles, an employer, employment agency, joint apprenticeship committee or labor organization (hereinafter collectively referred to as "employer") is responsible for its acts and those of its agents and supervisory employees with respect to sexual harassment regardless of whether the specific acts complained of were authorized or even forbidden by the employer and regardless of whether the employer knew or should have known of their occurrence. The commission will examine the circumstances of the particular employment relationship of the job functions performed by the individual in determining whether an individual acts in either a supervisory or agency capacity.

d. With respect to conduct between fellow employees, an employer is responsible for acts of sexual harassment in the workplace where the employer (or its agents or supervisory employees) knows or should have known of the conduct, unless it can show that it took immediate and appropriate corrective action.

e. An employer may also be responsible for the acts of non-employees, with respect to sexual harassment of employees in the workplace, where the employer (or its agents or supervisory employees) knows or should have known of the conduct and fails to take immediate and appropriate corrective action. In reviewing these cases the Commission will consider the extent of the employer's control and any other legal responsibility which the employer may have with respect to the conduct of such non-employees.

f. Prevention is the best tool for the elimination of sexual harassment. An employer should take all steps necessary to prevent sexual harassment from occurring, such as affirmatively raising the subject, expressing strong disapproval, developing appropriate sanctions, informing employees of their right to raise and how to raise the issue of harassment under Title VII, and developing methods to sensitize all concerned.

g. Other related practices: Where employment opportunities or benefits are granted because of an individual's submission to the employer's sexual advances o requests for sexual favors, the employer may be held liable for unlawful sex discrimination against other persons who were qualified for but denied that employment opportunity or benefit.

Case 45: Pressing a Harassment Suit

Case 45: Pressing a Harassment Suit
Name:

Case Log and Administrative Journal Entry

This case analysis and learning assessment is printed on perforated pages and may be removed from the book for evaluation purposes.

Case Analysis:
Major case concepts and theories identified:

What is the relevance of the concepts, theories, ideas and techniques presented in the case to that of public management?

Facts — what do we know *for sure* about the case? Please list.

Who is involved in the case (people, departments, agencies, units, etc.)? Were the problems of an "intra/interagency" nature? Be specific.

Are there any rules, laws, regulations or standard operating procedures identified in the case study that might limit decision-making? If so, what are they?

Are there any clues presented in the case as to the major actor's interests, needs, motivations and personalities? If so, please list them.

Case 45: Pressing a Harassment Suit

Learning Assessment:
What do the administrative theories presented in this case mean to you as an administrator?

How can this learning be put to use outside the classroom? Are there any problems you envision during the implementation phase?

Several possible courses of action were identified during the class discussion. Which action was considered to be most practical by the group? Which was deemed most feasible? Based on your personal experience, did the group reach a conclusion that was desirable, feasible, and practical? Please explain why or why not.

Did the group reach a decision that would solve the problem on a short-term or long-term basis? Please explain.

What could you have done to receive more learning value from this case?

46

Many Faces of Discrimination

by
C. Kenneth Meyer and Stephen E. Clapham

As a young woman, Sydney Ross was not drawn toward the same type of interests that were shown by her female counterparts. She had an abiding interest in "things mechanical" and marveled at the "mega equipment" often shown on the Discovery Channel — huge excavating equipment, mining trucks, tractor-crawlers, and the C5-A Galaxy. Her mother often stated that Sydney was obsessed with "trucks, trucks, and more trucks." Her father simply observed that Sydney was "tougher than crabgrass."

Sydney could recite detailed descriptions about full-traction vehicles and the sleek, highly "decorated with chrome" eighteen-wheel rigs and trailers they dragged — flat-beds, tankers, reefers, and refrigerated units. She could speak eloquently about gas and diesel-fired engines and knew the details about all the elements that factored into performance, such as stroke/bore in millimeters, compression ratio, maximum torque at engine speed, and maximum output at engine speed, and for a snow plow, minimum turning radius.

During her days of attending the local community college, she was frequently looked at strangely by her peer group, especially when the class discussion gravitated toward changing gender roles in society and the "traditional versus non-traditional" occupational designations for both men and women. Her favorite instructor once pointed out to her class that five percent of registered nurses in the United States are men, and the complimentary 95 percent are women. The instructor also stressed that the vast majority of clerical, secretarial, data-entry, and cashier positions are held by women with only a small but growing percentage of women holding jobs as truck drivers, construction equipment operators, plumbers, carpenters, and electricians.

The information she acquired in class was reinforced by data generated by the U.S. Census Bureau. The census provided evidence of the changing occupational status of women in the working world and the Bureau of Labor Statistics (BLS) gave added reinforcement to the general tendencies revealed in the enumerated census.

Knowledge of these trends gave some solace to Sydney and she knew in her own mind that she must realize the dream of driving a truck that had been seeded in her "heart-of-hearts" early on in her childhood. Sydney had struggled with the tension caused by her career choice and always responded to inquiries from her colleagues about her "idealized work life" with courtesy and an understanding of why they might question her interests. Gender roles as society defined them, at least for Sydney, were simultaneously viewed with "excitable interest" and "blatant disgust." She lamented the lack of women role models in her chosen "profession" and she saw no reason, biological, genetics, or otherwise, why women could not do the same things men do and become the best in the field. Of course, she had firsthand experience dealing with the biases and prejudices she faced from both men and women over her career choice. Like other workers, she too struggled with balancing life-work-family responsibilities, especially since she was a "sandwiched caregiver."

Her attitude of tolerance toward those who viewed her differently had often been tested in school, at work, and through the stereotypical roles played by women in the media. Her patience was exhausted when she read about a speech given by President Lawrence Summers of Harvard University. Although Summers had impeccable academic qualifications, he attempted, albeit inadequately, to call attention to whether or not there were "systematic differences" that existed between women and men. He went on to suggest in his speech that gender differences were present in attributes as diverse as weight, IQ, mathematics and scientific ability. He spoke as if there was empirical evidence that could be used to support genetic differences, and for Sydney, this made no sense. She interpreted his remarks, not unlike that of many in the academies of higher learning, as just another manifestation of "white-male paternalistic" bashing or down-playing of the capability of women to achieve in mathematics, physics, chemistry, biology, or whatever field their career took them, at comparable levels with the male members of society.

Sydney thought about Summers' statement and she could have understand it better if it had been uttered by a "mindless talk-show host," or "babbling ideologue," but how could this type of gender-inequity come from the mouth of the president of one of the leading universities in the world? She wondered whether his views were representative of those who are learned in the area of biology, genetics, and anthropology, or of those who are supportive of removing the barriers that actually impede the advancement of women whether in academia, the "hardwood" corporate suites, or as truck drivers working for city government.

Sydney had become accustomed to the many "tricks and pranks" that her co-workers had played on her over the years. Although she often felt embarrassed that her colleagues would treat her less than their equals and repetitively subject her to demeaning comments and jokes, in her attempt to become one of the guys she bore the burden without expressing her displeasure. Nevertheless, she often wondered why her male team members had to act with such immaturity and total disregard for personal feelings. In the final analysis she figured she was paying the cost associated with breaking the "barrier of entry" into a field that was traditionally male and this was the price she had to pay for being female — even if it provided clear evidence of gender inequity and discrimination.

Questions and Instructions:

1. What advice would you give Sydney on how to handle the comments, jokes, etc. of her associates? Please elaborate.

Case 46: Many Faces of Discrimination

2. Is Sydney the victim of sexual harassment? If yes, please explain.

   Yes she is b/c Title VII prevents against an objectively hostile work place

3. What are some of the major dimensions associated with gender inequity? Please discuss.

Part 2

Sydney was now faced with a challenge that brought her "closer-to-earth" as she would often say. As a driver of a snow plow, she lived eight miles away from her job. She was informed that she exceeded Brooksville's residential requirement associated with emergency personnel. That is, she would be treated similarly to law enforcement officers, fire fighters, and emergency medical personnel. Accordingly, she lived one mile farther than the seven-mile policy permitted and this was a violation of the municipal ordinance. What was she to do now? She had purchased a piece of land and built a modest three bedroom home several years ago and now she was in violation of the "law." She wondered if the "response time" expectation associated with other "emergency personnel" or "critical workers," should also apply to snow plow drivers. Was it equally critical for her as snow plow operator to respond to emergency situations with the same alacrity as police or emergency medical personnel? With her four-wheel drive F-250 Ford pickup, she felt she could respond equivalently, if not more quickly, than the other personnel who lived one or more miles closer to the public works depot. She was always tuned into the weather forecasts — after all, her job was to remove the snow from the streets and highways and keep them open for travel. Sydney understood the level of criticality associated with keeping the streets open, but she opined, should she be equally disposed to the code like other emergency responders in the city of Brooksville.

As a bright and perceptive woman, Sydney understood the fallout or lingering residues associated with long-term gender and racial discrimination in society. But what she was to experience next seemed to be both irrational and inexplicable. She wondered if the type of discrimination she had faced was built on a foundation of fear, ignorance, or whether there was a systematic attempt to single her out for disparate and unfair treatment.

What Sydney was about to learn from her immediate supervisor, Olaf Henderson, Department of Transportation, would place her job or her residency in jeopardy and she saw no easy way of complying with the public employee residency requirement of Brooksville. Olaf spoke to Sydney in a soft and gentle way and his Scandinavian upbringing clearly showed that he too felt uncomfortable bringing to her attention that she was considered an emergency employee and, therefore, required to live within seven miles of the city boundary.

Sydney Ross had faced the forces of discrimination that affected her career and had overcome them with graceful pride. Now she was threatened economically by a residency requirement that

Case 46: Many Faces of Discrimination

classified her as an emergency worker. If she failed to move in three months, she would lose her job, a job that she felt gave dignity to her life and one that she loved above all others.

Questions and Instructions:

4. When Sydney became a snowplow driver, the job was not considered an emergency job. Should she be "grandfathered in" relative to the emergency status of her job? If so, why? If not, why not? Please explain.

   I would ? the 7 mile limit. Essential job functions should be can you respond to this area by X min.

5. Should Sydney sell her home and move if she needs to meet the Brooksville ordinance for emergency public employees? Please elaborate.

   Yes b/c how else to make a living

6. Please consult several municipalities in your region of the state and ascertain what their residency requirements are. Please prepare the definitions for distribution to the class. Should administrative personnel be treated differently from non-administrative personnel or from emergency workers? Please explain.

7. Are there any state Supreme Court decisions that have been rendered regarding residency requirements for municipal employees? If so, please provide the court opinions and how "emergency" or "critical" employees are defined.

   Ohio passed legislation 2006 ; Ohio supreme court upheld
   McCarthy v Philidelphia US supreme court upheld

Case 46: Many Faces of Discrimination

Case 46: Many Faces of Discrimination
Name:

Case Log and Administrative Journal Entry

This case analysis and learning assessment is printed on perforated pages and may be removed from the book for evaluation purposes.

Case Analysis:
Major case concepts and theories identified:

What is the relevance of the concepts, theories, ideas and techniques presented in the case to that of public management?

Facts — what do we know *for sure* about the case? Please list.

Who is involved in the case (people, departments, agencies, units, etc.)? Were the problems of an "intra/interagency" nature? Be specific.

Are there any rules, laws, regulations or standard operating procedures identified in the case study that might limit decision-making? If so, what are they?

Are there any clues presented in the case as to the major actor's interests, needs, motivations and personalities? If so, please list them.

Case 46: Many Faces of Discrimination

Learning Assessment:
What do the administrative theories presented in this case mean to you as an administrator?

How can this learning be put to use outside the classroom? Are there any problems you envision during the implementation phase?

Several possible courses of action were identified during the class discussion. Which action was considered to be most practical by the group? Which was deemed most feasible? Based on your personal experience, did the group reach a conclusion that was desirable, feasible, and practical? Please explain why or why not.

Did the group reach a decision that would solve the problem on a short-term or long-term basis? Please explain.

What could you have done to receive more learning value from this case?

47

Many Sides of Downsizing

by
C. Kenneth Meyer

Budgets were running in the red throughout all levels of government. The federal deficit was at an all-time high; all but a dozen or so states were running in the red, and most of the cities and counties, especially those that required a balanced budget by law, were struggling with their budgets. Rochester was no different! As a medium size city of 55,000 people, the city council had voted to combine the Department of Public Works and the Department of Parks and Recreation into the new Department of Public Works, Parks and Recreation. Ravi Singh discovered he must invoke a reduction in force of nearly thirty unskilled or semi-skilled employees in the several departments that were historically under his direction including sanitation, street maintenance, sewer maintenance, engineering, sewage treatment, and the water treatment plant. Now, with the merger, he had additional staff positions he could possibly cut in the parks and recreation program and park maintenance. The easiest plan was to operate on a "last-in, first-out" basis. But Singh did not like the idea because layoffs based on longevity could result in the worst employees being retained and the best being let go. He also realized that the "last-in, first out" model of reducing the force was potentially disruptive of those gains that the City of Rochester had recently made in implementing its affirmative action plan and moving toward equal employment opportunity — a record the mayor and council were proud of and one that was of high priority for all department heads.

As one who was quite familiar with the management literature, Singh knew that women and minorities tended to be the last hired, and because they had the lowest level of seniority, tended to be terminated first during staff cuts. Singh preferred an alternative method, basing layoff decisions on an employee's performance. The drawback to this, however, was that Rochester had not developed an appraisal system that would be objective and unbiased for these workers and to establish such a system would take time — time which he didn't have. Furthermore, Singh feared layoffs based on this principle might result in lawsuits from those believing they were unfairly fired. He considered a third possibility, furloughs, which would give workers short, forced vacations without pay. Furloughs, he thought, might bring about short-term relief but would not be adequate if the fund shortage continued as he believed it would.

Whatever his own predilections were concerning the euphemism called "rightsizing," he now had to balance his own budget. Was this downsizing going to benefit, in the long run, the city of Rochester, or would it produce in the public sector what it had in the private sector — little or nothing in terms of positive results. He had memorized what Robert Reich had stated when he was the Secretary of the U.S.

Case 47: Many Sides of Downsizing

Department of Labor, "Corporate downsizing has shown to be bad for many companies in the long-term. Companies are discovering that they've overdone it. It also has negative consequences for the economy as a whole because it holds down wage gains and undermines consumer confidence."

Questions and Instructions:

1. If you were in Singh's position, what would you do?

2. What are some of the alternatives to downsizing that you might suggest? Please list. **Exhibit 1** presents some alternatives to downsizing. Are there any suggestions on this list that might help Singh with his reduction-in-force or "rightsizing" decision? Which ones would you suggest and why? Please be specific.

3. Which of the three layoff principles mentioned in the case study do you consider fairest to workers? Why?

4. Which would be in the best interest of the city of Rochester? Which would be in the best interest of the newly formed Department of Public Works, Parks, and Recreation? Explain.

Case 47: Many Sides of Downsizing

5. How would you go about establishing an appraisal system for laying off employees of the caliber being considered by Singh?

6. If you were terminated today, what basic emotions would you feel concerning the decision? Do you think that employees might have some of the emotions mentioned in **Exhibit 2**? Which ones and why?

7. If you were Singh, what emotional responses would you have to layoffs in your department? Please list. Now examine **Exhibit 3**. Are there any emotions on this list that you might also share? Which ones?

Exhibit 1. Potential Alternatives to Downsizing

Wage freeze
Flexible scheduling
Transfer of employees to other departments
Reduction of overtime
Cutting pay across the board
Voluntary termination
Early retirement
Re-engineering
Attrition
Reduction of operation costs
Pay lag
Open book management style
Recapture outsourcing
Reduction of employee benefits
Work sharing program
Golden parachutes
Use of more part-time employees
Extended vacations (for those who have unused vacation saved)
Leave of absence without pay
Employee development program
Diversification and acquisition
Voluntary scheduled layoff
Reassess executive incentive programs
Reduce work-week to 35 hours or less
Job sharing

Exhibit 2. Potential Employee Reactions to Being Downsized

Abandoned	Loss
Abused	Loss of confidence
Anger	Loss of credibility
Anxiety	Loss of identity
Apathy	Loss of pride
Betrayed	Loss of self-esteem
Cheated	Loss of self-worth
Confused	Loss of status
Disbelief	New possibilities
Expendable	Out-of-control
Failure	Panic
Fear	Pleased
Frustration	Rage
Frustility (frustration combined with hostility)	Retaliation
Grief	Relief
Happy	Sabotage
Helplessness	Scared
Homicidal	Shameful
Hostile	Sick
Humiliated	Suicidal
Incompetent	Terrified
Insecure	Troubled
Let down	Urge to vomit
	Violent

Exhibit 3. Potential Managerial Reactions Toward Implementing Downsizing Decisions

Anger	Marionette, with strings being pulled by others
Disbelief	Out-of-control
Denial	Opportunity for change
Emotionally exhausted	Pleased
Empathy	Pressured
Failure	Rage
Fear of reprisal	Relief
Fear of violence	Resentment
Feel of being distanced from other employees	Sadness
Guilty	Scared
Happy	Sick
Humiliated	Sorrow
In-control	Stressed
Indifferent	Sympathetic

Case 47: Many Sides of Downsizing

Case 47: Many Sides of Downsizing
Name:

Case Log and Administrative Journal Entry

This case analysis and learning assessment is printed on perforated pages and may be removed from the book for evaluation purposes.

Case Analysis:
Major case concepts and theories identified:

What is the relevance of the concepts, theories, ideas and techniques presented in the case to that of public management?

Facts — what do we know *for sure* about the case? Please list.

Who is involved in the case (people, departments, agencies, units, etc.)? Were the problems of an "intra/interagency" nature? Be specific.

Are there any rules, laws, regulations or standard operating procedures identified in the case study that might limit decision-making? If so, what are they?

Are there any clues presented in the case as to the major actor's interests, needs, motivations and personalities? If so, please list them.

353

Case 47: Many Sides of Downsizing

Learning Assessment:
What do the administrative theories presented in this case mean to you as an administrator?

How can this learning be put to use outside the classroom? Are there any problems you envision during the implementation phase?

Several possible courses of action were identified during the class discussion. Which action was considered to be most practical by the group? Which was deemed most feasible? Based on your personal experience, did the group reach a conclusion that was desirable, feasible, and practical? Please explain why or why not.

Did the group reach a decision that would solve the problem on a short-term or long-term basis? Please explain.

What could you have done to receive more learning value from this case?

48

To Quit or Not to Quit

by
C. Kenneth Meyer

Case A. An Intolerable Situation

Ever since Jason Hendrix became director of the state Bureau of Investigation, Alonzo Mercedes, deputy director for five years, had found himself at odds with his superior. Mercedes had been a candidate for the position of director on the retirement of an old friend and associate, but he had not really expected to be appointed. He realized that a new governor, elected on the promise of making a clean sweep, would search outside the state to find a director without established political friendships and loyalties. The governor's choice was Jason Hendrix, a retired army colonel whose latest assignment had been in military intelligence.

Introducing a bit of military spit and polish into the bureau was in Mercedes's view not a bad thing, but he thought Colonel Hendrix overdid it at times. As experienced peace officers, most staff members understood the need for concise and explicit orders and did not mind commands rather than requests. They regarded the colonel, however, as a martinet rather than a leader. Hendrix's chief fault as an administrator, Mercedes thought, was that he would not listen to people. His usual response to difficult situations was, "I want action, not explanations." Thus, as chief intermediary between the director and the staff, Mercedes developed a smoldering resentment of Hendrix.

This resentment grew when employees formed a chapter of the Fraternal Order of Police (FOP). Colonel Hendrix, believing the FOP a threat to his authority and to the orderly performance of investigations, told Mercedes that he would "bust" Henry Dryfus, supervisor of the intelligence section, who was serving as interim president of the FOP chapter. Hendrix threatened to disband the chapter because two other agents were also officers. Later he issued a memorandum to staff members warning them against joining the organization.

In the past Mercedes had not regarded unionization favorably but, in view of the low morale brought on by Hendrix's fulminations, he decided to defend the FOP. He felt that his continuance as deputy director, after the director's typical display of unreason, would be intolerable. He therefore delivered a letter of resignation to Hendrix, and made it available to reporters who had heard of the dispute. The letter stated:

Case 48: To Quit or Not to Quit

I think employees should not be treated as you have done this past week. Bureau employees have the same guaranteed constitutional rights as everyone else. They should not be continually subject to your whimsical and irrational fits of anger nor should that be a repeated excuse for disregarding employees' rights.

Mercedes explained to reporters that he had decided to resign because he wanted to stop talk that he was criticizing Hendrix because he wanted his job.

In response to reporters' requests for an interview, Hendrix prepared a statement read by a bureau spokesman. In it he said that he regretted Mercedes's resignation because he had been an asset to the agency, adding that he did not care to comment on the dispute over the FOP. "The bureau is bigger than any one person or any small group of people and is certainly as professional as any law enforcement agency in the nation," the statement said. "When this resignation is no longer newsworthy, the bureau will continue to work to the best of its ability with the resources available."

Case B. The Frustrated Assistant Director

After the Department of Human Welfare was faced with the need to reduce its expenditures six percent on orders of the governor due to declining tax collections, Herbert Mauro, assistant director of health services, found himself constantly on the losing side in proposals to effect savings.

The tendency was, Mauro believed, to cause the state's needy to suffer through decisions to reduce services rather than to eliminate waste in operations. For example, state welfare officers were ordered closed for one day a week for which employees were not paid, two emergency relief services were eliminated, and a home-heating program was suspended. It would be better, Mauro felt, to reduce a top-heavy administrative force, delay a job reclassification program that would create promotions with pay increases, cut travel allowances, and in general save on operations costs rather than to "rob the poor and the needy."

Frustrated by the curt rejection of his recommendations, Mauro felt that he could no longer find satisfaction in his job. His letter of resignation to the Welfare Commission said:

> Throughout my fifteen-year career with the department, I have believed that informed decisions can be made only when all of the facts, honest opinions, and best advice are gathered for evaluation. The decision-making process places an absolute duty on employees, particularly those in management positions, to express their opinions to superiors in the performance of their job responsibilities. It is also the employee's responsibility, once having offered his or her advice, to carry out with professional dedication and best effort the ultimate decisions of the commission and the director.

Case 48: To Quit or Not to Quit

Under the present circumstances, I find it increasingly difficult to fulfill these essential responsibilities. Unfortunately, the employee's opinion is often regarded by superiors as criticism or negativism. Given this situation, I have decided that I must resign.

Questions and Instructions:

1. How do the motives of Alonzo Mercedes and Herbert Mauro differ in their decisions to resign?

2. To what extent were their resignations a result of personality conflicts?

3. Was resignation with a critical blast against superiors an effective way to correct a situation that each felt was wrong?

4. What other courses of action were open to Mercedes and Mauro to improve the situations they found unbearable?

5. Discuss the pros and cons of bringing before the public an internal conflict over policy within an agency or department of government.

Case 48: To Quit or Not to Quit

Case 48: To Quit or Not to Quit

Case 48: To Quit or Not to Quit
Name:

Case Log and Administrative Journal Entry

This case analysis and learning assessment is printed on perforated pages and may be removed from the book for evaluation purposes.

Case Analysis:
Major case concepts and theories identified:

What is the relevance of the concepts, theories, ideas and techniques presented in the case to that of public management?

Facts — what do we know *for sure* about the case? Please list.

Who is involved in the case (people, departments, agencies, units, etc.)? Were the problems of an "intra/interagency" nature? Be specific.

Are there any rules, laws, regulations or standard operating procedures identified in the case study that might limit decision-making? If so, what are they?

Are there any clues presented in the case as to the major actor's interests, needs, motivations and personalities? If so, please list them.

Case 48: To Quit or Not to Quit

Learning Assessment:

What do the administrative theories presented in this case mean to you as an administrator?

How can this learning be put to use outside the classroom? Are there any problems you envision during the implementation phase?

Several possible courses of action were identified during the class discussion. Which action was considered to be most practical by the group? Which was deemed most feasible? Based on your personal experience, did the group reach a conclusion that was desirable, feasible, and practical? Please explain why or why not.

Did the group reach a decision that would solve the problem on a short-term or long-term basis? Please explain.

What could you have done to receive more learning value from this case?

49

Freda is Sick Again

by
C. Kenneth Meyer and Chris Ward

Oakdale was one of the five boroughs that made up Jeffersonville. It was a stable, largely middle-class, homogeneous community that prided itself on being a "healthy city." The city crest on its logo was adorned with a background of lush vegetation, towering palm trees, and a waterfall that "gushed" water into a blue-green lagoon. In the logo one got a glimpse of a well-groomed bike path winding its way through a pedestrian friendly neighborhood. Jeffersonville was portrayed as the city that had it all and an especially "family friendly" place to live.

Neighborhoods were important to Oakdale and residents took their associations seriously. Politically, they were a force to contend with that resulted in local politicians attempting to garner their support. In short, the residents felt a sense of attachment and community. This identity was proudly displayed on their school uniforms, sweatshirts, and on the banners strategically positioned on the major entrances to the borough. One resident stated it was "Mayberry with an attitude!" This opinion was further reflected on the "Character Counts" attributes printed on the bottom of the neatly hanging banners that adorned the light-poles.

As a community, when a need was identified, it was usually met, whether it was accessible buildings, the removal of architectural barriers, the inauguration of a "safe haven" program, the provision of a child friendly park and equipment, or a childcare center. The Oakdale Childcare Center (OCC) was built with funds generated from a campaign that posited the simple dictum: "Put children first!" As a new nonprofit organization, Stacey Olsen became its first professional administrator. Her degrees in early childhood development and learning, coupled with five years of teaching at a Montessori school, gave her the credentials valued by Oakdale.

One childcare provider, Freda Dixon, began her tenure at the center at the same time Stacy Olsen was hired. Freda was well liked by the children and her co-workers found her to be respectful and trustworthy — two of the several attitudes that were posted on the city banners.

Shortly after her probationary employment had ended, she approached Stacy Olsen and told her that she had received a medical diagnosis and to her chagrin it was a cancerous tumor. She presented herself as a strong woman and indicated that she wanted to continue her teaching and caring tasks at OCC while she underwent a combination of radiation treatments and stem-cell therapy.

Case 49: Freda is Sick Again

Stacy was proud of Freda's tenacity and the fact that she had taken "ownership" of her disease. She told Freda that "reasonable accommodation" would be made and that her door was always open for consultation. Freda asked that the parents of the children be informed of her medical diagnosis and routinely kept appraised of her treatment and prognosis. In the final analysis, she received support from the many "stakeholders" and several years later declared that her cancer was in remission. Of course, this was great news and the center celebrated her health status with zest.

Freda did not talk much about being a cancer survivor, but she did participate periodically in a local cancer support group. Several years passed and everyone thought Freda's recovery was miraculous. Then one morning she visited Olsen's office and repeated the medical story that she told earlier. Her disease had returned; she would be in therapy and she asked that the parents be notified once more of her condition.

The center did what it could to accommodate her treatment needs and was empathetic with the many absences due to her "illness." During this period she once more received an outpouring of support from the children, parents, team members, and the administration.

To demonstrate their "solidarity" with Freda, the center, based on a parent-driven initiative, had a hair shaving party. Parents and children that wished to participate shaved their hair in anticipation of her eventual hair loss due to chemotherapy. The children and parents demonstrated an uncommonly high level of cohesiveness and empathy for Freda; she was by all accounts an excellent care provider!

A few months had passed. Freda developed an attendance problem and, unbelievably, she did not lose her hair!

Stacy Olsen stood nervously at the front door of the center and shielded the children to the extent possible of seeing Freda being escorted from the building by the local police. Stacy and others discovered that Freda had engaged in a rouse — a level of deceit and deception. She had fabricated the cancer story. Freda had Munchausen syndrome (MS) and her medical plight was a call for attention.

Olsen and Freda's co-workers were devastated by the situation and couldn't believe they had been "taken-in" on such a bizarre case. To calm and alleviate the fears of the parents who had children in the center, Stacy Olsen wrote the following letter:

"Sickness and disease vary by type of acuity. Unfortunately, a permanent staff member, who had a wonderful record of care giving to the children, was recently dismissed from the center due to her illness — Munchausen syndrome (MS). There are different types of MS and in her case it was not MS by proxy. Instead, she feigned an illness to gain attention from others. Her motives were self-centered and she sought to generate empathy and attention from those in her circle of connections.

The OCC is conducting an immediate investigation concerning her behavior and the evidence to date shows that she did not physically injure any of her charges — your children. The center will keep you fully informed as to the proceedings it will be taking, while simultaneously insuring that the

Case 49: Freda is Sick Again

children's safety, rights, and interests come first and that they are fully protected at all times. The center is formulating a comprehensive response and concerned stakeholders should feel free to have their questions answered by Julia Johnson, our child learning and development consultant. Julia can be contacted at the telephone, fax and email addresses given below."

Question and Instructions:

1. What is Munchausen syndrome? How is it further delineated by type? Please explain.

2. As Stacy Olsen, what are your immediate concerns and how would you prioritize them? Please be specific.

3. The Americans with Disability Act (ADA) is a far reaching piece of legislation that affects either directly or indirectly nearly 80 million Americans. Under the provisions of the ADA, what course of action is permitted by OCC? Explain. Secondarily, what protection does the ADA give Freda Dixon? Please elaborate.

4. Did Stacey Olsen's letter to the parents, in your opinion, address the essential concerns and fears that might surround the feigned illness? If yes, why was it sufficient? If not, what would you have added, deleted, or kept the same? Please elaborate by giving examples that you would have placed in your letter.

Case 49: Freda is Sick Again

5. Under the provisions of the Health Insurance Portability and Accountability Act (HIPPA) of 1996, did Stacy Olsen's letter violate any part of this federal law? Please explain.

Case 49: Freda is Sick Again

Case 49: Freda is Sick Again
Name:

Case Log and Administrative Journal Entry

This case analysis and learning assessment is printed on perforated pages and may be removed from the book for evaluation purposes.

Case Analysis:
Major case concepts and theories identified:

What is the relevance of the concepts, theories, ideas and techniques presented in the case to that of public management?

Facts — what do we know *for sure* about the case? Please list.

Who is involved in the case (people, departments, agencies, units, etc.)? Were the problems of an "intra/interagency" nature? Be specific.

Are there any rules, laws, regulations or standard operating procedures identified in the case study that might limit decision-making? If so, what are they?

Are there any clues presented in the case as to the major actor's interests, needs, motivations and personalities? If so, please list them.

Case 49: Freda is Sick Again

Learning Assessment:
What do the administrative theories presented in this case mean to you as an administrator?

How can this learning be put to use outside the classroom? Are there any problems you envision during the implementation phase?

Several possible courses of action were identified during the class discussion. Which action was considered to be most practical by the group? Which was deemed most feasible? Based on your personal experience, did the group reach a conclusion that was desirable, feasible, and practical? Please explain why or why not.

Did the group reach a decision that would solve the problem on a short-term or long-term basis? Please explain.

What could you have done to receive more learning value from this case?

50

Regional or Racial Bias in Diversity Training

by
C. Kenneth Meyer, Megan O. Broin and Lance J. Noe

James Kaplan was known for his strong views on racism and ethnic discrimination when he was brought on board as a trainer in the state's Department of Personnel. Although he had tasted discrimination as a young Jewish male growing up in a small southern city in the United States, he felt he could control the anxiety, anger, and rage which sometimes bubbled to the surface when he discussed race relationships in America with his colleagues. Kaplan knew what was associated with unkind behavior and ignorance, and he had the uncanny ability to feel, within his own fiber, the indignities of racial, religious, and ethnic slurs directed toward others. Although he had matured with age, his skin could be easily pierced with remarks that were tinged, no matter how slightly, with insensitivities to the personhood of others.

Kaplan would often say, "Discriminate against others today, and someday, I don't know when or how, it will also affect you. You can't get out of this world alive without sometime being the target of discriminatory remarks. Perhaps it will be when you get older, or disabled, or if your appearance gets radically changed from an accident or injury."

Kaplan was in the agency for only a short time when it became quite clear to his associates that he had very strong views on the Southern region of the United States. He minced no words about the racial, religious and ethnic legacy there. Over the years, he had accumulated comparative information on the U.S. Census Bureau regions, and he was quick to point out how the Southern region scored on the American College Test (ACT) standardized examination, literacy, productivity levels, and on accessibility to health care. He also knew how the South ranked among the other states utilizing basic statistics such as infant mortality rates (IMR), maternal mortality rates (MMR), violent crimes — especially rape and homicide — and murder and assault of police officers. Kaplan enjoyed comparing the former eleven Southern states with their Western, Northeastern, and Midwestern census counterparts on more exotic metrics, such as the index of civility, civic enhancement, and engagement.

Kaplan was known for his strongly-held personal views on "right-to-work" legislation, employee-collective bargaining, and unionization rights and protections. He wanted to enhance "quality of life" throughout America and the world.

Case 50: Regional or Racial Bias in Diversity Training

In all of the forenamed areas, he had marshaled an elaborate set of statistics and measurements, and his ability to reference and cite studies that ranked the 50 states was a constant favorite of his. Overall, he had a repertoire of statistics that painted a less than bright and progressive looking picture of the South. His bias was clear! He liked the North and he felt that America had increasingly become "Southernized."

Marlene Brown knew of his strongly held views on race, ethnicity, and religion when she hired him. "You have to respect Kaplan," she would often say to others. "Who among us has been the target of religious bias and has delved into, researched, and explored the basis for this lack of civility and tolerance among us?"

Brown knew Kaplan had suffered adversity. He also determined that Kaplan was a "zero-tolerance" sort of guy when it came to discrimination and that he was particularly sensitive to the issue of race relations in America. Although only a small circle of his closest friends knew of his personally-held cherished beliefs and values, it would now become clear to the trainees, how deeply engrained his childhood experiences with race and religion had become. Few would ever know the stories of how his parents and grandparents suffered human indignities and degradation at the hands of those who were in positions of power in the city of his youth. He remembered, and he would never let the story remain untold.

"The story must be told and retold," Kaplan would exhort, "or it will be doomed to oblivion."

Of course, he was familiar with the Holocaust and he could speak passionately about what took place during the Third Reich and how Jewish people were terrorized and killed at the hands of Nazis. He understood the economic and political philosophy of Adolph Hitler, as well as most, and he was prone to caution his colleagues on the dangers of taking freedom and liberty for granted.

"Vigilance," he would argue, "must be demanded if we wish to protect what centuries of dedicated liberal thought has wrought."

The time had come for the staff diversity training and Kaplan was scheduled to present the assigned module on racial and ethnic discrimination. He had prepared for this day and he wanted everyone to experience the "insidiousness of discrimination however it reared its ugly head." The class was made up of 18 mid-level managers drawn from across the agencies, bureaus and departments of the state. They were generally representative of the gender, racial and ethnic diversity that characterized state employment.

Kaplan's darker than average face lit up and he graciously smiled at the group as he was introduced by Brown. Since this was his very first training course, she took special care in her remarks to present his academic and professional background, experiences, and qualifications without unduly embellishing them or raising the group's expectations to levels that Kaplan would find difficult to reach. The introduction went well, Kaplan thought, although he felt nervous and his heart had begun to beat faster and stronger. Now, he had to demonstrate that he had the intellectual ability to present the material that he had labored over and the personal "steel" to withstand any controversy that his prepared remarks might engender.

He thanked Brown for her remarks and told those in the training group how pleased he was to be teaching the unit on racial diversity. He attempted to establish eye contact with each member of the group as he made his introductory remarks and clicked on his multimedia presentation. He thought it was comforting to know that the system was working and he could rely somewhat on the notes embedded in the slideshow.

He assertively began his presentation in a loud and authoritative voice, "In the movie, *Roots,* Alex Haley's book is brought to life and racism is portrayed realistically and graphically. It shows people being ripped from their African homelands, tribal and family connections, suffering the excruciating pain and indignities of the Middle Passage, and after that, being auctioned off in public and sold into slavery to the highest bidder, not only debasing the enslaved persons, but also the human owners," he stated.

Kaplan had garnered the attention of the audience, and he knew he had the personal zeal to develop his thesis. He stated, "Plantation manuals of the day instructed slave owners on how to demean and diminish the value of being black. If a slave was light-skinned, the owner would talk about the inferiority of the color and vice versa if the slave was dark-skinned. Also, if the enslaved persons had straight hair, they would be told about the superiority of curly hair. There were no assets associated with one's own personal qualities and once more, the value of what was good or bad came from those in dominant societal positions — the owners."

Scanning the audience, Kaplan noted that he still had their rapt attention and observed some trainees writing his statements into their training manuals.

Kaplan continued, "Racism is based largely on the notion of separation that is rooted in patriarchy — the rule of society's organizations by men. Separation in all of its manifestations is rooted in the dominance and control of others by men and is further shown by the cleavage we experience today between men and women, between the haves and those who will never have, and the chasm between those who live in the Northern hemisphere and those who survive in the Southern hemisphere. Separation is essential to patriarchy! Racism assumes that some people are superior to others, albeit that people across the world are 99.999 percent genetically similar. Racism is an attitude and behavior that attempts to exclude, rule over, control, and show dominance and superiority by one race over another, and in some instances, even own another person."

Kaplan noticed a few raised eyebrows and some of the group looked at one another and winked.

"Of course," Kaplan remarked, "racism is certainly based on the attitude that one's genetic composition — which reveals itself most powerfully in the color or tone of one's skin and is therefore, visible — makes one superior to those who are different. With racism comes differential inequality — that is, those who possess the idealized, cherished physical traits or color are given access to privilege, status, deference, and, in the final analysis, ownership. With ownership comes control and those who own or receive the vast resources of wealth, income, stock ownership, and rental payments also control and have power over those who are dispossessed. Further, racial identity makes a statement about one's self-worth and how we come to value our own persons. In the most insidious forms, it shows itself in the Southern regions of the United States, especially in the eleven states that made up the rebellious South, in the culture of honor. One's own worth is based on how one feels one is perceived by others. So, African-Americans received their worth by displaying obedience and compliance with the male, aristocratic, white, and powerful expectations in Southern society. By displaying submissive behavior, they communicated their inferiority, and became subordinate or beneath their dominant white counterparts. A display of their inferior position would be met with recognition and a sense of respect by their owners. As a result of this "master-slave" relationship, the enslaved persons did not develop their own recognitions of human dignity, self-worth, and self-respect. In short, they failed to mature. Accordingly, they remained dependent, passive and immature in their emotional and psychological development."

Kaplan continued to look at the group and hoped that they were following his historical analysis of what constituted a basis for racism in the United States. He intensely observed the body language of the group, but now he began to worry that he was losing the interest of the group due to the complexity and sophistication of his argument.

He continued, "In the Northern region of the country, the notion of submission to a culture of honor was gradually observed as African-Americans migrated to the industrial, urban North. Today, one can probably show that this type of culture is associated with the rise of violent crime — a type of crime that was always high in the South; however, during the last 60 years, this violent crime has reared its ugly head in the Northern and Eastern regions of our country. In short, to confront one's honor meant everything, and people were prepared to kill for honor. In a peculiar sense, the United States increasingly became Southernized rather than the South becoming more like the rest of the nation!"

The presentation was finally drawing to a conclusion and he strayed from his prepared remarks to make a dramatic final closing. He wanted his closing observations on racism to reverberate in the minds of the group — to resonate loudly and be retained.

Kaplan's final remarks were stated with zeal and enthusiasm, "Racism shows itself most poignantly among those who are viewed as unequal on the basis of skin color. For example, *Ebony*, *Vibe*, and *Jet*, among other black mass-oriented and consumer-oriented magazines reveal that 'lighter' blacks are perceived to be more attractive — that is more desirable, more likely to be emulated than those men or women with very dark skin. This level of racism shows that even African-Americans frequently reject their own racial characteristics based on the idealized and valued perceptions of skin color by the dominant, white, male and propertied class in the United States. Indeed, ownership, but in a very different way than during the era of Southern slavery, still equates to control."

Case 50: Regional or Racial Bias in Diversity Training

Questions and Instructions:

1. Please provide a comprehensive introduction to Affirmative Action (AA), beginning with President John F. Kennedy's Executive Order 10925 to the present. The give and take of the political times would be helpful to understand the root beginnings of AA and its present status in the United States.

2. It would be extremely helpful to the class if the relevant statistics surrounding the efficacy of Affirmative Action in the United States would be presented. The demographics should be compiled and presented in a pre-affirmative action/post-affirmative action dichotomy, accompanied by the actual demographic profile of the population by major social status categories (age, ethnicity, race, gender, occupational type, and income). For the federal level of government, please present the statistics that show the distribution of the percent women (African American, Hispanic, Asian, etc.), relative to standard occupational categories of Professional (P), Administrative (A), Technical (T), Clerical (C), and Other (O) or PATCO. Similarly, present the relevant statistics for your own state. In what ways or demographic categories do the state and federal government differ? In which areas are they nearly the same? Elaborate.

Case 50: Regional or Racial Bias in Diversity Training

3. The statistics on who is entering American colleges and universities and who is graduating, the graduation rate, should be examined. Please contact your admissions counselor at your university/college or search the Web for the most recent admission and graduation statistics. Then, for comparative purposes, find the average family income by education level (based on education of head of household) for men and women based on level of educational attainment and race. For example, in the state of Iowa, 2000, the median household income was $39,469, whereas the median family income in 2000 was $48,005. Why is there a difference between these two measurements? For those with less than 9th grade education, the average family income was $29,547; 9th to 12th grade, no diploma, the average family income was $33,356. In contrast, those who graduated from high school had an average family income of $48,434 and those with bachelor, master, and doctorate degrees had an average family income of $85,423, $101,670, and $123,796, respectively.

4. There are a number of functional theories of inequality. Some have argued that inequality is beneficial to society and that is why it continues. Others have focused on Kuznets' inverted "U" hypothesis on race relations in society or Lieberson's theory of intrinsic differences as it pertains to new immigrants and the theory of economic development. Please explain these theories and determine their relevance to the case study.

5. Do we really know what the effect of AA has been on our society? One thesis with some currency today postulates that social scientists tend to be liberal on the ideological side and AA is a "sacred cow" that they protect even if they have to "lie" about its benefits. Please review President William Clinton's "Mend it, but don't end it" speech on AA after the Adarand Constructors, Inc. vs. Pena, Secretary of Transportation (1995) decision of the U.S. Supreme Court, and indicate the rationale for his argument. In the most recent Supreme Court decision on Affirmative Action (Gratz and Hamacher vs. Bollinger, 2003), the University of Michigan's admission criteria were upheld for their law school but ruled unconstitutional for admission to their undergraduate degree programs. What was the logic behind this decision and can you say that "Race does matter" today? Please explain.

Case 50: Regional or Racial Bias in Diversity Training

6. What are the alternatives to affirmative action? Some scholars have suggested that the goal should be to raise group consciousness and self-esteem of racial, ethnic or gender groups (women) rather than focusing on only anti-discrimination laws, regulations, and policies. What is the gap, for instance, between average years of education for men and women and for whites and African-Americans? Some economists have argued that labor shortages for higher, more specialized, technical positions are created by those in control of major professional organizations, educational institutions, and the like, who want to maintain the status quo by maintaining inequality. Or, if people resist AA because they dislike it and believe it to be illegal, then all one needs to do is provide more AA education and the dislike will go away as education is the key to better race relations in the final analysis. Please assess the veracity of these twin arguments.

7. Race is an elusive concept! It may be argued that race no longer has any meaning in our society from the demographic, molecular genetics, and evolutionary biology perspectives, and this is especially the case when advanced mathematical and molecular tools are used to study the migration and evolution of genes, and that it only has meaning in terms of cultural definitions and awareness. In fact one study notes that genetic differences are greater among Africans than among Africans and Eurasians. If it is true that we have greater genetic similarities than differences, what happens to the concepts of racism, separation, prejudice, and discrimination? Please explain.

Case 50: Regional or Racial Bias in Diversity Training

8. The Bureau of the Census, U.S. Department of Commerce, is required by the Constitution of the United States to conduct a complete enumeration of the population every decennial (ten year) period. If you were an enumerator, how would you be sure that the respondents you were interviewing were Caucasian, African-American, American Indian or Asian? Please report the definitions and their subtleties to the class as to what constitutes race and ethnic difference in the United States today. If your mother is black and your father is white, how would race be recorded by the census enumerator? If your mother is black and your father happens to be Chinese, would you be recorded as "Black or Chinese?" Are these racial distinctions meaningful in your opinion — especially since so many persons are of mid-racial parentage, or is racial identity only a historical legacy that is being carried forward? Please justify your response. Today, in our society, is color of skin more important than race? Explain. What are the advantages or limitations, if any, associated with color of skin? Please give examples.

9. Based on your research, are there any areas in which you would advise Kaplan to be more thoughtful and accurate in his training remarks? Please explain.

Case 50: Regional or Racial Bias in Diversity Training

Case 50: Regional or Racial Bias in Diversity Training
Name:

Case Log and Administrative Journal Entry

This case analysis and learning assessment is printed on perforated pages and may be removed from the book for evaluation purposes.

Case Analysis:
Major case concepts and theories identified:

What is the relevance of the concepts, theories, ideas and techniques presented in the case to that of public management?

Facts — what do we know *for sure* about the case? Please list.

Who is involved in the case (people, departments, agencies, units, etc.)? Were the problems of an "intra/interagency" nature? Be specific.

Are there any rules, laws, regulations or standard operating procedures identified in the case study that might limit decision-making? If so, what are they?

Are there any clues presented in the case as to the major actor's interests, needs, motivations and personalities? If so, please list them.

Case 50: Regional or Racial Bias in Diversity Training

Learning Assessment:
What do the administrative theories presented in this case mean to you as an administrator?

How can this learning be put to use outside the classroom? Are there any problems you envision during the implementation phase?

Several possible courses of action were identified during the class discussion. Which action was considered to be most practical by the group? Which was deemed most feasible? Based on your personal experience, did the group reach a conclusion that was desirable, feasible, and practical? Please explain why or why not.

Did the group reach a decision that would solve the problem on a short-term or long-term basis? Please explain.

What could you have done to receive more learning value from this case?

51

American vs. Immigrant Labor

by
C. Kenneth Meyer

There was nothing about the release of a contract to provide janitorial service for a training center of the Federal Aviation Administration that indicated any problems would arise. It was all routine. The training center had been having the work done under contract to a private company for years, competitive bids were asked, and the contract was let to the low bidder. The only new thing was that a local firm, Kleen-Sweepers, was taking over from an out-of-state firm, Magic Maintenance, which had held the contract the past three years. Kleen-Sweepers had won the contract with a first-year bid of $765,848. Acme Cleaning and Maintenance, another local firm, was second with a bid of $846,909, and Magic Maintenance was third with a bid of $876,300.

Trouble began when Darrell Sanger, manager of the procurement division at the center, learned from employees of plans by Kleen-Sweepers to not retain the Magic Maintenance employees and instead replace them by what they called "foreigners." Magic Maintenance had employed an average of sixty janitors and Kleen-Sweepers intended to reduce the number to fifty, all of them Koreans, either immigrants or persons with work permits.

Sanger did not like the idea of a 100 percent turnover of workers, especially one that replaced the present force with immigrants. The service contracting firm had the right to bring in its own workers, but in the past, as a general rule, it had interviewed and hired on a trial basis most of the old force. Sanger's chief objection, however, was that the wholesale firing of some workers and replacing them with persons of another race might "stir up" a storm. Five years earlier the local airport had fired a similar work force and employed Koreans, and a controversy raged for weeks. Picketers invaded the airport bearing signs and shouting slogans at the traveling public; television stations played up these activities on the news shows; unions issued denunciatory resolutions; and newspaper editorial writers condemned the loss of jobs by hard-working Americans.

In an attempt to avert a similar situation, Sanger met with Troy Ridgeway, president of Kleen-Sweepers, to persuade him to abandon the idea of utilizing replacement workers. But Ridgeway insisted that he could not change his plan. He believed the Koreans comprised a more efficient force than one made up of Americans, in that he had found them to be more industrious, reliable, and likely to do work of high quality. Ridgeway's low bid, $81,061 under that of the closest competitor, was made possible only because his profit depended on using a small force of the most productive labor available. He already had his workers lined up, he said, and it would be unfair to tell them they would not be hired.

Case 51: American vs. Immigrant Labor

Discrimination and affirmative action did not enter into Ridgeway's program. The common belief that immigrants would work for lower wages than Americans also was not at issue. The wages Ridgeway would pay were the same he would have to pay any work force. Under government regulations, an agency advertising for a service contract must request from the Department of Labor a determination of a minimum wage for each of the work categories — (e.g., clerk, janitor, and so forth). The determination was usually the prevailing wage in the area and usually comparable to union scales. Persons not of United States nationality must be either naturalized citizens or hold work permits.

Sanger's fear that the employment of Asians and the firing of Magic Maintenance employees would stir up a row did not materialize. It was only a short item in television newscasts and rated only one story carried on an inside page of the local newspaper. The only outcry was raised by a radio talk-show host, who for several nights complained against policies that allowed immigrants to "swarm over the country" and "take the jobs of loyal Americans." His urging his listeners and callers to write their representatives in Congress resulted in dozens of letters to the state's delegation in Washington, who did no more than ask the training center to provide them with information about the situation and an explanation of the hiring policy.

Although there had been perhaps no great change in American attitudes since the airport incident five years before, Sanger mused, the American people were very likely becoming more cosmopolitan. Japanese management had put to shame American management; foreign investors and manufacturers, Asian and European, were pouring billions into the economy while Americans contributed to the drain of the money supply by closing plants in the United States and having work done abroad to take advantage of cheap labor. Further, Asian youngsters, especially the Vietnamese, were winning many high school and college honor awards and figuring prominently on the merit scholar lists. In view of these achievements, Sanger asked himself whether the firing of Magic Maintenance janitors was perhaps an instance of reverse discrimination. Perhaps, he thought, future affirmative action programs would arise for the majority to balance those for minorities.

Questions and Instructions

1. What do you think of the following stereotypes associated with the employment of foreign labor, immigrants, and displaced persons: That they take jobs that should go to American citizens? That they work for lower wages than Americans and, therefore, tend to keep down wage levels? That they are needed to perform the difficult or menial labor Americans avoid? That they are exploited because of language difficulties, lack of education or skills, training, racial prejudice, and unfamiliarity with American ways?

Case 51: American vs. Immigrant Labor

2. Should the affirmative action policies established for such minorities as blacks, women, and Hispanics also apply to recent immigrants?

3. In the case of the training center, do you think the procurement manager should have protested more strongly against the replacement of the entire janitorial force by Koreans?

4. Do you agree with the opinion of the president of Kleen-Sweepers that in what many consider menial work, a Korean force would be more industrious, reliable, and likely to do work of higher quality than an American workforce?

Case 51: American vs. Immigrant Labor

Case 51: American vs. Immigrant Labor

Name:

Case Log and Administrative Journal Entry

This case analysis and learning assessment is printed on perforated pages and may be removed from the book for evaluation purposes.

Case Analysis:
Major case concepts and theories identified:

What is the relevance of the concepts, theories, ideas and techniques presented in the case to that of public management?

Facts — what do we know *for sure* about the case? Please list.

Who is involved in the case (people, departments, agencies, units, etc.)? Were the problems of an "intra/interagency" nature? Be specific.

Are there any rules, laws, regulations or standard operating procedures identified in the case study that might limit decision-making? If so, what are they?

Are there any clues presented in the case as to the major actor's interests, needs, motivations and personalities? If so, please list them.

Case 51: American vs. Immigrant Labor

Learning Assessment:
What do the administrative theories presented in this case mean to you as an administrator?

How can this learning be put to use outside the classroom? Are there any problems you envision during the implementation phase?

Several possible courses of action were identified during the class discussion. Which action was considered to be most practical by the group? Which was deemed most feasible? Based on your personal experience, did the group reach a conclusion that was desirable, feasible, and practical? Please explain why or why not.

Did the group reach a decision that would solve the problem on a short-term or long-term basis? Please explain.

What could you have done to receive more learning value from this case?

52

The Good/Bad Administrator

by
C. Kenneth Meyer

Timothy Kingsbury, secretary of the state Department of Natural Resources, considered it a coup when he hired George Krittenbrink as director of the Land and Water Resources Survey. The survey had grown in importance as the environmental consequences of increasing population become more worrisome, yet staff positions had been difficult to fill because the work was highly technical. Krittenbrink was a nationally known figure in his field and Kingsbury thought he could turn the survey over to him and devote his attention to matters he knew more about.

For his part, Krittenbrink was glad to take the position, for it gave him an opportunity to ride his hobby horse of long standing: high- and low-altitude photography and remote-sensing pictures obtained by satellites circling the earth. He was a pioneer in applying such information about the earth to better use land and other natural resources and he had contributed authoritative articles to technical journals.

Krittenbrink's interest in this field had begun with aerial photography studies while studying geography in college and he had been excited by the prospects for obtaining more information about the earth's surface from hand-held cameras in the early Gemini and Apollo space flights. Later he familiarized himself with the advances made in 1972 when the National Aeronautics and Space Administration launched the first land-resource survey satellites — Landsat-1, -2, and -3, which provided a wealth of information about the planet.

The Land and Water Resources Survey had done more than most comparable programs in other states in the practical application of electronically recorded and transmitted data via satellite. Krittenbrink determined to make it the foremost program in the nation. When visitors inspected the survey and inquired how its work would help the state, Krittenbrink had a speech prepared for them, as if a guide in a museum.

"There are roughly 300 million Americans depending upon approximately 2.3 billion acres of land," he would say. "This means that the per captain land share in 1983 is about 10.8 acres compared to a per capita share of nearly 17 acres in 1940. By the year 2010 the per capita land share will be approximately five acres. We need to use our land resources more effectively as our population grows and the amount of land taken out of production each year by highways, airports and urbanization increases."

Case 52: The Good/Bad Administrator

Satellite data, Krittenbrink would continue, would enable planners to identify land-use patterns and changes over time. He envisioned additional applications: monitoring crops for pest infestation and disease, solving hydrological problems, forecasting snow runoff, measuring water characteristics, providing regional indices of water availability, evaluating wildlife habitats, assessing damage in burned-out areas, identifying climatologically patterns and trends, mapping thermal pollution, identifying soil characteristics associated with mineral exploration, predicting flood damage, locating new sources of fresh water, forecasting crop yields, conducting soil-conservation studies, detecting archaeological sites and assessing timber-stand vigor.

The day Krittenbrink took over as survey director, he addressed a staff meeting to explain his management policies and goals. He stressed the importance of completing projects expeditiously, of teamwork and of meticulous attention to detail. The staff quickly learned that he was a strong-willed, nose-to-the-grindstone type of manager who believed that efficiency and organization produced successful results.

The staff of eight scientists and engineers came from diverse regions of the country and represented varied educational backgrounds, including geology, geography, civil, hydrologic and electrical engineering, computer programming, and planning. Much of their work consisted of preparing and analyzing maps produced from information transmitted from satellites to the Goddard Space Flight Center, where it was placed on computer compatible tapes and readied for use in research and experimentation.

Each time the survey received a request from a city, county or state agency, Krittenbrink evaluated the work to be done and assigned the project to members of the staff. He expected all projects to be completed on schedule and to meet his stringent quality specifications. When they were not, he was sharply critical and sarcastic in reprimanding the offender.

The most frequent victim of Krittenbrink's criticism was James Cartmill, a young, wisecracking geological engineer who, the survey director thought, lacked the serious purpose and devotion to detail required in scientific pursuits. On one occasion Cartmill failed to meet a deadline. The work had been proceeding according to schedule until the mainframe computer broke down, making Cartmill two days late in completing the assignment. Dismissing Cartmill's explanation that the delay was not his fault because it was caused by a computer malfunction, Krittenbrink angrily replied that he wanted results, not excuses.

The next day, Krittenbrink called Cartmill to his office and brought up the matter again. "Cartmill," he said, "you're capable of good work but you've got to change your attitude. Science demands a holy dedication to work. It has no place for fun and games. You waste not only your time but that of others when you chat and joke with them." Cartmill attempted to explain that the delay in completing the project had nothing to do with his relations with other staff members. A vital computer had malfunctioned, parts had to be flown in from Boca Raton, and a specialist had been called from Atlanta to make repairs, he said.

Case 52: The Good/Bad Administrator

"Cartmill, a man must take responsibility for the circumstances of his life," Krittenbrink replied. "He cannot let outside forces rule him. A man must anticipate external problems and control the exogenous forces in order to succeed." Recognizing that Krittenbrink was not going to accept his side of the story, Cartmill apologized and promised that in the future he would try to be the master of his fate.

Cartmill thought the matter was closed and was shocked when at the next staff meeting Krittenbrink scolded him before his fellow workers for nearly fifteen minutes. That Cartmill had taken lightly the injunction to control outside forces, Krittenbrink said, was clear from a flippant comment on being the master of his fate.

"Deadlines are a necessity of life," Krittenbrink said. "Without them we would not know what to do or when to do it. This is one characteristic of modern organizations that distinguishes them from the older ones. The professional engineer and technician pay attention to schedule and engages in contingency planning." The staff members returned to their work areas in quiet disbelief.

In the next few weeks, Krittenbrink frequently reminded Cartmill of the need for adhering to work programs and once blamed him for the breakdown of a photographic copying machine because he had not followed a careful schedule of preventive maintenance. After a few months on the job, Krittenbrink extended his fault-finding to Donald Fletcher, a young engineer and friend of Cartmill, as well as three other staff members who all had excellent work histories and records for reliability. Toward the end of Krittenbrink's first year as supervisor, two engineers requested and received transfers to other departments. Cartmill, however, remained in the division, saying that he liked the work and could put up with the fault-finding supervisor.

It was not easy, for Krittenbrink had informed Cartmill that he was recording all work-related problems and transgressions in his personnel file. Cartmill's treatment did not go unnoticed by other staff members, and one morning during a coffee break they decided that, for self-protection, they should keep careful notes on the work they performed, on all problems associated with receiving computer tapes and related data sets, on machinery malfunctions, and on all regulations and project specifications ordered by Krittenbrink.

Joyce Harman, a new employee who had worked three years in the interior department of another state, observed the low morale in the division and the tense atmosphere that made it difficult to meet the exacting standards that the tasks required. Priding herself on being a well-educated and independent woman — she was active in the women's rights movement — Harman was not one to submit to the petty tyrannies of a male supervisor. When Krittenbrink made general criticisms of her work, she demanded specific proof. Krittenbrink, accustomed to the submissiveness of the other employees of the division, usually had no concrete justification and retreated to commenting on the need for expediting projects and for scientific accuracy in the work of the division.

After holding the job for three months, Harman took the initiative in arousing the division staff to protest Krittenbrink's unreasonable demands, selective persecutions, and general denigrations of them as people and professionals. They compiled a list of grievances with documentation that they submitted to Kingsbury, the Natural Resources Department secretary, requesting that Krittenbrink's supervisory

Case 52: The Good/Bad Administrator

behavior be evaluated and a formal hearing be held so that their concerns could be discussed. Kingsbury was surprised to learn about the trouble in the division. He had felt lucky to have as the director so dedicated and knowledgeable a person as Krittenbrink, who was praised by state agencies using the services of the survey. It now appeared to Kingsbury that efficiency and productivity might not be the sum total of good administration.

Questions and Instructions

1. As Kingsbury, what would you do first in taking up the problem? Would you talk first to the staff or to Krittenbrink?

2. Do you think that the differences between Krittenbrink and the staff can be reconciled?

3. Should Kingsbury come to the support of Krittenbrink? Consider both Krittenbrink's ability to get along with his staff and the productivity and quality of the work done by the survey.

4. Is there any justification for transferring Krittenbrink? What implications are associated with transferring the problem employees of an agency?

5. How does one supervise a supervisor? Should problem supervisors be treated similarly to or differently from other problem employees?

6. Is there any way for Krittenbrink to become a more effective administrator? If you were Kingsbury, what suggestions would you offer him in the way of improving his interpersonal relations?

7. Should Krittenbrink be dismissed from all supervisory responsibility? What are the implications of this decision? Please elaborate.

Case 52: The Good/Bad Administrator
Name:

Case Log and Administrative Journal Entry

This case analysis and learning assessment is printed on perforated pages and may be removed from the book for evaluation purposes.

Case Analysis:
Major case concepts and theories identified:

What is the relevance of the concepts, theories, ideas and techniques presented in the case to that of public management?

Facts — what do we know *for sure* about the case? Please list.

Who is involved in the case (people, departments, agencies, units, etc.)? Were the problems of an "intra/interagency" nature? Be specific.

Are there any rules, laws, regulations or standard operating procedures identified in the case study that might limit decision-making? If so, what are they?

Are there any clues presented in the case as to the major actor's interests, needs, motivations and personalities? If so, please list them.

Case 52: The Good/Bad Administrator

Learning Assessment:
What do the administrative theories presented in this case mean to you as an administrator?

How can this learning be put to use outside the classroom? Are there any problems you envision during the implementation phase?

Several possible courses of action were identified during the class discussion. Which action was considered to be most practical by the group? Which was deemed most feasible? Based on your personal experience, did the group reach a conclusion that was desirable, feasible, and practical? Please explain why or why not.

Did the group reach a decision that would solve the problem on a short-term or long-term basis? Please explain.

What could you have done to receive more learning value from this case?

53

The Far Side of Fifty

by
C. Kenneth Meyer and Garry L. Frank

At the age of 56, Hazel Ridgeway became unhappy with her job as a cartographic drafter in the Engineering Division of the state Department of Transportation. She had joined the staff twenty-one years ago and now held what some of her friends considered a good job — a decent salary, excellent fringe benefits, and interesting work. But somehow that did not seem enough.

Ridgeway expressed her dissatisfaction in a letter to a friend, "For the next ten or fifteen years of my work life I want something more — I'm not sure what, maybe something different — a change of scene perhaps or even some other type of work. I don't think I can do as a woman in another department told me she had done — accept the situation and not think about it anymore. That doesn't seem to satisfy me or some other women of my age I know."

Engaging in a new hobby, becoming an activist in some movement, perhaps women's rights, involving herself in politics, enrolling as a part-time student in the local university to work toward a master's degree — none of these possible activities that occurred to Ridgeway to add interest to her life seemed attractive. Nor could she devote herself to family affairs. Except for a few years when her two children were young, Ridgeway had always worked in her field. Now her children had their own successful careers and her husband enjoyed his work as an accountant.

In the past, Ridgeway had not been much interested in a management-level job, believing the chance of getting one remote. Now, however, she thought there might be an opportunity for advancement because of the resignation of Donald Porter as chief of the cartographic section. On numerous occasions Ridgeway had served as back-up supervisor for Porter, and had always received good performance ratings and salary advances. She felt that her chances of promotion had improved because many ambitious if perhaps younger women were climbing up the professional ladder. If she did succeed in getting the job it would offer challenges that would improve her outlook on her profession. So she decided to submit an application.

It was not long before Ridgeway discovered that the selection procedure for a new chief of cartographics was not being routinely followed. The Department of Transportation had an internal promotion policy, but in this case Jerome Makins, head of the Engineering Division, was going outside to fill the classified-exempt position and had appointed a search committee to seek applicants. Ridgeway was pleased to be one of three finalists but disappointed when a 35-year-old man, Leonard Black, was chosen for the position.

With no previous management experience and fewer than ten years of employment background, Black did not seem to Ridgeway to have credentials equal to her own. She protested to the deputy director of the Department of Transportation, asserting that she had been discriminated against because of her age — she did not want to raise the issue of sexual discrimination — but was told he would not intervene in the selection. For one thing, he told her, Black might sue if his appointment was rescinded. She replied tartly that she felt she also had a cause for a suit.

The vague dissatisfaction that Ridgeway had felt about her job now turned to anger, and her spirits were raised by the prospects of a fight. She engaged a lawyer to file a complaint with the Equal Employment Opportunity Commission (EEOC), asking that she be given the job of section chief or an equivalent one. Shortly thereafter Ridgeway suffered what she considered retaliation for making her EEOC complaint. For the first time in her years with the section, she received a poor job evaluation and only a token raise when there was an across-the-board salary increase.

Failing to settle the case through negotiation with transportation department officials, the EEOC brought suit in the United States District Court. Testimony at the trial showed that Engineering Division Chief Makins had pressured the selection committee to hire Leonard Black, and that he had told Porter, the retiring head of the cartographic section, he was sorry there was no way "to keep old Hazel Ridgeway from applying for the job because of equal opportunity laws." Evidence revealed that, though Ridgeway had never held a management position herself, she had frequently served as back-up supervisor to Porter and had successfully maintained production standards. Witnesses also testified that Black at the job interview had acknowledged he had very little supervisory experience. After joining the cartographic section he had enrolled in courses in public management at the local university to make up for this lack of experience.

The jury took about two hours to reach a verdict that the transportation department had engaged in willful age discrimination and retaliation. In subsequent negotiations the Department of Transportation agreed to a settlement by which Ridgeway would receive $112,000 in salary adjustment, expenses, and legal fees in addition to a promotion to a supervisory position. It had taken Ridgeway three years to win her fight but, even though there had been times of discouragement, she had been rescued from the doldrums that preceded it and had the satisfaction in the end of being a victor.

Case 53: The Far Side of Fifty

Questions and Instructions:

1. Do you believe that the frustrations and disappointments felt by Hazel Ridgeway are common among working women today?

2. In the present conditions prevailing as to the employment of women, what can a woman of Ridgeway's age expect to attain?

3. Is it harder for a man than for a woman, after passing the middle years, to accept the truth of having failed to be as successful as he had hoped to be?

4. Is early retirement an acceptable solution to the problem of the older employee who has feelings of frustration or failure about his or her career?

5. What options are available to older employees who feel that they have been by-passed for promotions and are seldom consulted in policymaking decisions, or who see younger workers getting ahead at a quicker rate than they did in their early careers?

6. What counts most in successful management, experience and knowledge of an older person or the ambition and enthusiasm of a younger person?

7. What courses of action are open to an executive who doubts that an older employee is physically or mentally fit for promotion or is not competent to handle a better job?

Case 53: The Far Side of Fifty

Case 53: The Far Side of Fifty
Name:

Case Log and Administrative Journal Entry

This case analysis and learning assessment is printed on perforated pages and may be removed from the book for evaluation purposes.

Case Analysis:
Major case concepts and theories identified:

What is the relevance of the concepts, theories, ideas and techniques presented in the case to that of public management?

Facts — what do we know *for sure* about the case? Please list.

Who is involved in the case (people, departments, agencies, units, etc.)? Were the problems of an "intra/interagency" nature? Be specific.

Are there any rules, laws, regulations or standard operating procedures identified in the case study that might limit decision-making? If so, what are they?

Are there any clues presented in the case as to the major actor's interests, needs, motivations and personalities? If so, please list them.

Case 53: The Far Side of Fifty

Learning Assessment:
What do the administrative theories presented in this case mean to you as an administrator?

How can this learning be put to use outside the classroom? Are there any problems you envision during the implementation phase?

Several possible courses of action were identified during the class discussion. Which action was considered to be most practical by the group? Which was deemed most feasible? Based on your personal experience, did the group reach a conclusion that was desirable, feasible, and practical? Please explain why or why not.

Did the group reach a decision that would solve the problem on a short-term or long-term basis? Please explain.

What could you have done to receive more learning value from this case?

54

A Problem of Motivation

by
C. Kenneth Meyer and Jeffrey A. Geerts

Two years before, the Department of Human Services had hired six new employees with the assistance of the federal government's Work Incentive (WIN) program. Under the program, the federal government paid the employees' salaries for a six-month training period, after which the department had the option of hiring or releasing the employees based on their performance and the recommendations of their supervisors.

Julie Davis, one of the WIN employees, was placed in the Child Welfare Department. Initially she was very industrious and suggested several improvements in procedures relating to her job. She exhibited a high degree of initiative and performed her duties efficiently. After about six weeks, though, Jeff Baker, her supervisor, noticed that she was developing poor work habits, such as long coffee breaks, tardiness, and absenteeism.

Baker felt Davis's low performance had resulted from her association with two employees in the adoption unit of the department. Baker arranged a meeting with her and advised her of the unacceptability of her work behavior. He had received complaints from other employees that she was not carrying her share of the load. "Julie," he said, "generally your work has been very good but lately your job performance has not lived up to expectations. Although our standards are higher than other sections of this department, the chances for promotion and career advancement are a lot better for the hard-working employee. You can do a lot better than you have been doing!" After the session with Baker, Davis's work and behavior immediately improved. She volunteered to assist others whenever her work was completed and quickly acquired the necessary skills for several other positions in the section. She often worked as a substitute in the absence of other employees.

At the end of the training period Baker recommended that the agency hire Davis at the level of Grade 5. The quality of her work remained consistently high and she continued to assist others willingly. Six months later, when she had completed a year with the agency, she was promoted to Grade 6 and assigned additional responsibilities. Indeed, a bright future seemed on the horizon.

About two months later, one of the employees Davis had been assisting resigned because of a death in her family. The announcement for the newly opened position emphasized it was limited to employees of the department. Since Davis was familiar with many aspects of the position, she discussed

Case 54: A Problem of Motivation

applying for it with Baker, who advised her that even though she was the only staff member familiar with the job her chance of being on the list of applicants supplied by the Bureau of Personnel was small because she had only 14 months' experience instead of the required two years. He said she would make the list only if there were no applicants with the required experience. This was possible, though unlikely. Davis decided to apply and hope for the best. There were several applicants with the required experience and she did not make the list.

Davis's attitude changed immediately. She became irritable and her relationship with other staff members deteriorated. She developed intense feelings of insecurity. Each time a new employee was hired she felt as though she might be replaced. As a result of this constant fear she developed an ulcer. In another meeting with her, Baker reassured her of her abilities, explained the steps involved in employee termination, and outlined the grievance procedures available to employees should termination occur. Initially, she seemed to gain confidence and her work improved, though not to the level of her previous performance. Davis had become confused and felt angry toward Baker for what she considered to be unwarranted encouragement.

Since Baker felt he could no longer adequately motivate Davis, he recommended that she be transferred to another supervisor, Malcolm Tate. After a few weeks, her work performance and attitude improved considerably, and Tate soon considered her among the best employees he had ever supervised.

The problem in the department appeared to be resolved, but Tate worried he would soon be faced with the same problem as Baker. In the next four months, two employees under Tate's supervision retired. Both positions were grade 7 level. Davis was now qualified for both, but there were others in the agency who were better qualified. Even if she made the list, there was a good possibility she would not be selected for the position.

Questions and Instructions

1. Was transferring Davis the best course of action Baker could have taken? What other choices did he have?

Case 54: A Problem of Motivation

2. Do rules stating that a person must have two years' experience bear any relationship to the realities of an employee's efficiency and the needs of an organization? Should the rules be reviewed?

3. Do you feel that the manner in which Davis was hired affected her job performance?

4. Should Tate encourage Davis to apply for a new position when the possibility of not being selected exists?

5. What can Tate do to prevent the recurrence of the previous situation if Davis is not selected for one of the grade 7 positions?

6. Davis seems to be experiencing stress. What do you think could be the main cause of the stress? Is the stress-risk behavior related to the actions of others, or is it related to her own expectations? What can Baker do to reduce the level of personal stress that Davis is experiencing? What can Davis do about her own situation?

Case 54: A Problem of Motivation

7. Does Davis appear to be internally or externally motivated? What are the implications associated with both of these motivations?

Case 54: A Problem of Motivation

Case 54: A Problem of Motivation
Name:

Case Log and Administrative Journal Entry

This case analysis and learning assessment is printed on perforated pages and may be removed from the book for evaluation purposes.

Case Analysis:
Major case concepts and theories identified:

What is the relevance of the concepts, theories, ideas and techniques presented in the case to that of public management?

Facts — what do we know *for sure* about the case? Please list.

Who is involved in the case (people, departments, agencies, units, etc.)? Were the problems of an "intra/interagency" nature? Be specific.

Are there any rules, laws, regulations or standard operating procedures identified in the case study that might limit decision-making? If so, what are they?

Are there any clues presented in the case as to the major actor's interests, needs, motivations and personalities? If so, please list them.

Case 54: A Problem of Motivation

Learning Assessment:

What do the administrative theories presented in this case mean to you as an administrator?

How can this learning be put to use outside the classroom? Are there any problems you envision during the implementation phase?

Several possible courses of action were identified during the class discussion. Which action was considered to be most practical by the group? Which was deemed most feasible? Based on your personal experience, did the group reach a conclusion that was desirable, feasible, and practical? Please explain why or why not.

Did the group reach a decision that would solve the problem on a short-term or long-term basis? Please explain.

What could you have done to receive more learning value from this case?

55

Special Privileges for Officials?

by
C. Kenneth Meyer and Lance Noe

Sarah Jefferies had worked in the rehabilitation agency of the state Welfare Department for almost 20 year and had become the administrative secretary to the agency manager, Edward Foster. Jefferies always received superior job-performance ratings from her supervisors and had several letters of commendation for assuming responsibilities beyond those given in her job description. Foster, who had managed the agency for five years, was considered a "good man for the job" and respected for his ability "to get the job done right." The central office frequently depended on him for assistance.

During the past nine months Jefferies had noticed that Foster and other officials often reported to work late in the morning and left the office early in the afternoon. Every agency employee earned ten hours of annual leave a month and could receive payment for the unused portion of accumulated leave at the end of each year. In addition, employees received nine paid holidays per year. Overtime was compensated for by allowing employees to take the equivalent time off. Jefferies was responsible for recording employee hours and leave time and felt that the agency officials were taking more time off than allowed by the state. Her coworkers also noticed this and were becoming upset. At a water-fountain conference Jefferies was selected by the other employees to speak with Foster about the situation.

Jefferies told Foster that some of the employees were disturbed by the agency officials' disregard for the rules governing office hours, leave time, and compensation time. She also informed him that with his approval one official improperly received two weeks compensation. Foster explained that administrators had more privileges than subordinate staff members. "They are not punching a time clock," he said, "and if they get their work done, that's all that counts."

After her discussion with Foster, Jefferies wondered what she should do.

Case 55: Special Privileges for Officials?

Questions and Instructions

1. Suggest several courses of action that are open to Jefferies in resolving her dilemma.

2. What are the legal and moral implications of the perceived abuses? Are they too trivial to bother with?

3. Does Jefferies have an obligation to "blow the whistle" about the abuses? If she decides to do so, should she tell Foster of her intention?

4. Should Foster consider more carefully the impact of his behavior on the organization?

5. Would you suggest that the agency policy governing tardiness, absenteeism, and sick leave be applied equally to all employees or differentiated according to administrative rank?

6. Should a flextime approach be recommended in resolving the issues raised in this situation?

Case 55: Special Privileges for Officials?

Case 55: Special Privileges for Officials
Name:

Case Log and Administrative Journal Entry

This case analysis and learning assessment is printed on perforated pages and may be removed from the book for evaluation purposes.

Case Analysis:
Major case concepts and theories identified:

What is the relevance of the concepts, theories, ideas and techniques presented in the case to that of public management?

Facts — what do we know *for sure* about the case? Please list.

Who is involved in the case (people, departments, agencies, units, etc.)? Were the problems of an "intra/interagency" nature? Be specific.

Are there any rules, laws, regulations or standard operating procedures identified in the case study that might limit decision-making? If so, what are they?

Are there any clues presented in the case as to the major actor's interests, needs, motivations and personalities? If so, please list them.

Case 55: Special Privileges for Officials?

Learning Assessment:
What do the administrative theories presented in this case mean to you as an administrator?

How can this learning be put to use outside the classroom? Are there any problems you envision during the implementation phase?

Several possible courses of action were identified during the class discussion. Which action was considered to be most practical by the group? Which was deemed most feasible? Based on your personal experience, did the group reach a conclusion that was desirable, feasible, and practical? Please explain why or why not.

Did the group reach a decision that would solve the problem on a short-term or long-term basis? Please explain.

What could you have done to receive more learning value from this case?

56

Balancing Work and Life Activity

by
C. Kenneth Meyer, Stephen Clapham and Heidi Price

First Scenario:

Mary Ruppe, a client counselor with the Office of Urban Affairs in Thompson Park, began her job with zeal and enthusiasm and was pleased when her immediate supervisor, Irene Klaff, gave her a positive performance evaluation and told her she was one of the top performers in the agency. Mary was also happy with having satisfied her probationary employment period and having reached permanent employee status — a significant accomplishment during an era of downsizing and retrenchment in municipal government. And, as a graduate student in management, Mary was especially interested in how to deal with urban issues in a more effective and efficient manner, although she found it taxing to balance her work with the life demands she has accepted as part of her normal routine.

Irene Klaff had been a long-time administrator in city government and had nearly a decade of service with the Office of Urban Affairs. As such, she had learned how to manage and build a team environment and she was no stranger to conducting individual performance evaluations. In department meetings, Klaff had always championed the use of performance evaluations. She felt that they could be used successfully as a communication mechanism and as a way to provide useful documentation for merit increases and promotion. Her skills would now be put to a crucial test since she had scheduled an appointment to go over Mary Ruppe's annual performance evaluation. She knew it would be stressful to deal with Mary since this was the first-time Mary would receive an assessment in which she was rated poorly in several critical areas of work performance.

Klaff made the needed arrangements to jointly review with Ruppe her work performance. She sent Ruppe her annual evaluation and had generally prepared Ruppe for the upcoming counseling meeting. After exchanging pleasantries and a limited amount of "chit-chat," it became apparent to Klaff that Mary was involved in so many activities outside of work that it was difficult for her to come to the office fully rested and ready to work. Klaff asked Mary what she felt had contributed to her change of attitude and the malaise she had observed during the performance period. Mary said she felt stretched and over-whelmed in balancing her work/life obligations. In response, Klaff listened carefully to what Mary had to say and gave her a sympathetic ear. Klaff asked Mary if she wanted her assistance in regaining her level of extraordinary performance, and provided that Mary agreed with her, she would help her more effectively prioritize her "life-activities" and assist her in what she perceived to be "time-management difficulties."

Case 56: Balancing Work and Life Activity

Mary Ruppe appreciated the open, frank, and honest discussion she had with Irene Klaff and indicated that she liked her job, enjoyed the level of responsibility she had been given, and had respect for her co-workers — some that she regularly socialized with after work. In preparation for the next counseling session, Mary was asked to keep tabs on all those activities that consumed her time during the next week and provide a summary statement for Klaff to review and analyze, in order to provide feedback during the next session. Also, Mary was asked to differentiate between "essential" and "non-essential activities" and indicate how those activities which she assigned a higher priority could be more fully met, while simultaneously reducing the time spent on "non-essential" activities.

Mary diligently worked on the assignment she was given and prepared the activity report displayed as **Exhibit 1**. Although she had done her homework, she felt an above average level of anxiety as she braced herself for Irene's evaluation. She told her closest friend at work, that she hoped Irene would be patient with her. After all she said, "I am at a fragile state in my life and I hope Irene realizes this and goes easy on me."

Exhibit 1. Mary Ruppe's Personal Activity Log

Monday morning, I get up at 5:00 a.m., shower, and watch the news as I get ready for work. Then, I say hello to my grandma as I walk out the door by 6:00 a.m., so that I can arrive on time at the agency. On the way to work, I stop at Quick Trip for a doughnut and tea, and arrive at the office between 6:30 and 6:45 a.m. – depending on traffic. At work, first I review the memos that were sent after I left on Friday, and then complete my 7:00 a.m. to 5:00 p.m. workday.

During the day, I take anywhere from 25-75 phone calls, answering various questions from homeowners and bankers. I go home at 5:00 p.m., fix dinner for my family, and spend time with my grandma if my school work allows. If not, I head to my living area in the house where I spend anywhere from 2-4 hours reading and doing research, and go to bed around 11:30 p.m. Tuesday, I get up around 6:00 a.m. and replicate the same routine as on Monday just a little later. I head to the office at 6:45 a.m. This time I go directly to our branch office in Thompson Park next to the Maid-Rite. I do all of the paperwork there and follow up work with mortgage servicing companies for our state-assisted clients, then leave the office around 5:00 p.m. – just in time to head home, grab my stuff for class, throw a load of laundry into the washer and drive to the university campus.

When classes are over, I leave campus between 9:00 and 9:15 p.m. – depending on when class gets out. Today, I drove to my friend's house on 65th Street to give her a half hour breather from her three small children. I play with the children for a half hour while their mother gets ready for bed. It's not always quiet, but she doesn't have to pay attention to the noise; then I leave and get home around 11:00 p.m. Next, I check in with my cousin from central Missouri who just moved in with us about two months ago, and make sure things are going well for him. Wednesday, I repeat Monday's schedule at work, but now I add one-hour to make calls to our state-assisted clients who have fallen delinquent with the home mortgages and remind them that their payments are overdue.

Also, I assist the three new employees we have whenever they need help. At 4:00 p.m. I finally get off the phone and I help the new employees for one-hour, and then I try to catch up on my own work that has managed to pile up on my desk throughout the day. I leave the office around 5:30 or 6:00 p.m., eat dinner in my room, and try to get some more reading done. Thursday is the same routine as Wednesday, but I leave work at 5:30 p.m. This leaves me just enough time to stop at Quick Trip and grab water before I head to class. Thursday night I am in bed by 10:30 p.m., if at all possible. Friday I repeat Thursday, only now I am able to leave work at 2:00 p.m. I head to my dad's office and from 2:30 p.m. to usually 8:00 or 9:00 p.m. I work there. Then I return home, say hello to my family and go to bed by 10:00 p.m. Saturday morning, I get up and head to work at my dad's office around 7:00 or 7:30 a.m. I work for about three hours then drive to Airborne Express by the airport. I'm supposed to be there by 11:00 a.m.

The weekend has arrived, and I drive to Valley Hill for my weekly gab session with my mother. We run errands all day, and purchase office supplies and shop for everyday household supplies we need. We head home around 4:00 p.m. I spend the next hour trying to help mother sort laundry. I usually give up after an hour. I try to catch up with my friends on Saturday night, but typically there is still too much reading and research to be done, so I spend half an hour on the phone telling everyone to have a drink for me and retire to what they have affectionately named the Dungeon (my room). I work until around 12:30 or 1:00 a.m. trying to finish all my reading and research for the week. Sunday morning I get up around 8:00 a.m. and prepare for church attendance. Church is usually over by 10:30 a.m. and I am back at home by 10:35 a.m. Usually, I then suit up for the afternoon Harley ride and take off for the day to wherever my dad decides to lead the pack.

When I get home I try to make a schedule for the following week, but I usually just shower, eat dinner and sit in front of the TV for a few hours and spend some quiet time with my family. And in all of this I still manage to see my five year old nephew, three year old niece, and my six month old nephew and have numerous fights with my sister about how much candy they can really handle. I hold my position that Mountain Dew is not good for a three year old. The next week is about to begin, and I start all over with my week Monday morning at 5 a.m. This is my typical week. Makes me tired just writing it and it's only Sunday night.

Questions and Instructions:

1. After reviewing the Personal Activity Log submitted by Mary Ruppe, what conclusions would you draw from the log of activities? How would you categorize Ruppe's activities? Please be specific.

2. In the bifurcation of work/non-work activities, managers frequently find it difficult to draw a line of distinction. What would you advise Mary Ruppe concerning her busy schedule away from work that is negatively impacting her job performance at work? Please be specific in your

recommendations. What recommendations, if any, would you make to help Mary overcome her performance problems? Explain.

3. The issue of balancing work with other life activities is of increasing concern to those in the "work-a-day-world." Even though we are supposed to have more leisure time by having more conveniences, accessible technology, new software, and electronic equipment, etc., dissatisfaction with work and work/life balance is increasing. This phenomenon is called "Progress Anxiety." What recommendation would you personally make to Mary Ruppe in order for her to overcome her final statement in the log: "This is my typical week. Makes me tired just writing it and it's only Sunday night!" Please develop the outline of a plan that you could discuss with Mary.

Second Scenario:

Fred Jones is a ten year career employee in the Office of Urban Affairs and Irene Klaff, his supervisor, noticed that he too, like Mary Ruppe, was increasingly concerned with how to more effectively manage and maintain a life/work balance. Irene had just discussed the same sort of issues with Mary Ruppe, his co-worker, and she was a bit puzzled that Fred displayed some of the same difficulties. In the course of evaluating Fred, she asked him if he would like to present a personal log of his weekly activities for her to review and analyze. Fred responded to Irene's suggestion with some reluctance and only consented to the "in-depth analysis," when Klaff assured him that the log and the nature of the counseling that followed would remain confidential. Klaff looked him squarely in the eye and gave him the assurance he had requested. "Fred," she asserted, "what happens here, stays here! Just like being in Las Vegas."

During the counseling session, the discussion was far-reaching between Fred and Irene. They mutually agreed that downsizing in the office had shifted a larger than normal work-load to the average employee, and to some extent, Fred said, "I've felt this added burden. I need to perform the tasks initially assigned to my own position and the work once performed by other employees who have left the agency." Fred went on to say, "In the final analysis, Irene, I don't have enough time to do my work well, provide quality client relations, and remain productive." Both Fred and Irene mutually agreed that downsizing or what they laughingly called "right-sizing," had come to the agency and they were candid and mature enough to understand that they were facing the likely prospects of lowered morale, job-satisfaction and even burnout.

Fred Jones left the counseling session and made a commitment to himself that he would do the best job he could in keeping a detailed record of his typical activities for the week. At week's end he reflected upon the many work-related tasks and activities he had performed, and as he created a word document and entered the following information, as displayed in **Exhibit 2,** he was surprised at what he found.

Exhibit 2. Fred Jones' Personal Activity Log

A sampling of my work-week looks like this. Monday through Friday, I get up at 6:00 a.m., shower, wake up the kids, get out their clothes (which will never be ironed), make breakfast for the kids and myself, and make all the beds. Then, I get dressed, throw a load of laundry in the already overloaded washer, drop off the children at school by 7:00 a.m., then brace myself for the Interstate "race-track." I arrive at the employee parking lot, wait like a "shark" to find a vacated parking spot, pushing the time clock to the limit and arrive for another "fun-filled day at the office."

The lunch hour is used to run errands like most of my other colleagues. Lunch? Are you kidding? I literally throw some money at one of the interns, begging that they return with something that looks edible. I work until 4:30 p.m., on a good day, then race back home. I check the schedules for the children, call the kids at home to make sure all the water bottles are filled, uniforms or practice clothes are on, and that they are ready to "play ball." Then, I change the laundry, check the mail, and drive at least one child, if not more, to a practice or game, or on some nights, watch all three kids play soccer, baseball, or softball at different parks located throughout the city. Dinner? How many times a week can you have hot dogs or macaroni and cheese? Pull laundry out of the dryer, throw the next load in – I learned how to do this really well. Next comes the homework assignments, it must be done and all four of us pick up the house, fold laundry, and, at last, retire for the evening –yes, go to bed!

What about reading the popular press? Newspapers and magazines – only on vacations. Dry cleaning? No thanks, too much time and too much money. Oh, I nearly forgot, I'm on call 24 hours a day for work and if there happens to be a problem, I have to run down to the agency at all hours of the night or day.

The weekends don't bring much free time either. Here is a small sampling of the activities that consume my time and energies: the lawn needs to be mowed and trimmed – suburban life-style demands it; laundry needs to be completely done; housekeeping chores must be fulfilled, including dusting; floors need to be vacuumed and scrubbed; bathrooms need to be cleaned; and the floors are a constant maintenance problem, due to the debris that is brought into the kitchen, living room, and bathrooms that is unending. And, the grocery store beckons and between sporting events for the children, all other errands must be handled. And, someone always "urgently" needs something from the mall or Wal-Mart that "just can't wait," for it seems we all have too many friends who have birthday parties. Of course, there is always the unforeseen event of a broken nose, ankle, and arm – and the summer months have just begun. Finally, quiet time – maybe, if my own homework is done, I can watch the 10:00 p.m. news on television.

Case 56: Balancing Work and Life Activity

Questions and Instructions:

4. How would you characterize the information presented in Fred Jones Personal Activity Log? Explain. Are there any broad categories or grouping that you would construct? What categories would you recommend using? Please list.

5. Do you see any similarities or differences between what was presented in Exhibit 1 and 2? Be specific.

6. What do you think about asking Mary and Fred to consider the following questions in preparing their log? List the five essential tasks associated with your present job; the five most important time-wasters; and, list all work activities that might be changed in some way to free-up more time. Why are these either good or bad suggestions in preparing a time-management analysis? If possible, give specific examples.

7. Would recommendations for Irene or Fred be any different if their years of experience in the agency were flipped or had more or fewer years of service? If their gender was reversed? Please explain.

8. An enduring question of management is, "If what is being done away from work affects job performance, should it concern you as a manager?" How would you answer this question? Justify your answer.

9. Some private firms offer fringe benefits to employees to assist the employees with their "outside of work distractions" such as a service that runs errands for employees during the work day, onsite auto service and repair, onsite dry cleaning pick and delivery, grocery shopping services and dinner preparation. Should organizations offer these types of benefits? If so, why? If not, why not? What are your thoughts about the public sector offering these types of benefits?

Case 56: Balancing Work and Life Activity
Name:

Case Log and Administrative Journal Entry

This case analysis and learning assessment is printed on perforated pages and may be removed from the book for evaluation purposes.

Case Analysis:
Major case concepts and theories identified:

What is the relevance of the concepts, theories, ideas and techniques presented in the case to that of public management?

Facts — what do we know *for sure* about the case? Please list.

Who is involved in the case (people, departments, agencies, units, etc.)? Were the problems of an "intra/interagency" nature? Be specific.

Are there any rules, laws, regulations or standard operating procedures identified in the case study that might limit decision-making? If so, what are they?

Are there any clues presented in the case as to the major actor's interests, needs, motivations and personalities? If so, please list them.

Case 56: Balancing Work and Life Activity

Learning Assessment:
What do the administrative theories presented in this case mean to you as an administrator?

How can this learning be put to use outside the classroom? Are there any problems you envision during the implementation phase?

Several possible courses of action were identified during the class discussion. Which action was considered to be most practical by the group? Which was deemed most feasible? Based on your personal experience, did the group reach a conclusion that was desirable, feasible, and practical? Please explain why or why not.

Did the group reach a decision that would solve the problem on a short-term or long-term basis? Please explain.

What could you have done to receive more learning value from this case?

57

Management: Helpful or a Hindrance?

by
C. Kenneth Meyer and Amy Polson

Jeffrey Worthington worked in Christian Charities as a part-time employee while he pursued a degree in Child and Family Development from the state university located with an easy commute from his home. Later on, he worked as a social worker for a non-profit agency that had a mediocre reputation for rendering quality and professional services to families. While pleased up to now with the work experiences he garnered there, he told his wife that he was "…ready to bail and work for a living wage!" With the demand for social workers high in the state and supply found wanting, he signed on with the state Department of Human Services (DHS) and received what in horse racing terms would be considered a trifecta: full backing of the juvenile court system, ability to make an impact on both children and families in his community, and pay which was much higher and the benefits more comprehensive than any of the other agencies he had researched.

Worthington was first assigned by the DHS to a mid-sized metropolitan area of nearly 200,000 citizens. Not large by metropolitan standards, it was considered a major service area in the state.

Jeffrey was the kind of person who "never met a stranger," and he made friends quickly. His sense of humor and "hail good fellow" attitude was infectious and he had well-developed listening and other interpersonal skills. The department he had just joined, however, was not measuring up to his expectations in the area of having a professional organizational culture. For instance, he found his co-workers to be disgruntled and frustrated and, overall, as he told his friends, "…it reeked with the stinking attitude of negativism and pettiness." It did not take long for him to take on some of his colleagues' negativism and this was not in character with his natural *persona*. Of course, Jeffrey kept his "eye on the ball" and did not want to submit to the strong, pervasive, cultural impulses that were embedded in the organization.

To withstand being infected with negativism was not easily accomplished for he witnessed, in disbelief, how fresh ideas on changing the processes and new standards of service were shot down when they were brought to higher authority and dismissed with managerial disrespectfulness. In some instances, he heard the "old saw" that "We've always done it this way, it's worked perfectly well over the years, and we're not going to change now!"

Case 57: Management Helpful or a Hindrance?

The list of frustrations began to pile up in his mind and produced a feeling of uneasiness about what he was doing. Within the first few months on the job, he encountered the "sacred cow" regulations related to budgeting and financing. He found it nearly impossible to meet the needs of the families he was charged with serving. Management frequently asked him and the other social workers to cut back on the service level given to their case-loads — an euphemism for children and families. His judgment on how he provided services was routinely challenged and he felt his professionalism was regularly questioned. Additionally, he felt the stressful results of the DHS and Juvenile Court System being at loggerheads with one another, as he told John Phillips, his office-mate, "I feel like the knot in the middle of the rope that is used in a tug of war game — first being pulled in one direction and then in another."

The judges would order certain family services based on demonstrated needs and he would not be able to deliver the counseling or assistance that was ordered because the money was simply not there or the services were not available. Consequently, he had to spend much of his time bargaining and negotiating with management attempting to reach a compromise that would appease the court, satisfy his superiors, and effectively and appropriately serve his client families. This proved to be exasperating in terms of his motivation, job satisfaction and morale.

If the set of problems presented above was not enough to produce dissatisfaction and alienation, his caseload was routinely increased without consultation or approval. He wondered how much further he could be stretched before his spirit and effectiveness would "snap." Added to this already volatile mixture of stress, case overload, and unresolved interagency issues, was the added dose of reality brought about with the methamphetamine or "meth" epidemic. Meth had a ruinous impact on many vulnerable families in Jeffrey's county and nearby cities. Of course, meth was taking its toll on families all over the city and his experienced co-workers said, "It has scrambled and fried the brains of our children and families in an unforgiving and ravenous way. It is, simply, a scourge on society." The last straw for Jeffrey, however, was the increased need for the state to remove children from their parental care and place them in the care of foster parents. Meth had taken its toll on families to be sure, but it was also having its "nasty way" with the state's social service agency.

Jeffrey Worthington was no stranger to politics and he understood the legislative process better than the typical layperson. He told one of his trusted co-workers that it would be difficult for the department to get more funding from the state legislature due to fiscal austerity and the competing demands for limited resources. While he felt frustrated with being unable to match the services rendered to family needs, he too had reconciled in his own mind that this was simply an enduring political problem and the Department of Human Services would have to take its own lumps and share the budgetary shortfalls and accompanying pain.

This unresolved tension between meeting family needs and budgetary constraints fell beyond his purview, or as he would jokingly say, "…my job description." The budgetary dilemma was well beyond his ability to control or influence, and this further exacerbated his personal feelings of estrangement from and anger toward the agency. Jeffrey had reluctantly accepted what he felt could not be changed, but what he found difficult to accept was the culture of a department that was unresponsive to its employees and the issues they faced on a daily basis. This irresolvable tension had begun to seriously erode his spirit and zest for his job. "Perhaps," he said to himself, "am I experiencing cognitive dissonance?"

Case 57: Management Helpful or a Hindrance?

In Jeffrey's office there were approximately sixty foster care workers and another fifty or so social workers involved in child abuse investigations, adoptions or dependent adult casework. The complex issues that each of these social workers had to address daily created a chaotic environment. Jeffrey and his co-workers shared a common reaction when they approached their managers for support. Instead of receiving empathy and understanding, they received discouragement. Management, however, reluctantly acknowledged the frustrations associated with the budget constraints, but dismissed their demands with ease and with seemingly uncaring disregard for the families.

Most of the 100 or so social workers in the building, including Jeffrey, were unionized employees. While Jeffrey wholeheartedly believed in the union and the benefits and security it provided, he found that the union had a downside as well. He felt it shielded employees who no longer cared about the families they were working with, aided poor employees (laggards) in biding their time until retirement, and provided cover for non-productive employers. Also, Jeffrey found the disparity that existed between workers caseload to be unacceptable—he carried a caseload of seventy families, while others had caseloads of only thirty-five families or less. Jeffrey and his fellow "hardworking and competent" employees were discouraged by this fact and had little reason to believe that assignment of caseloads would improve.

In addition, Jeffrey Worthington observed that top management seemed to take an unreasonable response toward employees who did not follow official protocol and under most circumstances, they would face with disciplinary action. Instead of addressing the individual transgressions of caseworkers, management would "crack down" by initiating a new set of rules that would extend to everyone, even if only one employee had erred. This was particularly frustrating to the social workers who had followed the sundry agency and program rules and regulations, because they felt the offending employee who had violated agency policy or had a record of poor performance should be addressed—not the group *en masse*. Further, when management tightened the reins on employees who were already doing the best they could with the limited resources available, this further diminished an already suffering morale. The social workers also felt that management would shift their focus from things that really mattered to that of giving inordinate attention to those things it could easily control such as late reporting—the theory of inverse proportionality.

The more stressful and frustrating the working environment became for Jeffrey, the more it seemed to him that management would make rash, "knee-jerk" decisions regarding the larger and more important issues, and focus less and less on those issues that really mattered. Jeffrey observed a clear divide between employees and management and within the first nine months on the job he noticed that the gap had actually widened. Jeffrey watched his frustrated co-workers respond to this unsupportive environment by submitting their resignations and saying farewell to the agency. In fact, within the last month, twelve workers had submitted their resignation notices, often leaving for lower paying, nongovernmental jobs; some of his colleagues even left without having any prospect for outside employment. Jeffrey felt he too was reaching his wits end.

He had repeatedly tried to approach his supervisor with suggestions on how things could be improved, and had voiced his concern about the negative culture, worker turnover problem, and the added stress that had been placed on those who remained. Each time Jeffrey voiced his concerns his supervisor,

Case 57: Management Helpful or a Hindrance?

Ed Rourke, told him, "He did not have time to listen to him, things have always been this way in the department, and there was nothing that he could do to correct the problems." Feeling caught himself, his manager finally unloaded on Jeffrey and said:

"Jeffrey, you can rightfully be angry and it is clear that you are frustrated and disappointed with me. What am I supposed to? I'm not a magician! I have no genie that I can summon and 'poof' our budget will be increased several millions of dollars so that I can meet your expectations and demands. Get serious. We are all professionals around here and none of us relish the current state of affairs. I, like you, am trying to do the best that I can with a bad situation. There is no need to come to me with the same old and worn set of demands because I cannot fix them. Until my name is embossed on the stationery you use and the program carries my name, it is the states' problem and that is the end of the story!"

Jeffrey did not buy into Rourke's remarks and felt that although he was working for a bureaucracy that was resistant to change, it did not have to be this way. Jeffrey liked the responsibility associated with his job and enjoyed working with the families and he did not want to separate from DHS. Regrettably, however, unless the environment improved he had no other choice but to resign like those before him; he would not submit to becoming a mere "paper-rat."

Questions and Instructions:

1. Please identify the major management issues that are connected to this scenario. Are these management and policy difficulties easy to rectify? If yes, how would you resolve the major issues you identified.

2. To what extent does the union contribute to the overall negative organizational culture and climate of the Department of Human Services? Please differentiate between what constitutes organization culture and organization climate.

3. How did you react to Ed Rourke's statement of frustration when he let off steam and unloaded on Jeffrey Worthington? How would you have reacted if faced with same troublesome problems? Please elaborate.

4. Should the Department of Human Services be completely revamped and if so what 21st century characteristics would you like DHS to possess? Please enumerate and justify your listing of idealized organizational traits.

Case 57: Management Helpful or a Hindrance?

Name:

Case Log and Administrative Journal Entry

This case analysis and learning assessment is printed on perforated pages and may be removed from the book for evaluation purposes.

Case Analysis:
Major case concepts and theories identified:

What is the relevance of the concepts, theories, ideas and techniques presented in the case to that of public management?

Facts — what do we know *for sure* about the case? Please list.

Who is involved in the case (people, departments, agencies, units, etc.)? Were the problems of an "intra/interagency" nature? Be specific.

Are there any rules, laws, regulations or standard operating procedures identified in the case study that might limit decision-making? If so, what are they?

Are there any clues presented in the case as to the major actor's interests, needs, motivations and personalities? If so, please list them.

Case 57: Management Helpful or a Hindrance?

Learning Assessment:
What do the administrative theories presented in this case mean to you as an administrator?

How can this learning be put to use outside the classroom? Are there any problems you envision during the implementation phase?

Several possible courses of action were identified during the class discussion. Which action was considered to be most practical by the group? Which was deemed most feasible? Based on your personal experience, did the group reach a conclusion that was desirable, feasible, and practical? Please explain why or why not.

Did the group reach a decision that would solve the problem on a short-term or long-term basis? Please explain.

What could you have done to receive more learning value from this case?

Appendix A

Case Histories Keyed to Topics

The text gives major emphasis to topics marked by asterisks.

1. **Keep Your Stick on the Ice or Your Views to Yourself**
*Discipline, *Freedom of Speech, Political Violence, *Public Employee Rights, Resistance to Change, Workplace Violence

2. **Patronage or Cronyism at DHS**
Accountability, Communication, Complaints of the Public, *Consultants, *Contracting Out, *Cronyism, Legislative Oversight, Legislative-Executive Relations, News-Media Relations, Nonprofit Organization, Outsourcing, Partisan Politics, *Patronage, *Political Favoritism, *Reorganization, Teamwork

3. **Jimmy's 53 Questions: Team Interviewing**
Diversity, Employee Rights, Equal Employment, Fair Labor Standards Act (FSLA), Human Resource Management Issues, *Interview Panel, Job Classification and Placement, Job Description, Negligent Hiring, Nonprofit Organization, Recruitment and Selection

4. **What Questions are Lawful or Unlawful?**
Affirmative Action, *Application for Employment, *Civil Rights Act of 1964 (CRA, 1964), *Ethical Questions, Hiring Quota, *Interview Questions, *Interviewing, Privacy and Confidentiality Issues, *Recruitment and Selection, *Recruitment Applications Form, *Recruitment Discrimination

5. **Making Meetings Work**
*Brainstorming Technique, Conflict Resolution, Interpersonal Relations, *Meeting Planning and Management, *Nonverbal Behavior, Organization Behavior and Change, *Relevancy Challenges, Small Group Behavior

6. **Time and Time Again**
*Absenteeism, Anger Management, *Annual Leave, *Attendance Management, Employee Benefits, Child Care, Elder Care, *Emergency Leave, Health Care Policy, Job Satisfaction, Morale, Problem Employee, Productivity, *Professionalism, Retention, *Time Management, Wellness, Work-Life Balance

7. **The Dress Dress Code**
*Conduct Codes, *Dress Code/Grooming Standard, Professionalism

8. **Supervising God**
Censorship, Civil Rights Act of 1964, Civil Rights Act of 1991, Communication, Conflict Resolution, *Employee Rights, Freedom of Religion, Interpersonal Relations, Leadership, Organization Behavior and Change, *Religious Discrimination, Religious Practices, *Supervisor-Staff Relations

Appendix A

9. Ergonomics in the Workplace
*Ergonomics, *Health and Safety, Kaizen, Liability

10. Severe Acute Respiratory Syndrome (SARS)
*Americans with Disability Act (ADA), Communication, *Emergency Management, Employee Rights, *Health Care Policy, Health Law & Regulations, Human Resource Management Issues, Interpersonal Relations, *Pandemic Disease, *Severe Acute Respiratory Syndrome (SARS)

11. Pictures are Worth a Million Words
*Clientele Relations, Communication, Employee Counseling, Employee Evaluation, Image Management, *Marketing, Motivation, Organizational Culture, Organizational Behavior and Change, *Perception, *Supervisor-Staff Relations, *Training

12. Interns: An Underutilized Asset
*Intern Evaluation Form (Sample), Intern Selection and Placement, *Intern Supervision, *Internship Memorandum of Understanding (Sample), *Internship Program (Sample), *Internship Program Management, Pollution Prevention Intern Program

13. Lingering 9/11 Concerns
*Absenteeism, Conflict Resolution, Diversity, *Employee Counseling, Employee Rights, *Equal Employment, Human Resource Management Issues, *Immigration Issues, Interpersonal Relations, *Problem Employee, *Racism, *Religious Discrimination, Rules & Regulations, *Terrorism, Workplace Security

14. A Hiring Dilemma: Recruitment from In-house Versus from Outside
Administrative Advocacy, Administrative Discretion, *Recruitment and Selection, *Field-Central Office Relations, *Human Resource Planning, Interviewing Panel, Interview Questions, Interviewing, *Job Description, Natural Resources Management, Organizational Structure and Design, Patronage, Performance Evaluation, *Succession Planning, Supervisor-Staff Relations

15. Other Duties as Assigned
Conflict Resolution, *Cutback Management, Delegation of Authority, *Hostile Work Environment, Interpersonal Relations, *Job Description, Leadership, Organization Behavior and Change, *Power and Authority, *Privacy and Confidentiality, *Professionalism, Sexual Harassment, *Supervisor-Staff Relations, *Termination Policy, Wrongful Discharge

16. City Bargaining
Arbitration, *Collective Bargaining, *Compensation and Benefits, Contract Negotiation, *Cost of Living Allowance (COLA), Cutback Management, Downsizing, *Fiscal-Budgetary Matters, Fraternal Order of Police (FOP), Inter-Agency and Intra-Agency Relations, International Association of Firefighters (IAFF), International Brotherhood of Teamsters (IBT), Participatory Management, Professional Air Traffic Controllers Association (PATCO), Reorganization, Right-to-Work, Unfair labor Practices (ULP), *Union-Management Relations

Appendix A

17. Doing the Zoo
*Board of Directors, Conduct Codes, *Conflict of Interest, Contracting for Service, Entrepreneurialism, *Ethical Questions, Fiduciary Responsibility, Fundraising, *Interpersonal Relations, Management Style, *Nonprofit Organization, Philanthropic Organization, Planning & Goal Setting, Power and Authority, *Professionalism, *Recruitment and Selection

18. Printing, Politics and Personal Preference
Communication, *Conflict of Interests, *Contract Administration *Contracting for Service, Hiring, *Invitation-to Bid (ITB), *Marketing, News-Media Relations, Outside Employment ("Moonlighting"), Outsourcing, *Purchasing/Procurement, Turnover

19. Employee Health Benefits
*Benefits, *Change, *Compensation and Benefits, Fiduciary Responsibility, Fiscal-Budgetary Matters, *Health Care, Health Care Policy, Health Insurance, Health Law and Regulation, Human Resource Management Issues, Human Resource Planning, *Motivation, Organization Behavior and Change, Outsourcing, Planning and Goal Setting, Policy Formulation and Implementation, Recruitment and Selection, Re-Engineering, Supervisor-Staff Relations

20. Was Her Privacy Violated?
Health Care, Health Insurance Portability and Accountability Act (HIPAA), *Interpersonal Relations *Privacy and Confidentiality Issues

21. New Direction for the Department of Personnel
*Centralization-Decentralization, *Change, *Compensation and Benefits, Delegation of Authority, Employee Retention, *Entrepreneurialism, Flex-time, Flexible Benefits, Internet, Job Classification and Placement, Leadership, Organization Behavior and Change, *Organization Structure and Design, *Planning and Goal Setting, *Policy Formulation and Implementation, *Program Evaluation, *Quality Management, *Quality of Work Life (QWL), *Recruitment and Selection, *Re-Engineering, *Reinvention, *Reorganization, Rules and Regulations, Total Quality Management (TQM), *Women in Management

22. Betting on Family Life
*American Federation of State, County and Municipal Employees (AFSCME), *Americans with Disability Act (ADA), Child Care, Family Friendly, *Flex-time, Gambling, Quality of Work Life (QWL), Work-Life Balance

23. AIDS in the Public Workforce
*Acquired Immunodeficiency Syndrome (AIDS), Health Care Policy, Hepatitis, *Human Immunodeficiency Virus (HIV), Infectious Diseases, Privacy and Confidentiality, Tuberculosis

24. The Sweet Smell of a Good Appearance Policy
Discipline, *Dress Code/Grooming Standard, *Employee Counseling, Interviewing, Marketing, Personal Hygiene, Recruitment

Appendix A

25. Leave it to Bereavement
Absenteeism, Benefits, *Bereavement Policy, Collective Bargaining, Communication, Conflict Resolution, Cultural Values, Discipline, Emergency Leave, Ethnocentrism, Multiculturalism, *Polycentrism, Problem Employee, Supervisor-Staff Relations

26. Madison County's Zero Tolerance of Harassment and Discrimination Directive
Discrimination, Diversity, *Homophobia, *Homosexuality/Lesbianism, *Hostile Work Environment, Minority Relations, Sexual Harassment, *Sexual Orientation, Strategic Planning, *Training, *Zero Tolerance Policy

27. A Proud Tradition of Affirmative Action
*Affirmative Action, Affirmative Action Goals, Diversity, Hiring Quota, Recruitment and Selection, *Underutilization

28. Competition from Behind Bars
Change, Employee Rights, Entrepreneurialism, Equal Employment, Outsourcing, *Prison and Business Relations, *Prison Labor, *Prisoner Rehabilitation, *Prisoner Rights, Public and Community Relations, Recruitment, *Stereotyping, *Union-Management Relations, Workplace Security

29. Life at Quality Care House (QCH)
Assisted Living Center, *Clientele Relations, *Communication, Conflict Resolution, Discipline, *Echolalia, *Employee Counseling, Employee Rights, *Hostile Work Environment, Leadership, Mental Health Issues, Nonprofit Organization, *Organization Behavior and Change, Professionalism, Quality Work Life (QWL), Privacy and Confidentiality Issues, Rules and Regulations, Sexual Harassment, *Staff-Client Relations, *Supervisor-Staff Relations, Termination, Termination Policy, *Vulnerable Person, Wrongful Discharge

30. The Expectant Mother
*Contingent Employee, Equal Employment, Family Medical Leave Act (FMLA), Health Care, *Health Insurance Portability & Accountability Act (HIPAA, 1996), Human Resource Management Issues, *Pregnancy Discrimination Act (1978), Privacy and Confidentiality Issues

31. Managerial Succession
Absenteeism, *Complaints of the Public, Conflict Resolution, Employee Evaluation, Employee Placement, Recruitment and Selection, *Incompetence and Inefficiency, Intergovernmental Relations, Power and Authority, *Preferential Treatment, Productivity, Stress Management, *Supervisor-Staff Relations, Time Management, *Turnaround Management

32. Crossing the Ethical Divide
Client Relationship Management System (CRMS), *Clientele Relations, *Computer "Hacking," Conflict of Interest, *Dishonesty and Corruption, *Ethical Questions, Internet, *Intranet, Professionalism, *Secrecy and Confidentiality, *Theft, Workplace Security

Appendix A

33. The Downward Spiral of Founder's Hospital
*Board Membership, *Board of Directors, Communication, *Community Relations, *Compensation and Benefits, Complaints of the Public, Conflict Resolution, *Consultants, Cronyism, Job Satisfaction, Leadership, Legal Requirements, Morale, Nonprofit Organization, Outsourcing, *Program Evaluation, *Strategic Management, *Succession Planning

34. Daughter Dearest: Nonprofit Nepotism
Accountability, Board of Directors, Bureaucratic Abuse, *Conduct Codes, *Conflict of Interest, Ethical Questions, *Fiduciary Responsibility, Leadership, *Management Style, *Nepotism, Nonprofit Organization, *Planning and Goal Setting, *Preferential Treatment, Professionalism, *Recruitment and Selection, *Rules and Regulations, Teamwork and Cooperation, Telecommunication, Termination Policy

35. Entrepreneurialism or Exploitation?
Contracting Out, *Entrepreneurialism, Fiscal-Budgetary Matters, *Homeless Persons, *Prison Labor, Public and Community Relations, *Reinvention, Rules and Regulations,*Workfare/Work Program, Workplace Security

36. An Instance of Racial Bias
*Equal Employment, Equity, Interpersonal Relations, Job Classification & Placement, Recruitment and Selection

37. What Should it Be? CEO or Executive Director
*Affirmative Action, *Board of Directors, *Executive Search Company, Gender Discrimination, *Management or Leadership Title, *Nonprofit Organization, Planning and Goal Setting,*Promotion Policies, Recruitment and Selection, *Reorganization, Rules and Regulations, Strategic Planning, *Succession Planning, Supervisor-Staff Relations

38. The "Pink Slip" Support System
*Community Services Block Grant (CSBG), *Economic and Planning District, Fiscal-Budgetary Matters, *Green Job Growth, Offshoring, One-Stop Shop, Outsourcing, *Plant Closure, Retrenchment, Tax Increment Financing (TIF), Termination Policy, Unemployment, Union-Management Relations, *Wagner-Peyser Act, *Worker Adjustment and Retraining Notification (WARN), *Workforce Development Programs, *Workforce Investment Act of 1998 (WIA, 1998)

39. Language has Meaning
*Communication, *Diversity, *Employee Counseling, Equal Employment, Equity, Leadership, *Marketing, Leadership, *Public & Community Relations, *Speech Writing, Value Clarification, *Women in Management

40. A $5,000 Anonymous Phone Call?
Administrative Discretion, Bureaucratic Abuse, Centralization-Decentralization, *Complaints of the Public, Conduct Codes, Discipline, *Dress Code/Grooming Standard, Employee Rights, *Field-Central Office Relations, Professionalism, Public and Community Relations, Resignations

Appendix A

41. A Campaigner for Equal Rights
Employee Rights, *Equal Employment, *Gender Discrimination, Grievances, Interpersonal Relations, Management Style, Supervisor-Staff Relation, Union-Management Relations, Women in Management

42. Sick Leave or AWOL
*Absenteeism, *Annual Leave, *Attendance Management, *Conduct Codes, *Discipline, Ethical Questions, *Insubordination, Interpersonal Relations, *Military Administration, Problem Employee, Secrecy and Confidentiality, Sick Leave, Work Schedules, Work-Life Balance

43. What Color is Your Coded Message?
Clientele Relations, *Communication, Community Relations, Email, *Emergency Management, Human Resource Management Issues, Human Resource Planning, Quality of Work Life (QWL), Staff Relations, Training, *Workplace Security, *Workplace Violence

44. Problems with Volunteer Workers
Clientele Relations, *Delegation of Authority, Interpersonal Relations, Ombudsmen, Recruitment, Teamwork and Cooperation, Training, *Volunteerism, Volunteer Management, *Volunteer Workers

45. Pressing a Harassment Suit
*Civil Rights Act of 1964, Employee Rights, *Equal Employment, Hostile Work Environment, Professionalism, Quality of Work Life (QWL), *Sexual Harassment, Workplace Stress

46. Many Faces of Discrimination
Discipline, Diversity Training, *Employee Rights, Equal Employment, Equity, Gender Discrimination, Intergenerational Issues, Interpersonal Relations, Legal Requirements, Policy Formulation and Implementation, *Rules and Regulations

47. Many Sides of Downsizing
*Downsizing, Fiduciary Responsibility, Fiscal-Budgetary Matters, Policy Formulation and Implementation, Termination Policy

48. To Quit or Not to Quit
Clientele Relations, Employee Rights, *Employee Separation, Fiduciary Responsibility, Interpersonal Relations, Job Satisfaction, Morale, Retrenchment, *Termination Policy, Union-Management Relations

49. Freda is Sick Again
*Americans with Disability Act (ADA), Attendance Management, *Clientele Relations, *Community Relations, Discipline, Employee Counseling, Ethical Questions, Family Medical leave Act (FMLA), Health Care, Interpersonal Relations, Job Classification and Placement, *Munchausen's Syndrome, *Negligent Retention, Nonprofit Organization, *Problem Employee, *Public and Community Relations, Supervisor-Staff Relations, Termination Policy, Workplace Security

Appendix A

50. Regional or Racial Bias in Diversity Training
Conduct Codes, *Diversity, *Equal Employment, *Ethical Questions, Freedom of Speech, *Interpersonal Conflict, Interpersonal Relations, Lifestyle, *National-Origin Discrimination, Organization Change and Behavior, Problem Employee, Racism, *Training, *Union-Management Relations

51. American vs. Immigrant Labor
Complaints of Public, * Contracting for Service, Employee Rights, *Immigrant Employees, *Immigration Issues, Interpersonal Relations, News-Media Relations, Policy Formulation and Implementation, Public and Community Relations, Recruitment and Selection

52. The Good/Bad Administrator
Communication, *Discipline, Employee Counseling, Employee Rights, Equity, *Interpersonal Relations, Job Satisfaction, *Management Style, Morale, Motivation, Organization Behavior and Change, Performance Evaluation, *Protests Organized by Employees, Responsibility, *Small Group Behavior, *Teamwork and Cooperation

53. The Far Side of Fifty
*Age Discrimination, Equal Employment, Gender Discrimination, Intergenerational Issues, Job Satisfaction, Performance Evaluation, *Promotion Policies, *Recruitment and Selection, Succession Planning

54. A Problem of Motivation
Communication, Job Satisfaction, *Motivation, *Performance Evaluation, Productivity, *Stress Management, *Workfare/Work Program

55. Special Privileges for Officials?
Benefits, Employee Orientation, Equity, Ethical Questions, *Flex-time, Management Style, Morale, Preferential Treatment, Professionalism, *Rank and Privilege, *Rules and Regulations, Whistle Blowing, Work Schedules

56. Balancing Work and Life Activity
Discipline, *Employee Counseling, *Interpersonal Relations, *Management Style, Participatory Management, *Performance Evaluation, Problem Employee, Quality of Work Life (QWL), Stress Management, Teamwork and Cooperation, *Time Management, *Women in Management, *Work-Life Balance

57. Management Helpful or a Hindrance?
Bureaupathology, *Case Workload/Overload, *Clientele Relations, *Cutback Management, Downsizing, *Employee Retention, Fiscal-Budgetary Matters, Incompetency and Inefficiency, Job Satisfaction, Leadership, Management Style, Morale, Motivation, Organization Behavior and Change, Public and Community Relations, Reorganization, Rules and Regulations

Appendix A

Appendix B

Index of Names, Positions and Organization Types

A

Abbott, Phil
  representative, House of Representatives 31
Andrews, ... 300, 301
Aquinaldo, ... 333, 334
Arnold, ... 334
Atkinson, ... 316
Aura, Maria
  governor 213
Avery, Chris
  division administrator, Department of Natural
    Resources 122, 125, 126

B

Baker, Jeff
  supervisor, Child Welfare Department 395, 396
Bartlett, Jack
  governor 29
Bauer, Joe
  personnel analyst, Bureau of Personnel 194
Baxter, Gina
  marketing director, Sunnyside General Hospital
    .... 157, 158, 159, 160
Bergman, Marcia
  senator, State Senate 31
Bevington, John
  job candidate, Department of Natural Resources
    .... 120, 121, 122, 123, 124
Bird, Bernard
  philanthropist 151
Black, Leonard
  applicant, Department of Transportation 390
Blake, ... 299, 300, 301
Bly, ... 293, 294, 295
Bowers, ... 327, 328
Brown, Marlene
  director, Department of Personnel 368
Buckman, Max
  director, Scottsville Parks and Recreation .203, 204

Burns, Marion
  supervisor, Quality Care House 230, 231
Butler, ... 284

C

Carlson, Marge
  employee, Birdland Zoo Foundation 153
Cartmill, James
  geological engineer, Department of Natural
    Resources 384, 385
Clark, Kevin
  labor relations manager, city of Scottsville 203
Clark, Roger
  city manager, city of Union City 273
Coleman, Harry
  warehouse supervisor, World Parcel Service 79, 81
Colton, Fred
  vice president of outreach services, Sunnyside
    General Hospital 157, 158, 159, 160
Comer, K.L.
  founder, Comer, Welch and Rassel Group 69
Comer, Welch and Rassel Group
  policy research firm 69
Cummings, Samantha
  fundraiser, Birdland Zoo Foundation 153, 154

D

Dalby, Kaitlin 29
Dandurand, ... 300
Davidson, Doug
  state auditor 31
Davis, Julie
  employee, Child Welfare Department 395, 396
Davis, Maxie
  director of human resources, Children's Hospital
    86
Dawson, ... 305, 306, 307
Dixon, Freda
  employee, Oakdale Childcare Center 361, 362

Appendix B

Doe, Tom
  executive board chairman, Capital Housing Authority 139
Donovan, Elizabeth
  assistant division administrator, Department of Natural Resources 124, 126
Drapier, Chris
  trainer, Good Mission Community Training Center 199, 200
Dryfus, Henry
  supervisor, Bureau of Investigation 355

E

Elmore, Cheryl
  employee, Allied Health Care 251
Erica
  administrative assistant, Clay County Treasurer 177
Everest, ... 305

F

Fairfield, ... 267
Fairfield, Herbert: 268
Farnsworth, ... 293, 294, 295
Fiedler, ... 333, 334
Flanagan, ... 334
Fong, Carolyn
  county manager, Madison County 210
Ford, Austin
  director of operations, Metropolitan Transit Authority 239, 240
Forrester, Donald
  chief financial officer, Children's Hospital 85, 86
Forrester, Jessica 85
Foster, ... 333
Foster, Debra
  director, Department of Human Services 29, 31
Foster, Edward
  manager, State Welfare Department 401

G

Glassner, Harold
  organizational and leadership consultant and facilitator 90
Golfman, ... 268, 269
Grayson, Dan
  program director, Credit Builders Association 259, 260, 261, 262
Green, Ron
  president and chief executive officer, Lutheran Social Services 31
Greene, Amy
  Braxston Public Engineering and Consulting Group 97, 98, 99, 100
Greenwood, Edward
  human resource specialist, State Medicaid Program 113, 114, 115
Grimly, Marcus
  employee, Benton City Casino 189
Grunwald, ... 305, 306, 307

H

Hanson, Jim
  union steward 225
Harman, Joyce
  employee, Department of Natural Resources .. 385
Harris, Jenny
  employee, Capital Housing Authority 137, 138, 139
Harvey, John
  union secretary 221
Henderson, Olaf
  supervisor, Department of Transportation 343
Hendrix, Jason
  director, Bureau of Investigation 355, 356
Herzberg, Frederick 89
Hills, Raymond
  director, Quality Care House 231
Holbrook, ... 285, 289
Hoyt, Robert
  director, Bureau of Personnel 193, 194
Hyde, Emily
  employee, Quality Care House 229, 230
Hyde-Watson, Sylvania
  superintendent candidate, Hope for Boys Center 278, 279

J

Jacobson, Paula
  temporary, Kent and Company 235
Jahoda, Frank
  consultant 251, 252, 253, 254
Jefferies, Sarah

Appendix B

administrative secretary, State Welfare Department 401
Johnson, ... 299, 300, 301
Johnson, Julia
    child learning and development consultant 363
Jones, Barry
    CEO, Birdland Zoo Foundation 152, 153, 154
Jones, Fred
    employee, Office of Urban Affairs 408
Jones, Kathy
    nurse practitioner, Springfield Cancer Research Center 64, 65
Jones, Maggie
    human resources training specialist, Madison County 209
Jones, Paula
    chief of customer service, Department of Natural Resources 123, 124, 125
Jones, Roscoe
    employee, Regency County Department of Assessment 73, 74
Jorgeson, Jim
    department manger, Center for Justice .55, 56, 57, 58

K

Kahoe, ... 315, 316, 317
Kaplan, James
    trainer, Department of Personnel 367
Kash, Dr. Harold
    pediatrician 177
Kate
    employee, Capital Housing Authority 138
Kimball, Christina
    intern, Braxston Public Engineering and Consulting Group 97, 98
Kimmer, John
    personnel director, Good Mission Community Training Center 199, 200
Kingsbury, Timothy
    secretary, Department of Natural Resources .. 383, 386
Klaff, Irene
    supervisor 405
Klean, Jordan
    CEO, Tractor Works 219, 220

Klinesmith, Mary
    tool and dye maker 222, 223, 225
Klineworth, Jason
    Team Selection Committee, Northrup Community Center 35
Knoll, ... 267
Kolini, Lani
    applicant, city of Union City 273
Kramer, Kathy
    consultant, Department of Human Services 29, 30, 31
Krittenbrink, George
    land and water resources survey director, Department of Natural Resources383, 384, 385, 386

L

Lester, ... 285
Lewis, Elaina
    director of human resources, World Parcel Service 79, 81
Lightfoot, James
    director, Human Resources of Northrup Community Center 35
Lightner, ... 315, 316, 317

M

MacArthur, ... 327, 328
Madison, ... 333, 334
Makins, Jerome
    head of engineering division, Department of Transportation 389, 390
Maner, ... 299
Martin, Cynthia
    employee, Clay County Treasurer 177
Maslow, Abraham 89
Mason, Margaret
    employee, Horizon Place 167
Matthews, Rachel
    director, Department of Personnel ... 181, 182, 185
Mawisa, D.
    maintenance, Scottsville Parks and Recreation203, 204
McGregor, Sherry
    executive director, Capital Housing Authority 137, 138

Appendix B

McHenry, Charles
 assistant chief, Department of Natural Resources 119, 123, 124, 125
McKnight, ... 283, 284, 285, 286, 289
Mead, Orville
 board president, Hope for Boys Center 279
Meier, ... 286
Mercedes, Alonzo
 deputy director, Bureau of Investigation . 355, 356
Meyer, George
 mayor, city of Woodward 31
Mi, Herbert
 assistant director of health services, Department of Human Welfare 356
Miller, Robert
 supervisor, Mount Pleasant Hospital 235
Mills, Erin
 director of h.r., Horizon Place 167, 168, 171, 173
Moody, Jeffrey
 chief recruiter, Horizon Place 169
Morgan, Mackenzie
 accounting graduate 170, 171
Mortenson, Bill
 college friend 56, 57, 58, 59
Murphy, Mandy
 employee, Credit Builders Association 260, 261
Murphy, Tina
 executive director, Credit Builders Association 259, 260, 261

N

Newman, Dennis
 speaker, House of Representatives 30

O

Olsen, Stacey
 administrator, Oakdale Childcare Center . 361, 362

P

Parker, Sarah
 data coordinator, Springfield Cancer Research Center 64, 66
Paulette
 secretary, Scottsville Parks and Recreation 204
Pearson, ... 328
Perth, ... 316, 317

Petersen, Marietta
 workforce planner 181, 182, 183, 184, 185
Peterson, ... 316, 317
Phillips, John
 employee, Department of Human Services 414
Porter, Donald
 cartographic section chief, Department of Transportation 389, 390
Powers, Sydney
 business school graduate 170, 171, 172, 173

Q

Qazsi, Muhammad
 employee, State Medicaid Program . 113, 114, 115
Quade, Gloria
 wife 120

R

Radick, Jim
 county manager, Regency County 73, 74
Ramsey, Mark
 job candidate, Department of Natural Resources 120, 121, 122, 124
Reagan, ... 327
Reagan, Ronald
 president, United States of America 146
Reich, Robert
 Secretary, U.S. Department of Labor 347
Rex
 resident, Quality Care House 230, 231
Reynolds, Diane
 senator, State Senate 31
Rhines, Julia
 city manager, city of Park Wood 145, 146, 147
Ridgeway, Hazel
 cartographic drafter, Department of Transportation 389, 390
Ridgeway, Troy
 president, Kleen-Sweepers 377
Rodriquez, Jorge
 administrative assistant, Capital Housing Authority 138
Rosen, Barb
 director, Scottsville Department of Human Resources 203, 204
Ross, Maureen

senior consultant, Viva Consultant Group....89, 90, 91
Ross, Sydney
  emergency responder, Brooksville Department of Transportation 341, 342, 343
Rourke, Ed
  supervisor, Department of Human Services..... 416
Ruppe Mary
  client counselor, Office of Urban Affairs ..405, 406, 408

S

Sam
  engineer... 98
Sanger, Darrell
  procurement manager, Federal Aviation Administration 377, 378
Schilling, Matt
  consultant, Department of Human Services 29, 30, 32
Schlick, Rebecca
  applicant, city of Union City 273
Schwabe,.. 284
Shapiro, Larry
  State Office of Education................................45, 46
Sim, Greg
  benefit counselor, Horizon Place.......168, 169, 170
Singh, Ravi
  director, Department of Public Works and Parks and Recreation 347
Smith, Arnold
  chief of law enforcement bureau, Department of Natural Resources 123, 126
  chief, Department of Natural Resources 125
Smith, Kay
  registered nurse, Springfield Cancer Research Center...63, 64, 65, 66
Smith, Maggie
  manager, Metropolitan Transit Authority.239, 240
Smith, Megan
  financial counselor, Horizon Place....168, 169, 171, 172
Snow, John
  Human Resources Counselor, city of Plainview 23, 26

Sparks, Nancy
  director of human resources, State Medicaid Program...113, 114, 115
Springfield Cancer Research Center 63
Stanton, Sophie
  human resources manager Mount Pleasant Hospital 235
Stone, Richard
  representative, House of Representatives 31
Sullivan, Leslie
  employee, Comer, Welch and Rassel Group 69
Summers, Lawrence
  president, Harvard University 342

T

Tate, Annie
  manager, Metropolitan Transit Authority .239, 240
Tesh, Hale
  mayor, Kinross 219, 220, 221, 224
Thomas, Mark
  zoo director, Birdland Zoo 152
Throckmorton, Brock.............................245, 246, 247

W

Wabanaki, Niles
  employee, World Parcel Service....................79, 80
Wells, Peggy
  manager, Clay County Treasurer 177
Wells, Tammy
  project manager, Springfield Cancer Research Center...63, 64
White, Gordon
  superintendent, Hope for Boys Center 277, 278
Wiesener,...315, 316, 317
Wise, Melinda
  interim CEO, Founder's Hospital 251
Worthington, Jeffrey
  employee, Department of Human Services 413, 414, 415

Y

Yamamoto, Joan
  employee, Hope for Boys Center 277

Appendix B

Appendix C

Summary Guide to Application Pre-Employment Questions*

	ACCEPTABLE	INADVISABLE**
1. Age	Whether candidate meets minimum legal age requirements for the job.	Age, date of birth, any inquiry aimed at identifying age or excluding persons of a particular age (e.g., high school or college attendance, graduation dates, what are your retirement plans, how long do you plan to work, how can someone so young handle this job?)
2. Arrest Records	None. (For convictions, see No. 5)	Number and kinds of arrest.
3. Availability for Work on Weekends, Evenings	If asked of all applicants and is a business necessity for the person to be available to work weekends and/or evenings.	Any inquiry about religious observance, child care, inquiries directed only to persons of one sex.
4. Citizenship, Birthplace & National Origin	The only legitimate concern here is whether the applicant is eligible to work in the United States, under Terms of the Immigration Reform and Control Act of 1986. There is a fair and advisable way to obtain this information. The best approach is to ask: Are you EITHER a U.S. citizen OR legally authorized to work in the United States? The "Yes" or "No" answer that follows provides all needed information while not disclosing citizenship or national origin information.	Birthplace, national origin, ancestry, or lineage of applicant, applicant's parents, or applicant's spouse.
5. Conviction Records	Inquiry into convictions if job-related. Include disclaimer stating that conviction does not automatically bar candidate, depending on the job, time, nature and seriousness of the conviction and related rehabilitation.	Any inquiry about conviction unrelated to job requirements.
6. Creed or Religion	None, except where religion is a bona fide occupational qualification.	Applicant's religious affiliation, church, parish, or religious holidays observed.

Appendix C

	ACCEPTABLE	INADVISABLE**
7. Credit Records/ Finances	None, unless job-related.	Inquiries about charge accounts, bank accounts, car and home ownership, credit rating, garnishments, fidelity bonds, etc., that do not relate to performing the particular job.
8. Disability	Whether applicant can perform essential functions of the job, with or without accommodation.	To ask applicant if he/she is disabled and/or to list illness or disabilities or any inquiries that elicit information about disabilities or health, e.g., "Do you have any medical limitations that would prohibit performance of this job? How many sick days did you use in your last job? Have you ever sought treatment for a mental condition?"
9. Drinking	May ask if an applicant drinks alcohol or has ever been arrested for driving while under the influence.	Any questions that could elicit information about alcoholism, which is a disability.
10. Family Status	Whether applicant has responsibilities or commitments which will prevent meeting work schedules, if asked of all applicants regardless of sex.	Marital status, number and age of children, spouse's job.
11. Height & Weight	None, unless job-related.	None, unless job-related.
12. Language	Language applicant speaks or writes fluently, if job-related.	Language used by applicant or family members at home, or how applicant acquired the ability to read, write, or speak a foreign language.
13. Marital Status	None, other than if candidate can meet work schedule of the job, whether candidate has activities, responsibilities, or commitments that may hinder work requirements. (Should be asked of both sexes.)	Whether applicant is married, single, divorced, separated, engaged or widowed.
14. Military Service	Military experience or training, or education.	Type or condition of discharge, unless it is the result of a military conviction.
15. Name	All previous names used by applicant.	The original name of an applicant whose name has been legally changed or the national origin of an applicant's name.

Appendix C

	ACCEPTABLE	INADVISABLE**
16. Organizations	Applicant's membership in professional organizations if job-related.	All churches, clubs, social fraternities, societies, lodges, or organizations to which an applicant belongs.
17. Photographs	None except after hiring.	Photograph with application or after interview, but before hiring.
18. Pregnancy	None.	Any inquiry into pregnancy, medical history of pregnancy or family plans.
19. Race or Color	None.	Applicant's race or color of applicant's skin.
20. References	Name/s of references.	Name of applicant's pastor or religious leader.
21. Relatives/ friends	Names of applicant's relatives, friends already employed by employer if employer has assignment policies, practices related to friends, relatives and/or an anti-nepotism policy. Employer may not give preference if women and minorities are underrepresented in its workforce.	Names of relatives, other than those working for the company, names of friends, relatives working for a competitor.
22. Sex	None, except where sex is a bona fide occupational qualification (BFOQ).	Any inquiry except where BFOQ.
23. Sexual Orientation/ Gender Identity	None, except for the narrow exceptions specified in the law.	Any inquiry except for the narrow exceptions specified in the law.
24. Workers' Compensation	None.	Past workers' compensation claims.

*Permission to use "Summary Guide to Application Pre-Employment Questions" excerpted from *Successful Interviewing Guide* granted by the Iowa Workforce Development, 1000 East Grand Avenue, Des Moines, Iowa 50319-0209, www.iowaworkforce.org and Iowa Civil Rights Commission, 400 East 14th Street, Des Moines, IA 50319-1004, www.state.ia.us/government/crc.

** These are questions considered inadvisable, and in some very limited instances, illegal on their face, by the U.S. Equal Employment Opportunity Commission and the Iowa Civil Rights Commission.

Appendix C

Appendix D

Avoiding Discrimination During the Hiring Process

Discrimination in hiring practices is prohibited in Iowa under several state and federal laws, as well as a Governor's executive order. A summary of the most important of these laws follows.

Discrimination on the basis of sex, race, color, religion, or national origin is prohibited by the Civil Rights Act of 1964, specifically Title VII of that Act which deals with employment. Discrimination on the basis of age is prohibited by the Age Discrimination in Employment Act of 1967 ("ADEA").

The Americans with Disabilities Act of 1990 ("ADA") requires all employers and private employers of 15 or more employees to ensure equal employment opportunities to persons with physical or mental disabilities who are qualified for the jobs they seek. Employers are required to make "reasonable accommodations" for disabled employees who are qualified to perform the essential functions of their jobs, unless such accommodations would impose an "undue hardship" on the operation of the employer's business.

The Federal Rehabilitation Act of 1973 requires government contractors and subcontractors to ensure equal employment opportunities to persons with physical or mental disabilities who are otherwise qualified for the jobs they seek. Employers are required to make "reasonable accommodations" for disabled employees who are qualified to perform the essential functions of their jobs, unless such an accommodation would impose an "undue hardship" on the operation of the employer's business.

The Iowa Civil Rights Act prohibits employment discrimination against any applicant or employee on the basis of age, race, creed, color, sex, national origin, religion, or disability. Iowa's commitment to equal employment also was established by Governor Robert Ray's Executive Order No. 15 (1973), which affirms the U.S. Civil Rights Act of 1964. The term "creed" has been interpreted by the Attorney General's office to mean "religion."

The Iowa Civil Rights Act is enforced by the Iowa Civil Rights Commission ("ICRC") and covers employers with four or more employees. Anti-discrimination cases may also be filed with a local human rights commission and/or the U.S. Equal Employment Opportunity Commission ("EEOC").

An employer seeking to hire an applicant, or make other employment decisions, should inquire about skills, education and past experiences *that relate to actual job performance.* Although Title VII and the Iowa Civil Rights Act do not expressly prohibit the use of any specific question in an interview or on a job application, they do prohibit the use of non-job-related information solicited for a discriminatory purpose. It can be very difficult for an employer who has included non-job related questions in an interview to prove the information generated by such questions was not part of a final hiring decision.

An employer should keep in mind that the goal is to find the best possible match between the requirements of the job and the experience, skills, education, and characteristics of the applicant. Application and interview questions should be related to that goal.

The EEOC and the ICRC have found the following questions to be discriminatory, or primarily aimed at collecting information to be used for discriminatory reasons, and thus should be avoided.

AGE, DATE OF BIRTH

The Age Discrimination in Employment Act ("ADEA") prohibits discrimination on the basis of age against individuals who are 40 years of age or more. However, the ADEA does not prohibit employers from favoring an older employee over a younger employee.

In Iowa, the prohibition of age discrimination is broader than that imposed by federal law. The Iowa Civil Rights Act prohibits discrimination on the basis of age against individuals who are age 18 and older, or otherwise considered by law to be adults.

Most people graduate from high school and college around specific ages, so this information can be used to approximate an applicant's age. Asking an applicant what years they attended high school, and/or what year they graduated from high school or college, does not directly violate the ADEA, but could be interpreted as a method of discriminating against the applicant based on age. Unless graduation dates are needed for a specific purpose, it is preferable to ask where the applicant went to school, how many years they attended, and what degree they obtained.

ARRESTS & CONVICTIONS (OTHER THAN TRAFFIC VIOLATIONS)

As you are aware, an arrest is no indication of guilt. Because members of some minority groups are arrested substantially more than whites in proportion to their numbers in the population, making employment decisions on the basis of arrest records involving no subsequent convictions has an adverse impact on the employment opportunities of those groups. Thus, such records alone cannot be used to routinely exclude persons from employment. Exclusion is justified only if it appears that the applicant or employee engaged in the conduct for which he was arrested and the conduct is job-related and relatively recent.

Similarly, an employer's policy or practice of excluding individuals from employment on the basis of their conviction records has an adverse impact on minority populations. The EEOC has found that an employer may exclude an individual from employment on the basis of a conviction record only if the employer's decision was "justified by business necessity." The relevant factors, the EEOC says, include:
(1) the nature and seriousness of the offense;
(2) the time that has passed since the conviction and/or completion of the sentence; and
(3) the nature of the job held or sought. Thus, a blanket exclusion based on conviction records can seldom be justified. Application forms that ask about conviction records should include a statement to the effect that whether a conviction will disqualify an applicant depends on the

nature of the offense, the nature of the job, and the length of time since the conviction and incarceration.

BACKGROUND AND REFERENCE CHECKS

Before making a conditional job offer, an employer may not ask previous employers, family members, or other sources, any questions about the job applicant that cannot be directly asked of the applicant. The employer may inquire about job-related issues, but should not make any inquiry related to age, sex, national origin, race, color, creed, religion, or physical or mental disability.

If an employer uses an outside firm to conduct background checks, the employer should make certain that this outside firm complies with all relevant discrimination laws. Such a firm is an agent of the employer, and the employer is responsible for the actions of its agent. The agent may not do anything through a contractual relationship that the employer may not do directly.

For example, the EEOC warns that an employer or its agent should not ask a previous employer or other sources about the following:

☐☐ How old is the candidate?
☐☐ Has the candidate ever filed a discrimination charge with any local, state or federal agency?
☐☐ Has the candidate ever filed a workers' compensation claim?
☐☐ Does the applicant have a disability or suffer from any illness?
☐☐ Any subject that the employer may not directly ask the applicant during the pre-offer stage.

A previous employer may be asked about:
☐☐ job functions and tasks performed by the applicant,
☐☐ the quality and quantity of work performed,
☐☐ how job functions were performed,
☐☐ overall attendance record, or
☐☐ other job-related issues that do not relate to disability.

If an applicant has a known disability and has indicated the ability to perform a job with a reasonable accommodation, a previous employer may be asked about accommodations made by that employer.

CHILDBIRTH AND PREGNANCY

The federal Title VII law prohibits discrimination based on pregnancy, childbirth, and related medical conditions. Therefore, employers should not ask questions regarding pregnancy or future child-bearing plans.

The Iowa Civil Rights Act requires that women affected by pregnancy or potentially affected by pregnancy and related medical conditions, must be treated the same as other job applicants and employees on the basis of their ability or inability to work. Accordingly, employers are prohibited under Iowa law from refusing to hire, or promote, or terminate the employment of a women because she is pregnant or has had an abortion, or medical conditions related to those conditions. The Iowa Civil Rights Act also specifically provides at Section 216.6(2.)(b) that an eligible employer must provide a leave of absence for a woman disabled by pregnancy, childbirth, or related medical conditions, for the time period the woman is disabled, or for eight weeks, whichever is less. The employee is required to provide timely notice of the need for leave. Before granting the leave, the employer may require medical verification of the need for the requested leave.

CHILD-CARE AND FAMILY RESPONSIBILITIES

Questions asking about number of children, how many children are under the age of 18, and child-care are often used to discriminate against women. The EEOC considers it a violation of Title VII to require preemployment information about child-care arrangements from female applicants only, and employers cannot have different hiring policies for men and women with pre-school age children. Information about dependents needed for tax, insurance, or Social Security purposes can be obtained after the applicant is hired.

CITIZENSHIP AND IMMIGRATION

The federal Title VII law extends coverage to both United States citizens and non-citizens with respect to employment within the United States. Although Title VII and the Iowa Civil Rights Act do not specifically prohibit discrimination on the basis of citizenship, questions about citizenship, or requirements that an applicant be a citizen of the United States, may violate the law where they have the purpose or effect of discriminating on the basis of national origin.

Imposing a citizenship requirement for the purpose of excluding people on the basis of national origin violates Title VII. Even if a citizenship requirement is not intentionally discriminatory, Title VII can be violated if the requirement disproportionately excludes persons of a particular national origin and the employer cannot establish that the requirement is job-related and consistent with business necessity. See the next two subsections for information on federal law prohibitions against employing undocumented workers and related non-discrimination provisions.

ELIGIBILITY TO WORK, PROOF OF IDENTITY

The federal Immigration Reform and Control Act of 1986, makes it a crime to knowingly hire an unlawful alien and requires all employers to verify the employment eligibility of all newly hired applicants before they are put to work. Asking an applicant if they are a citizen of the United States--which would make them eligible for employment within the U.S.--puts an employer at risk for national origin discrimination. The appropriate inquiry is, "Can you, after being hired, verify your legal right to work in the United States?" Another acceptable inquiry is, "Are you a U.S. citizen or otherwise eligible to work in the United States?" The answer of yes or no to that question does not divulge national origin information.

About the "I-9 Process"

The federal Immigration and Reform Act requires that before putting a new employee to work, the new employee must show proof of their identity and eligibility to work in the United States. This is often called the "I-9" process. Employers are required to maintain such I-9 compliance records.

Documenting identity and employment eligibility should not be difficult. An applicant who produces a valid driver's license and an original social security card has met these requirements. In addition, a passport, certificate of U.S. citizenship, or alien registration card, or unexpired foreign passport with employment authorization stamp may be sufficient to show both identity and eligibility to work. Another approach is to use two documents to show: (1) identity; and (2) employment eligibility. For example, a state-issued driver's license is sufficient under the federal immigration law to establish identity. A birth certificate or original social security card is sufficient to demonstrate employment eligibility. There are other documents that in tandem may satisfy the identity and employment eligibility requirements. A list of those documents can be obtained from the U.S. Citizenship and Immigration Services.

Use of Native Language

The EEOC, the ICRC, and the courts have interpreted Title VII and the Iowa Civil Rights Act as barring employment policies that require speaking English only on the job, unless the employer can show the English-only policy is job-related and consistent with business necessity, such as safety, communication with customers, co-workers, or supervisors.

DISABILITY AND HEALTH

Employers have a legitimate concern in hiring employees who are physically and mentally able to do their jobs. Many persons have been screened out from employment because of real or perceived physical or mental conditions which may not be related to their ability to perform the work.

Under the federal Americans With Disabilities Act ("ADA"), it is specifically unlawful to ask whether an applicant is disabled, or to inquire about the nature or severity of an illness or disability. The Iowa Civil Rights Act's prohibition on disability discrimination follows the federal ADA. These laws prohibit disability-related questions on application forms, during job interviews, or in background or reference checks. Employers may ask an applicant questions about the person's ability to perform the essential functions of the job. Employers may also ask an applicant to describe or demonstrate how, with or without reasonable accommodation, that the applicant can perform job-related functions.

An applicant or employee must be qualified for the job, that is, they must satisfy the job requirements for educational background, employment experience, skills, licenses, or other job-related qualification standards. The ADA and Iowa Civil Rights Act do not interfere with the employer's right to hire the best qualified applicant. Nor do these laws impose any affirmative action obligations. The law simply prohibits the employer from discriminating against a qualified applicant or employee because of a disability.

Under the ADA, a disability is defined as a physical or mental impairment that substantially limits a major life activity. The ADA also protects individuals who have a record of such impairment, or who are regarded as having such impairment. The Act makes it unlawful to discriminate against a qualified applicant or employee because of the disability of an individual with whom the applicant or employee is known to have a family, business, social or other

Appendix D

relationship or association.

An employer may not use a physical or mental condition to disqualify an applicant merely because the employer believes the applicant's condition would pose a health or safety threat. The employer must show that the condition poses a "significant risk of substantial harm." An assessment of the condition must be based on valid medical evidence.

For example, under the ADA, merely making the following types of inquiries during the interview/ pre-job-offer stage is unlawful:

- Do you have a disability or major illness?
- What is the nature or severity of your disability?
  (Or the nature and severity of any conditions or diseases for which an applicant has been treated.)
- Have you ever been hospitalized?
- Have you ever been treated for a mental illness?
- Questions about an applicant's past record of a disability, his record of drug/ alcohol addiction or the nature of related treatment.
  (Note: It would be unlawful to decide not to hire the applicant based only on the knowledge that the applicant had a record of disability, or had received related treatment for it.)

- Have you ever filed a worker's compensation claim or suffered a disabling injury in a previous job?
- Will you need time off for medical treatments or for other reasons associated with your disability?

During the interview/pre-offer state, an employer may ask an applicant the following:

- Whether they can perform the duties of the job, with or without accommodation. (This should be asked of all applicants.)
- If the applicant has the necessary ability and experience related to the specific duties and essential functions of the job?
- If the applicant has the necessary licenses, diplomas, training certificates, or other required qualifications?
- Ask the applicant to describe or demonstrate how he/she will perform the specific functions, if this is required of everyone, regardless of disability.

(Note: The EEOC advises that an employer may single out an applicant to ask for a description or demonstration of performance of specific functions if the applicant has a known disability that the employer reasonably believes could interfere with the performance of those job functions. If a demonstration is requested, the employer must be ready to provide a necessary accommodation to allow a person with a disability to perform the demonstration or reschedule the demonstration to allow the employer to provide the necessary accommodation.)

- If the applicant can meet the requirements of the employer's work hours, overtime

WORK, TRAVEL, AND ATTENDANCE POLICIES.

- Ask a previous employer about job functions and tasks performed by the applicant, the quality and quantity of the work performed the applicant's attendance record and other job-related questions that are not likely to disclose disability.

Reasonable and Necessary Accommodations During the Hiring Process

The ADA requires that reasonable accommodations be made for applicants with disabilities during every step of the hiring process. (Note: This section only deals with the hiring process and not potential issues of accommodation during the actual employment process.)

The ADA requires that people whose disabilities impair sensory, speaking or manual skills be given tests in a format that does not require use of the impaired skills, unless the test is designed to measure that skill. Some examples of accommodation include:

- Substituting a written test for an oral test (or written instructions for oral instructions) for people with disabilities that impair speaking or hearing;

- Giving the test in large print, in Braille, by a reader, or on a computer for people with visual or other reading disabilities;

- Providing the services of a sign language interpreter during the interview or testing procedures for applicants with impaired hearing.

Medical Examinations

Under the ADA it is unlawful for the employer to require an applicant to take a medical examination before making a job offer. After a job offer is made and prior to the commencement of employment duties, an applicant may be required to take a medical examination if everyone who will be working in the job category must also take the examination. The job offer may be made conditional on the results of the medical examination. However, if an individual is not hired because a medical examination reveals the existence of a disability, the employer must be able to show that the reasons for exclusion are job-related and necessary for the conduct of business. Also, the employer must be able to show that there was no reasonable accommodation that would have made it possible for the individual to perform the essential job functions.

While a person is employed, an employer cannot require that an employee undergo a medical examination or inquiry unless it is job-related and consistent with business necessity. The employer's evidence of job-related problems should be objective. When an employee is injured on or off the job, becomes ill, or otherwise disabled, a medical examination may be necessary to determine if the person can continue to perform the essential functions of the job, with or without a reasonable accommodation. The examination may also be necessary to determine the need for or extent of reasonable accommodation.

Employers may conduct periodic examinations and other medical screening and monitoring required by federal, state or local laws. Employers may also conduct **voluntary** medical examinations and screening as part of an employee health and wellness program.

Information obtained from an employee medical examination or inquiry may not be used to discriminate against the employee. All information obtained from employee medical examinations and inquiries must be maintained in secured files separate from personnel files, and must be used in accordance with ADA confidentiality requirements.

ALCOHOL AND DRUG ABUSE

In dealing with alcohol and drug abuse, a distinction needs to be made between a past history of, and recovery from such abuse, and current abuse of alcohol or drugs. Under state and federal law, recovery from alcoholism or drug addiction is considered a covered disability by virtue of "having a history" of an impairment. An applicant should not be rejected from employment solely because of a history of and recovery from drug or alcohol abuse. The Iowa Administrative Code Section 161-8.27(1)(b) allows an employer to reject an applicant whose current disability, such as alcoholism, would create a danger to the life or health of co-employees.

Under the ADA, an individual who is currently engaging in illegal use of drugs is not an "individual with a disability," and is specifically excluded from coverage under this law. However, someone who currently abuses alcohol is not excluded from coverage under the ADA, and may need accommodation in undergoing treatment should the employee voluntarily undertake treatment. This does not mean, however, that an employer has to tolerate an employee under the influence of alcohol on the job site. Lastly, a person seeking treatment for alcoholism may have leave rights under the Family and Medical Leave Act ("FMLA").

An alcohol test is considered a medical examination under the ADA. Therefore, if an employer has a policy of pre-employment testing for alcohol use, an applicant can be tested for alcohol only after a conditional offer of employment has been made. Because the illegal use of drugs in not protected by the ADA, an employer can test an applicant for illegal drugs at any time in the screening and hiring process.

Iowa law, Section 730.5, allows private sector drug and alcohol testing of prospective and current employees in a limited number of circumstances, and with a carefully worded testing policy. (See pg. 15 & 16 for details.)
The federal Drug-Free Workplace Act of 1988 requires that employers having federal contracts of $25,000 or more or receiving federal grants, establish a drug use policy and maintain drug-free awareness programs. That figure was recently changed to $100,000 for all contracts entered into on, or after December 1, 2003.

AIDS

AIDS (Acquired Immune Deficiency Syndrome), ARC (AIDS-related Complex), and testing positive for HIV (Human Immunodeficiency Virus) have become matters of concern for employers because of fear about the communicability of AIDS. Present research shows there is no transmittal of disease through casual contact, and that where there is a slight risk of infection through contact with body fluids, precautions can be taken to reduce that risk.

Persons with AIDS and HIV disease are protected from discrimination under the Americans with Disabilities Act of 1990. The Rehabilitation Act of 1973, as amended, Section 503, prohibits federal government contractors and subcontractors from discrimination against qualified disabled applicants and employees. Several recent court rulings have determined that AIDS is considered to be a disability covered under federal law. Iowa Code Section 216.2(5) states that a positive HIV test result, a diagnosis of AIDS, AIDS-related Complex or other conditions related to AIDS, is considered to be a disability.

Iowa Code Section 216.6(1.)(d.), prohibits requiring as a condition of employment that any employee or prospective employee take a test for the presence of the antibody to HIV, or to use the test or results of such a test to affect the terms, conditions or privileges of employment or to terminate an employee solely as a result of the test.

DRESS AND APPEARANCE

An employer may have a legitimate business interest in having employees present the company's desired image and appearance to its customers and public. Courts have ruled that reasonable dress and appearance codes are a proper exercise of management authority, so long as the standards are directly related to the requirements of the position, and do not have an adverse impact on any protected class, such as sex, race, or religion. Employers should be aware that an appearance requirement based on offensive or demeaning sex stereotypes may be a Title VII or Iowa Civil Rights Act violation.

In addition, if an employer has a dress or grooming policy that conflicts with the practices or beliefs of an employee's religion, the employee may ask for an exception to the policy as a reasonable accommodation. For example, religious grooming practices may relate to shaving or hair length. Religious dress may include clothes, head or face coverings, jewelry, or other items. Absent undue hardship, an employer must accommodate the employee's religious dress or grooming practices.

FIDELITY BONDS

Asking if an applicant has ever been denied a fidelity bond presumably represents an indirect effort to find flaws which may exist in an individual's past. A fidelity bond may have been denied for totally arbitrary and discriminatory reasons and the individual did not have an adequate opportunity to know of, or challenge the action. The regulatory agencies recommend that this method of ascertaining an individual's past financial history, if related to the job requirements, be dropped in favor of some other method.

FINANCIAL STATUS: HOME, CAR OWNERSHIP, CREDIT RECORD

Rejection of applicants because of poor credit ratings can have a disparate impact on minority groups. If so, asking for credit information is unlawful unless a business necessity can be shown. Such inquiries also might have a disparate impact on women because many women do not have a credit history separate from their husband's credit history.

Inquiries about an applicant's financial status, such as bankruptcy, car ownership, rental or ownership of a house, length of residence at an address, if used to make employment decisions, may also violate Title VII. For example, asking how an employee is going to get to work could solicit information about car ownership. The more appropriate inquiry is whether the applicant will be able to get to work at the scheduled time.

FRIENDS OR RELATIVES WORKING FOR US?

Asking an applicant for the names of the applicant's friends or relatives already employed by the employer is acceptable if the employer has a policy or practice about work assignments of employees who are related or friends, and/or an anti-nepotism policy. Be aware, however, that Title VII may be violated if the employer' work force consists primarily of one race or ethnic group and the employer hires only friends and relatives of employees.

GARNISHMENTS

Iowa law, specifically Section 642.21(2)(c), prohibits an employer from discharging an employee because the employee's wages are being garnished. In addition, federal courts have ruled that discharging an employee because of a wage garnishment(s) violates Title VII because minorities incur wage garnishments more often than non-minorities, and wage garnishments do not affect an employee's ability to perform his/her job.

HEIGHT AND WEIGHT

Minimum height and weight requirements are considered unlawful if they screen out a disproportionate number of minority group individuals (e.g., Hispanics or Asian Americans) or women, and the employer cannot show that these standards are job-related and consistent with business necessity.

MARITAL STATUS

Because the question, "what is your maiden name" generally applies only to women, and it is not relevant to a person's ability to perform a job, the EEOC and ICRC warn that responses to it could be used for discriminatory purposes. If an employer needs the information for purposes of a pre-employment background investigation, a permissible alternative is to inquire as to all the names used by an applicant. Information about marital status needed for tax, insurance, or social security purposes may be obtained after making the offer of employment to the applicant.

Similarly, questions as to whether an applicant is married, single, separated or divorced should be eliminated because they are not job-related.

An employer also would violate Title VII if it refused to hire a married woman or pay her the same as a married man for the same work. In addition, an employer cannot refuse to hire a married woman because of the employer's beliefs concerning morality or family responsibility.

Finally, asking an applicant if they prefer to be known as Ms., Miss, or Mrs. is considered another way of inappropriately asking the applicant's sex or marital status.

MILITARY SERVICE

Discharge Status

An employment policy which arbitrarily eliminates candidates who have less than an honorable military discharge may violate Title VII and Iowa law because it could have an unfair impact on minority applicants. There is evidence that proportionately more minority males than white males are given dishonorable discharges from military service.

Veteran's Preference:

Federal and state laws forbid discriminating against veterans in employment decisions. In addition, Iowa Code Section 35C.1. states that veterans are entitled to preference over other applicants of "no greater qualifications" with regard to all state, city, county, and public school positions. Iowa Code at Section 400.10 also calls for special scoring for veterans with regard to civil service grading. Lastly, federal law requires that recipients of federal contracts in excess of $100,000 take affirmative steps to employ qualified covered veterans.

RELIGION - SATURDAY AND SUNDAY WORK

Although it is perfectly reasonable to ask if an applicant can work on weekends if there is a need, government regulators advise the question may discourage applicants of certain religions which prohibit working on Friday nights, Saturdays, or Sundays. If there is a business necessity for asking this question, an employer should explain the regular work schedule in terms of days (including weekends), shifts, and hours, and ask to the effect, "Is there anything that would prevent you from meeting this work schedule?" The employer should make it clear that it will make a reasonable effort to accommodate the employee's religious practices without undue hardship on the employer's business.

SALARY

(LOWEST ACCEPTABLE)

Questions such as "what is the lowest salary you will accept," or "how much salary do you need," or "how much money does your husband make," are not permissible. The EEOC reasons that women generally have been relegated to lower-paying jobs than men, and paid less for the same work. As a result, a woman might be willing to work for less pay than a man in the same job would find acceptable. Pursuant to the Equal Pay Act, men and women performing substantially the same job must be paid equal wages. If the employer's objective is to find out an applicant's desired salary, the employer should ask all applicants about their salary expectations.

SEX

Title VII and the Iowa Civil Rights Act prohibit discrimination in employment on the basis of sex except in the few instances in which sex may be a "bona fide occupational qualification ("BFOQ") reasonably necessary to the normal operation" of the employer's business. There are virtually no jobs which can be performed by only one sex or the other. For this reason, any question asking the applicant's sex should be omitted from an application form.

SEXUAL ORIENTATION/GENDER IDENTITY

The Iowa Civil Rights Act was amended July 1, 2007 to prohibit discrimination on the basis of sexual orientation and gender identity. Several municipalities in Iowa also consider sexual orientation a protected classification. The federal Title VII law does not include sexual orientation as a protected classification. Title VII and the Iowa Civil Rights Act also prohibit harassment on the basis of sex, which has been interpreted by the courts to prohibit "same sex" harassment.

SPOUSE'S NAME & SPOUSE'S WORK

To the extent this question asks for marital

status, the comments made above about marital status apply, and questions about a spouse's name and work should not be asked. A spouse's name also can be used as an indication of religion or national origin. If there is a need for a spouse's name or contact telephone number for a spouse in case of an emergency, such information can be collected after an applicant is hired.

TESTING
Pre-Employment

The purpose of any pre-employment testing procedure is to help the employer accurately select employees on the basis of their ability to do the job. Testing procedures are more than just paper and pencil tests; other examples include performance testing, training programs, educational or work experience requirements, and probationary periods. The test must be job-related and consistent with business necessity.

Under the Americans with Disabilities Act (ADA), employers must also make it possible for a person with a disability to participate in the application process. For example, if an applicant is blind, the employer must provide assistance with the written application and any required written test. The personnel office and testing site should be accessible to persons with disabilities, or alternate arrangements must be available.

The state and federal regulations on test validation and selection procedures are highly technical. But in general, an employer should not use any testing or selection procedure that has an adverse impact on members of a racial, ethnic, age, sex group, or people with disabilities. At a minimum, an employer should review job requirements to be sure that they are job-related and appropriate for the job classification.

A uniform, scored interview process will also assist the employer in keeping selection decisions as objective as possible. Keeping records of applicant flow and selection rates for each job category will enable the employer to determine if any adverse impact is occurring.

For technical assistance in test validation, an employer can contact state or federal civil rights agencies or a professional testing consultant.

Lie Detector (Polygraph)

Iowa Code Section 730.4 prohibits employers from requiring job applicants or employees to take a polygraph or lie detector test, including a voice stress analyzer, as a condition of initial or continued employment. This law does not apply to peace officers and correctional officers.

The Federal Employee Polygraph Protection Act prohibits most private employers from requiring or suggesting that a job applicant or employee take a lie detector or polygraph test. The law does allow some very limited private employer exceptions. The law does not apply to the United States government, or any state, local, or political subdivision employer.

Drugs and Alcohol Testing

Recent changes were made in Iowa's law on drug and alcohol testing in the workplace that expand an employer's role in testing applicants and employees for drug or alcohol abuse.

The law, found at Iowa Code Section 730.5, applies only to private sector employees. The state and its political subdivisions, as well as Native American tribes and the federal government, are excluded from the definition of "employer." The Act also provides that its requirements do not apply to drug or alcohol tests of employees required to be tested by federal law.

In order to engage in drug or alcohol testing, an employer must have a written policy, available to employees and prospective employees, governing drug or alcohol testing. The policy must also spell out the uniform disciplinary or rehabilitative actions an employer will take following a positive test.

An employer also must establish a drug and alcohol awareness program in the workplace before conducting testing. Employees must receive notice of the benefits and services available under an employee assistance program, or information on community services concerning alcohol and drug abuse.

The law permits testing of job applicants. It also permits unannounced drug or alcohol testing of employees selected from the entire employee population, or who work at a particular work site, or from all employees working in a safety-sensitive position. Testing also is permitted based on reasonable suspicion of being under the influence, or to investigate an accident at work. Confidentiality of test results is required, except for use of the results as allowed by the Iowa testing law.

The Iowa testing law provides that an employer shall not be liable for actions taken in good faith based on a positive drug or alcohol test. It also establishes that a test conducted in accordance with the Act is presumed valid, and that an employer is not liable for monetary damages if the employer's reliance on a false positive test was reasonable and in good faith.

An employer interested in drug or alcohol testing should obtain a copy of the Iowa statute and consult with legal counsel before starting such a program.

---

*Permission to use "Avoiding Discrimination During the Hiring Process" excerpted from *Successful Interviewing Guide* granted by the Iowa Workforce Development, 1000 East Grand Avenue, Des Moines, Iowa 50319-0209, www.iowaworkforce.org and Iowa Civil Rights Commission, 400 East 14th Street, Des Moines, IA 50319-1004, www.state.ia.us/government/crc.

Appendix E

Selected Online-Resources for Human Resource Management Topics and Issues

Any attempt to be exhaustive in listing the thousands of websites that are available in the area of public personnel management would be inadequate. The following websites represent a highly select number that the authors have found useful in their own research and consulting and ones that have been recommended by practicing personnel specialists. The websites which follow are listed by area of interest, accompanied by a brief description of each websites' salient feature(s). They are provided in an attempt to get managers to go online. Our experience instructs us that the more we use these sites in preparing for class and conducting research, the more they get incorporated into our everyday world of management. The websites referenced here are listed in the following order:

1. Performance Appraisal and Work Quality
2. Pay/Compensation/Benefits/Merit Systems
3. Recruitment
4. Unions
5. Collective Bargaining/Labor Relations
6. Equal Employment
7. Affirmative Action
8. Federal Personnel Systems
9. Gender Issues
10. General Personnel Issues
11. Legal Aspects (EEOC and Anti-Discrimination)
12. Disabilities
13. State, Regional, County, and Municipal Organizations
14. Productivity
15. Reinvention, Re-engineering of Government
16. Jobs and Careers
17. Comprehensive Access for Government
18. Budgeting and Finance
19. Ethics
20. Miscellaneous

1. Performance Appraisals and Work Quality

http://www.mapnp.org/library/perf_mng/perf_mng.htm: This website specifically addresses performance management and includes activities to ensure that organizational goals are consistently met in an effective and efficient manner. Performance management also focuses on performance of the organization, a department, or process to build a product or service, and employees. This website provides some of the overall activities involved in performance management. Your understanding of performance appraisals can be enhanced by reviewing closely related library topics referenced on this website.

http://performance-appraisal.8m.com/index.htm: This site is dedicated to educating managers, supervisors, human resource professionals and staff so they can maximize the value they gain from performance management and performance appraisal.

www.aqp.org: Association for Quality and Participation AQP) is an international, non-profit association that provides research and commentary on how to improve the quality of the workplace through different types of participatory management in hospitals to factories.

http://www.workteams.unt.edu/: The Center for the Study of Work Teams is based at the University of North Texas and was created for the purpose of education and research in all areas of collaborative work systems. The center was officially incorporated as a nonprofit organization in 1992, although the first conference took place in 1990.

http://www.peoplemanagement.co.uk/Index.html: People management from the United Kingdom.

http://www.pmn.net/: The Performance Management Network Inc. is an incorporated Canadian company focusing on management consulting, education, and the exchange of ideas in all areas of performance improvement, including resource management, organizational design/development, and outcomes management.

http://www.ispi.org/: Founded in 1962, the International Society for Performance Improvement (ISPI) is the leading international association dedicated to improving productivity and performance in the workplace.

http://www.siop.org/: The Society for Industrial and Organizational Psychology is the premier membership organization for those practicing and teaching industrial and organizational psychology.

http://www.essential.org/: Founded by Ralph Nader in 1982, Essential Information encourages citizens to become active and engaged in their communities and provides information to the public on topics neglected by the mass media and policy makers.

http://www.iaqc.org: The International Academy for Quality Certification endeavors to enable organizations and people to obtain high standard, internationally recognized levels of certification for quality and people development programs.

http://www.dol.gov/_sec/media/reports/dunlop/dunlop.htm: Department of Labor site with information related to workplace productivity and practices related to union-employer collective bargaining.

http://managementhelp.org/perf_mng/perf_mng.htm: Provides resources about performance management's overall goal and basic steps; brief overview of key terms generic to performance management; performance plan; performance appraisal; development plans; benefits and concerns of performance management; performance management during rapid change; guidelines, myths and examples of performance measurement; and general resources.

http://www.opm.gov/perform/plan.asp: Provides links about U.S. Office of Personnel Management's staff recommendations, policy documents, resources, newsletter articles, performance plans, goal setting, linking to organizational goals and book reviews that is related to performance management.

http://www.govbenefits.gov: Provides easy online access to government assistance programs and benefits.

http://www.gao.gov The U.S. Government Accountability Office (GAO) is the "congressional watchdog" for Congress. As such it assesses the performance of federal programs and agencies and researches requests from members of Congress. There is no item too small or too large for the GAO to research.

http://www.ipma-hr.org: IPMA-HR is an organization that represents human resource professionals at the federal, state and local levels of government by providing information to improve their job performance.

2. Pay/Compensation/Benefits/Merit Systems

http://management.about.com/smallbusiness/management/library/weekly/aa041498.htm?pid=2737&cob=home: This site is listed as an article; however, it has several links to other compensation and benefit sites that managers will find useful.

http://www.worldatwork.org/worldatwork.html: A professional association with information about compensation, benefits, and total rewards.

http://www.benefitslink.com/topics.shtml: BenefitsLink.com is the King Kong of benefits listing and references.

www.compensationlink.com: Compensation Link is the global on-line service that unites principal compensation Internet based resources from the United States, Canada, Europe, Asia, and Latin America with compensation and human resource professionals around the world.

www.benefitnews.com: Benefitnews.com, the Internet's most comprehensive resource for benefits professionals, is now a free, members-only site, but registration is required.

http://www.opm.gov/lmr/html/flexible.htm: U.S. Office of Personnel and Management - The Federal Employees Flexible and Compressed Work Schedules Act of 1982, codified at 5 U.S.C. § 6120 et seq. (the F&CWS law), authorizes a versatile and innovative work-scheduling program for use in the federal government. In recent years, the importance of flexible and compressed work schedules has been enhanced by the emergence of work and family issues.

http://www.usda.gov/da/employ/ffwg.htm: The Department of Agriculture's "Family Friendly Guide" provides many examples of a federal agency addressing family friendly issues, such as flextime, child care, elder care, domestic violence, adoption, fatherhood support, domestic partners, and nursing mothers.

Appendix E

http://www.opm.gov/oca/leave/index.htm: U.S. Office of Personnel and Management provides the law, regulations, and forms for such family-friendly leave polices as FMLA, organ donor leave, and sick leave to care for a family member.

http://www.snc.edu/socsci/chair/336/group1.htm: If you are interested in career development, salary compression, and pay for performance and other incentive systems, this site will be particularly interesting.

http://www.aflcio.org/corporateamerica/paywatch/: Those who are interesting in monitoring the bonuses and compensation for CEO's will find that the American Federation of Labor/Congress of Industrial Organization (AFL/CIO) keeps a watchful eye on executive perks and other forms of compensation.

http://www.mspb.gov/: The U.S. Merit Systems Protections Board serves as guardian of the federal government's merit-based system of employment, principally by hearing and deciding appeals from federal employees of removals and other major personnel actions.

http://www.osc.gov/: The U.S. Office of Special Counsel's (OSC) primary mission is to safeguard the merit systems by protecting federal employees and applicants from prohibited personnel practices, especially reprisal for whistle blowing.

http://www.opm.gov/studies/: The U.S. Office of Personnel Management-Special Studies on the Federal Civil Service studies human resource management issues and policies that have a critical effect on the federal civil service.

http://www.opm.gov/feddata/factbook/index.htm: *The Fact Book: Federal Workforce Statistics*, from the Office of Personnel Management, contains statistics on employee demographics; compensation, payroll, and work years; performance management and the Senior Executive Service (SES); retirement and insurance programs; and student employment programs.

http://www.opm.gov/ovrsight/index.htm: The U.S. Office of Personnel Management Office of Merit Systems Oversight and Protection's mission is to ensure that personnel practices are carried out in accordance with Merit Systems principles.

3. Recruitment

http://www.erexchange.com/: A great site for articles on selection, retention, training, interviewing and screening, metrics, employment law, and general employee referral programs. It also has information on college recruiting, Internet recruiting, and orientation and assimilation. Click on "Jobs" and the senior executive recruiter, manager recruiter, technical recruiter and recruiter consultant world unfolds before your eyes.

www.hr-guide.com: This is a huge website for human resources information and Internet guidance within the comprehensive field of human resources management. If you can't find it here, you aren't looking!

Appendix E

http://www.best-in-class.com/: This website is for Best Practices, LLC. It has a link for information regarding human resources. Best Practices, LLC is a recognized leader in the field of human resources benchmarking and process improvement.

http://www.interbiznet.com/eeri/index.html: Internet recruiting sites.

www.shrm.org: The Society for Human Resource Management website is a must for any serious student or professional in the field of personnel management.

http://www.hr.com: "HR.com is a free website that is in business to help build great companies by connecting them to the knowledge and resources they need to effectively manage the people side of business. As the largest social network and online community of HR executives, we provide thousands of worldwide members with easy access to shared knowledge on best practices, trends and industry news in order to help them develop their most important asset – their people" (www.hr.com).

http://www.bls.gov/oco/ocos021.htm: This link is listed as an article in Bureau of Labor Statistics' (Occupational Outlook Handbook, 2008-09 Edition) website. However, it provides good information about human resources, training, labor relations, other qualifications and advancement; employment; job outlook; projections data; earnings; OES (Occupational Employment Statistics) data; related occupations; and sources of additional information.

4. Unions

http://www.unions.org: "Unions.org manages a database of union organizations across the United States. Unions.org serves as an advertising platform for unions, with its proprietary Internet marketing software. Our members find us through a combination of online and print advertising, as well as word of mouth from local union chambers."

http://www.union-organizing.com: "Resources for Labor Union Organizing is designed to provide help to U.S. workers in their efforts at organizing themselves and their co-workers into labor unions. It is also a resource for union leaders to assist in their operations, organizing, and bargaining efforts."

www.aflcio.org: The official website for the American Federation of Labor-Congress of Industrial Organizations (AFL-CIO).

http://www.nlrb.gov/: The National Labor Relations Board is an independent federal agency created by Congress to administer the National Labor Relations Act, the primary law governing relations between unions and employers in the private sector.

http://www.afge.org: The American Federation of Government Employees (AFGE).

Appendix E

5. Collective Bargaining/Labor Relations

http://homepages.uhwo.hawaii.edu/clear/CB-FAQ.html://www.opm.gov/cplmr/html/labrmgmt.html-ssi: The U.S. Office of Personnel Management -Labor-Management Relations Guidance Bulletin.

http://www.law.cornell.edu/topics/collective_bargaining.html: A legal discussion about collective bargaining and labor arbitration.

http://www.fmcs.gov/: The Federal Mediation and Conciliation Service (FMCS) was created by Congress in 1947 as an independent agency to promote sound and stable labor-management relations. FMCS offers services in dispute mediation, preventative mediation, alternative dispute mediation, arbitration services, and labor-management grants.

http://www.dol.gov/esa/olms/regs/compliance/cba/index.htm: Provides U.S. Department of Labor's Office of Labor-Management Standards' (OLMS) online listings of private and public sector collective bargaining agreements.

http://www.nlrb.gov/: The U.S. National Labor Relations Board (NLRB) is an independent federal agency created in 1935 to enforce the National Labor Relations Act. NLRB conducts secret-ballot elections to determine whether employees want union representation and investigates and remedies unfair labor practices by employers and unions.

6. Equal Employment

www.eeoc.gov: The official website for the U.S. Equal Employment Opportunity Commission (EEOC).

http://disabilities.about.com/health/disabilities/library/weekly/aa092500a.htm: This link is a thorough site to articles with resources such as court cases and other material that would be useful in courses that discuss current issues of personnel management.

http://classiclit.about.com/cs/gendertheory/index.htm: A listing of related human resource material.

http://www.dol.gov/dol/topic/discrimination: Department of Labor's website about its two agencies that deal with Equal Employment Opportunity (EEO) monitoring and enforcement.

http://www.gsa.gov/Portal/gsa/ep/contentView.do?contentType=GSA_BASIC&contentId=11939: U.S. General Services Administration's link to its Office of Civil Rights. The website also provides several resources/links about equal employment opportunity.

http://www.ada.gov: U.S. Department of Justice's Americans with Disabilities Act homepage.

http://www.eeac.org: Equal Employment Advisory Council is "the nation's only employer association dedicated exclusively to the advancement of practical and effective equal employment opportunity and affirmative action compliance programs to eliminate workplace discrimination."

Appendix E

http://www.seattle.gov/civilrights/: The city of Seattle, WA, has had a program in place since 2004 to end institutional racism and promote citizen participation and multiculturalism. The Seattle Race and Social Justice Initiative (RSJI) recently issued a report on the steps it has taken to counter racism and systemic disparities in Seattle government in areas such as economic fairness, health, education and environmental justice. Also included are insightful ideas directed toward ending systemic racism by confronting it in Seattle's workforce and communities, budget, policy analysis and public engagement policies and practices.

7. Affirmative Action

http://www.washingtonpost.com/wp-srv/politics/special/affirm/affirm.htm: An Affirmative Action website that lists key stories, editorials, and stories from the *Washington Post*.

http://aad.english.ucsb.edu/: This site presents diverse opinions regarding Affirmative Action topics. Rather than taking a singular pro or con position, it is designed to help lend many different voices to the debates surrounding the issues of Affirmative Action. This site is an academic resource and it provides scholars, students, and the interested public with on-site articles and theoretical analyses, policy documents, current legislative updates, and an annotated bibliography of research and teaching materials.

http://www.now.org/issues/affirm/: A National Organization of Women and Affirmative Action website.

http://www.affirmativeaction.org/: The American Association for Affirmative Action is the association of professionals managing Affirmative Action, equal opportunity, diversity and other human resource programs.

http://www.naacp.org/: The National Association for the Advancement of Colored People (NAACP) is the nation's largest and strongest civil rights organization.

http://www.now.org/issues/affirm: National Organization for Women's archives and latest news articles that deal with affirmative action.

http://www.infoplease.com/spot/affirmativetimeline1.html: *Columbia Encyclopedia* presents major milestones in the history of Affirmative Action.

http://www.dol.gov/dol/topic/hiring/affirmativeact.htm: Department of Labor provides several links about Affirmative Action.

http://www.feminist.org: The Feminist Career Center provides information related to Affirmative Action and other topics related to gender based employment disparities and inequalities.

http://www.apa.org/ppo/aa.html: American Psychological Association website on Affirmative Action issues.

Appendix E

8. Federal Personnel Systems

http://www.fedguide.com/: The Federal Personnel Guide home page.

http://www.opm.gov/fedclass/fwsintro.pdf: Introduction to the Federal Wage System Job Grading System.

http://www.ustreas.gov/jobs/ses.html: The U.S. Senior Executive Service website.

http://www.usajobs.opm.gov/a.htm: Current job listings for the federal government.

http://www.opm.gov/oca/payrates/: U.S. Office of Personnel Management website on salaries and pay rates.

http://www.fpmi.com/: FPMI Communications offers consulting and technical assistance services to federal agencies in all aspects of human resources, management and EEO. They can assist your agency by providing experienced professionals to perform specific tasks in virtually any human resources field from labor relations to position classification.

http://www.whitehouse.gov/WH/Services: The official White House website.

http://www.library.vanderbilt.edu/central/staff/fdtf.html: The Government Documents Round Table is a large, multiple listing of federal government websites.

http://www.usa.gov/: This is a large web portal for the U.S. federal government and should be one of the first stops on your way to accessing what is available in cyberspace.

http://www.doleta.gov/: U.S. Department of Labor Employment and Training Administration.

http://www.ipma-hr.org/: The International Public Management Association for Human Resources (HR) is an organization that represents the interests of human resource professionals at the federal, state and local levels of government. Its goal is to provide information and assistance to help HR professionals increase their job performance and overall agency function by providing cost effective products, services and educational opportunities.

http://www.mspb.gov/: The U.S. Merit Systems Protection Board (MSPB) protects the integrity of the federal merit systems and the rights of federal employees working in the systems.

http://www.osc.gov/: U.S. Office of Special Counsel's (OSC) primary mission is to safeguard the merit systems by protecting federal employees and applicants from prohibited personnel practices, especially reprisal for whistle blowing.

http://www.opm.gov/studies/: The U.S. Office of Personnel Management-Special Studies on the Federal Civil Service provides studies on human resource management issues and policies that have a critical effect on the federal civil service. These studies are prompted by analyses of personnel trends, the findings from oversight reviews of agencies, and by such stakeholders as Congress and other interested parties.

http://www.opm.gov/feddata/factbook/index.htm: "The Fact Book: Federal Workforce Statistics" from the Office of Personnel Management, contains statistics on employee demographics; compensation, payroll, and work years; performance management and the Senior Executive Service (SES); retirement and insurance programs; and student employment programs.

http://www.opm.gov/ovrsight/index.htm: The U.S. Office of Personnel Management Office of Merit Systems Oversight and Effectiveness' mission is to ensure that personnel practices are carried out in accordance with merit systems principles.

http://www.opm.gov/ses/: Office of Personnel Management: Senior Executive Service.

http://publicservice.monster.com/articles/classification/: This website contains information about the federal job classification system including example job ads.

9. Gender Issues

http://www.diversityinc.com/: DiversityInc's mission is to bring education and clarity to the business benefits of diversity.

www.now.org: National Organization for Women is a good resource for all women in the workplace issues.

http://www.transitionsinc.com: Transitions into Parenting Incorporated covers lactation issues that assist in making the workplace more employee-friendly.

http://www.storknet.org/: StorkNet is a good place to look for topics related to pregnancy issues.

http://www.uakron.edu/lawrev/robert1.html: Sexual Harassment in The Workplace: A Primer.

http://www.nolo.com: Nolo provides a plethora of material on topics as diverse as sexual harassment, health and safety, fair pay and time off, discrimination.

www.workingmother.com: *Working Mother* magazine website.

www.shrm.org: The Society for Human Resource Management website has everything you need to know about human resources.

http://www.aflcio.org/issues/jobseconomy/women/equalpay/: The American Federation of Labor and Congress of Industrial Organizations' webpage on equal work for equal pay. You can find out what the lack of equal pay costs you each year and for your career.

Appendix E

http://www.advancingwomen.com/: Advancing Women's website is devoted to women and the many issues they face in the workplace.

http://www.lwv.org/: The League of Women Voters, a nonpartisan political organization, encourages the informed and active participation of citizens in government, works to increase understanding of major public policy issues, and influences public policy through education and advocacy.

http://www.nclrights.org/site/PageServer: National Center for Lesbian Rights (NCLR) "is a national legal resource center with a primary commitment to advancing the rights and safety of lesbians and their families through a program of litigation, public policy advocacy, free legal advice and counseling, and public education. In addition, NCLR provides representation and resources to gay men and bisexual and transgender individuals on key issues that also significantly advance lesbian rights." (OU library)

http://muse.jhu.edu.ezproxy.lib.ou.edu/journals/nashim: An e-journal that was "co-founded in 1998 by the Hadassah-Brandeis Institute at Brandeis University and the Schechter Institute of Jewish Studies in Jerusalem, *Nashim: A Journal of Jewish Women's Studies & Gender Issues* provides an international, interdisciplinary academic forum the only one of its kind for the innovative work being done in the many areas of research that comprise the field of Jewish women's and gender studies. It regularly includes articles on literature, text studies, anthropology, theology, contemporary thought, sociology, the arts, and more.

10. General Personnel Issues

http://www.mapnp.org/library/topics.htm -This site has it all. Everything you could possibly imagine in relation to human resource management and administration. It has superb links to advertising and promotion, benefits and compensation, career development, communication, crisis management, customer service and satisfaction e-commerce, creativity and innovation, evaluations, employee performance management, ethics, financial management, group performance management, interviewing, legal information, leadership development, organizational change, training and development, staffing, and social entrepreneurship, and quality management.

http://www.aspanet.org/: With a diverse membership composed of more than 10,000 practitioners, scholars, teachers and students, ASPA is the largest and most prominent professional association in the field of public administration. As students in public administration, this site will be accessed frequently. It also provides many excellent links to governmental agencies and other professional associations.

http://www.napawash.org: The National Academy of Public Administration is an independent, nonpartisan organization chartered by Congress to assist federal, state, and local governments in improving their effectiveness, efficiency, and accountability.

http://www.dot.gov/ost/dapc/: U.S. Department of Transportation Office of Drug and Alcohol Policy and Compliance's mission is to provide expert advice to industry representatives regarding implementation of the controlled substances and alcohol testing rules. And where possible, they have attempted to simplify and standardize testing operations across the United States.

Appendix E

http://www.kepner-tregoe.com/: Kepner-Tregoe, a worldwide management consulting firm, helps integrate an organization's knowledge base and critical thinking skills with its strategy, its structure and systems, and the processes by which goals are accomplished.

http://www.public-policy.org/: National Center for Policy Analysis

www.ipma-hr.org: International Personnel Management Association

www.shrm.org: Society for Human Resource Management home page.

http://www.workforce.com/: This website is for business leaders in human resources. It includes a variety of practical HRM information that is useful to the personnel administrator on a day-to-day basis.

http://www.hrlive.com/: A monthly digest of news, views, tips, and trends.

http://www.hrworld.com/: A quarterly magazine on using informational technology effectively in human resources.

http://www.fpmi.com/: This U.S. site has a listing of HR publications, a daily government news feature, and two HR lists on general personnel and training for government agencies.

http://www.bcsolutionsmag.com/: U.S. magazine with featured articles on human resources management.

http://www.humanresourcesinfo.com/: A Canadian newsletter focusing on the issues of compensation, productivity, restructuring, performances management, and managing change.

11. Legal Aspects

http://www.eeoc.gov/: This site is a clearinghouse for all issues relevant to the Equal Employment Opportunity Commission (EEOC).

http://www.corporateinformation.com/: A place to find corporate information by state and country. It also has links to other sites such as the state's Supreme Court archives and decisions.

http://www.whistleblowers.org/: The National Whistleblower Center is a nonprofit, tax-exempt educational and advocacy organization committed to environmental protection, nuclear safety, civil rights, and government accountability and protecting the rights of employee whistleblowers. Established in 1988, the center has successfully established many of the most important precedents protecting employee whistleblowers throughout the United States and has revolutionized the protection afforded them. If you want to study what happens to whistleblowers, this site is a must.

http://www.ahipubs.com/: Good resource for legal information pertaining to all phases of employment.

Appendix E

http://www.osc.gov: The U.S. Office of Special Counsel Whistleblower Disclosure Section provides a safe channel through which current and former federal employees, and applicants for employment, may disclose information that they believe shows a violation of law, rule or regulation, gross mismanagement, gross waste of funds, abuse of authority, or a substantial and specific danger to public health or safety.

http://www.thecre.com/fedlaw/default.htm: FedLaw was developed to see if legal resources on the Internet could be a useful and cost-effective research tool for federal lawyers and other federal employees. Fedlaw has assembled references of use to people doing federal legal research and which can be accessed directly through "point and click" hypertext connections.

http://www.naspaa.org/: The National Association of Schools of Public Affairs and Administration (NASPAA) is an institutional membership organization that exists to promote excellence in public service education. The membership includes 245 U.S. university programs in public affairs, public policy, public administration and nonprofit management. Visit this site and see what the issue of program accreditation is all about and whether your MPA program is accredited.

http://www.lawlink.nsw.gov.au/lawlink/adb/ll_adb.nsf/pages/adb_eeo_affirmative_action: This website links to "Discrimination, EEO and Affirmative Action," a fact sheet that explains the difference between discrimination, equal employment opportunity (EEO) and Affirmative Action, in relation to employment.

http://www.usa.gov/Topics/Reference_Shelf.shtml#laws: Wonderful source for EEOC laws ranging from Title VII of the Civil Rights Act, 1964, as amended to Age Discrimination Employment Act of 1967, and Civil Rights Act of 1991.

http://www.eeoc.gov/types/sexual_harassment.html

http://www.eeoc.gov/mediate/facts.html

http://www.lectlaw.com/temp.html: Useful site for standard topics such as the Fair Labor Standards Act (FLSA), Americans with Disabilities Act (ADA), and rights to workplace privacy.

http://www.lawatwork.com: Site for current labor laws, Affirmative Action, and different types of discrimination.

http://www.osc.gov/discl.htm: The U.S. Office of Special Counsel Whistleblower Disclosure Section provides a safe channel through which current and former federal employees, and applicants for employment, may disclose information that they believe shows a violation of law, rule or regulation, gross mismanagement, gross waste of funds, abuse of authority, or a substantial and specific danger to public health or safety.

http://www.dol.gov/dol/esa/public/regs/compliance/whd/1421.htm: The U.S. Department of Labor's "Family and Medical Leave Act (FMLA) Compliance Guide" summarizes the FMLA provisions and regulations and provides answers to the most frequently asked questions.

Appendix E

http://www.opm.gov/oca/leave/index.htm: The U.S. Office of Personnel Management provides government-wide leadership on federal leave policies and programs. This is accomplished by developing and maintaining government-wide regulations and policies on the administration of leave, including the Family and Medical Leave Act, family-friendly leave policies, federal leave sharing programs, annual leave, sick leave, and time off for special circumstances.

http://www.dot.gov/ost/dapc/: The U.S. Department of Transportation's Office of Drug and Alcohol Policy and Compliance provides expert advice to industry representatives regarding implementation of the controlled substances and alcohol testing rules.

http://www.opm.gov/family/wrkfam/index.html: U.S. Office of Personnel and Management website on family friendly workplace advocacy.

12. Disabilities

http://www.aarp.org/: This site is dedicated to the American Association of Retired Persons (AARP).

www.ahipubs.com: This is a good site to utilize if looking for information about employing persons with disabilities. In addition, this site also has legal information regarding a full range of employment issues.

http://www.dredf.org/: Founded in 1979 by people with disabilities and parents of children with disabilities, the Disability Rights Education and Defense Fund, Inc. (DREDF) is a national law and policy center dedicated to protecting and advancing the civil rights of people with disabilities through legislation, litigation, advocacy, technical assistance, and education and training of attorneys, advocates, persons with disabilities, and parents of children with disabilities.

http://www.eeoc.gov/: U.S. Equal Employment Opportunity Commission (EEOC).

http://www.dol.gov/whd/fmla/APPENDIXF.htm: The U.S. Department of Labor Family Medical Leave Act (FMLA) Compliance Guide summarizes the FMLA provisions and regulations, and provides answers to the most frequently asked questions.

http://www.opm.gov/oca/leave/index.htm: The Office of Personnel Management provides leadership across government on federal leave policies and programs. This is accomplished by developing and maintaining government-wide regulations and policies on the administration of leave, including the Family and Medical Leave Act, family-friendly leave policies, federal leave sharing programs, annual leave, sick leave, and time off for special circumstances such as early dismissal or closure for weather emergencies. However, each federal agency is responsible for administering leave policies and programs for its own employees.

http://www.ada.gov: U.S. Department of Justice's Americans with Disabilities Act homepage.

Appendix E

http://www.disabilityinfo.gov: Disability.gov is a federal government website where new resources are added daily across ten main subject areas – benefits, civil rights, community life, education, emergency preparedness, employment, health, housing, technology and transportation.

http://www.access-board.gov/: The Access Board of the Federal Government is an independent federal agency devoted to accessibility for people with disabilities.

13. State, Regional, County, Municipal Organizations

http://www.naco.org/: The National Association of Counties (NACo) is the only national organization that represents county governments in the United States. If the county level of government is your interest, then this website will be a high priority on your browsing list.

http://www.geocities.com/CapitolHill/1389/: This website serves as a collection of city-related URL's from throughout the United States.

http://www.statelocal.gov/: A state and local government link.

http://www.icma.org/: The International City/County Management Association (ICMA) is the professional and educational organization representing appointed managers and administrators in local governments throughout the world. If your interest is in the area of county management, this is the capstone website.

http://www.nga.org/: The National Governors Association (NGA) is the only bipartisan national organization of, by, and for the nations' governors. Its members are the governors of the fifty states, the commonwealths of the Northern Mariana Islands and Puerto Rico, and the territories of American Samoa, Guam, and the Virgin Islands. Through NGA, the governors identify priority issues and deal collectively with issues of public policy and governance at both the national and state levels.

http://www.nlc.org/: The mission of the National League of Cities (NLC) is to strengthen and promote cities as centers of opportunity, leadership, and governance. NLC was established in 1924 by and for reform-minded state municipal leagues. NLC now represents 49 leagues, more than 1,700 member cities, and through the membership of the state municipal leagues, NLC represents more than 18,000 cities and towns of all sizes.

http://www.usmayors.org/: The United States Conference of Mayors is the official nonpartisan organization of cities with populations of 30,000 or more. There are about 1,100 such cities in the country today. Its chief elected official, the mayor, represents each city in the Conference.

http://www.natat.org/: The purpose of the National Association of Towns and Townships (NATaT) is to strengthen the effectiveness of town and township government. It does so by educating lawmakers and public policy officials about how small town governments operate and by advocating policies on their behalf in Washington, D.C.

http://www.narc.org/: The National Association of Regional Councils (NARC) is a nonprofit membership organization serving the interests of regional councils nationwide.

14. Productivity

www.astd.org: American Society for Training and Development. Anything and everything you need to know about if training is your *forte*.

http://www.suite101.com/welcome.cfm/training_and_development: Offers numerous links related to training and development.

15. Reinvention and Re-engineering of Government

www.icma.org: The International City/County Management Association (ICMA) website is your essential source for information on managing the municipality or the county. This site is also, a great source for international management initiatives that help break-down our own ethnocentric biases concerning how a large number of problems might be remedied.

http://www.afscme.org/private/index.html: The American Federation of State, County and Municipal Employees (AFSCME) offers a comprehensive website for those who wish to learn the union perspective on topics, such as privatization and contracting out. This site special feature and strength is found in the many links to labor unions, both domestic and international, and the traditional listing of topics including bargaining, classification, compensation, diversity, gay and lesbian issues, health care, labor studies and resources, testing, women's issues and workers' compensation.

http://www.orau.gov/pbm/links/npr1.html: National Partnership for Reinventing Government's article titled "Balancing Measures: Best Practices in Performance Management."

16. Jobs and Careers

http://www.ajb.dni.us: Excellent site for those seeking employment. On this site employers list their job openings and keep the information up to date.

http://www.allstarjobs.com: All Star Jobs is an extremely useful site since it includes job openings in all 50 states and Washington, D.C. It also is a valuable resource for resume writing, salary information, career fairs, career planning, job information and student careers.

http://www.aspanet.org: The American Society for Public Administration (ASPA) provides information about new developments in public administration as a field of study and as a career field.

http://www.bestjobuse.com

http://www.careerbuilder.com

Appendix E

http://www.careercruising.com

http://www.careeronestop.org/

http://www.careersingovernment.com: On this website a national listing of government jobs is posted. Users may view postings by specific words or view the list of employers by region or state.

http://www.chicagojobs.org

http://www.collegegrad.com/topemployers

http://www.collegerecruiter.com

http://www.diversitycareers.com

http://www.employmentguide.com/site/index.html

http://www.govtjobs.com: Govtjobs.com has an extensive pool of individuals seeking public service careers. Cities, counties, states, executive search firms and advertising agencies all post jobs to this site.

http://www.governmentjobs.com: "GovernmentJobs.com is the only government sector job board created from the world's foremost fully integrated recruitment, selection and applicant tracking system called NEOGOV Insight designed specifically for public sector employers." (www.governmentjobs.com)

http://www.hightechcareers.com

http://www.hotjobs.com

http://www.hrcrossing.com: HRCrossing.com claims to seek out human resources job postings from multiple sites in order to provide them all in one place.

http://www.humanresourcesjobs.com: This website assists users in finding top jobs in human resources.

http://www.indeed.com

http://www.interns.org

http://www.jobfox.com: This site provides more than a list of job openings. It has helpful material on nearly every topic related to recruitment, hiring, and placement.

http://www.jobsfed.com: A place to look for government job listings.

http://www.jobs4HR.com: Jobs4HR.com is a local employment website for job seekers and employers.

Appendix E

http://www.jobsearch.vacareers.va.gov

http://www.jobweb.com

http://www.jobsingovernment.com/: A website devoted to jobs and employment in the public sector.

http://www.makingthedifference.org: Great site for federal job information.

http://www.makingthedifference.org/federaljobs/hotjobs.shtml: This Hot Jobs/Cool Internships eNewsletter is an essential site for "cool applicants."

http://www.monster.com: Monster.com is one of the largest and most well-known career websites.

http://www.napawash.org The National Academy of Public Administration (NAPA) lists useful information about public service as a profession.

http://www.nationjob.com

http://online.onetcenter.org/

http://www.ony.unu.edu/internships: Internship information with the United Nations is provided through the University Office at the United Nations. One popular program is the Junior Professional Fellows (JPF) Program. This UN agency acts as a think tank in order to enable policy makers and members of academia to partner in such areas as marketing, policy research, and partnerships in fundraising.

http://www.opajobs.com/: Find job opportunities in public affairs on this website.

http://www.ourpublicservice.org: The Partnership for Public Service provides students with useful information about federal job opportunities and federal internships. This nonpartisan and nonprofit organization is devoted to the revitalization and transformation of the federal government and is oriented toward providing solutions to problems facing the U.S. federal government.

http://www.paidinterns.com

http://www.preferredjobs.com

http://www.publicservicecareers.org: Public Service Careers is the American Society of Public Administration's (ASPA) online career center. The site enables members to post resumes, search job databases and make online applications.

http://www.simplyhired.com: Simply Hired consolidates millions of job postings in a variety of fields from all throughout the country.

Appendix E

http://smartcareermove.com/

http://www.stats.bls.gov/oco: Bureau of Labor Statistics website with occupational information.

http://www.studentjobs.gov: Studentjobs.gov is an essential portal for federal governmental jobs for those at nearly any level of formal education — high school through graduate school.

http://www.summerjobs.com

http://www.usajobs.com: Senior executive service current job openings.

http://www.usajobs.org: USAJobs.org is the official job site of the government of the United States and lists thousands of federal employment opportunities.

http://www.usajobs.opm.gov/: The U.S. Government's official site for jobs and employment information provided by the United States Office of Personnel Management.

http://www.vault.com

http://www.wetfeet.com

http://www.workforamerica.com: Essential site for those who have special interest careers or want to learn about the federal hiring process, benefits and so on.

http://www.workforcehrjobs.com: Workforce HRJobs provides an online career center and job postings in the human resources field.

http://www.workiniowa.com

http://www.workinpr.com

http://www.wsj.com: *Wall Street Journal.*

17. Comprehensive Access for Government

The following provide comprehensive materials on selected institutions and organizations of government and provide many valuable links to topics associated with modern personnel management practices.

http://www.lcweb.loc.gov/: Library of Congress — need we say more.

http://www.si.edu/: Smithsonian Institute.

http://www.whitehouse.gov/: The White House website includes valuable links to other federal executive agencies and congressional organizations.

http://www.usa.gov/: A comprehensive site that can link to almost all government sites, which are easily listed as executive, legislative, and judicial branches and offices. This is the "real McCoy" of federal government websites and is touted as the one single best source for information on the U.S. government.

http://www.epa.gov/: The Environmental Protection Agency (EPA) website keeps up to date information about environmental programs and Superfund site clean-ups.

http://www.wto.org/: The World Trade Organization website.

http://www.searchgov.com/: An in-depth site for links to federal and state governmental programs and agencies.

http://www.census.gov/: The U.S. Census Bureau site provides information about recent census data, people, business, geography, news, and additional topics. A top notch site for demographic, social, and economic data compiled nationally, by state and locale.

http://www.supremecourtus.gov/: The official website for the U.S. Supreme Court.

http://www.dhhs.gov/: The Department of Health and Human Services is the United States government's principal agency for protecting the health of all Americans and providing essential human services, especially for those who are least able to help themselves.

http://www.va.gov/: The Department of Veteran Affairs website contains *information* about health, compensation, education, insurance, special services, and links to state and local sites.

http://www.fda.gov/: Food and Drug administration's official website.

http://www.doi.gov/: The official website for the Department of the Interior.

http://www.uscourts.gov/outreach/resources/fedstate_lessonplan.htm: A website that aims to help an average person to understand the differences between federal, state and other special courts. It also provides links to "locate courts" in your own state and city and other judiciary websites.

http://www.ojp.usdoj.gov/bjs: U.S. Department of Justice's Bureau of Justice Statistics.

http://www.fec.gov: The Federal Election Commission (FEC) administers and enforces the Federal Election Campaign Act (FECA) - the statute that governs the financing of federal elections.

18. Budgeting and Finance
http://www.whitehouse.gov/omg: The website of the U.S. Office of Management and Budget.

http://www.cbo.gov: The Congressional Budget Office (CBO), legislative arm of the federal government for budgeting purposes.

http://www.nncls.org: The National Conference of State Legislatures (NCSL) provides massive amounts of budget information on state government budgets and public finance.

http://www.abfm.org: Association for Budgeting and Financial management (ABFM) is a national association that provides detailed and specialized budgetary and financial information for all levels of government.

19. Ethics

http://www.usoge.gov: This website from the U.S. Office of Government Ethics provides a survey of federal employees on their ethical perspectives and a "Standards of Ethical Conduct for Employees of the Executive Branch" publication.

http://www.house.gov/ethics: The official website for the U.S. House of Representatives Committee on Standards of Official Conduct.

http://www.ethics.senate.gov: The official website for the U.S. Senate Select Committee on Ethics. This site includes a handbook for its membership and employees.

http://www.mspb.gov: The Merit Systems Protection Board of the U.S. Government, a must visit site for those interested in civil service reform and its protection.

20. Miscellaneous

http://www.napawash.org: The National Academy of Public Administration provides useful information on a myriad of public administration/public affairs topics and publishes specialized reports on, among many others, the federal civil service and the future of federal employment.

http://www.nasbo.org: the National Association of State Budget Officers (NASBO).

http://www.nga.org: The National Governors Association (NGA).

http://www.ncsl.org: The National Conference of State legislatures (NCSL).

http://www.brookings.edu: The Brookings Institution is widely known for its research and publications on topics as varied as poverty, globalization, and human resources management.

http://www.flra.gov: The U.S. Federal Labor Relations Authority (FLRA).

http://www.bls.gov/: The U.S. Bureau of Labor Statistics (BLS).

Appendix E

http://www.usa.gov/: The official web portal of the U.S. government.

http://www.ncpp.us/: Public Performance studies sponsored by Rutgers University — a national leader in this important area of measurement.

http://www.nationalpriorities.org: National Priorities of the U.S. Government.

http://www.constitutioncenter.org: The National Constitution Center (NCC) provides an informed presentation on the Articles and Amendments to the U.S. Constitution. This is a handy website for public employees wishing to know more about the Bill of Rights and other protections, freedoms and liberties.

http://www.msha.gov/: This site provides useful information on the Mine Safety and Health Administration.

http://www.workinglife.org/wiki/resources: The website of the Labor Research Association.

http://www/concordcoalition.org: The Concord Coalition provides up-to-date information on federal and state budgeting, taxation and spending trends from a non-partisan perspective.

http://www.aspeninstitute.org: For the person interested in developing executive leadership skills, The Aspen Institute is known world-wide.

http://wwwafscme.org: The American Federation of State, County and Municipal Employees (AFSCME) website has employment related data, human resource management links, and is current on work-place trends.

http://www.nlc.org: The National League of Cities (NLC) provides useful information on data and trends in American cities.

http://www.pti.org: The Public Technology Institute (PTI) was designed for city and county governments and is focused on technology issues. This site has useful information for organizations interested in partnering, collaboration and innovation that improves government performance and service delivery by using state-of-the-art technology.

http://www.data.gov: This website provides thousands of links to federal data that are accessible for use by researchers, students and by the public at large. The data deal with topics as different as mass layoffs to toxic releases. This site is intended to reduce the duplication of data generation and facilitate the sharing of information between the many agencies and different levels of government. This data will be useful in the general area of performance management.

http://www.usaspending.gov: This site operationalizes the Obama-Coburn Act that requires the federal government to create a database of all its contracts, grants, and loans. In brief, it provides a detailed listing of federal government spending and the recipients of federal monies.

Appendix E

http://www.federalreporting.gov: This site is managed by the Office of Management and Budget (OMB). The American Recovery and Reinvestment Act requires the federal government to track the flow of recovery dollars to the recipient and sub-recipient level. It requires that the amount of funding granted to state agencies be recorded as well as who was contractor. It also requires that state agencies report on whether the awards were made competitively or on a non-competitive basis.

http://www.naspe.org: The National Association of State Personnel Executives (NASPE) is a key resource on human resource issues, trends, practices, and policies at the state level of government. It strives to improve the quality of human resources management under tight finances and budgets at the state level.

http://www.surveymonkey.com: A useful online tool for collecting and analyzing survey data. In short, everything you will need to prepare and analyze an online survey or questionnaire.

http://www.america2050.org: The issues associated with the infrastructure of the United States — its needs and spending — are assessed and novel ways to finance projects are presented that could generate long-term returns on investments from institutional pension funds, retirement accounts, corporate investments, and small investors (IRA's, 401k's).

http://www.bestplacestowork.org: Researchers can customize their own analysis of 278 federal agencies on the basis of trend analysis (2003, 2005, 2007 and 2009) on ten dimensions associated with the workplace environment.

http://www.accel-team.com: Building successful teams.

http://www.csmonitor.com/2003/0729/p01s03-usgn.html: White-collar jobs moving abroad.

http://www.shrm.org/hrmagazine/articles/0404/0404covstory.asp: America's newest export: white-collar jobs.

http://www.sullivan-county.com/nf0/dispatch/white_collar.htm: Contains an article about white-collar jobs joining blue-collar counterparts overseas (funny picture).

http://www.interviewprep.com/articles/white_collar_casualties/: Contains an article about white-collar layoff casualties taking what they can get.

http://www.bls.gov/data/home.htm: Bureau of Labor Statistics.

http://www.opm.gov/fedclass/fwssupv.pdf: Federal Wage System Job Grading Standard for Supervisors.

http://federaljobs.net/occupations.htm#GENERAL%20SCHEDULE: Good web resource on General Schedule (GS) Occupational Groups.

http://www.riskinstitute.org: Public Entity Risk Institute.

Appendix E

http://www.1105govinfo.com: Contains a state and local government information technology report.

http://www.slge.org: Center for State and Local Government Excellence (CSLGE).

http://www.ipma-hr.org: International City/County Management Association (ICMA).

http://www.ilsg.org/: Institute for Local Government (ILG).

http://www.kff.org: The Kaiser Family Foundation.

http://www.pewtrusts.org: The PEW Charitable Trusts sponsors research on the federal and state levels of government in human resources management, contracting-out, employee satisfaction, and financial management and in the general areas of health, environment and economic policy.

http://www.Markle.org/: Markle Foundation.

http://www.governing.com: *Governing* Magazine.

http://www.govexec.com: Government Executive

http://www.ksg.harvard.edu/TheBehnReport/

http://www.osha.gov/oshstats/work.html: The Occupational Safety and Health Administration maintains this great site for data on occupational and work-place injuries and illnesses.

http://www.globaledge.msu.edu/ibrd/ibrd.asp: The Center for International Business Education and Research at Michigan State University provides this site with trade information and other human resource information on a country by country basis.

http://www.astd.org: The American Society for Training and Development (ASTD) provides specialized information in the area of human resources training and development.

http://www.sympatico.workopolis.com: If you are looking for a solution to a work situation/problem, this might well become a favorite site. You might compare your solution in contrast with that of Sympatico's.

http://www.vistaprint.com: Resource for free business cards.

http://www.whitehouse.gov/fsbr/esbr.html: If statistics on economic issues such as output, income, production, money, and prices are your interest, this site provides federal economic indicators from U.S. governmental agencies.

http://www.hrisolutions.com/index2.html: Great site that links other human resources websites and search tools.

Appendix E

http://www.shrm.org: A premier site sponsored by the Society for Human Resource Management (SHRM) dealing with all aspects of human resource management including law, recruitment, evaluation, interviewing, training, and much more.

The authors wish to acknowledge the helpful assistance of Brian Hanft and Frank Baxter in helping to compile these useful websites.